LÉON HARMEL

Catholic Social Tradition Series

Preface to the Series

In *Tertio millennio adveniente,* Pope John Paul II poses a hard question: "It must be asked how many Christians really know and put into practice the principles of the church's social doctrine." The American Catholic bishops share the pope's concern: "Catholic social teaching is a central and essential element of our faith . . . [and yet] our social heritage is unknown by many Catholics. Sadly, our social doctrine is not shared or taught in a consistent and comprehensive way in too many of our schools." This lack is critical because the "sharing of our social tradition is a defining measure of Catholic education and formation." A United States Catholic Conference task force on social teaching and education noted that within Catholic higher education "there appears to be little consistent attention given to incorporating gospel values and Catholic social teaching into general education courses or into departmental majors."

In response to this problem, the volumes in the Catholic Social Tradition series aspire to impart the best of what this tradition has to offer not only to Catholics but to all who face the social issues of our times. The volumes examine a wide variety of issues and problems within the Catholic social tradition and contemporary society, yet they share several characteristics. They are theologically and philosophically grounded, examining the deep structure of thought in modern culture. They are publicly argued, enhancing dialogue with other religious and nonreligious traditions. They are comprehensively engaged by a wide variety of disciplines such as theology, philosophy, political science, economics, history, law, management, and finance. Finally, they examine how the Catholic social tradition can be integrated on a practical level and embodied in institutions in which people live much of their lives. The Catholic Social Tradition series is about faith in action in daily life, providing ways of thinking and acting to those seeking a more humane world.

Michael J. Naughton
University of St. Thomas

Todd David Whitmore
University of Notre Dame

LÉON HARMEL

Entrepreneur as Catholic Social Reformer

JOAN L. COFFEY

University of Notre Dame Press
Notre Dame, Indiana

University of Notre Dame Press
Notre Dame, Indiana 46556
www.undpress.nd.edu
All Rights Reserved

Copyright © 2003 by University of Notre Dame
Published in the United States of America

Paperback edition published in 2017

The author and publisher thank the Archives Jésuites in Paris for the photographs of Figures 1–6 and permission to reproduce them. These photographs can be found in *Léon Harmel, 1829–1915* by Georges Guitton, S. J., 2 vols. (Action Populaire-Éditions Spes, 1927).

Library of Congress Cataloging-in-Publication Data
Coffey, Joan L., 1944–
Léon Harmel : entrepreneur as Catholic social reformer / Joan L. Coffey.
    p. cm. — (Catholic social tradition series)
Includes bibliographical references and index.
ISBN 978-0-268-15919-1 (paperback)
ISBN 978-0-268-03360-6 (hardback)
    1. Harmel, Léon, 1829–1915. 2. Social reformers—France—Biography.
3. Social problems—France—Reims Region.   4. Social problems—France.
5. Catholic Workers Movement.   6. Church and social problems—Catholic
Church.   I. Title. II. Series.
HV28.H336 C64   2003
338.7'677'0092—dc21

2003009033

∞ *This book is printed on acid-free paper.*

TO

Edward Charles Coffey,
exemplary Christian businessman,
for his inspiration and unfailing support

CONTENTS

Acknowledgments ix
Introduction 1

CHAPTER ONE   Family History and Legacy   11

CHAPTER TWO   The Corporation at Val-des-Bois   49

CHAPTER THREE   The World Beyond   101

CHAPTER FOUR   Pilgrimage to Rome   145

CHAPTER FIVE   New Directions   193

Conclusion 233
Notes 251
Bibliography 307
Index 329

ACKNOWLEDGMENTS

NO WORK OF THIS SCOPE CAN BE ACCOMPLISHED WITHOUT THE SUPPORT of numerous institutions and individuals. Early on, the University of Colorado provided abundant assistance. The Department of History helped fund my initial research trip to France and Italy, Interlibrary Loan filled request after request for books housed in depositories across the nation, Professor Emerita Julia Amari translated archival material written in Italian, and Professors David L. Gross, Barbara A. Engel, and Robert A. Pois of the Department of History helped me conceptualize and organize the original project.

In Europe, the Gilbert Chinard Scholarship, sponsored by the Institut Français de Washington, helped me financially, while personnel at the National Archives of France, Monsieur G. Dumas and Madame Marceline Deban of the Archives of the Marne, and Père Josef Metzler of the Vatican Archives kept me well supplied with precious materials. On a more personal level, Father George Lawless introduced me to the wonders of Vatican City, as well as the historic plazas and buildings of Rome; Monsieur and Madame Pierre Trimouille graciously hosted a working lunch during my lengthy stay in Châlons-sur-Marne (now

Châlons-en-Champagne); and M. Trimouille continued to assist my research on Léon Harmel through informative letters and telephone calls.

As I made repeated trips to France and Italy and the manuscript took shape, I became indebted to Sam Houston State University (SHSU) for its generous assistance. The History Department at SHSU helped to fund additional research trips, the Interlibrary Loan team, headed by Bette Craig, located books I thought might be too ancient or too obscure to appear at my office door, Professor Mark Leipnik created maps, and Professor Tracy Steele acted as cheerful courier on many occasions. Finally, the university awarded me a faculty developmental leave at a point in the manuscript's life when it was most critical to have a semester to think and write without classroom responsibilities.

Additional archives enriched my work as research drew to a conclusion, and so I am grateful also to the staff of the Archives of the French Ministry of Foreign Affairs, as well as Père Noye, archivist of the Archives of Saint-Sulpice, for their assistance. A huge *merci beaucoup* goes to the several readers of earlier versions of this study whose valuable suggestions assisted in the final stages and also to the editorial team at the University of Notre Dame Press, especially Sheila Berg, copyeditor, for her careful reading and suggestions, and Jeffrey L. Gainey, associate editor, for his guidance throughout.

Moral support is a far less tangible commodity but an important one for any author who has experienced moments of disappointment amid the thrill of discovery. I owe special thanks to those who had the capacity to buoy my sagging spirits during difficult times. This list is a long one indeed and includes family, friends, colleagues, and students, as well as medical professionals, but I do want to single out just a few individuals who helped this educator learn some useful lessons. Father Francis J. Murphy taught me the real meaning of kindness, Professor James S. Olson taught me how to research and write despite medical problems, Professor Martha Hanna taught me how to enjoy Parisian cemeteries on a Sunday afternoon, Professor Thomas A. Kselman taught me when to move on to the next project, Dr. John W. Durst taught me the meaning of compassion, Dr. Raymond Alexanian taught me to always have the next research trip to France planned, and Edward Coffey, to whom this book is dedicated, taught me what moral support really means.

INTRODUCTION

> God shall send against him the fury of
> his wrath
> And rain down his missiles of war
> upon him.
> —*Job 20:23*

DEFEAT WAS SWIFT AND IGNOMINIOUS. ON JULY 19, 1870, NAPOLEON III (1808–1873) declared war on Prussia, and surrendered at Sedan on September 2. The German army convincingly demonstrated its superiority in numbers, organization, and materiel and pushed west, by way of the French Ardennes, toward Paris. A contingent of the German army accompanying the crown prince of Prussia, however, paused for forty-eight hours at Val-des-Bois, a textile spinning mill located on the outskirts of Warmériville, approximately eleven miles northeast of the cathedral city of Reims. From September 5 to 7, Léon Harmel (1829–1915), *patron* of the family enterprise, played host to the uninvited Germans. The visit was extremely cordial given the circumstances. Harmel guided the crown prince about the factory premises, taking him to the workrooms and the chapel and introducing him to workers and their organizations. Harmel reported that the crown prince was interested in everything. The prince, gracious guest par excellence, spoke to his hosts of the horrors of war, his distress over the spilling of French as well as German blood, and his determination to avoid future war at all cost.[1]

Unfortunately, events played out otherwise. The crown prince succeeded to the German throne in 1888 but died three months afterward. In 1914 German troops, acting on orders from William II (r. 1888–1918), emperor of the Second German Reich, once again marched through the Ardennes and stopped at Val-des-Bois. This time the visit was far less cordial. For a while the Harmel factory continued to function marginally because the Germans were interested in cloth for military uniforms, but in February 1915 the army took control of Val-des-Bois, carrying off what they could and destroying what they judged worthless, including factory records.

The military events of 1870 and 1914 obviously were tremendously significant for Léon Harmel and his factory at Val-des-Bois, as they indeed were for all of France. For Harmel, the Franco-Prussian War (1870–1871) and the opening years of World War I (1914–1918) served as bookends to a long and productive public life; the intervening years brought Harmel and his factory national and international attention. As for France, despite the national humiliation of 1870, the country experienced exciting though stressful times, producing what Gérard Noiriel has characterized as a virtual "laboratory of ideas" politically and socially.[2] *La belle époque* was made to order for the privileged set, while the lower classes, victimized by the industrial revolution, waited impatiently for the government to gradually ameliorate their living and working conditions. Not willing to stand by until the government enacted labor reform, Harmel began earlier and operated amid the political, economic, and social vortex of the times.

Léon Harmel became the chief executive of his family's spinning mill at Val-des-Bois in 1854. As *patron*, or boss, he not only inherited the family business, but the family legacy of social reform as well. Léon followed in the footsteps of his father, Jacques-Joseph Harmel (1795–1886), in carrying out reform in the workplace, the motivation of which was rooted firmly in their Catholic religion. Carefully balancing his duties as chief executive and social reformer, Léon Harmel weathered the turbulent economic cycles that typically plagued the textile industry and swept under less stable enterprises while simultaneously transforming the mill into a model workplace for the times. Moreover, he distinguished himself beyond factory reform at Val-des-Bois during the years of the early Third Republic (1870–1914). Harmel contributed immensely to Catholic social teaching through his involvement in the social Catholic and Christian democratic movements during some of their most crucial developmental years. He was a veritable force majeure.

Harmel's commitment to social activism received considerable impetus from the humiliating military defeat of France by Prussia in 1870 and the ensuing mayhem of the last French revolution of the nineteenth century, the Paris Commune (March–May 1871). Indeed, these two events caused virtually all of France to redefine itself. Politically, military defeat meant the collapse of the Second Empire (1852–1870) and the inauguration of the Third Republic (1870–1940). The new government, intent on reestablishing the secularism of the First Republic (1792–1804), earned a reputation for militant anticlericalism, but it also became notorious for its political scandals, which rocked and seriously threatened the life of the Republic, exposing political and social cleavages left raw from the Revolution of 1789 and exacerbated by events of 1870 and 1871. The Panama Canal Affair, the Boulanger Affair, and the Dreyfus Affair reinforced old enmities, created new ones, and stimulated profound distrust of government officials and societal structure. Nationalism and anti-Semitism grew as France looked for ways to redeem national pride, deeply wounded by political scandal coming so soon after military defeat.

German influence of French society extended beyond political repercussions, however. Militarily, defeat at the hands of the Germans initiated a lengthy period of self-examination inside the French army, resulting in a multifaceted program of reform that continued right up to the outbreak of war in 1914. With one eye on innovations within the German military and the other on the climbing German birthrate, France saw its population growing at one-third the German rate, while its marriages declined by 20 percent between 1872 and the end of that decade.[3] France also was aware of increasingly losing economic ground after 1870 to the industrial giant to its east, a trend reflected in German advances in science and pedagogy.[4] France imported and assimilated such German ideologies as Kantianism and Marxism into its universities and political parties. The German welfare program was worthy of imitation too in the years after 1870, as socialism made inroads among French workers and forced even the bourgeoisie to question capitalism's laissez-faire methods.[5] Meanwhile, Catholics interested in social reform looked to the work of Wilhelm Emmanuel von Ketteler, Bishop of Mainz (1850–1877), for inspiration.

The aftermath of the 1870 defeat was particularly significant for the Roman Catholic Church in France. Having enjoyed a privileged position early in the Second Empire, the Church rediscovered that republicans under the Third Republic intended to eliminate the Church's perquisites and shift the French government toward a decidedly more secular and anticlerical stance. The Catholic Church responded by both digging in its heels and engaging in dialogue with the state. The episcopacy bargained with government officials whenever they could as schools, hospitals, and cemeteries became laicized, patois was cleansed from regional catechisms and sermons,[6] young priests and seminarians began serving in the military, religious orders were dissolved, and the Concordat was replaced by a formal separation of church and state. Religiosity among the French at once faded and intensified. Men, in particular, neglected their Easter duty and generally kept away from Church functions. Yet religious fervor was apparent in the resurgence of devotion to Mary and the Sacred Heart, in the popularity of pilgrimages, in the vitality of the religious orders, and in the growth of social Catholicism and Christian democracy. Catholic reformers joined their like-minded Belgian and German coreligionists in addressing the ills of industrialism and promoting the political empowerment of the workers. Thus, despite depressed attendance at Mass and other quantitative markers of weakened religiosity, there remained considerable vibrancy in the French Church during the 1870–1914 period.

As for Léon Harmel, the events of 1870–1871 brought to a dramatic head all that had plagued French society since at least the Reformation but especially since the Revolution of 1789, which had ushered in the First Republic. Initially, Harmel decried the return of republican France, because in his view it signaled the restoration of the godless state of the earlier Republic, but later he was one of the first to rally to the Republic once the papacy signaled a shift in its policy. The death of his beloved wife, Gabrielle, in 1870 only exacerbated his grief; he mourned in that historic year as a husband, as a Catholic, and as a *citoyen* of France.

Nevertheless, Harmel hoped to turn defeat into victory, and so he rededicated himself to God and nation in 1870. To anchor himself for the task ahead, he planted his feet squarely in two places, Val-des-Bois and Rome. The workers at the Harmel factory became his raison d'être; his every act responded to their needs or was intended for their benefit. The papacy likewise provided a source of direction and opportunity for service, and during his long life, Harmel devotedly served four popes.[7] However, the pope who is most closely identified with Harmel is Leo XIII (r. 1878–1903). Not only did the years of their public lives coincide most perfectly, but there was a mutual respect established between the two men that can only come from shared concerns and joint endeavors, and which perhaps is best exemplified by the papal encyclical *Rerum Novarum* and the worker pilgrimages to Rome. Significantly, Harmel's major literary works, *Manuel d'une corporation chrétienne* (1876) and *Catéchisme du patron* (1889), and his prodigious social activism date from this time. The Christian corporation at Val-des-Bois with its family wage and factory council, the Catholic worker circles (L'Oeuvre des Cercles Catholiques d'Ouvriers), the Patrons du Nord for factory employers, the worker pilgrimages to Rome, the Christian democratic congresses, the factory chaplain project (Aumôniers d'Usines) and Social Weeks (Semaines Sociales) program for young clergy, the study circles for workers interested in *Rerum Novarum* (Les Cercles Chrétiens d'Études Sociales), the fraternal union for workers in commerce and industry (Union Fraternelle du Commerce et l'Industrie), and the Christian trade unions are among his most noteworthy achievements and took place during the 1870–1914 period.

The Franco-Prussian War of 1870 and the outbreak of World War I in 1914 are two significant points on a historical time line by which to study the life of Léon Harmel. While the German invasion of 1870, with its brief occupation of Val-des-Bois, was an incentive to a younger Harmel to plunge headfirst into social reform, the German invasion of 1914, coming in his eighty-sixth year, marked the closing months of his life and of his tenure as *patron* of Val-des-Bois. Harmel reluctantly departed for Nice with some members of his family as the German army moved into eastern France and civilians from the Warmériville area were advised to evacuate to Reims. Harmel's son attempted for a time to keep the enterprise operating, but German occupation of the factory grounds and requisitions for textiles drove the business under. The senior Harmel kept abreast of developments at the factory from his sickbed in Nice. He steadfastly maintained his faith in the will of God until his death on November 25, 1915, but he was visibly heartbroken by events taking place at Val-des-Bois. The factory reopened after the war under the Harmel family aegis but without its most famous *patron*.

The prewar years were turbulent times, and reaction to perceived and real change characterized the epoch and bred reformers of diverse agendas. Léon Harmel fits neatly into this context of reform. Since his deep religious faith was the inspiration for social reform, historians have taken note of both aspects of the man. Gérard Cholvy, for instance, has described Harmel as an "authentic mystic and one of the numerous laic saints of the century."[8] Other historians applaud him as an exemplar of paternalistic management,[9] as "the most important pacesetter of the second Christian democracy in France,"[10] as a man "who reconciled the classes,"[11] as an "inexhaustible spokesman of social Catholicism and a man of the pope,"[12] and as a man "a half-century ahead of his time."[13]

The French scholars Georges Guitton and Pierre Trimouille have produced major works on Léon Harmel.[14] The biography by Guitton, a hefty two-volume study (1927), is essential introductory reading for students and admirers of Harmel. It relies on Harmel's voluminous correspondence with family, friends, and professional associates, organizational reports, and oral and written testimonies of those who knew Harmel personally. The result is a book of remarkable intimacy, particularly with regard to the Harmel family, and a loving tribute to a man of the Church. But the book suffers from two shortcomings. Although Guitton makes no claim to do so, it lacks a certain historical objectivity and does not attempt to place Harmel in a political, economic, or social context.

Trimouille's book (1974), by contrast, possesses greater objectivity. It also remains unsurpassed in its treatment of the factory at Val-des-Bois, the organizational structure of a Christian corporation, and Harmel's role in the creation of Christian trade unionism in France. Trimouille devotes the first half of his study to the spinning mill at Val and the process of forming a Christian corporation at the factory and the second half to an examination of the growth of Christian syndicalism and Harmel's relationship to it in its formative years before World War I. The Trimouille account, moreover, benefits from access to the excellent secondary works by Henri Rollet, Jean-Baptiste Duroselle, Jean-Marie Mayeur, Robert Talmy, and René Remond. But while Trimouille places Harmel, his factory, and his work with various organizations in the context of early Christian syndicalism in France, he does not discuss the worker pilgrimages to Rome or create a cultural or religious context or a national or international political setting; neither does he develop the important nexus between Léon Harmel and the papacy.

It is the purpose of this study to provide a third extensive account of Léon Harmel, one that incorporates the excellent scholarly material that has come to light since 1974 while also attempting to delve into the heart and soul of the man. Whenever possible, Harmel speaks directly through extant correspondence, speeches, and publications. But this study also attempts to determine whether Harmel's thoughts and actions merely reflected his epoch and culture or if he was truly distinctive. In addition to the general texts on the social Catholic and Christian democratic movements used by Trimouille, this study employs such now standard works as those by John McManners, Paul Misner, Parker Thomas Moon, and Alec R. Vidler. It also introduces numerous other scholarly works by American, British, and French scholars who have contributed enormously to an understanding of the world of Léon Harmel.

In the area of general history, for example, texts by Louis Bergeron, Jeremy D. Popkin, Eugen Weber, Gordon Wright, and Theodore Zeldin provided general background material for nineteenth-century France. Discussion of economic factors and the labor situation benefited from the work of Kathryn E. Amdur, Susanna Barrows, Edward Berenson, Lenard R. Berlanstein, Rondo Cameron, François Caron, William B. Cohen, Marianne Debouzy, David M. Gordon, Tamara K. Hareven, Jules Houdoy, Steven L. Kaplan, Richard F. Kuisel, David S. Landes, Roger Magraw, Allen Mitchell, Leslie Page Moch, Gérard Noiriel, Michelle Perrot, William M. Reddy, François Sellier, William H. Sewell Jr., Francine Soubiran-Paillet, Peter N. Stearns, Carl Strikwerda, and Judith F. Stone. Work by Patricia Prestwich helped in defining the social world of the worker.

Studies by Elinor A. Accampo, Marilyn J. Boxer and Jean H. Quataert, Gloria Fiero, Laura L. Frader, Rachel G. Fuchs, Madeleine Guilbert, Patricia Hilden, Olwen Hufton, Gerda Lerner, Mary Lynn McDougall, Karen Offen, Joan W. Scott, Bonnie G. Smith, Mary Lynn Stewart, and Louise A. Tilly added to a fuller understanding of the societal role of women. David Herlihy and James F. McMillan also contributed significantly on the subject. Formal education, particularly vocational training for workers, involved men as well as women and was important to an appreciation of the full range of benefits at Val-des-Bois. The work of Linda L. Clark, Robert Gildea, Sandra Horvath-Peterson, and Martha Hanna enlightened me on the French educational system, whether for upper or laboring classes.

Religious history of the nineteenth century is central to this study. The work of Fernand Boulard, Jean-Yves Calvez, Richard L. Camp, Gérard Cholvy, Paul M. Cohen, John F. Cronin, Suzanne Desan, Donal Dorr, Caroline Ford, Ralph Gibson, Etienne Gilson, Y.-M. Hilaire, Thomas A. Kselman, Lester K. Kurtz, James G. Murtagh, Joseph Moody, Claude Langlois, Pierre Pierrard, Paul Seeley, Claude Willard, Stephen Wilson, and Marie Zimmermann provided insights into the theology and structure of the Roman Catholic Church, as well as popular religion as expressed by the French. Michèle Sàcquin supplied valuable information on Protestantism. And Pierre Birnbaum, Jean-Denis Bredin, and David McCullough helped in the area of anti-Semitism. On pilgrimage and sacred sanctuaries, the work of Jean Chelini and Henry Branthomme, Raymond Jonas, Roger Lipsey, Mary Lee Nolan and Sidney Nolan, and Edith Turner and Victor Turner framed this study's treatment of the worker pilgrimages to Rome. Studies by L'Abbé Emmanuel Barbier, S. William Halperin, and Lillian Parker Wallace helped to place material from the Vatican Archives in perspective.

Works by Anthony Black, Gail Bossenga, Edward Hyams, Steven D. Kale, Steven L. Kaplan, Philippe Levillain, Benjamin F. Martin, David McLellan, William H. Sewell Jr., Catherine Bodard Silver, and K. Steven Vincent contributed in the area of corporatism and its place in the context of social Catholicism. Those of J. E. S. Hayward and Judith F. Stone assisted in the discussion of Solidarism, which brought together several ideologies, including that of traditional corporatism, at the turn of the century. Treatment of foreign affairs, so crucial in assessing the role of papal politics in the joint ventures of Harmel and Leo XIII, benefited from the work of Federico Chabod, Martin Clark, C. J. Lowe and F. Marzari, Humphrey Johnson, William L. Langer, Maurice Larkin, Martin E. Schmidt, and Edward Tannenbaum and Emiliana P. Noether.

This book is divided into five chapters, with each chapter unfolding another forum from which Harmel lived out his developing social program. Chapter 1 introduces Léon Harmel on a personal level. Learning about his family and the early years of Harmel's life leads naturally to an understanding of his philosophy and social vision. It also explains his talent for entrepreneurship. Chapter 2 focuses on Val-des-Bois. It is here that Harmel operated as *patron* of the family business and as social reformer. Expanding the factory reform started by his father, he successfully turned the spinning mill into a Christian corporation and one that, for the most part, operated with a profit. Chapter 3 tests Harmel outside terra firma, that is, outside the familiar, outside his family and family business. *Provocateur* amid fellow factory owners and heir to a rich legacy of French social reform, he soon made a distinctive mark in nineteenth-century social Catholicism. Not surprisingly, he caught the eye of the pope. As Leo XIII prepared his great encyclical on labor, *Rerum Novarum,* he was inspired by what had occurred at Val-des-Bois. But the worker pilgrimages propelled the pope into action. Chapter 4 delves into the French worker pilgrimages, which put to use Harmel's exceptional organizational talents, displayed the religiosity of the male worker, and uncovered the political nature of the pilgrimages to Rome. The pilgrimages put Léon Harmel on the European stage too. Not above using theatrical gimmicks or the press to their advantage, both entrepreneur and pope demonstrated their finesse in using modern media techniques to achieve religious and political goals. Success bred suspicion, however, especially among Italian nationalists, and an incident at the Pantheon in Rome during the 1891 pilgrimage halted ambitions and turned Harmel in yet another direction. Chapter 5 documents Harmel's role in the founding of Christian democracy in France, a movement that absorbed time and energy in the waning years of his life. The Conclusion documents his rich legacy as entrepreneur and as social reformer, assuring him a permanent place in the social history of France as well as in the social teaching of the Roman Catholic Church.

CHAPTER ONE

Family History and Legacy

> Neither cleric, priest, nor layman
> Can from women turn away
> If he does not wish to stray,
> Sinfully from the good Lord; ...
> — The Virtues of Women[1]

THE FAMILY HISTORY AND PERSONAL PHILOSOPHY OF LÉON HARMEL predisposed him to success as an entrepreneur and also to dedicate his life to the service of others. It is important then to understand why the Harmel family settled in the Suippe River valley of northern France and how the successes and failures of early business attempts often were tied to national political events, as well as to the entrepreneurial acumen of the Harmel patriarchs, who frequently weathered seemingly overwhelming odds to keep their factory going. Resilience in times of economic adversity and entrepreneurial creativity were just two family traits passed on to Harmel, who, after taking over the spinning mill in 1854, successfully ran the business until forced to abandon the enterprise during World War I. Equally significant to Harmel's personal development was the family legacy in the area of social reform. Grandparents and parents, brothers and sisters, spouses and children all had a hand in making Léon Harmel the person he was, none more influential than those who nurtured him in his early years. Those who shaped Léon's character and values enabled him to embrace life with boundless confidence and enthusiasm. Likewise, his atttitudes toward clergy, women, and workers, all of whom played key roles in his philosophy and life agenda, largely were formed by early life experiences.

Roots

Léon-Pierre-Louis Harmel was born on February 17, 1829, at Neuville-les-Wasigny, a town in the French Ardennes not far from the Belgian border, in the house of his maternal uncle. Naming the baby Léon curiously seemed to foretell the future: it was also Pope Leo XIII's given name, a fact that the pope delighted in.[2] Destiny also seemed apparent when the second son in a family of eight children ultimately assumed the role of patriarch in the Harmel family and, thereby, became heir to a business and to a legacy initiated by his paternal grandfather and developed by his father.

The grandfather, Jacques Harmel (1763–1824), worked as a blacksmith in the Belgian Ardennes as a young man, but when revolutionary armies destroyed the family forge in 1793, he looked for greater security by changing occupations and relocating. He became interested in the textile business, specifically the wool industry, and in 1810 constructed, near Sainte-Cécile in the Belgian Ardennes, one of the first mechanized (steam-powered) spinning operations in the French empire. The business flourished for a time, with a putting-out system that encompassed neighboring villages, but the fall of Napoléon Bonaparte's empire in 1815 meant that Belgium was once again master of its own house and, consequently, subject to the *douane,* or customs duty. The reimposition of the tax financially ruined Jacques;[3] all of his savings were tied up in the factory.[4]

Undaunted, Jacques Harmel packed up his wife and five surviving children (nine were born to the couple) and crossed the border into France where he established a workshop at Signy-l'Abbaye in the French Ardennes. He tried for two years to make a go of it single-handedly, but as debts mounted and the business faltered, he summoned home from schooling in Reims his two older sons, Jacques-Joseph and Hubert, to help. Jacques-Joseph, the younger of the two but the more inclined to business, inherited the family enterprise at age twenty-five.[5]

Jacques-Joseph Harmel (1795–1884), Léon's father, "incarnated the industrial *bourgeois* in full ascension."[6] He was a workaholic and an entrepreneur. Tireless when it came to putting in hours at the family business, he lived at home and accepted no remuneration until he married in 1824, the year of his father's death. When one venture stumbled, he went on to the next with a resilience that was astounding. The family and the business relocated several more times in the region of the French Ardennes before settling in 1841 on the outskirts of Warmériville. His wife and life partner, Alexandrine Tranchart de Rethel, struck by the beauty and peacefulness of the chosen site along the Suippe River, named the new family spinning mill "Val-des-Bois,"[7] or Wooded Valley.

This last relocation was permanent, and the enterprise eventually was successful but not before the Harmel family once again experienced anxious times. The wool industry was new to Warmériville, a village of approximately 1,134 inhabitants at the time the Harmels were constructing their steam-powered factory along the Suippe. The cost of construction, coupled with the fact that Jacques-Joseph was dedicated to having the latest equipment in the factory, resulted in considerable debt. There were particular problems associated with the Revolution of 1848, which disrupted trade and commerce throughout France as revolutionary embers flared in February, simmered in March, April, and May, and reignited in June before finally being extinguished in Paris that same month.[8]

While Jacques-Joseph worked at the factory, often collapsing among the balls of wool at night for a few hours of sleep, Alexandrine gave birth to eight children in eight years (three died before the age of one year), managed the bustling household with efficiency and joy, and on occasion traveled to Reims to see to bills and debts. She counted every sou and was not above personal sacrifice. In an era when every proper *haute bourgois* (and the Tranchart family were members of the upper middle class, of the *bonne bourgeoisie*) donned a chapeau before stepping outside, Alexandrine gave up buying hats.[9] Her participation in the day-to-day affairs of the mill was not that unusual for wives whose husbands owned textile enterprises in northern France during the eighteenth and early nineteenth century. In fact, women often took over the financial duties of these firms, tending to accounts and balancing the books.[10] In addition to acting as a partner in the business, Alexandrine shared her husband's deep religious faith and no doubt encouraged him when he began the process of turning Val-des-Bois into a Christian factory.

In some ways, Jacques-Joseph was not unique in his ardent religiosity. As a middle-class male (although not as distanced from the artisan class as other members of the middle class since his father originally was a blacksmith), he would have been more likely to be a practicing Catholic than someone who worked with his hands for a living. That the family originated in Belgium also increased the likelihood of religious practice; nineteenth-century Belgian men of all classes went to church more frequently than did French men of the era.[11] It is not surprising then that Jacques-Joseph was disturbed by the irreligion and immorality of the workers at his new factory in the French Ardennes.

He moved from dismay to concrete action by attempting to re-Christianize his workers at first by personal example. The lackluster response to this initial overture led Jacques-Joseph to attempt a more vigorous and systematic course of action. Soon he established institutions and associations that demonstrated his concern for the spiritual and material conditions of the workers at the Harmel factory. For example, in 1842 he created a savings bank for the workers, and in 1846 he organized a relief fund to provide material assistance during illness by guaranteeing to the worker half of his or her salary, free medical care, and, if the worst arose, a Christian burial. To buttress the family unit, he paid wages collectively and personally; as the head of each worker household went into Harmel's office to pick up the family paycheck, Jacques-Joseph bantered with the worker about his children and other personal matters. To provide his workers and their families with wholesome entertainment and informal education, he enlisted his three sons—Jules, Léon, and Ernest—to organize a musical society and give instruction on Sunday. The workers reciprocated by awarding him the sobriquet *le bon père*,[12] or the good father.

To what extent Jacques-Joseph Harmel's social program at Val-des-Bois was inspired by reform begun earlier in the century by concerned Catholics is hard to know, but the effort made at the factory to mitigate the effects of the industrial revolution certainly falls within the framework of social Catholicism. In offering his workers an array of benefits outside of but including traditional Christian charity, he joined others in recognizing a new kind of poverty, pauperism—poverty so pervasive that "large sections of society were degraded and deprived of tolerable conditions of livelihood and of a tolerable life in common with others."[13] His programs at Val also indicated an awareness of the new class stratification brought about by the industrial revolution, one that defined the classes not only by economic disparity but also by religious observance; the French working class, as demonstrated by the Harmel workers, were neglecting if not out and out abandoning religious practice.

While social Catholicism found expression in Belgium, Italy, and Germany, it flowered most profusely and extensively in France, where it began shortly after the onset of industrialization.[14] Its early years, when it at times cross-pollinated with pre-Marxist socialism, were its most creative. But a certain weeding out had to take place. If social Catholicism was to become part of the social teaching of the Catholic Church, it had to manifest a certain doctrinal orthodoxy, and individuals unprepared to commit to a Church whose ideas did not match their own or who were unwilling to wait for change in some distant future parted ways with institutional Christianity. In terms of political periodization, the era of the Bourbon Restoration (1814–1830)[15] and the July Monarchy (1830–1848)[16] most closely matches this time.

Beginning in 1822, the Society of St. Joseph ministered to the workers of Paris and, in so doing, called attention to the needs of the industrial poor. Félicité de Lamennais (1782–1864) championed the efforts of the Society of St. Joseph and fashioned an ideology for what would be known as social Catholicism by decrying the demoralizing effects of the French Revolution, with its breakup of the trade guilds, and advocating the return of artisanal associations as a solution for contemporary worker atomism. Lamennais is considered the founder of social Catholicism in France, just as he is recognized as the man most responsible for suggesting to Catholics interested in social reform that their chief advocate resided in Rome and not among the national episcopacy. Henceforward, social

Catholics were identified with ultramontanism, or adherence to Roman policy, while those more comfortable with the status quo clung to the notion of a national church, or Gallicanism. When Lamennais felt his ideas could no longer be reconciled with the social teaching of the Catholic Church, he left the Church to become a socialist.[17]

Other reformers contributed to social Catholicism too. Antoine-Frédéric Ozanam (1813–1853) founded the Society of St. Vincent de Paul, which had as its express purpose the ministry of the urban poor. Philippe Buchez (1796–1865), who was convinced philosophically that Christianity was the appropriate response to contemporary ills because it emphasized the brotherhood of mankind, pointedly refused to become a practicing Catholic because that would lessen his credibility as intermediary between Catholics and socialists. Even Charles Fourier (1772–1837) can be given some credit for influencing social Catholicism as he stressed societal "harmony."[18] Certain other aspects of his ideology, such as the dismantling of the traditional family, kept the Fourierists and social Catholics respectfully distanced, however.

Just as the Revolution of 1848 disrupted national political life by bringing down the July Monarchy of Louis-Philippe (r. 1830–1848) and putting into place, albeit ever so briefly, the Second Republic (1848–1852),[19] and just as it wreaked havoc with commercial enterprises like that of the Harmel factory, it also initiated a period of sobering reassessment within the ranks of social Catholics. For many, flirtation with socialism ended on the barricades in 1848. Those Catholics who had identified themselves as democrats or republicans or Christian socialists in the years from 1830 to 1848 became disillusioned with the shortcomings of both church and state in 1848.[20] They would have to wait until later in the nineteenth century and the appearance of a new generation of reformers such as Léon Harmel to rekindle dreams. In the meantime, most social Catholics became dedicated monarchists who did not support the current occupant of the French throne, Napoléon III (r. 1852–1870),[21] but instead held out hope of a Bourbon restoration. As so-called Legitimists, they envisioned a new alliance of Throne and Altar as a means to implement their social program.[22]

From 1852 to 1870, the period of the Second Empire, the Harmel family, as bona fide social Catholics, were ultramontane and Legitimist. Léon in particular looked to the pope as a partner in all his endeavors on behalf of the French workers. And since the pope resided in Rome, center of religious cosmology for Catholics, ultramontanism was not only something to support intellectually, but to feel physically, emotionally, and spiritually when visiting the papal city. The Harmels positively thrived on being in Rome. Walking its streets and smelling its air were tactile and emotional experiences that exhilarated, especially when their visits typically included a papal audience. In 1860, for example, Léon accompanied his seventy-year-old father to Rome, where the men had a private audience with Pius IX. Jacques-Joseph had been ill, and Léon wondered as they set out from Val if the excursion to Rome would prove foolhardy. To his delight, his father appeared rejuvenated by the Roman sojourn, adding to the sacredness of the city in the eyes of father and son. Perhaps because his father seemed to recover in Rome, Léon disclosed that the visit had been inspirational for him. It was then and there that he decided to organize pilgrimages to Rome.[23] That the idea for the worker pilgrimages came to him while in Rome in 1860, years in advance of their occurrence, was in keeping with the notion that religious centers are loci of revelation.[24] Rome would retain its sacredness for Léon Harmel; it was here that he was energized and inspired.

Léon's commitment to the Bourbon pretender[25] and to the throne of France was considerably more fragile than his commitment to the occupant of the Chair of St. Peter. He became one of the first to shake off the Legitimist chains once Leo XIII endorsed the republican form of government for the French in 1892. Nevertheless, as ardent Catholics living not too far from Reims, Léon and his family gravitated quite naturally to Legitimism. Reims was the geographic center and symbolic capital of Legitimism. According to tradition, when Clovis (466–511), king of the Franks, converted to Christianity, holy oil descended from heaven in a vial to be used at his baptismal ceremony. Because of the miracle, the holy oil was reserved for rightful kings of France; their legitimacy was tied to a miracle and a ceremonial anointment at Reims. Beginning in the twelfth century with Louis VIII, kings of France were anointed at their coronation ceremonies with a mixture of sacred chrism and holy oil from the vial.[26] During the Hundred Years' War, for example, Joan of Arc (1412–1431) escorted the Valois claimant to the throne of France from the Loire Valley to the Cathedral of Notre Dame in Reims for his coronation and anointment. She persisted in calling him "dauphin" rather than "king" until the moment of legitimization,[27] but once duly crowned and anointed at Reims, Joan, as well as most other French men and women, recognized Charles VII as rightful ruler of France. The tradition persisted through twenty-five coronations. The Bourbon king, Charles X, observed the sacred ceremony of French kings in 1824, but he would be the last to do so. When the count of Chambord died in 1883 both the tradition of anointment at Reims and Legitimism as a political movement died with him.

Tied to political Legitimism was devotion to the Sacré Coeur. The Bourbon Louis XVI had prayed to the Sacred Heart to bail him out of political difficulties, and though his prayers obviously went unanswered, he placed France under the protection of the Sacred Heart as he neared the end of his life. His death produced a bona fide martyr for the Legitimist cause.[28] Devotion to the Sacred Heart, therefore, seemed especially appropriate in times of national turmoil, an abundant commodity in France during the eighteenth and nineteenth centuries (one need only be reminded of the major political revolutions of 1789, 1830, 1848, and 1870). From the French Revolution forward, the Sacred Heart was the emblem of the Catholic Church in France and intrinsically linked to the restoration of the Bourbons. Legitimism, at least until the death of the count of Chambord in 1883, was regarded as politically subversive.[29]

The building of the basilica of the Sacré Coeur in Montmartre in what was in 1871 the very heart of radicalized Paris displayed a certain bravado to be sure. As Raymond Jonas points out, though, the site was irresistible. Saint Denis, the first bishop of Paris, had been martyred there in the third century, and thus the hilltop, high above Paris, represented sacred ground worthy of a grand religious edifice dedicated to national retribution for past sins.[30] Psychologically, many French Catholics were more inclined to attribute defeat on the battlefield during the Franco-Prussian War to the de-Christianization of the nation than to any military weakness. The Romanesque-Byzantine basilica, constructed from 1873 to 1919, served as the modern political emblem of the power of the Sacred Heart for Catholic France.

The Harmel family saw devotion to the Sacred Heart as essential not only for political reasons but for religious and social reasons as well. The heart of Jesus represented a compassionate Christ, an aspect of the divine nature that would have special significance for the suffering of society, which in nineteenth-century France essentially meant the worker.[31] On a more personal level, the cult of the Sacred Heart became established in the family with Alexandrine and Jacques-Joseph Harmel,[32] and Léon and his wife, Gabrielle, became ardent followers. Gabrielle Harmel, for example, performed her two principal duties, that of wife and mother, by drawing inspiration from the Sacred Heart,[33] while Léon spent the closing days and hours of his life, literally dragging himself from his deathbed, meditating before the Blessed Sacrament, the adoration of which was a fundamental part of the devotion to the Sacred Heart.[34] Devotion to the Sacred Heart was stimulated further once Leo XIII issued the *Annum Sacrum* (May 25, 1899) encouraging personal commitment to the Sacred Heart.

While somewhat typical of other social Catholics in their endorsement of ultramontanism and Legitimism, the Harmel family was decidedly atypical in the passion of its commitment to changing the factory environment for workers. Jacques-Joseph initiated the program of reform at Val-des-Bois, but when illness prevented him from continuing as *patron* and Jules, his eldest son, was away helping his father-in-law with his business, he turned to his second son, Léon, in 1854 to run the factory and to carry forward reforms already put into place. Jacques-Joseph nevertheless continued to actively participate as best he could in life at Val, and now both father and son were affectionately called *bon père* by their workers. Jacques-Joseph had lived with his son since 1848 when widowed and continued to do so until his death on March 4, 1884. As he aged, Léon lovingly cared for him. In a moving acknowledgment, Jacques-Joseph observed, "He is more than my son, he is like my father."[35] As in so many other things they shared, Léon was twenty-five years old when he became *patron* of Val-des-Bois. He accepted the responsibility without hesitation. In a way, he had trained for the position all his life.

Léon Harmel attended the Collège[36] Saint-Vincent de Senlis from 1843 to 1850 where his formal education was traditional and classical, and his performance mediocre. He studied the Middle Ages, the Renaissance, and the French Revolution and thought of those epochs of history that departed from close alliance with religion as pagan and godless. He welcomed nineteenth-century Romanticism with its fresh appreciation of Christian virtues. He enjoyed the literature of Chateaubriand and

Lamartine, for example, and delighted in playing the most popular new instrument of the century, the pianoforte.[37] Harmel easily passed his exit exam, the *baccalauréat,* at the Collège, but that did not stop him from criticizing the French educational system, both laic and confessional. Elementary schools, in his opinion, neglected to prepare children adequately in the practicalities of everyday living, and the classical programs followed in the secondary schools erred by completely ignoring study of the Bible. Still, Harmel's education at the Collège Saint-Vincent de Senlis succeeded in nourishing his natural curiosity.[38]

His thoughts with regard to school curriculum clearly indicated a preference for the pragmatic. Léon Harmel was an empiricist in an age enamored with the wonders of science. Theories, he believed, only divided men of goodwill who wasted their eloquence, passion, and efforts in attempts to dominate by having the last word.[39] Thus, while he was a man of conviction when it came to personal beliefs, he was open to new ideas and ways, even when in the eighth decade of life, and firmly believed circumstances often directed a fresh course of action. Because his life's work was immersed in what he called "the social side of things," which by its very nature, Harmel reasoned, was "the truly practical side of things," he found it necessary to return always to the pragmatic, and that was not to be found in theories but rather in life itself.[40] The human personality in all its fullness and with all its idiosyncrasies was his "living book."[41]

Besides being a pragmatist, humanist, and devotée of the Middle Ages, Romanticism, and the piano, Harmel possessed numerous noteworthy character traits, many of which were inherited from the paternal side of the family. The Harmel men were known for their tenacity, entrepreneurship, indefatigability, simplicity of lifestyle, and religiosity. Léon acquired all these traits. He demonstrated an iron will from youth on, which resulted in the stubbornness of a bulldog and a righteousness that expressed itself in impatience and intolerance of others. His headstrong nature energized him. His involvement in organizations and events such as L'Oeuvre des Cercles, L'Association des Patrons du Nord, the congresses of Christian workers, the worker pilgrimages to Rome, Notre Dame de l'Usine, and the Social Weeks at Val all bore the Harmel stamp and suggested long days and short nights. He was a classic example of an overachiever and frequently became overextended in his commitments.[42] His strong will led one journalist to describe him as the "pontiff of Val," and of even greater consequence, his bullheadedness put a halt to the canonization process started shortly after his death in 1915.[43]

Harmel's inclination to modest living was less controversial. Sensitive to the fact that a luxurious lifestyle would in all likelihood put off their workers, neither father nor son was inclined toward the display of wealth.[44] Léon never tired of preaching against luxury and despite his notoriety preferred always to present himself simply and unpretentiously as "mill owner of Val-des-Bois."[45] Still, there was always time and money for those in need.[46] Unostentatious living was de rigueur in the Harmel household as Léon was growing up, not only because of personal philosophy but also because of economic necessity. In this, as in the matter of religious piety, Alexandrine Tranchart Harmel joined her husband in the socialization of their children. Again, that she exercised considerable control over the household was typical of women of northern France.[47]

In fact, there is considerable indication from the correspondence between mother and son when he was away at school at the Collège Saint-Vincent de Senlis that Alexandrine Harmel was the most instrumental family member in forming Léon's character and imparting values, with perhaps his grandmother Tranchart a close second.[48] But as Léon entered adulthood, Alexandrine came to rely on her son increasingly as spiritual advisor. While still in school, he routinely offered her moral advice, typically recommending Christian resignation, when she encountered difficulties with regard to the family's business.[49] Earlier, it was she, who in the process of tucking in Léon each evening at bedtime, had him examine his conscience before falling asleep. She would admonish the imperfections and applaud the virtues of the day's activities.[50] Léon must have responded especially well to her spiritual guidance, as there were hints early on that he might become a priest.

Grandmother Tranchart nurtured the notion of a religious vocation for her grandson, and she, like her daughter, doted on the boy. She had hoped that one of her sons would become a priest, but when that dream failed to become a reality, she turned to Léon as a fresh possibility. She furnished him with a complete "chapel" where the six-year old "said" Mass and then afterward enlisted his siblings and other children to process through the village streets to their maternal grandparents' home in Boulzicourt.[51] Grandmother Tranchart took her grandson's vocation seriously; she willed her Bible to Léon on one condition: he would have to become a priest to get it.[52]

Léon's mother also encouraged her son to consider the priesthood as a vocation, and he gave it serious thought during the last two years at the Collège (1848–1850). But his spiritual advisor at the school recognized that Léon was better suited for the lay apostolate,[53] and circumstances moved him in that direction. When his favorite younger brother, Ernest, became ill, Léon left school in 1850 to care for him. Being a caregiver came easily and naturally to him, and it was a role he would practice throughout his life. He routinely, for example, visited the sick at Val-des-Bois, and apparently had the knack for consoling the suffering.[54]

Alexandrine Harmel and her second son were especially close, and Léon had nothing but the highest praise and admiration for his mother. Indeed, she appeared to be the consummate French woman. She possessed an eye for detail that brought beauty and grace to the household, worked wonders in the garden, played the piano, and quite seriously wondered why she was exhausted at night.[55] Léon regarded his mother as vivacious, imaginative, pious, and intelligent. She was untiring in her good humor, creative in turning the bustling household into a place of understated bourgeois elegance, unstinting in her attention to the religious instruction of her children, and a woman of clear, good sense.[56] Alexandrine Harmel seemingly embodied every Christian virtue and was the ideal nineteenth-century middle-class lady, a true bourgeoise.[57] But perhaps Léon paid her the ultimate compliment when he characterized her as a "femme de tête."[58] She died peacefully on November 18, 1856,[59] having bequeathed to her son a fertile imagination and an eternal optimism in the face of life's difficulties.[60]

In 1854 Léon would be able to put into practice all that he had learned from his family when his father's retirement and the inability of Jules to manage the factory at Val-des-Bois meant that he would become *patron*. It was time to begin his life's work, and his goals were consistent with his family's values. In his own words, his was to be a "life absorbed by three great loves: the union and sanctification of the family, the happiness of the workers, and the service of Jesus Christ."[61]

The Union and Sanctification of the Family

When Léon Harmel decided not to pursue a vocation in the priesthood, he opted for the married state as the alternative best suited for a lay apostolate. In 1852, not long after leaving the Collège Saint-Vincent de Senlis, he married Gabrielle Harmel, a cousin, who caught his eye and won the approval of his mother. By marrying his cousin and receiving the benediction of his mother, Harmel acted according to standards set for young scions of northern textile enterprises. Cousins married to keep wealth within the family, to assure the protection of financial and production secrets, and to lessen influence and scrutiny from outsiders;[62] and women from the region routinely saw to matters involving marriage and vocation, as well as distribution of parental largesse and love.[63] Practical matters aside, Gabrielle was the perfect complement to her headstrong and energetic husband. She was "soft and humble of heart," a masterpiece of tenderness, more temperate than he. When Léon demanded the children be up and doing at five o'clock in the morning in order to begin the very regimented day he had outlined for them, she typically tried to intervene on their behalf and begged relief from the rigorous schedule.[64] Like her husband, she was religious and preferred simple living. The young couple wasted no time in establishing a large family. In eighteen years of marriage, they produced nine children, one of whom died at an early age, before Gabrielle died of peritonitis[65] on October 13, 1870,[66] forty-one days after Napoléon III surrendered to the German army at Sedan on September 2 and forty-four days after the Prussian crown prince visited Val-des-Bois on his way to the German victory parade in Paris. Widowed at forty-one, Léon never remarried. He attempted after 1870 to be both mother and father to the children, making an extra effort to provide them with the tenderness so characteristic of Gabrielle Harmel.[67] Two women assisted Léon in raising his large family after the death of Gabrielle; his widowed sister stepped in after 1870, until his daughter took over with the younger children in 1888.[68]

The Harmel family, in both its nuclear and its extended forms, was close, brought together by their shared faith, their care and concern for one another, and their trials.[69] It also was a family accustomed to labor. Léon Harmel refused simply to hand over spending money to his children, for he believed that men were to earn money by the sweat of their brow.[70] In the role of patriarch, he warned his numerous relatives that the "worst thing was to do nothing,"[71] and consequently, as various Harmel family members came to live at Val-des-Bois, they were housed, helped, and put to work.[72] Though a bit of a martinet, he demanded of himself in equal measure.

The Problem

Outside his immediate family, however, Harmel detected serious trouble: "Children no longer obey their parents and parents no longer know how to command. Within households there is dissension and hate, and indeed charity seems to have departed from the Earth."[73] Unfortunately, the problem was not confined to the individual family unit, according to Harmel's assessment, because in destroying the family, civil society ultimately became unraveled too.[74] The basic causes of the problem, according to Harmel, were political and economic in nature and linked to the events of 1789.

As early as the sixteenth century, Harmel argued, "forensic surgeons" set out to destroy Christian society not only by beginning the drive toward secularization of the national state but also by eliminating artisanal associations. Although he never specifically identified the "forensic surgeons," he no doubt referred to thinkers and writers of the early modern period who wanted to move society away from church domination and toward secularization. These same intellectuals also wanted to eliminate guilds, the medieval craft associations that regulated the quality and quantity of goods produced in the shops, provided for their members when ill, and established an ethos of brotherhood among its members and their families. But without associational life, moral structure disintegrated and workers experienced an aimlessness, or anomie, which Émile Durkheim, the greatest social scientist of the era, wrote about at great length and considered a prominent factor in antagonism between labor and management.[75] Reformers wanted to expunge medieval craft associations from society not because they detested workers or devalued human labor but because they saw them as restricting trade and representative of exclusivity since the associations were limited to skilled workers. But Harmel's interpretation was dramatically different. For him, sixteenth-century "legalists" believed that working with one's hands was "degrading," had no "social value," and was a "humiliating necessity from which mankind ought to escape."[76]

The forensic surgeons-cum-legalists, Harmel continued, succeeded politically in 1789 when the workers' corporations, along with professional representation, were "brutally destroyed, thereby reducing the worker to an isolated being, abandoned in the midst of his enemies who organized themselves against his faith, his family, his dignity, and his wage."[77] Harmel referred here to the Chapelier Law of 1791 that made illegal all professional associations, such as the corporate guilds, on the grounds that they were elitist and protected only a certain segment of the working class. With the worker left unprotected just as the industrial revolution was set to take off in France, Harmel was outraged at what had happened to the laboring class in the aftermath of the French Revolution. The Revolution of 1789, in his opinion, unleashed the "thirst for riches" and the "desire for success" that soon became emblematic of nineteenth-century economic liberalism. The results, he thought, had been devastating for the workers and for French society as a whole, for egoism, once considered a vice, had been transformed into a virtue.[78]

Harmel further believed that the Revolution of 1789 established a certain pernicious pattern in France, for revolution had become the "mistress of our country."[79] And, indeed, events of 1830, 1848, and 1870 lent credence to his supposition. Harmel conceded that tactically revolution appealed to a nation that characteristically shied away from half-measures. But while revolutionary rhetoric flattered the worker, it reduced him to a state of economic servitude; in reality, revolution was the "enemy" of the worker.[80] He witnessed firsthand the destructive nature of revolution when he found himself in Paris in 1848 and became convinced that revolution only worked to the disadvantage of the workers.[81]

He thought that the political system instituted during the French Revolution held the seeds of its own destruction, and this prospect gave him hope. By recognizing the right to redress grievances and gradually expanding the scope of political suffrage, the state unwittingly allowed a "secret plan of divine justice" to unfold; the enfranchised worker now had the means to reform laws and re-Christianize France.[82] Harmel consequently was willing to concede that certain aspects of the French Revolution were, at least, handy. Perhaps political empowerment of the underprivileged would end the cycle of revolution that had been the national plague since 1789. Consistent with his pragmatic nature, Harmel eluded unqualified political labeling. He began as a monarchist, albeit it as a subversive Legitimist, and ended up as a republican. Philosophically, he was a lifelong "democrat"; governmental institutional form was of secondary importance to him. His bête noire was the godless state, the uncaring state, which Harmel associated with the secularization of society.

Economic fallout from political events surrounding the French Revolution was all too visible in late-nineteenth-century France, and Léon Harmel was not alone in noting the contemporary evils associated with unbridled industrialization. For example, Dr. Louis Villermé's reports of the 1830s and 1840s on the physical and moral destruction inflicted on the French working class generated considerable interest among politicians for reform modeled after so-called English legislation. Books such as *L'Ouvrière,* written by Jules Simon in 1860, noted the particular problems associated with female labor.[83] Indeed, this was an era characterized by high infant mortality, shortened life spans for adults, child labor, exploitation of workers, discord between labor and management, and pauperism.[84]

Pauperism, as defined by Harmel, was a product of "industrialization without religion and without faith. It united material misery with moral abasement and was the incurable malady of modern society." In short, the "progress of misery followed the progress of industrial riches."[85] For this reason, "millions of workers without work have asked despairingly, 'Where is the prosperity that was promised by the utilitarian school of economics? ... They [the liberal economists] have stimulated luxury and encouraged consumption without limit, but only by the sale of our material misery.'" Furthermore, economic liberalism remains "powerless to remedy the evil that it has produced,"[86] as one need only look to the workshops for a "living condemnation" of liberalism.[87] The net result, Harmel posited, was the total ruin of the new working class, the proletariat.[88]

His sharp censure of classical economic liberalism argues in favor of placing Harmel among nineteenth-century Christian socialists. He observed that laissez-faire economics had not succeeded in establishing a trickle-down economy in which society's poorest members shared in the prosperity of its wealthiest members. He also called attention to the fact that contrary to utilitarianism's notion that there should be laws for the greatest happiness for the greatest numbers, liberal representatives of the Third Republic lagged behind their counterparts in Great Britain and elsewhere when it came to government intervention in the workplace. We have no evidence that Harmel monitored parliamentary records and debates, especially outside of France, or knew of specific reforms or reformers, but the records allow us to say that he greatly admired Germany, Great Britain, and the United States,[89] all countries that had demonstrated not only their industrial might but also their willingness to enact legislation implementing workplace reform. He also noted that the industrial revolution tantalized workers with a plethora of consumer goods but that abysmally low wages often kept new products out of reach for the average family. The scenario Harmel painted was a ringing indictment of economic liberalism, made all the worse, in his estimation, by the displacement of religion from society.

Pauperism was merely the exterior sign of an interior disorder, or in his words, "a sickness of the soul," brought on by the godless state. The egoism and individualism so esteemed in contemporary society were, in fact, vices that instead of serving personal interest, led to the "collapse of fortunes" and the "destruction of families." For Harmel, virtue was the necessary base for prosperity and vice the source of material and moral ruin.[90] Trimouille purports that Léon Harmel had all the earmarks of a puritan; material success indicated moral virtue and divine approval.[91]

Harmel repeatedly expressed admiration for the American people whom he perceived as God-fearing, thrifty, hardworking, and adventuresome. A virtuous nation would naturally be rewarded with material blessings, and the economic history of the United States supported his claims, he observed. His reasoning in the general broke down in the particular, however. For example, Harmel esteemed both Theodore Roosevelt and Andrew Carnegie, Roosevelt for his "hardiness in the face of life's adversities" and Carnegie for his business acumen and the decision not to ruin his children by endowing them with his vast wealth.[92] (Coincidentally, these traits were not dissimilar to those associated with the Harmel family.) What Harmel seemingly failed to notice was the egoism and the rugged individualism present in Roosevelt and Carnegie, which admittedly allowed the former to achieve feats such as the completion of the Panama Canal, a project started by the French but finished with remarkable flourish by the Americans,[93] and the latter to accumulate vast sums of wealth built on the backs of American labor. Harmel perceived American cupidity as both romantic and virtuous, while those same qualities, when packaged in the French context, he typically construed as vice.

For Harmel, the evils of contemporary society could not be obliterated without addressing the moral order. He wrote in 1879 that "there has always been a fight against good and evil, and today the evil was economic liberalism."[94] In his Manichaean vision of the world, France was at a crucial point in its history. It either would fall into complete atheism or once again, as eldest daughter of the Church, climb to the "heights of faith."[95] And there was to be no compromising with principles or with the enemy. Harmel thought that since 1789 the state had attempted to play God, but, in reality, this was both a gross misjudgment of the proper order of things and blatant atheism. Some Christians erroneously imagined that economic liberalism, in its present godless form, and Catholicism could somehow reach an accommodation, but this, for Harmel, writing in 1876, would be like fusing the "oui" with the "non," the result being a "hybrid doctrine."[96] Later, as state legislation moved toward helping the worker, he withdrew from such an absolutist analysis and his criticism became somewhat less stinging. Yet, as Claude Langlois has pointed out, the very excessiveness of such oratory—and Harmel was not alone in this regard—suggests that the issues were real and that there were indeed two distinct philosophical camps in nineteenth-century France, the Catholics and the seculars.[97]

But in the immediate aftermath of the military fiasco of 1870 and the installation of the secular Republic, and with the industrial revolution in full swing and the laboring class suffering enormously because of it, Léon Harmel surmised that drastic action was needed; simple philanthropy, a mere "palliative" in his estimation,[98] had not been adequate. If the spiritual and temporal worlds were ever to be reunited, traditional agents of religious propagation had to be summoned anew. He turned to the institutional Church and to women to help him reintroduce religion into society.

The Solution

According to Harmel's interpretation of history, "the centuries of faith were the centuries of social peace."[99] Consequently, he idealized the Middle Ages. The medieval family was "strong, traditions were respected, and households taught religious faith which became engraved in the hearts of the children."[100] His explanation of medieval society masked certain realities, however, for this was a period when peasant revolts disrupted social peace, when serfdom kept most of the peasantry in abject poverty and without human or civil rights, and when popular religion often blended orthodoxy with beliefs and practices that predated the arrival of Christianity. Harmel also held to the idea that the Middle Ages represented a time when the workers' social position was recognized and honored[101] and the economy was protected from the "voracious" usury of the present.[102] Here he stood on firmer ground for several reasons. First, in the traditional society of orders, every individual contributed to the welfare of the whole and was, theoretically at least, important for the functioning of society: peasants provided food, artisans and shopkeepers provided necessary goods and services, nobles provided military protection and government, and, most important, clergy provided the means (by administration of the sacraments, for example) for salvation. Second, to prevent anyone from preying on the misfortune of another, the Church outlawed Christians from charging interest on loans to coreligionists; usury would be left to the Jew, who was shut out of most other means by which to earn a respectful living and, as a result, a frequent victim of anti-Semitism. The Church shifted its position on the use of usury once bank loans became part and parcel of the business expansion associated with capitalism. But defaulting on loans drove under not only the rural family farm but also the urban shopkeeper during the latter half of the nineteenth century, and as a result, usury and its association with the Jew remained present in French society. In his comparison of contemporary society with an earlier epoch, Harmel's assessment was not always historically accurate, but many nineteenth-century Romantics were just as guilty of idealizing the Middle Ages.

Outwardly at least, the Middle Ages stood in stark contrast to fin-de-siècle France in which a godless state presided over a society replete with industrial evils, the most critical, for Harmel, being the breakdown of the family. Since the Church always incorporated the spiritual into the material, Harmel perceived the Church as the most logical agent to solve contemporary social problems.[103] Indeed, Harmel argued, the current persecution of the French Church was acknowledgment that it "harbored the poor and the oppressed" and that it operated with a "concrete program while the pagan state did not."[104]

In fact, Harmel continued, the Church through the ages had involved itself in the temporal world. By overseeing worker and commercial associations, as well as rules that promoted justice and brotherhood, the Catholic Church expressed its traditional concern for such mundane affairs as commercial prosperity.[105] Peter and the other early Christians, he pointed out, focused their efforts on the commercial cities of the Hellenistic world, such as Antioch and Rome. They accepted the challenge of these cities of trade and industry and their attendant corruption and were rewarded with souls for Christ. From the first Christian centuries to the later ones of the Crusades and the discovery of the New World, he went on, the Catholic Church was associated with urbanization and commercialization. Not until the pernicious influences of the Renaissance, beginning with the sixteenth century and culminating with the suppression of the worker corporations (guilds) during the French Revolution was the bond between Church and commercial society broken. Simply stated, secularization was the culprit.

Yet, despite the adverse conditions of the present, the Catholic Church, in Harmel's opinion, was ready for the challenge, a challenge that would be met by employing traditional methodology, that is, by juggling conservative and progressive measures.[106] For example, the Church campaigned for justice in all commercial transactions by condemning exorbitant interest rates and the law of supply and demand, the principal modus operandi of economic liberalism. The Church also supported the worker cause by endorsing Sunday as a day of rest, morality in the workplace, and a just remuneration for all who labored.[107]

Harmel assigned the role of societal mediator to the Catholic clergy. He envisioned them breaking down barriers between employers and employees, between government and governed, and by dealing severely with the important people (*les grands*) and by showing compassion for the weak and humble (*les petits*).[108] Yet Harmel was not prepared to delegate complete and uncritical executive power to the hierarchy of the Catholic Church. With the exception of the bishop of Rome, he was capable of taking the clergy to task,[109] and he believed that priests were limited in how much they could influence contemporary society. He noted in particular the lack of scientific knowledge the average priest was exposed to in this new age of science, and felt in general that the clergy lacked schooling in practical matters.[110] For this reason, beginning in summer

1887, Harmel invited seminarians to spend part of their summer recess at Val-des-Bois. The Semaines Sociales introduced the young men to science, encouraged discussion of current social questions, and, of course, allowed them to observe firsthand the social experiment conducted at the Harmel factory. In this, Harmel anticipated the more secular education of the modern seminarian, as well as such later innovations as the worker-priest movement of the 1950s. Involvement in the formation of future generations of priests reflected Harmel's view that the Catholic Church as a whole had to keep abreast of the latest knowledge and societal changes. He wrote, for example, that it was necessary for the Church to develop a "Catholic science" for the latest economic works just as it routinely did for liturgy and dogma.[111]

Harmel did not coin the term "Catholic science." It apparently entered usage with the followers of Lamennais who wanted to find a place in modern Catholic theology for advances in science and was part of the ongoing debate between Catholics and seculars over the sensitive issues of science and ethics. Since science had only become a separate discipline from theology in the seventeenth century and secularized during the Revolution, Catholics looked for a way to reunite science and theology. The need to develop a "Catholic science" became apparent after 1860 but more urgent after 1870, when German philology and Darwinian biology questioned traditional thinking on biblical matters. Catholics also wanted to know how to respond to pointed inquiries about such uncomfortable events in Church history as the trial of Galileo and were relieved when a scientist of the stature of Louis Pasteur could be counted among ardent believers.[112] Harmel, for one, evoked the Pasteur name with great assurance.

Knowledge of the contemporary world was mandatory then if the Catholic Church was to reassert its influence in society and effectively mediate difficulties between individuals or institutions. And when Harmel spoke of a resurgent Church, he typically placed its locus of operation within the public sphere. The Church, with its male hierarchy, best related to the male world of business and government on its own turf. Priests, armed with practical knowledge, were to join forces with employers and employees, newly instilled with religious conviction, to become modern crusaders for Christ. Furthermore, if Christ were returned to the world of commerce and industry, young men would be situated in a proper moral environment for the nurturing of vocations. The disquieting erosion of the priestly ranks, according to Harmel, would be halted.[113]

If the principal instrument for the re-Christianization of France in the public sphere was the Church, women were the chief agents for the private or domestic sphere, as "the family is essentially the domain of the woman."[114] But by the same token, responsibility for the moral condition of society was not shared equitably between the genders. Women traditionally shouldered an inordinate part of that responsibility, and in this, Harmel merely reflected past history and present culture. In his words, "the woman in all societies was the foremost moralizing element, the foundation of all society,"[115] so much so that "without good women, there is neither family, nor society, nor social work in the fullness of the word."[116]

Moreover, not all categories of women were empowered to the same degree, because "to make households Christian it is necessary that the *mothers* be Christian. If the mothers are hostile, or only indifferent, there will arise a nearly insurmountable obstacle. No matter the milieu, the mother saves or causes the others to perish; she is Eve or Mary."[117] The Eve-Mary dualism referred to by Harmel and held by Christian theologians since the early days of the Church gave women an extraordinarily important role in Christian salvation but, at the same time, pinned the primary responsibility for sin and corruption on the female of the species. Women were complex creatures, physiologically and psychologically, their nature possessed of complementary and contradictory moral counterparts,[118] according to this view. Eve overturned the natural hierarchy by acting authoritatively in the Garden of Eden when she, not Adam, responded affirmatively to the serpent, and by upsetting the natural order of things, she brought evil to the world. Mary, by agreeing to become the mother of God, erased the sin of Eve and restored woman's dignity. Her loving and long-suffering nature earned her a place at the right hand of her Son; she became Queen of Heaven. It is no coincidence that within Catholic culture there are so many churches and institutions dedicated to Our Lady—Notre Dame—that honor Mary, mother of God.[119]

Feminists extol motherhood for other reasons: it conferred distinction and authority. Christine de Pizan, for example, wrote of women's uniqueness because of their monopoly on childbirth.[120] Gerda Lerner asserts that motherhood not only conveys societal authority but also results in a so-called ideology of motherhood, which goes beyond the physical act of giving birth by assuring women a primary source of identity.[121] She further points out that the meaning of motherhood depended on class. Peasant women probably had in mind additional workers in the fields as they produced large families, whereas noblewomen were especially intent on producing male heirs.[122] By the nineteenth century, the wives of factory workers (and mine workers if we use Émile Zola's *Germinal* as an example) continued to produce large families, but the difficulty of feeding children in the face of insufficient wages made the rationale of having large families increasingly dubious, whereas middle-class women, largely isolated from economic deprivation, produced children not for economic motives but for cultural and religious reasons.

Although Harmel seems not to have commented directly on the general French concern with the declining birthrate and high infant mortality,[123] his ideas on motherhood were shaped by contemporary secular and religious culture. Both Church and nation celebrated the family, and mothers were thought integral to that societal unit. His own family history bore witness to the importance attached to motherhood; the Harmel couples had large families, and in the case of his immediate family, that is, his siblings and his children, numbers of live births exceeded the norm among the northern bourgeoisie.[124] His devotion to and admiration for his mother (who delivered eight children) and wife (who delivered nine children) were genuine but no doubt reinforced sentiments already present in French, particularly Catholic, culture.

Martin Luther, not the Roman Church, frequently is credited with emphasizing the critical role of the mother in the religious education of the family's children. His translation of the Bible into German not only empowered Christian laity in general; by encouraging women to learn to read in order to better instruct their children in God's word, he went a long way in advancing female literacy. Luther further empowered the married woman by eliminating religious communities. The religious life, once considered the most perfect vocation,[125] and convents, once considered respectable depositories for daughters, were no longer options for Protestant women.

Léon Harmel, of course, did not look to Martin Luther on the topic of French womanhood, but he had inadvertently absorbed what had taken place in cultural history since the Reformation: married life had become in many French households the preferred vocation for its women. Although French women entered religious life in record numbers throughout the nineteenth century, Harmel remained relatively silent about his own daughter who became a nun. To what extent demographic concerns played a role in his exalted notions of motherhood remains uncertain, but since he had a pragmatic bent, the cloistered life might have appeared less conducive to the overt proselytizing he had in mind than did the vocation of motherhood.

Not all women were born to goodness, however. Although daughters might be considered the "ornament" of the marital union because of their "purity" and "softness," and they often gave "dignity" and "joy" to households, parents had to exercise constant vigilance.[126] The teenage years were fraught with danger as then girls experienced a "bubbling up" (*bouillonnement*) of passions, their imaginations ran wild, and indeed all sorts of physical forces were at work.[127] Marriage, but especially motherhood, tamed this darker side of the female persona. This analysis of the female nature by Harmel indicates he assimilated traditional religious and physiological beliefs dating from at least the time of Artistotle: women were less cerebral and more passionate than men.[128] (We do not see a similar diatribe on the hormonal surges experienced by young men, for example.) This ideology led to the justification of traditional patriarchal society in which women, since they were less capable than men of analytic thinking, were best left in a subordinate role.[129] Still, one cannot leave the subject before being reminded that Harmel considered Alexandrine Tranchart Harmel, his mother, a *femme de tête,* an intelligent woman.

When discussing women, particularly in their role as mothers, Harmel ascribed to them an almost mystical relationship with God. In a somewhat veiled, perhaps unwitting allusion to the physical and emotional burden carried by married women, Harmel described the life of women as "a road of sorrow," which if "voluntarily offered" to God for the "salvation of mankind, could save the world."[130] And certainly he had ample opportunity to observe firsthand the extraordinarily long days and short nights of his mother and wife as they went about the business of raising large families while simultaneously running a household and, in the case of Alexandrine, seeing to paying bills and arranging loans in Reims. He observed further that "mothers came to God without effort and almost naturally."[131] Again, he must have based this theory on female saintliness on observations of the Harmel family, since other women of the era resorted to prostitution, abortion, and infanticide to survive,[132] not ideal ways of experiencing motherhood.

With considerable hyperbole, Harmel bowed to the economic power wielded by mothers within their households when he declared them the "sovereign motor of the economy" and maintained that it was impossible to do anything in that area without their concurrence.[133] It seems, then, that while Harmel certainly was capable of traditional biases against women, he also demonstrated both sincere respect for women and certain sensitivity to the difficulties they experienced in industrialized France. His thoughts on the female factory worker illustrated these points.

Like many of his contemporaries, Harmel was troubled by the conditions under which women worked, for if the "factory evils are distressing for a man, they are ten times worse for a woman."[134] He especially noted a "profound and nearly universal degradation of women in the modern workshops" because of sexual harassment "from on high," that is, from the boss or his foreman.[135] For this reason, he advocated not only a morally responsible supervisory staff but also the separation of the sexes in the workplace as much as was practically feasible, and in this, he was again in agreement with most of his contemporaries. Indeed, that women were in the workplace at all was not considered ideal. For the "good of society," doctors and economists advised against women working outside the home,[136] and most French women sought employment in the public sphere only when their husbands were in a "precarious economic situation."[137] Harmel was in perfect agreement, for he wrote in 1891 of the satisfaction a parent experienced when a daughter met a respectable man, one who was active, hardworking, and able to make his own way, because men who were supported by their wives were in an "inferior situation."[138]

Harmel also observed that the female factory worker was not as sophisticated as the *couturière* (ladies' tailor) or the daughter of the *petit marchand* (small shopkeeper). But while naïveté often worked to her disadvantage, the same simplicity of spirit meant that once on the "right road," she would more easily maintain a virtuous life.[139] Nevertheless, certain steps should be taken to prepare a young woman for the dangers of the public sphere. In dress and deportment, women must avoid all show of luxury and frivolity and instead embrace simplicity.[140] Furthermore, Harmel suggested that young women receive a *virile* (manly) education.[141] He apparently was not advocating that women be given access to traditional male schooling or jobs but rather that these young women of the Victorian era be given at least a modicum of sex education. Delicacy, or squeamishness, should be cast aside and "traps" normally hidden from them revealed because catastrophe usually followed *la chute* (the fall).[142]

In his concern for the morality of the female factory worker, Léon Harmel anticipated what has only recently been deemed an appropriate part of female education. Yet it was crucial to his plan for the revitalization of the family. If the family, and indeed all of society, were to be saved from the current crisis threatening its existence, women needed to be virtuous; once that was assured, the feminine influence, or in Harmel's word, the *levier* (lever), could be used to help win over men.[143] But he was not content to rely solely on these two traditional agents, the Church and women, to re-Christianize his world. Additional ideas crystallized around the societal segment that was most at risk, the world of work and the worker. Here he plowed new territory.

The Happiness of the Worker

The Setting

In contrast to those who portrayed work as a necessary evil, Léon Harmel followed traditional Catholic social teaching by elevating work to a supernatural level. It was, after God and family, the "primary good of the people," and provided the setting in which man was capable of becoming morally perfect. In short, the community of labor had a moral dimension. According to Harmel, this had not been the case under liberalism, which, with its laissez-faire philosophy, had encouraged men "to destroy one another," thereby reversing the divine directive. The proper order of things, as outlined in the Gospels, told men instead to "love one another."[144] Thus Harmel insisted that Christian charity become the essential ingredient in the establishment of a harmonious work environment. For Harmel, this "union of hearts" achieved substance and assumed form within the institution known as the association, or corporation.

What Harmel created, then, at Val-des-Bois was his version of the Christian organization of work.

He defined the Christian corporation as an "association between bosses and workers of the same profession, or similar profession, that had for its end the reign of justice and charity."[145] The corporation's raison d'être, however, was to turn a profit, and one of the best ways to ensure the smooth running of an enterprise to realize profitability was to maintain order and peace. Harmel turned to the family structure as a guide to orderliness, since this was what God had established to safeguard peace in the workplace.[146] The father of a family and the boss of a factory were, in Harmel's opinion, more "natural" authority figures than those elected by the people. Consequently, in structure and in spirit, Harmel's corporation modeled itself after the human family; the *patron* was the father and the workers his sons and daughters.[147] The Christian corporation blurred the physical boundaries between human family and worker family and between home and workplace, especially since most of the workers and management personnel, in the instance of Val, for example, lived on site.

Harmel's corporation both looked to the past and anticipated the future. The inspiration for the nineteenth-century corporation originated with the medieval guild, in which masters, journeymen, and apprentices were of the same profession and faith and provided mutual assistance to its members and their families in time of trouble. Because the individual was subsumed within the whole, it was corporate in nature; the good of the whole was paramount to the good of the part. Corporatism as a *mentalité* became much more of a continental phenomenon in the nineteenth century than an Anglo-American one, where individualism reigned supreme, but as Anthony Black reminds us, it largely was the provenance of intellectuals for it never became a grassroots movement.[148] Later on, that is, in the twentieth century, corporatism took its hierarchical and paternalistic inclinations and turned them into fascist authoritarianism, which nineteenth-century theorists and reformers would have abhorred for its subordination to state control.[149]

The Patron

Paternalism was a natural corollary to a corporate mind-set. According to Harmel's interpretation of paternalism, the authority of the *patron* came directly from God[150] and was expressed through natural law.[151] This "social paternity," the caring for the *petits* by the *grands*, merely reflected humanity's relationship to God and was the real source of fraternity in the world. But fraternity did not imply equality, except in the moral sense that all mankind was equal in terms of grace, or innate worth, before God. Instead it took into account natural differences, such as intelligence or physical health, among men, and it admonished the stronger to watch over the weaker. Harmel cited the two laws of God, that is, to love God and to love one's neighbor, to corroborate his words and further explained that "neighbor" did not suggest "persons of your own rank and blood" but rather those who were less fortunate.[152] In this, he no doubt had in mind Gospel accounts such as the story of the Good Samaritan in which the lesson to be learned is that it is rather easy to love those who are mirror reflections of ourselves; the difficulty and consequently the merit of good deeds becomes more apparent when good deeds are directed at those who are dissimilar to ourselves in socioeconomic circumstances.

Given that this was the era when the second industrial revolution and the New Imperialism were making considerable headway, his thoughts on natural hierarchies, with their references to *petits* and *grands*, might have received subtle support from contemporary notions addressing the inequalities of the human race. In the late nineteenth century, as industrialized nations of the West gobbled up most of the world outside Europe and the Americas, ministering to the less fortunate, whether at home or abroad, operated under various guises, called, depending on time and place, *noblesse oblige, mission civilisatrice,* or the "White Man's Burden." Harmel's thoughts on natural hierarchies as reflected in Gospel lessons and medieval Thomistic theology are clear enough and traditional in origin. What is left unsaid are his notions with regard to racial inequality. Did he assimilate recent scientific theories of Social Darwinism to extend the scope of his hierarchical world to include all the peoples of the globe? His correspondence and speeches are silent on the subject, although his evocation of the term "Catholic science" tells us he was a traditionalist in this matter. His anti-Semitism, as will be demonstrated later, was more religious than racial. As far as can be determined, Léon Harmel's philosophical beliefs largely were based on his experience at Val-des-Bois, and here the operating principle was paternalism.

He believed that the managing classes themselves had to reform so that words became meaningful through good example.[153] In fact, the *patron* was unable to fulfill his duties in full measure unless motivated by the divine.[154] This required him to forgo luxury and the love of riches,[155] as well as to overcome his most formidable enemy, egoism.[156] Exemplary conduct extended to his life inside and outside the factory, in both its private and its public aspects, because it was only in this way that he could hope to assert "indirect control," that is, provide a continuous good example for his own workers' conduct.[157] During work hours, the *patron* must take special cognizance of the virtues of justice and charity, for these are crucial to the maintenance of factory order,[158] and when present, justice and charity largely were responsible for the creation of a Christian spirit among all in the workplace, which could reap such practical side benefits as fewer strikes.[159] It was only by becoming morally virtuous himself, then, that a *patron* displayed his superiority and thereby earned the respect of his workers and acquired his "natural" authority.[160] For Harmel, moral reform started at the top.

Authority was not unconditional, however, and therefore the *patron* operated under several constraints. He had to take into account "written and tacit controls," such as human and divine law, work contracts, and "legitimate custom."[161] If a custom was not an abuse against God or opposed to the best interests of the workers, then it was considered a "quasi-contract" and binding.[162] Nevertheless, under the paternalistic system, and most remarkably during an era when economic liberalism prevailed, the state allowed management substantial leeway in factory governance. For this reason, Harmel considered it necessary to delineate the specific rights and duties of the *patron*.

No doubt in recognition of the need for reform within the factories under paternalistic management and the free hand given to factory owners under the laissez-faire system, Harmel gave but a cursory glance at the rights of the *patron* while dwelling at considerable length on his duties. Simply stated, management's rights consisted of determining the quantity and quality of the product and expecting obedience from all on the factory premises.[163] His responsibilities "before God, before Church, and before society," on the other hand, were substantial and ones he could not dismiss.[164] The factory was to reflect his revitalized morality.

Organizationally, the Christian corporation required rules of conduct and support personnel to assure its smooth operation. Discipline was as essential to the workshop as it was to the family, the schools, and the army,[165] and included rules against blasphemy, "evil" books and newspapers, and conversations contrary to "morality."[166] Utmost care was to be used in choosing the foreman and other personnel in supervisory positions not only because of past abuses but also because of their critical role in the hiring of congenial workers, that is, workers noted more for their placidity than their troublemaking ways; in the case of a Christian factory, practicing Catholics were the ideal. Supervisors also were important in the maintenance of factory discipline and the overall harmonious atmosphere of the workrooms. The moral character of supervisory personnel was to mirror that of the *patron* so as to assure correct, that is, exemplary, behavior to all factory personnel but most notably to women and apprentices, the principal objects of factory abuse.[167]

Once the proper organizational structure and atmosphere were in place, the *patron* was free to carry out his duties to four specific groups: the Catholic Church, civil society, the *famille ouvrière* (work-family, or corporation), and the family of the individual worker. As far as the Catholic Church was concerned, the *patron* needed to "pay attention to" the bishops, the parish priest, and the laws of the Church; whereas the obligation to civil society consisted of obedience to its laws, especially those concerning workshops, factories, apprentices, and other workplace matters.[168] Obviously, the *patron* had more direct control over events within his factory than he did over those occurring in the Church or in civil society. Consequently, Harmel elaborated at greater length when describing the duties of the *patron* in the realm of the Christian corporation and the workers' families.

On the factory premises, the *patron* was obligated to "know each of his workers," always to demonstrate "goodwill" on their behalf, and to generate "good" and eliminate "evil" by having the workers practice "virtue."[169] For example, time was to be allocated to worship God, so keeping Sunday as a day of rest was unquestioned.[170] It also meant the regulation of factory hours to allow workers, in their alternate and primary roles as fathers, mothers, and children, sufficient time to fulfill their individual duties to God, society, and each other. In other words, time spent at factory work stations was not to be "overwhelming."[171] Moreover, as an extension of the employment contract between the *patron* and the worker, management was to provide a just wage to the worker, one "proportionate to his work and as sufficient as possible to support his needs and those of his family."[172] However, should the situation arise in which the factory was suffering a financial "crisis," both management and labor were expected to adjust and make temporary "sacrifices."[173]

The personal and pervasive nature of the paternalistic commitment became even more apparent when Harmel addressed the *patron*'s obligations in the private world of the worker. Here the *patron* was duty-bound to care financially for those who were ill, or the victim of an accident, or those who had suffered the loss of a mother or father.[174] Housing was to ensure that family members were not exposed to "dangerous promiscuity or immorality"; that is, it was to guarantee a certain degree of privacy.[175] Furthermore, the working mother was to be given sufficient time and freedom to tend to her duties to husband and children.[176] And children, if not sufficiently protected by civil law, came under the aegis of natural law; they were not to be allocated tasks beyond their physical strength, were to be provided with instruction that prepared them spiritually and professionally for adulthood, and, if apprentices, were to be given special paternalistic protection. This was the case since parents, particularly if not employed at the same factory, had in reality surrendered certain parental rights to the *patron*. Being physically separated, these parents could no longer tend to the moral or educational upbringing of their offspring. The *patron*, therefore, had a special duty to see to the spiritual and physical needs of these children.[177]

In sum, the *patron* was to protect the body and, above all, the soul of the worker and his entire family.[178] Because he was motivated by the divine, his sentiments were ideally those of a father for his children. For this reason, workers were no longer "vulgar men, weak and fickle but rather souls redeemed by the blood of Jesus Christ."[179] Although Harmel's paternalism contained much that was traditional, he departed from convention by increasing his support of worker autonomy and, thereby, ultimately undermined the whole paternalistic structure.

The Workers

According to Harmel's schema, the worker also had specific rights and duties.[180] To begin with, he was, of course, guaranteed those rights entitled to him as citizen of a state and as head of a family, above all, adequate resources to raise his family.[181] More specifically, his work hours were to be reasonable, not above what was prescribed by human or divine law; his wage needed to be commensurate with the assigned task,[182] which largely was determined by the regional pay scale; and finally he was to be professionally represented.[183] His sole duty as worker was to labor hard and produce the best work he could.[184]

Harmel defined the worker as a skilled tradesman who worked for a *patron* at home, in a small workshop, or at a larger establishment. His definition excluded the self-employed, for example, the entrepreneur or the individual artisan, and the unskilled.[185] Sounding once again like a bona fide Christian socialist, he also said that the worker, rather than the product fashioned at the workplace, was the essential ingredient in determining the value of the work undertaken.[186] The debilitating demands placed on the worker often forced participation in "ruinous" strikes,[187] resulting in fatigued and disheartened workers who gave the appearance of irreligion. But worker de-Christianization was deceptive; Christian baptism had put down solid roots, and thus, given the proper setting, the worker's faith could be rekindled.

These were not necessarily idle dreams on Harmel's part, for the nineteenth century, especially after 1831, was a time of theological renewal and evangelization. The Concordat and the Organic Articles were silent on the matter of proselytism, so initially there was considerable activity by both Catholic and Protestant missionaries, particularly in the rural areas. Catholics were concerned enough with their Protestant rivals to take them to court in these new wars of religion, but since French courts generally ruled in favor of the Catholics, by the time of the Second Empire, Protestant missionary activity had been severely blunted.[188] Yet proselytism continued in the face of declining Mass attendance and observance of the Easter duty. Indeed, the whole system of interior missions set up by the Catholics premised its work on the notion that there were souls to be won for Christ.[189] The net result of the heightened evangelization meant that one could speak in terms of not only de-Christianization when referring to the state of religion in postrevolutionary France but also of re-Christianization. Harmel certainly intended that the Christian corporation nurture the worker's soul as well as his body, because ultimately he wanted workers from Christian corporations to proselytize in the factories throughout France. He set his sights high: he envisioned the building of a new "social reign of Jesus Christ" and the spiritual regeneration of the French nation.[190]

Harmel's system promised autonomy to the worker in several areas.[191] Of course, he wanted his workers to take an independent stand vis-à-vis the godless state and secular society, but he also seemed to be hinting that once the worker had returned to practicing his faith, he would be ready for greater freedom within the Christian corporation itself, and this in fact would be the case in the Conseil d'Usine, or factory council, at Val-des-Bois. The practice of one's Catholic religion, therefore, held the implicit promise of loosening paternalistic ties at the factory.

In anticipation of tangible rewards and in preparation for workplace evangelization, Harmel asked the worker to participate in a self-development program for the lay apostolate that emphasized faith, study, and action.[192] Faith was to be nurtured through observance of religious practices. Harmel supported placing religious objects, such as crucifixes, in the factory workrooms, building chapels on factory grounds, and establishing l'Archiconfrérie de Notre Dame de l'Usine, a confraternity designed to oversee the installation of religious artifacts and practices on factory premises. He founded the organization in 1875 after what he interpreted as a miracle occurred at Val-des-Bois. On September 13, 1874, a fire broke out, causing extensive damage to the factory. The blaze stopped just at the foot of a statue of the Blessed Mother in one of the workrooms, convincing Harmel of a miracle. Devotion to Mary, under the title Notre Dame de l'Usine (Our Lady of the Factory) was concentrated in the Nord, and the organization became controversial as socialists, for example, objected to religious artifacts in honor of Our Lady of the Factory displayed at work sites.[193] Nevertheless, the establishment of the confraternity and whatever popular support it had would have been in keeping with the strength of Marian miracle cults prevalent in nineteenth-century France.[194]

Harmel also deemed essential the study of religious doctrine and contemporary social problems if truth were to successfully combat error and if successful proselytizing were to occur; this became the impetus for Harmel's involvement with workers' study groups in L'Oeuvre des Cercles Catholiques d'Ouvriers[195] and Les Cercles Chrétiens d'Études Sociales.[196]

Finally, Harmel wanted social action, the outward sign of the workers' spiritual renewal, to be a source of inspiration for the entire Church.

The worker-family at Val-des-Bois assiduously tended to the needs of one another in sickness and in health and because of the notoriety of the Harmel factory, became exemplars to Catholics of the era.

Harmel formulated a major role for the Catholic worker of France. In his plan for the regeneration of the nation, the worker was as essential a component as the small particles in the living organisms that Pasteur described to the scientific world;[197] the worker became, for Harmel, an increasingly important ingredient in his social plan. This reflected both the growth of the French labor movement in the closing decades of the nineteenth century and Harmel's ability to absorb societal changes. Because he always had the utmost regard for the basic goodness and common sense of the worker, he was willing to acknowledge that even the Christian corporation, in its original form, needed to change with the times. With increased literacy and political enfranchisement, with increased wages and benefits, with greater worker representation and avenues to discuss grievances with management, the lines between the *grands* and the *petits* became less distinct for society in general and Harmel in particular with the passage of time.

Harmel wrote in 1876, for example, that he had noticed from living with workers on a daily basis that they needed protective authority, and "the stronger that authority was, the better the workers liked it." If *patrons* were timid in exercising their authority, they would not be respected by their workers.[198] But by 1898 he advised sacrificing paternal authority when it interfered with the love and respect the managing class owed the worker, because recognition of the human dignity inherent in each individual and the special bond between followers of Jesus Christ demanded a softer touch. In order not to offend the legitimate pride of the worker, management needed to operate with a "particular delicateness" in their dealings with workers. Even if the *patron* possessed greater expertise, he ought to encourage the personal initiatives of the worker so that the worker would gain confidence and thereby ready himself for greater responsibility in factory affairs.[199]

The same confidence in the worker surfaces elsewhere. Harmel suggested, for instance, that worker councils be allowed to operate with as much latitude as possible[200] and that *patrons* ought to listen to the suggestions of workers on matters concerning the materials, the machinery, and the business of the factories.[201] He went so far as to assert that workers be more fully brought into the management of the enterprise by becoming familiar with buying and selling prices and the balance sheet. Yet this is one area where his credibility was questionable when it came to putting words into practice. Harmel resisted relinquishing any financial control at Val-des-Bois to workers, even to the most capable and religious among them. The same reluctance to embrace at Val what he actively encouraged for others occurred over the matter of workers' unions after 1884. As discussed in chapter 2, Harmel endorsed in theory the *syndicat separé,* or union without management personnel, but refused to abandon the *syndicat mixte,* or union made up of labor and management, at his factory.

His equivocation over surrendering total control at Val-des-Bois to his workers seemed to have two bases. From the days of his childhood, Harmel directed and managed others and from what the records disclose, always with honorable goals in mind. He was the one who said Mass and then led the procession through the village streets to his grandparents' home; he was the one, though not the eldest son, who took over the business when still a young man from his father, Jacques-Joseph Harmel. To step aside and let others direct at Val would have been totally out of character, particularly when his all-consuming preoccupation was the happiness and well-being of the worker. He undoubtedly felt the workers would profit best under his direction. In his words, "[T]he workers[,] . . . how I love them with a passion, how I have consecrated my life to them, my health, all that God has given me of fire and ardor, I wish to come to their aid, to save them, to give back to the Church and to the nation the wayward children."[202] Given his personality and character, his inability to give up at Val-des-Bois what he readily endorsed elsewhere in the way of control is not so puzzling or disingenuous as it might seem. A life lived without personal association with the worker was inconceivable, even if that meant the continuation of certain paternalistic ways at Val-des-Bois.

The Service of Jesus Christ

The principal source of Léon Harmel's dedication and fervor on behalf of the worker was his deep religious faith. This is not to say that he never pondered the ways of the divine. For example, he appreciated the irony of the contemporary world in which such marvels of technology as the steam engine and electricity existed alongside incredible human misery.[203] But ultimately he bowed before divine wisdom and providence. After all, if God had wanted to, He could have created the world by uttering one word instead of spending days at the task,[204] and thus, he concluded, divine will often worked in mysterious ways. This profound trust in God consistently sustained him in difficult times.

Harmel further believed that personal and societal salvation hinged on acceptance of the Christian faith. It was necessary to be a Christian in order to be morally good and, therefore, capable of earning eternal salvation.[205] That he lived in an era that predated twentieth-century ecumenism generated by Vatican II partially explains his concern over the influence exerted by republican liberals, Jews, and Freemasons on French society, and why his mission to re-Christianize the French worker became not only an apostolic work but also a patriotic duty to which he devoted his life. He believed that if the workers were not Christian, charity, the spiritual bulwark against "mistrust, jealously, and discontent that makes rapport so difficult," would be absent from the workplace.[206] And the consequences, for Harmel, were predictable. Harmonious relations among the classes would remain unrealized dreams, for indeed non-Christian workers would have trouble accepting paternalism.[207] In short, Harmel's social blueprint would suffer an irreparable breakdown if workers rejected the Christian faith.

His own spiritual life was noteworthy. Beginning in 1860, he affiliated with the Third Order of St. Francis, a lay organization that sought personal sanctification for its members while attempting to alleviate human misery.[208] After the death of his wife, Gabrielle, in 1870, there was a new intensity in his interior life, and he became even more committed to the organization and its twin goals.[209] Choosing this road to personal sanctification entailed considerable commitment. Harmel took three religious vows, those of chastity (a short time after he was widowed), poverty, and obedience (to his spiritual director).[210] "Poverty" in this instance meant the denial of "useless" things.[211] Harmel's frugality was thereby encouraged spiritually, but this in no way meant that he celebrated poverty: pauperism, for him, was a societal evil.

In addition to committing himself to the three vows, Harmel gave up smoking cigarettes. For him, this personal sacrifice was particularly difficult because he was a heavy smoker[212] in an age when smoking among bourgeois males was a social event as well as a personal habit; gentlemen smoked together and separate from women. He also structured his daily schedule so as to allow for two hours of private prayer and meditation, which included the taking of Communion and visits before the Blessed Sacrament. The quiet moments before the Tabernacle yielded the greatest spiritual gratification for him personally, although he recognized the benefits of public worship for the development of communal spirit. Because of his frequent travels, he lamented the times when this part of his daily routine was disrupted and, for this reason, welcomed insomnia as an additional opportunity for prayer.[213]

Notwithstanding his dedication to solitary prayer and meditation, family tradition and personal conviction taught Harmel that religion was not to be confined to the private sphere.[214] It was not enough to "know" one's duties, one had to "fulfill" them.[215] In a more poetic rendering of the same idea, Harmel wrote that "he knew that the Gospel said that man was not nourished by bread alone, but neither was man nourished only by the word of God."[216] Christianity entailed social involvement.

Harmel's perception of the ideal Christian was not in accord with the medieval notion that idealized the detached mystic who physically and psychologically removed himself or herself from the material world in order to reach perfection. No less an authority than Thomas Aquinas devoted considerable space (Questions 180–189) in the *Summa Theologica* to demonstrating why the contemplative life was "absolutely more excellent" than the active life, and why those who dedicated their lives to religion were more perfect than those who did not. The great medieval scholastic postulated that just as love of God takes precedence over love of mankind, religious life, because it is consecrated to God, is a more perfect vocation than others.[217]

Léon Harmel was too much of an extrovert, too much of a humanist, to agree with Aquinas on this matter; he embraced this life despite all its suffering. He did so because by nature he was an optimist, and as a Christian, he believed there was spiritual merit in enduring suffering. Consequently, although Harmel maintained a constant awareness of life's ultimate goal, namely, union with God in heaven, he advised the young to prepare to "live" and not to prepare to "die" because "life is the great and important mission of man. Life is what makes our Eternity."[218]

His admiration for the Middle Ages was shared by many in an epoch renowned for its neo-Romanesque but above all neo-Gothic architecture and Romantic literature and music, featuring Wagnerian opera and medieval heroes and heroines. But to use the sage words of Thomas Wolfe, one cannot go home again, and Harmel was too pragmatic to force a medieval paradigm on a nineteenth-century world. Rather than insist on traditional roles for the social orders, he preferred to commingle their functions and reverse hierarchical order whenever appropriate. Clergy were not only to be educated in Thomistic theology, but also in recent scientific developments and current Catholic social teaching on matters dealing with the workplace, and they were not necessarily more spiritually perfect than the laity. Women, particularly in their roles as mothers, were perceived as the most effective of traditional agents for the re-Christianization of France, while workers offered the greatest hope among the more nontraditional elements for their *loci communes* were where evil was rampant. The factory had become the principal home of Satan, according to Harmel,[219] and so henceforth there was but one remedy: "Baptize industry and make it the servant of Jesus Christ."[220] This Léon Harmel first attempted at Val-des-Bois.

CHAPTER TWO

The Corporation at Val-des-Bois

"Come in, do come in," she repeated to her guests. "We are not putting anybody out.... Once again, isn't it clean? And this good woman has seven children! All our families are like this.... As I was explaining to you, the Company rents them the house at six franc a month. A large room on the ground floor, two rooms upstairs, cellar and garden."

The dazed expression and vaguely staring eyes of the decorated gentleman and the lady in the fur coat showed that they had dropped only that morning from the Paris train into a new world which had thrown them off their balance.

"And garden," echoed the lady. "One really could live here oneself. Quite delightful!"

"We give them more coal than they can burn," went on Madame Hennebeau. "A doctor sees them twice a week, and when they are old they are given a pension although no deduction is made from their wages."

"Arcadia!" murmured the gentleman in ecstasy. "A land flowing with milk and honey!"

— *Émile Zola,* Germinal

ALTHOUGH TECHNICALLY OUTSIDE THE NORD REGION, THE HARMEL factory possessed features indistinguishable from many of the textile enterprises located in the region immediately to the northwest. The reasons included geographic proximity, factory size and product, and personnel—both management and labor—whose origins and ethos could often be traced to the Nord. In addition, Léon Harmel maintained associational ties with numerous of the Catholic *patronat* of the Nord through organizations such as the Patrons du Nord. These practitioners of paternalism were vividly portrayed in the naturalist novels of Zola such as *Germinal* and pose an interesting comparison to the paternalistic paradigm established by Harmel at Val-des-Bois.

If Harmel was to be acknowledged as a social reformer and his program for the regeneration of France marketable, the social experiment at his factory needed to triumph. But his social experiment did not operate in a vacuum, and the French textile industry experienced turbulent times throughout the nineteenth century. To remain financially solvent when other enterprises went under, the Harmel mill updated its technology, expanded its product line, developed foreign markets, and, in a tight job market, aggressively recruited workers. Harmel was as attentive to business details at Val-des-Bois as he was to transforming his factory into a model Christian corporation.

The Textile Industry

The first French industrial revolution took place between 1830 and 1880, with maximum intensity occurring between 1840 and 1860. Then, after a period of stagnation in the 1880s and early 1890s, a second industrial revolution took off in the twenty years preceding World War I.[1] During the course of the industrial revolution, France saw its dominant position slip as it moved from the first phase to the second phase, dropping from second to fourth place in worldwide production of goods by the end of the nineteenth century.[2]

The first industrial revolution was characterized by iron and coal production, by the prominence of the textile industry, and, above all, by the use of steam power in factories. With the exception of lagging behind Great Britain in the production of iron and coal, products that needed to be imported throughout the nineteenth and early twentieth century, and in the transportation of raw materials to manufacturing sites, France was one of the leaders of the first industrial revolution alongside Great Britain and Belgium. Between 1852 and 1870 its industrial production doubled, its foreign trade tripled, its use of steam power expanded fivefold, and its railroad mileage multiplied sixfold.[3]

The second industrial revolution was noted for its steel production, the development of the chemical industry, and the use of electrical power in factories, but by this time France had fallen behind the front-runners, who included some new players, most notably, the United States and Germany, but Russia, Japan, and Italy challenged too. Commentators noted that entrepreneurial spirit was in short supply in France and that the political elite of the Third Republic was untrained in business matters,[4] offering as an example the fact that the French were slow to adopt such modern devices as the telephone.[5] Economists pointed out that France was late in turning its eyes east, toward the Pacific with its growing markets, and that France really never recovered from the Franco-Prussian War of 1870.[6]

The above rendition of the French industrial revolution is the traditional account but may not be the most accurate, especially when it comes to the second industrial revolution and the decades before World War I. From 1870 to 1914 industrial output tripled, national income doubled, and French investments abroad rose sixfold; whereas from 1896 to 1914, the real boom period, prices increased by 40 percent and trade by 75 percent.[7] Scholars justifiably have questioned the notion that France declined significantly during the second industrial revolution and have argued instead for the uniqueness of France. Jeremy Popkin, for example, points out that since France's agricultural sector retained its hold on the economy and since agriculture was slow to modernize, the perception existed that the economy *en toto* became obsolete by the turn of the century.[8] Richard F. Kuisel elaborates by suggesting that France was an interesting blend of tradition and modernity, often resisting mass production in favor of retaining handcrafted methods that had long been its hallmark.[9]

There were some dynamic sectors of the French economy during the later stage of the industrial revolution that belie the notion that France was stagnant during this period. The aluminum industry flourished, thanks to large deposits of bauxite and the development of hydroelectric power. The automobile industry, although not nearly as adept at mass production as the American factories of Henry Ford, nevertheless was

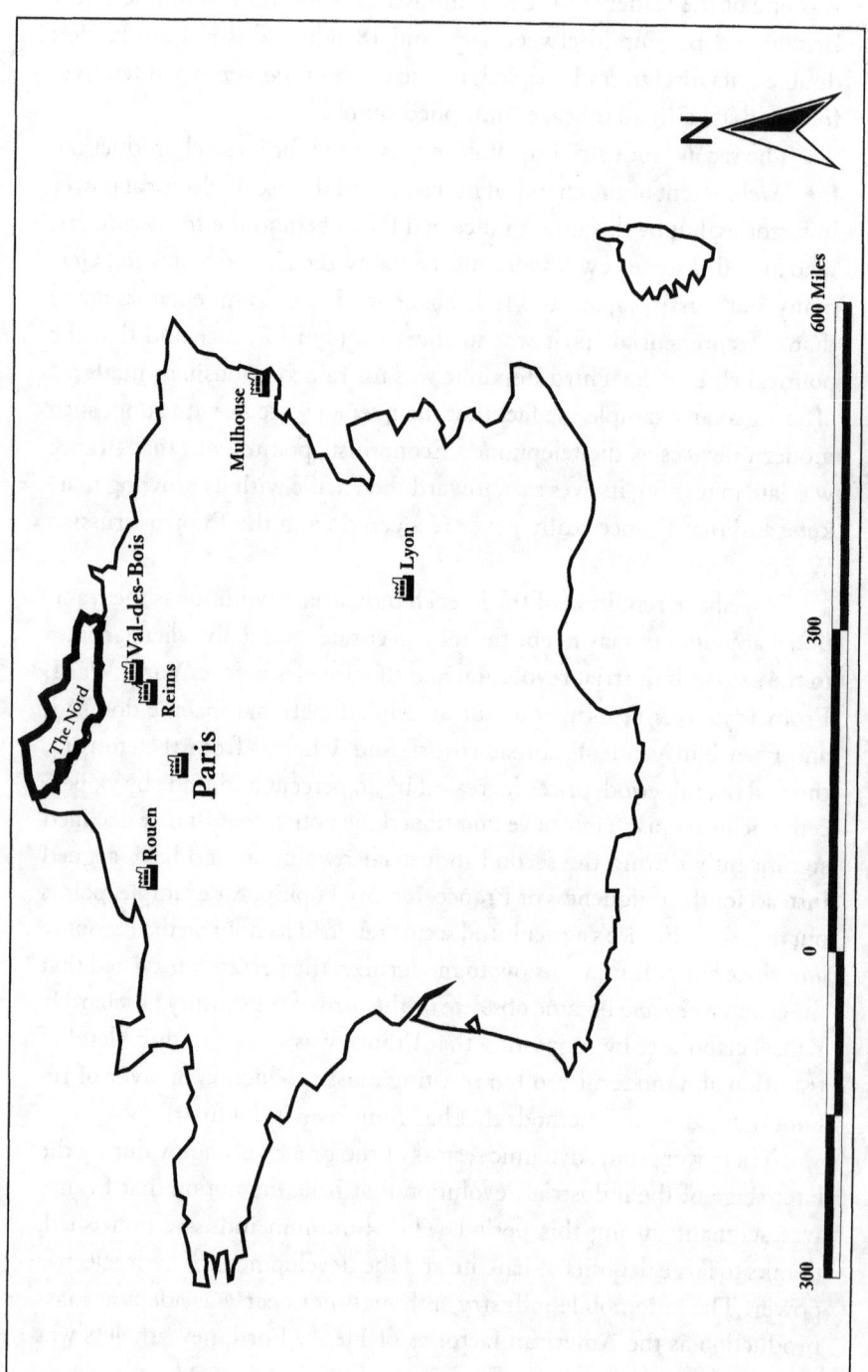

Map 1. Factory sites and the Nord Industrial Region. Cartography by Mark Leipnik.

impressive. Renault, for example, produced just six cars a year in 1898 but was delivering 4,481 cars to customers by 1913. And the motion picture industry highlighted French advances in science and technology when the Lumière brothers, together with Thomas Edison, strung multiple photographs together so as to give the perception of motion when projected on a screen.[10] Still, it was only in the marketing of bicycles and automobiles that France registered an increase in exports during the years from 1899 to 1913.[11] In short, France presented a complex economic picture during its industrial revolution, and the reasons were several.

Unlike Great Britain during the first industrial revolution or Russia during the second, to cite but two examples, France experienced no specific "take-off" point in its industrial revolution, resulting in a rather undramatic economic history when compared to other nations at this time.[12] The more moderate performance of French industrialization can be attributed in part to the lively political history of the nation in the eighteenth and nineteenth centuries; wars and revolutions interrupted economic development. Another consideration was the strong attachment to the land and the concomitant reluctance on the part of the French to relocate permanently to new industrial centers far from the family farm, which meant that industrialization frequently went to the people. This *enracinement*, or deep rootedness, of the French rural worker frustrated Karl Marx on more than one occasion,[13] and was indicative of French traditional ways. Factories in France often were located in rural areas, were organized under a paternalistic structure,[14] and were considerably smaller than the new, large enterprises being built in other industrialized states during the latter part of the nineteenth century. In the 1840s spinning factories that specialized in wool or cotton averaged sixty to seventy workers, while weaving enterprises counted thirty or forty workers. Only six thousand factories in France had more than twenty employees during this period,[15] among them the Harmel spinning mill. In 1914 one-third of France's industrial workers still were employed in shops of not more than ten workers, and more than one-half worked in enterprises of no more than one hundred employees.[16]

Looking at the traditional three economic sectors—agriculture, industry, and service—from 1781 to 1881, one is offered a striking example of the slow evolution of French economic life. Agriculture dominated throughout the period, representing 55 percent of the workforce in 1781 and still commanding 47.5 percent in 1881; industry represented 15 percent of the economic pie in 1781 but had edged up to 26.7 percent by 1881; service took 30 percent of the whole in 1781 but had dropped to 24.9 percent in 1881.[17] France had a larger portion of its workforce in agriculture than any other industrialized nation,[18] with 40 percent still involved in agriculture in 1900.[19] A word of caution is in order, however. Depending on region, officials categorized differently, and consequently statistics risk being more approximate than absolute, although in the main the picture painted is reliable.[20]

The size of enterprises in the industrial sector can also present a problem for the interpreter. Although this clearly is not the case with factories the size of Harmel's, there were many small businesses, some with no more than two workers for one boss,[21] in which it becomes difficult to distinguish between *patron* and *ouvrier* when employer and employee worked side by side.[22] It then becomes harder to talk about an authentic proletariat in significant numbers until the end of the nineteenth century, when, for example, the worker suburbs, or *banlieues,* sprang up to accommodate the growing numbers of factories being built on the outskirts of Paris.[23] In the smaller workshops, the average worker had less sense of existing in a separate class with a distinct consciousness and future until much later, especially when most workers lived only for the moment.[24] Given that some industries were seasonal and that significant numbers of workers continued to have ties to the family farm, work in a factory might be determined by the rhythm of the agricultural season, with part-time work the norm for many. Factory work might be a temporary matter for the young woman before her marriage or the young man before going off to fulfill his military service.[25]

Still some would argue that the machine is what transforms the worker into a member of the proletariat, and if that interpretation is valid, then a genuine proletariat in the textile industry, which was the first to become mechanized in France, appeared much earlier in the nineteenth century. Further authentication of a true proletariat in France before the end of the century stems from the fact that the worker's low wage kept him from acquiring the means of production and made him totally dependent on the functioning of the machine.[26] In fact, for some, mechanization was an effective means by which to discipline the worker. The machine, not the worker, fashioned the product, with the net result that management now controlled production. In short, according to this view, mechanization diminished the worth and influence of labor once foremen and other supervisory personnel made decisions that previously belonged to the worker.[27] But since Léon Harmel placed control of the workroom environment increasingly in the hands of his workers, labor more readily retained its dignity at his factory.

Industrialization took place throughout France, but the principal clusters were located in the north, in Lorraine, and in the region around Lyon. In the French industrial sector, the textile industry dominated, continually edging out mining, metallurgy, and construction, for instance. Its chief center was Normandy where one-third of all spindles were located in 1894, but because the factories of Normandy were slow to modernize, areas such as the Nord, which converted sooner to steam power and other technological advances, would be economically stronger.[28] The textile industry had its own hierarchy; cotton commanded the largest segment, with 245,000 people, or 35 percent of the industry, at the end of the July Monarchy in establishments with more than ten people. During the same period, silk factories counted 165,000 persons and represented 24 percent of the industry; wool factories claimed 144,000 persons and represented 20.8 percent of the industry; hemp and flax factories had 56,000 persons and represented 8 percent of the industry; and factories involved with diverse other textiles accounted for 80,000 persons and claimed 11.6 percent of the industry.[29] Forty percent of French workers remained in the textile and clothing industries as late as 1914, with more than one-half of these working in the home.[30] The textile industry was a conservative industry in that, once mechanized, it did not change very much from the beginning of the twentieth century until the 1950s.[31] In the case of the Harmel factory, once it was renovated after the disastrous fire of 1874, there were no major capital improvements during the remainder of Léon's term as *patron*. But the industry as a whole needed to respond to important events that occurred in the French economy during the mid-nineteenth century.

The year 1860 often is viewed as the turning point in French industrial history in general but especially in the textile industry for several reasons. While France was still the dominant industrial power on the continent in 1860, its position increasingly was being eroded by nations with faster-growing and more diversified industrial sectors. The New

Imperialism ushered in an age of globalization of trade and industry, but it also brought increased competition, with the competitive threat sometimes coming from colonies and former colonies of European nations. The United States, for example, touted its cotton as the best in the world. But India and Egypt were also known for the quality of their cotton, and because of Great Britain's efficient factories, raw materials sent from these British colonies to the mother country for manufacturing had the capability to undercut sales of French products at home and abroad. Mechanization of the cotton industry occurred ahead of the wool industry and more rapidly,[32] with mechanization making its greatest impact in spinning mills.[33] Cheaper and more comfortable than wool, cotton became the textile of choice for many Europeans and thereby had the effect of destabilizing or driving under enterprises specializing in wool or other textiles that did not adapt by modernizing their factories and diversifying their product lines. Diversity, however, often took the form of luxury threads and fabrics, and the wool industry was not geared to mass consumption like the cotton industry was. In fact, the cotton industry was the first to benefit from rising incomes.[34] But the wool industry was more stable and took advantage of the more volatile cotton industry in the 1860s by modernizing technologically and aggressively marketing the new luxury products. In sum, instability characterized the textile industry in its cotton and its wool sectors.

During this crucial period, the Harmel enterprise, which specialized in wool thread but also produced cotton thread, as well as various derivatives of the two, not only distinguished itself by surviving and prospering financially, largely by putting its entrepreneurial skills to work, but simultaneously increased efforts to convert the factory into a Christian corporation. Capital improvements (particularly after the 1874 fire), product diversification, global marketing, vocational training for its workforce, and cultivation of morale by offering workers social and economic amenities, as well as engagement in factory management, marched side by side with a program to re-Christianize the workforce. The spinning mill also offered its workers considerably greater job security than many other enterprises in the textile industry at the time.

Since nearly half of the laboring population in French industry still worked in the textile factories in the later decades of the nineteenth century (48.8 percent in 1872 and 40 percent in 1914, for example), industrial uncertainty touched the lives of a significant portion of the population.[35] Insecurity became especially acute after 1860 when France and Great Britain concluded the Cobden-Chevalier Treaty, a commercial pact that lowered tariffs and established a period of relative free trade that lasted until the return of protectionism in 1892. A protected segment of the economy since the time of Colbert, the textile industry was unaccustomed to the crests and troughs of the business cycle under a free-market system. Public opinion believed that the treaty only served the interests of Great Britain, and indeed the iron and textile industries encountered stiff competition from across the channel.[36] France quickly learned that it was smarter to complement Great Britain than to compete, especially when high-quality goods, aimed at the international carriage trade, remained the hallmark of the French textile industry.[37] Similar treaties with other industrialized nations quickly followed, introducing the only free-trade period in French history. The introduction of free trade was a controversial step that is still debated today, especially because an economic slump began almost before the ink had dried on official trade documents.[38]

The early 1860s also saw the drying up of cotton imported from the United States, which in 1860 had furnished 93 percent of the raw cotton arriving in France.[39] Attempts at growing cotton in France and Algeria proved unworkable, and it was only with the discovery of Indian cotton and the resumption of the American cotton trade at the end of the decade, with the conclusion of the American Civil War, that cotton supply and quality again became satisfactory. In the interim, the price of imported cotton increased, production of cotton products decreased, and workers saw wages lowered, hours shortened, or positions eliminated completely; factories that relied on manual production methods closed, and pauperism grew.[40] After 1870, however, cotton textile factories benefited from the loss of Alsace to Germany, because the great cotton textile center of Mulhouse, which was located in the eastern province, henceforward ceased to be a domestic competitor.[41]

When the McKinley Tariff of 1890 initiated a renewal of protectionism, France responded with the Méline Tariff of 1892, which established a two-tiered system: there was a tariff *minimum* for those countries with which France had reached commercial accord and a tariff *maximum* for those countries with which no commercial agreement had been set.[42] The tariff rates were set even higher in 1910, securing the French tariff a fourth-place position on the world scale.[43] In any event, any advantage offered by the resumption of protectionism was offset by foreign competition for export markets. French textile exports fell from 180 million francs in 1890 to 128 million in 1897 to 93 million in 1900 and 72 million in 1902.[44] The result was that during the last third of the nineteenth century many textile manufacturers in France permanently closed their doors. The Harmel factory was one of the survivors, but location might have contributed to its endurance.

Relative to other regions of France, the Nord was somewhat of an exception, at least until the 1880s. Although most small factory owners were forced to shut down in the wake of the 1860s shake out, there was increased production and factory expansion in the north of France.[45] Textile enterprises of the Nord imported wool from Great Britain and, after the 1850s, from Argentina and Australia, and exported combed and carded wool, cotton, linen, jute, wool thread and yarn, hemp rope, and various finished fabrics.[46] Because the Nord experienced prosperity in the period from 1814 to 1860,[47] that is, during the first industrial revolution, it was economically in better shape than the rest of France when free trade became the modus operandi after 1860 and therefore more likely than other regions to weather the tough times. Northern factories specializing in wool survived by modernizing their factories and expanding their product line in order to compete with foreign rivals, and the Harmel enterprise is a principal example of this commitment to capital improvement and product diversification.

But the survivors often became more secretive with the uncertain times. Factory owners, intent on protecting their family's patrimony, released vague statistics on production figures, profits, and working conditions to inquiring state bureaucrats in the closing decades of the nineteenth century,[48] which, of course, complicates matters for historians attempting to interpret cryptic figures. As far as can be determined, and no doubt because he had little if anything to hide, Léon Harmel released valid statistics on his spinning mill. Other industrialists of the region, particularly as their numbers dwindled, increasingly defied national labor laws and resisted workers' demands.[49] Yet being better off financially meant that larger companies of the North could buy, if they chose, newer, more efficient machinery[50] and had an advantage in finding workers since the population density in the North facilitated the recruitment of factory labor.[51] The Harmel factory realized these benefits; it was large and geographically situated to take advantage of the greater numbers of workers in the area. But the Harmel spinning mill also enjoyed a favorable reputation as an ideal place to work and thus may have experienced fewer problems in recruitment and retention than other enterprises in the region.

Notwithstanding the region's firmer economic footing, it too experienced difficulties and change after 1860. Factory owners opted to invest abroad rather than modernize equipment or technology, workers turned anticlerical and militant, and the workforce increasingly was drawn from foreigners and women. Though complete statistical records with regard to his workforce are not available, it is clear that Harmel actively recruited and employed Belgian workers during his tenure, but it may have been as much for their overt religiosity as their willingness to work. Women, though surely employed at his factory, were intended principally to be anchors of the worker home, and married women at least were discouraged from working. How typical Harmel was in recruiting foreigners and women is therefore difficult to pinpoint. But in 1880, for example, 40 percent of the foreign workforce in France was Belgian, most of whom had come to France in search of higher wages and could be found in the Nord.[52] After 1880, however, the worker influx from Belgium slowed considerably,[53] as increasingly they became *fontaliers,* or daily commuters, who lived in Belgium but worked in France.[54] The best-paid workers were those employed in metallurgy, but ironworkers, blacksmiths, and mechanics also were of the elite with regard to wages,[55] with some of these industries paying twice as much as other industries.[56] Not surprisingly, the heavy industries rarely employed women or children and had a lower percentage of foreign workers than those, such as the textile industry, that did not pay as well.

The French textile industry traditionally depended on female labor, and during the second half of the nineteenth century and the first decade of the twentieth century, mechanization allowed women to join the work pool in even greater numbers. But other segments of the economy opened up to women too. In 1866, 30 percent of people working in industry were women, with 70 percent of women working in textile factories.[57] By 1906, and despite church and state promoting the domestic ideal of the stay-at-home wife and mother, women represented 37 percent of the workforce, although now they only represented 51 percent of textile workers.[58] The number of women in the workforce clearly was growing, and the more work became mechanized, the more women could be found in factories and sweatshops. This was especially true in the spinning mills, where in one case an enterprise counted 93 men and 327 women.[59] The invention of the sewing machine gave women the added option of working in the home where children could be tended.[60] Women also increasingly participated in the tertiary sector of the economy as office workers, waitresses, sales clerks in the new department stores, and nannies but, above all, as domestics, where in Paris, for example, they represented 85 percent of household help at the beginning of the twentieth century and, not surprisingly, were the most exploited in terms of low wages.[61] By 1914 women represented 40 percent of the total workforce.[62]

That women typically were employed in lower paying jobs meant that employers usually did not have to worry about a strike. For those already enduring meager wages, union dues were out of the question, and the thought of trying to do without any wages, as would be the case in a strike, jolted any would-be striker into economic reality. A single woman, for example, could only survive with some sort of economic assistance; a family member could contribute to her support, or she could turn to prostitution as a means to supplement scanty wages. As a consequence, women workers were prized for their (perceived) docility.[63]

One found more women and children in cotton factories than in wool factories, not only because of mechanization and lower wages, but also because cotton was lighter than wool and thus easier to carry and handle.[64] Depending on the amount of humidity in the air, wool fibers could add up to 40 percent more to their weight.[65] Although working with cotton was healthier than working with linen, for example, since there were fewer particulates in the air, many suffered from "cotton pneumonia" in an industry notorious for its air pollution.[66] According to Louis-Réne Villermé, a physician who wrote on the living conditions of French textile workers, beating cotton was the most unhealthy of activities, although the harmful effects of the task elicited enough concern on the part of employers that they periodically rotated these workers.[67] Nevertheless, pulmonary problems were common in the textile industry, as fabric particles could be found on eyelashes and hair and lodged in the nostrils of the workers. The elevated temperatures and high humidity in the workrooms only exacerbated the problem.[68] At the Harmel enterprise, however, temperatures in the workrooms were well below industry levels.

Although there was less of a discrepancy between wages paid to men and wages paid to women in France than in other European countries at this time,[69] French women routinely were paid one-half less than men.[70] For good reason, the typical factory girl was single and under the age of twenty,[71] for her gender, youth, and inexperience meant that her wages would be among the lowest in the factory and therefore a desirable commodity for any employer, even Léon Harmel, interested in maximizing profits. Contemporary justification for the wage differential argued that women had fewer "needs" than men because they ate less and did not smoke or frequent the cabarets. The underlying and real reason, though, was that society assumed a woman's wage to be largely supplementary to that of her father or her husband.[72] Children, of course, were paid even less, about one-fourth of what men earned.[73]

A word of caution is in order before proceeding with this discussion. Gordon Wright tells us that price and wage studies for the 1815–1848 period are not totally reliable,[74] and Patricia Hilden and David Landes disclose that factory owners during the *belle époque* not infrequently masked pertinent information from state bureaucrats with regard to their businesses so as to keep a competitive edge. Furthermore, the government of the early Third Republic had no consistent policy on gathering data; inquiries made by the regional prefect moved down to the local mayors, only to be met with vague responses by the *patronat,* or civic boosterism by local chambers of commerce, or the bias of a local *conseil des prud'hommes*.[75] Further complicating the issue is the matter of old and new value of the franc. Between 1795 and 2001 the value of the franc changed several times, and thus one cannot always be assured that wage values, for example, are consistent for comparison purposes.[76] In short, the advice of Roger Magraw to view French statistics with a healthy dose of skepticism seems prudent.[77] Nevertheless, despite discrepancies in statistical data, the overall picture drawn is more than impressionistic.

Villermé, using information from the early decades of the nineteenth century, gives us the following wage scale for textile workers: 2 francs per day for men; 1 franc for women, 0.75 franc for adolescents (thirteen to sixteen years old), and 0.45 franc for children (eight to twelve years old).[78] In the context of 1828 conditions, most of what the family earned had to be used for basic living needs; from 30 percent to 50 percent of its budget went for bread, and only a small percentage of workers ate meat more than once or twice a year.[79] In 1848 a husband and wife, in times of full employment, could earn 765 francs per year, and 300 francs typically was spent on bread, 100 or 200 francs on other foods, 150 francs for rent, heat, and household goods, and another 100 francs for clothes.[80] In 1890, 65 percent of the household budget went for food and 12.6 percent was spent on clothing; in 1905, 63.6 percent of the budget was spent on food, but 12.6 percent was still spent on clothing.[81]

Throughout the nineteenth century and continuing into the opening decade of the twentieth century wages were low enough that any crisis sent the individual or family into destitution, and few worker families had saved for a rainy day. One such situation occurred in Lille, where 60 percent of textile workers were unemployed in 1844–1845. There were, of course, no employment contracts, no welfare benefits, no unions, and no legalized strikes. To cushion in times of disaster, charitable organizations helped, but they could not begin to cope with the needs of the vast majority of the working class.[82]

While wages in general rose in France throughout the nineteenth century and into the early years of the twentieth,[83] and the average French worker of the second industrial revolution was better off than his counterpart of the first industrial revolution in absolute terms, real wages declined[84] as wages were not keeping up with the cost of living. Factory workers also were troubled by the fact that their wages noticeably lagged behind their *petit bourgeois* countrymen, as the wage spread between blue-collar and white-collar workers in France was greater than in other European countries.[85] Between 1866 and 1906, wages for public servants, bankers, and employees of insurance companies doubled. Resentment stemmed from the fact that members of the lower middle class often had worker origins; some 26 percent of teachers in 1896 did, for instance.[86] What had occurred was a classic case of boot-strapping largely because of mandatory elementary education that was put into place in the 1880s by Jules Ferry. Those who were left behind, that is, those who were still workers, became bitter toward those who had advanced on the socioeconomic ladder.

The wage situation resulted in the further deterioration of the relationship between mill owners and their workers. Basic necessities, not to mention the new consumer goods, stretched family budgets to the breaking point. In human terms, it meant that at the birth of an additional child in a textile worker's family, wages could be insufficient to support the family.[87] Yet children were needed, because if they survived the first years of life, to help meet family expenses they could be sent off to the factories, where they were appreciated for their agility and suppleness. In the spinning mills, for example, children accounted for about one-third of the manpower and typically began work at eight or nine years of age.[88] In 1841, when France inaugurated the first of its labor laws by prohibiting children under the age of eight from working in factories and shortened the hours of youths below the age of sixteen, 12 percent of the workforce were children. However, since factory inspectors who saw to the enforcement of the law were drawn from the ranks of retired mill owners, the law was not iron clad; in 1870, children constituted 7 percent of the workforce.[89]

France continued to lag behind other industrialized nations in labor legislation. In 1876 women in the textile industry typically put in a thirteen-hour day (5:00 A.M. to 8:00 P.M., with two hours off for meals). In 1900 a law was passed that restricted women and children to a ten-and-a-half-hour workday, but although the subsequent law of 1904 reduced the workday for women and children to ten hours, factory owners, except individuals like Léon Harmel, continued to ignore state regulations and imposed eleven-hour days on female workers.[90]

As a rule, the single worker, especially a single male worker, fared better than the married worker.[91] If married, the man could expect his wife and children to work too, but to the detriment of family life.[92] In addition to the paltry wages and lack of what today is commonly known as quality family time, the long hours and brutal conditions presented hazards to the health and general well-being of family members. Between 1861 and 1870 Mulhouse averaged thirty-three infant deaths per one hundred legitimate births, and forty-five of every one hundred illegitimate babies died before they reached their first birthday.[93] In the textile factories of the Nord, the life expectancy for the *ouvrier* was forty-five years, while the average *ouvrière* died in her mid-thirties. The reason for the lower life expectancy among female factory workers was twofold:

they typically spent their entire lives, from childhood onward, working in the factory; and marriage and childbirth added to a health history already made precarious by the perils associated with the factory. Most female textile workers in the Nord were married and averaged four to six surviving children. Attempts to limit family size by means of abortion met with resistance because it was illegal and costly and, more important, because of religious condemnation.[94] It was only later that worker families significantly limited family size, but women continued to carry the extra burden of home and child care. As for the men, and no doubt reflecting the fifteen-hour workday of the average male worker, military records for the July Monarchy indicate that 90 percent of army draftees from the industrial areas of France were rejected for physical deficiencies.[95]

Paris, with its population density and chronic housing shortage, offers the most dramatic illustration of the dehumanizing effects of the industrial revolution.[96] The sheer growth of the city was astounding. In roughly three quarters of a century, it had quadrupled in size, from a population of 500,000 in 1800 to 2 million in 1879.[97] The capital city had always attracted single people seeking employment who found lodging in dormitories, attics, and just about any nook and cranny available. What was new, beginning about 1850, was the number of families who moved there looking for work who often had to settle for the same housing arrangements as the single workers. Cramped housing, with several families living in one room, and poor nutrition (soup and potatoes constituted three-fourths of their daily diet) and poor hygiene led to promiscuity and disease. In addition to periodic disasters such as the cholera epidemic of 1832 that killed 102,000 French,[98] workers confronted routine infectious diseases that decimated on a regular basis the malnourished and overworked; typhoid, meningitis, tuberculosis, and syphilis claimed the lives of many. In the industrial neighborhoods of Paris at the end of the Second Empire, that is, toward 1870, 70 percent of the people died before the age of forty, and one-half of all children under the age of five did not survive.[99] Those who achieved life expectancy could anticipate living marginalized lives characterized by violence, alcoholism, *concubinage* (cohabitation), and illegitimate liaisons.[100] One-third of all births in Paris were illegitimate.[101] And those who outlived the actuarial prognostications could look forward to being eased out of their jobs when they were forty-five years old with, in most instances, no retirement benefits to replace, even partially, lost wages.[102] The Harmel factory, in stark contrast to the seemingly uncaring world of industrial urban life, offered its workers and their families security and care from cradle to grave.

What impact did the lifestyle of the textile worker and his family have on their religious observance? In a working-class neighborhood of Lille, where there were considerable numbers of the ostensibly more religious Belgians, only 1,500 out of 18,000 inhabitants observed the Easter duty in 1855. The working-class neighborhoods of Paris, Belleville and Montmartre, were similarly weak in religious practice.[103]

DE-CHRISTIANIZATION/RE-CHRISTIANIZATION

In the closing decades of the nineteenth century, in a total population of 40 million, from 87.5 percent to more than 95 percent[104] of the French were nominal Catholics who remained attached to traditional rites of passage in the Church, namely, baptism, first communion, marriage, and burial. Not surprisingly, given the numbers, Catholic institutions and monuments maintained high visibility throughout the period,[105] while nominal Catholics exhibited a healthy dose of anticlericalism and neglected many of the religious observances as defined by the official Church. This phenomenon of irreligion, or de-Christianization, characterized the French working class in particular. De-Christianization has been much noted, but measurement of the diminution of spiritual life remains elusive. There were certain indications, of course, such as the neglect of the Easter duty by the vast majority of the men and ever more frequently by their wives, as well as the numbers of civil marriages and burials[106] and the practice of onanism (coitus interruptus).[107] Then too there was living together before marriage, the frequenting of cabarets, and the replacement of the "jour du seigneur" (Sunday) with "la saint-Lundi" (Monday) as a day of rest among the workers.[108] Indeed, the cabaret enticed many men away from Sunday Mass. By 1914 France had a higher concentration of drinking establishments than any other industrial nation.[109]

The popularity of the cabaret not only diminished attendance at Mass on Sunday, but because of the inevitable hangover on Monday, reduced workplace productivity too. Alcohol abuse was perceived as a moral vice and was of concern to the Church as well as to other segments of society that had a vested interest in, if not the moral life of the worker, then his productivity. Drinking was a favorite male pastime.[110] Workers typically began drinking seriously after work on Saturdays and continued until late on Monday night. Since Monday frequently was written off for work purposes in many factories, this meant that some of Tuesday also was lost, leaving effectively four days of work (Wednesday through Saturday).[111] Villermé, writing in 1839, suggested that drinking was a particular problem in the Nord because of the colder climate, and the statistics he cited were chilling: the Englishman drank 33.1 gallons (125.3 liters)[112] of alcohol per year, the Frenchman 32.2 gallons (121.9 liters) per year, the German 29.9 gallons (113.2 liters) per year, and the American 14.2 gallons (53.75 liters) per year.[113] Eugen Weber says that by the end of the nineteenth century, France led the world in alcohol consumption, as well as the number of alcoholics.[114] Patricia Prestwich offers additional sobering statistics: by 1900 the per person consumption rate amounted to 4 gallons (15.14 liters) of pure alcohol each year, which translated into 160 bottles of wine for every man, woman, and child in France. For comparison purposes, British men, women, and children each consumed 2 gallons (7.571 liters) during the same period, and each American 1.5 gallons (5.678 liters).[115] Taking into account the fact that men consumed proportionately more alcohol than women or children, French men indeed imbibed in record and injurious amounts.

Alcoholism was the third major health problem after tuberculosis and syphilis in Belleville, a working-class neighborhood in Paris where alcohol abuse was considered normal and linked to the increase in worker wages.[116] And while the French worker might consume wine with meals, the real problem was drinking in the cabarets or *estaminets* (beer halls) where one could order aperitifs, absinthe, and other alcohols. Absinthe, the most toxic alcoholic drink, was consumed in ever-increasing quantities after 1890, with national intake rising from 211,320 gallons (8,000 hectoliters) in 1874 to more than 5,283,000 gallons (200,000 hectoliters) in 1905.[117] Once the reserve of the wealthy, it became popular with workers as the cost of a drink decreased with less expensive production methods.[118] Indicative of the growing problem, in 1881 there were 367,825 dram shops, but by 1911 the number had risen to 482,704. Beginning in 1891, 3,300 new bistros opened every year for the next twenty years, and by one count in 1906, Paris workmen consumed 0.7925 gallon (3 liters) of wine a day.[119] Consumption of alcohol at the local cabaret absorbed about 8 percent of the worker's wages.[120]

The effects of drinking were widespread. In the view of the Church, alcohol abuse contributed to moral decline and irreligiosity because men often preferred to spend Sundays in the cabaret rather than at Mass or with family, and increasingly excessive drinking resulted in physical abuse of family members, murder, or other crimes of violence. At the end of the Restoration (1830), crimes against persons represented 26 percent of the total, and in the first decades of the Second Empire (1850s and 1860s), 36 percent of total crimes were crimes against persons; but at the beginning of the twentieth century, crimes against persons had climbed to 44 percent, and experts linked the rising crime rate to increased intake of alcohol.[121] Factory owners registered concern over weekend drinking because it resulted in lost productivity on Mondays and Tuesdays, and thus argued against increasing wages that only served to support the worker's drinking habit. Harmel attempted to curtail alcohol consumption among his workers by making Monday, instead of Saturday, payday and by handing over wages of young male workers to a senior member of his family.

Yet throughout the same period and despite problems with lax morality and insalubrious drinking habits, popular religiosity was often expressed in traditional pilgrimages to places like Lourdes, and religious vocations remained plentiful, particularly among women. In 1878, for example, nuns made up 58 percent of the religious in the Church.[122] It is interesting to note, moreover, that while religious vocations among women flourished, vocations among men held their own in an era much noted for the feminization of religion. Fernand Boulard maintains that despite the laic laws that restricted religious education in the public schools, which attracted more boys than girls, who continued to attend religious schools, and thereby caused a drop in priestly vocations, one still can see evidence of significant numbers of vocations among men throughout the nineteenth century. His studies show that the 1886–1905 period witnessed an upward trend in vocations, behind only that of 1825–1847 and 1871–1890, in numbers of priests ordained nationally.[123] In analyzing the same phenomenon, Ralph Gibson suggests that, at least in the waning decades of the nineteenth century, the strength of priestly vocations might have reflected the *esprit nouveau* of the 1890s; or that it might have been a result of anticlericalism, attracting young men who viewed a vocation to the priesthood as arduous and challenging.[124] Weber interprets the data somewhat differently, citing 1868 as the peak year for ordinations, with falling numbers in the last quarter of the century.[125]

All agree that the real crisis period for priestly vocations began in 1905 and lasted until 1919. By 1914, for example, the number of incoming seminarians had declined by 50 percent from pre-1905 days,[126] and national ordinations had plummeted to 704.[127] Two factors influenced the decline in ordinations. Once church and state separated in 1905, the state no longer paid clerical salaries, and henceforth clergy served two years in the military alongside their secular peers[128] rather than the original one-year obligation stipulated by the Military Law of 1889. In short, the law of separation eliminated two major perquisites attached to the priestly life in France, and those who were attracted to religious life because it was in some ways less demanding than laic life henceforward did not pursue it.

Was the phenomenon of de-Christianization, then, more imaginary than real? Did practical considerations—birth control, clerical salaries, and military exemptions, for example—determine the religiosity of French men? If so, they appeared to be rather ephemeral commodities, ones that might be manipulated or stimulated as circumstances dictated. Thus environmental considerations might also play a role in the augmentation or diminution of de-Christianization.

One historian has found that religious practice remained more widespread in the textile industry than among miners or glass workers,[129] but even in that industry, religious observance depended on geographic location. For example, in the north of France, in the rural Champagne district where the Harmel factory was located, there was weak religious practice and considerable anticlericalism,[130] whereas the city of Lille, located in the Nord proper, was noteworthy for its adherence to traditional religious practices.[131] Seemingly, the presence in significant numbers of the more outwardly Catholic Belgian workers,[132] who represented 25 percent of the workers of the Nord,[133] contributed to the appearance of religiosity in this textile center.

The factors contributing to weak religious practice among the French working class are many. Pierre Pierrard suggests parental indifference, religious pragmatism, anticlericalism, the mediocre example given by the upper classes, and the weakness of religious education as causes.[134] Yves-Marie Hilaire points to onanism as a major reason men stayed away from the sacraments in droves. In the nineteenth century, one customarily confessed before receiving the Eucharist, and since the Church forbade the practice of onanism as a method of birth control, many men neglected their Easter duty.[135] Joseph Moody cites a clergy inadequately trained in the social sciences, social distancing between clergy and worker, and the attraction of the clergy to the political right and the wealthier classes. He also mentions as a reason the perception among workers that the bourgeoisie, that is, the factory owners, were abandoning revolutionary principles, which encouraged the worship of the divine under the guise of Deism rather than as part of institutionalized religion, and returning to traditional religious practice. In short, if the bourgeoisie were returning to the religion of the *ancien régime*, the workers would need to show their contrariness to their bosses by staying away from the Roman religion. The Church also, in Moody's opinion, discouraged religious practice among workers by failing to build churches near factory sites, a clear indication that most Catholic lay leaders remained blind to the deteriorating situation of the industrial worker.[136] Harmel was not guilty on this count, as his spinning mill had a chapel on the premises to facilitate Mass attendance and the receiving of the Sacraments.

Moody argues, moreover, that the French Revolution—or at least its memory—had a powerful impact on the worker, wedding him to revolution and to the ideologies of 1789 rather than to those of traditional religion.[137] At least one other historian, however, suggests that Moody may overstate the lure of myth on this matter. Suzanne Desan posits that to pull religion from culture was not so simple, and in fact the French people consider religious freedom one of the rights established in 1789, and thus most of the French continued to profess belief both in institutional religion and in the principles of the French Revolution.[138]

But as the Revolution ended and Throne and Altar returned to France at the beginning of the nineteenth century, the effects of 1789 on institutionalized religion were as yet undetermined. Proselytism on the part of both Catholics and Protestants began in earnest after 1815, and the result was a veritable war of religion in rural France. The Concordat signed by Napoléon I and Pius VII in 1802 remained silent on the matter of proselytization,[139] and the two leaders actually initialed a program of religious pluralism, but this concept took a while to become part of the public consciousness.[140] Although Protestants represented only 2 percent of the population at the time, they were perceived as a potent threat to Catholicism because Catholics linked them to freethinkers, Freemasons, philosophes, republicans, anticlerics, and even militant atheists.[141] Catholics and Protestants tangled over the distribution of the Bible (whose version?) in rural areas by *colporteurs,* or traveling salesmen, religious teaching in the schools, and who would minister to the poor, the sick, and prisoners.[142] Later Catholics carried out their anti-Protestant rhetoric in newspapers and Christian democratic congresses, and Léon Harmel and Leo XIII added to the oratory on this matter. In short, anti-Protestantism existed alongside anticlericalism and anti-Semitism in French society during the nineteenth century.[143]

Even though Catholics were able to curtail Protestant evangelization through legal action in courts disposed to them, they continued to aggressively reach out to lapsed Catholics throughout the nineteenth century.[144] State officials were most open to the missionary effort during the Second Empire and least so during the early Third Republic. As a consequence, missionaries reported immediate and sometimes spectacular results during the Second Empire,[145] while having to work deceptively during the Third Republic made evangelization more difficult and often less effective, especially in the cities.[146]

Religious orders intensified their efforts at evangelization by means of a network of interior missions during the second half of the nineteenth century, but in fact the concept of interior missions began in the seventeenth century with the work of Vincent de Paul (1581–1660). Hilaire's study, based on the numbers of confessions as recorded by the religious orders involved in the missionary work, demonstrates that the venture was in part successful. The overall number of confessions did not change significantly, but the number of bourgeois men who once again became practicing Catholics was larger than the number among the working class. In fact, there was a continuing decline in religious observance among workers, and in support of Moody's contention, this was in part because their bosses were again observing their Easter duty. Thus there was a slowdown in de-Christianization in those communities targeted for missionary work, most notably among the bourgeoisie.[147]

Léon Harmel invited missionaries to Val-des-Bois to assist in the re-Christianization of his workers, a necessary first step in transforming his spinning mill into a Christian corporation. Would the workers' response be as lackluster at the Harmel enterprise as elsewhere?

WARMÉRIVILLE AND THE VALLEY OF THE SUIPPE

The Suippe River valley, where the Harmel factory was located, was considered a cultural and economic extension of Reims, the nearest large city and the ancient center of the French wool industry, where only one-fourth of labor worked inside the city walls, and most of these workers fell into the category of traditional artisans. As the wool industry mechanized in the 1860s, taking advantage of hard times in the cotton industry during the years of the American Civil War, the artisans of Reims became victims of modernization.[148] The vast majority of factories were located in the rural areas surrounding the city, and its workforce might alternate between working on the family farm and working in a factory.[149]

Unlike other nations where large industrial centers sprang up during the industrial revolution, France did not experience great migrations of people to new industrial cities (Mulhouse probably was the exception to this rule), although the rural exodus picked up after 1871.[150] In 1861 only 11 percent of the populace lived in a department other than the one in which they were born; in 1881 the number had risen to 15 percent.[151] Leslie Moch tells us that workers left their rural homes in teams, migrated short distances (often never leaving the region of their birth), and went to places where family or neighbors welcomed them.[152] Whether the worker in the countryside was better off than his counterpart in the city is a matter of debate, but certainly working in remote areas in which the worker concentration of true industrial centers was absent made for fewer spectacular accounts of worker suffering.[153] Disruption of past work environment and family lifestyle may not have been as traumatic for rural workers as for those living in the working-class neighborhoods of Paris, for instance.[154]

Textile factories located within the radius of Reims fitted into the economic and social picture described above. The city began a depression five years later than the rest of France, beginning in 1878, the apogée of the textile industry as it turned out, and lasting until 1895. Afterward, there was further decline.[155] Between 1876 and the end of the century, forty-one establishments permanently closed their doors, signaling a major weeding out process.[156] The majority of workers experienced significant de-Christianization, while at the same time they observed the traditional Catholic rites of passage. Manpower was a mélange of local laborers and transients from the northern and eastern districts of France and included Belgians. Warmériville was one of the fortunate textile communities of northern France as it was able to maintain economic and demographic strength despite the series of depressions and factory closures plaguing industrial France at this time. The reason was twofold. The town was in part an agricultural community, and it was home to two textile mills— the Simonnet enterprise (founded in 1878) and the Harmel factory— that withstood the periodic business crises.[157] While other enterprises in the area floundered from 1878 on, Val-des-Bois flourished until 1900 and was recognized as a successful spinning mill in the Champagne region.[158]

The Factory

> Behold what awaits me when I return to Val-des-Bois,
> to my paradise where what matters to me is:
> the tenderness of my children, the love of my workers,
> the singing of the birds in green foliage
> and the sun of the North, always a little gloomy yet splendid.
> —Léon Harmel to M. Gabriel Ardant,
> July 3, 1889[159]

The worker population of Léon Harmel's earthly paradise vacillated between 375 and 678 in the years from 1867 to 1914, the number varying with the fluctuating business cycle and peaking at 678 in 1899, the year before the crisis of 1900.[160] In 1906 only 10 percent of French labor worked in factories of more than five hundred employees,[161] so Val-des-Bois was a relatively large enterprise by French standards. Taking into account all members of the workers' families, the population expanded to about 1,400 in peak times. Institutionally, the factory was a

Christian corporation, specifically designed to offer a third alternative to a French nation grappling with capitalist and socialist ideologies.[162] Within its confines, Harmel intended that the spiritual as well as temporal needs of the workers and their families be met by seeing to the professional education, health, improvement of lifestyle, and, of course, salvation of each soul in the factory community.[163] The formation of the corporation was not left to chance. Harmel initiated a three-step process to assure that religious matters took precedence from the outset but with the overall welfare and happiness of the workers and their families a constant consideration.

The first step called for a small group of workers and their families, all of whom were to be well grounded in their Catholic faith, to form a cell community that served as the nucleus of the corporation. By their good example and low-key proselytizing, the cell group inspired fellow workers to renew their baptismal commitment to the Church and once again take up religious practices long neglected. When this religious "association" was strong enough, the workers were ready to commit to the second stage and establish economic organizations such as savings banks and consumer cooperatives for the material and social benefit of the factory community at Val. Finally, with religious, economic, and social structures in place, the enterprise inaugurated the third step and organized professionally by becoming a union, or *syndicat*.[164]

Harmel wanted the Christian corporation, then, to attend to the immediate spiritual and material needs of the workers and their families while simultaneously carrying out the regeneration of the French nation. Although the original groundwork had been laid almost from the founding of the factory at Val-des-Bois in 1840, Harmel transformed the spinning mill into a Christian corporation in the years from 1861 to 1875.

Step One: Religious Renewal

According to Harmel, the evils that plagued his factory before 1861 included drunkenness, neglect of Sunday observance, few marriages "with honor," and lack of proper religious education for children.[165] Since these same factors were cited as signs of the de-Christianization rampant throughout the Champagne district, Harmel's experience in this matter was not unique. The means by which he chose to combat moral malaise at Val-des-Bois, however, demonstrated a certain creativity if not originality. He opted to build a chapel on the factory premises and to establish a series of religious associations for the purpose of re-Christianizing his workers.[166]

The rationale for building a factory chapel in 1862 was simple and straightforward: it offered workers accessibility to the Sacraments and ease in observance of religious rituals. Since only about 25 percent of the factory workers and their families regularly attended the parish church in Warmériville,[167] having a chapel close at hand seemed to serve its intended purpose; beginning in 1862, Sunday Mass was held at Val, and by 1864, daily Mass was offered too.[168] Its mere existence, however, was cause for criticism. To those outside the factory community who were not sympathetic to the creation of a Catholic atmosphere in the workplace, the chapel at Val-des-Bois represented an infringement on the workers' freedom of conscience.

Yet accounts are unanimous in pointing out that chapel attendance, as well as participation in religious events in general, was a matter of individual choice. Workers who chose to abstain from participation in the various religious functions testified that their actions were not used against them.[169] Indeed, Harmel repeatedly cautioned against overt pressure as, in his opinion, an authentic spiritual life could not be forced. Nevertheless, as in any closed community, there were no doubt psychological forces at work to conform. Once lapsed Catholics began observing the Easter duty and other traditional religious rituals in significant numbers at Val, were the minority who did not resume Catholic practices marginalized, if not overtly, then in subtler ways? Extant records regrettably offer no hint about the group dynamics at work on this matter.

If the chapel at Val-des-Bois was the spiritual center of factory life, the associations were the organizational network that facilitated re-Christianization. Key to the initial undertaking were the individuals selected to form the core group. For this, Harmel sought out families who were "profoundly Christian," finding them not in the Suippe valley but instead in the French and Belgian Ardennes.[170] Recruitment from outside the local area was not uncommon. Because of the chronic shortage of manpower, area factory owners routinely hired "les oiseaux migrateurs" (migratory birds) from Alsace, the Nord, Flanders, Savoy, Piedmont, and Germany.[171] In 1840, for example, when the Harmel family relocated to Val-des-Bois from Boulzicourt in the Ardennes, they brought with them workers from their former home and place of business. It was natural, then, that Harmel again recruited in the Ardennes in the 1860s when looking for additional factory personnel, for these workers of the Ardennes were prized not only for their work skills but also for their Catholic demeanor.[172]

A point that Trimouille raises is whether these Catholic recruits of the 1860s should be considered more as religious "plants" than as part of the bona fide conversions (or reconversions of lapsed Catholics?) touted by Harmel. But given the apparent success of the re-Christianization process at the Harmel factory, an equally intriguing question to raise is how it occurred so quickly within an admittedly de-Christianized workforce. Trimouille points out that by 1878, "the vast majority of the worker population had returned to a religious practice which was nearly unknown in 1865."[173] The trend only continued. In a letter written on August 13, 1883, Harmel jubilantly declared that on Easter Sunday of that year, "a great number of women, young girls, and men made their communion in the church." Specifically, he claimed that out of a thousand-member community, seven hundred took communion that Sunday. Furthermore, there had been consistent growth in the numbers taking communion during the previous years: 5,300 in 1872, 7,300 in 1873, and 10,500 in 1882. Even attendance at Sunday and weekday Masses was impressive: on ordinary Sundays, two hundred regularly heard the Low Mass and six hundred the High Mass, and one could count on seeing seventy to eighty at the weekday Masses.[174]

Here one certainly has to acknowledge the presence, beginning in 1861, of the religious personnel invited to Val by Léon Harmel for the purpose of reintroducing religious practice among the workers. First to arrive were Jesuits and Lazarists, who organized religious associations and served as chaplains-in-residence.[175] During subsequent years, priests, brothers, and nuns occupied themselves principally with the children, young girls, and the sick but were also on hand to administer the sacraments and conduct religious services. The Harmel factory became part of the *missions intérieures* and, like others who were recipients of the missionary work in France at this time, experienced positive results.

There was one major distinction in the case of Val-des-Bois, however. The success story at the mill was not of bourgeois management once again observing the Easter duty but rather the re-Christianization of the workers. The Harmel family—both its men and its women—were not lapsed Catholics but ardent practitioners of the faith. By contrast, his workers, with the exception of those imported from the Ardennes, had been negligent in their religious observance. Their return to regular religious practice was unusual among a segment of the population that increasingly was noted for its irreligiosity. Thus once the workers confessed and received the Eucharist on a regular basis, the factory at Val was on its way to becoming a Christian corporation, and the religious associations assisted in the process.

Religious associations were first established in 1863, and by the late 1870s, they counted 75 percent of the population at Val-des-Bois as members.[176] These associations were grouped by sex and age and were not mandatory. The Society of St. Joseph, founded in 1867, was perhaps the most important of the religious associations for Harmel's plans for a Christian corporation, since it was the first association intended for the reputedly less religious male workers. The society enjoyed respectable membership.[177] For example, in 1897, when 435 men were employed at the factory, 315 chose to join one of the two adult male organizations, thereby leaving 120 men outside membership in a religious group. The same freedom of action was extended to women at Val with regard to associational membership.[178] As further proof that Harmel wanted religious commitment to be free from direct patronal control, each association had its own government and was responsible for its own propaganda and recruitment.[179]

Nevertheless, Harmel insisted that the associations be "Catholic, hierarchical, and universal, or general." In other words, he expected that once one joined the organization the annual Easter duty would be fulfilled, that the governing structure would follow a familial model, and that the associations' agendas would "embrace all the needs of the associates."[180] In practice this meant that each member of the association took seriously the religious commitment to the organization, that the governing bodies of the various associations included members of the Harmel family, as well as representatives from the religious personnel on the premises, and that membership in these groups demanded time devoted to others. For instance, members of both the men's and the women's religious associations attended marriages and funerals and visited the sick of the

Harmel community. The women and girls who belonged to associations also were responsible for reaching out to women of the community at moments peculiar to a woman's life, such as visiting a new mother after the birth of a child and presenting her with a hand-stitched *petit trousseau* that had been prepared for the occasion. The women's associations, therefore, under the guidance of the Harmel bourgeoisie, nurtured the charitable traditions prevalent in France of this era among ladies of the middle class.[181]

Harmel clearly was assertive in tackling the problem of moral malaise among his workers by importing religious personnel to Val-des-Bois and establishing religious organizations to re-Christianize his labor force. But the idea of assistance from religious personnel was an amplification of the whole *missions intérieures* project and, as such, not all that original. And whereas the founding of religious associations at the mill can be viewed as an innovation, the actual organizational prototype for the groups was the religious orders themselves and therefore represented a bit of "old wine in new bottles." Only in the self-regulated diminution of his own authority did Harmel break from past and contemporary French traditions among members of his class and occupation, for French industrialists preferred to keep a tight rein on their workers.[182] He, earlier than the vast majority of *patrons* and not waiting for strikes or labor laws to move him to action, began loosening patronal ties. While the Harmel family were members of the associations, their authority was diluted. Association programs were self-directed by the group as a whole, and Harmel acknowledged that it would have been "impossible for the patron to organize and govern the worker-family without the help of the associations."[183]

Step Two: Communal Improvement

Harmel wanted justice to be the underlying determinant for the compensation system at Val-des-Bois. He based his wage scale on three factors: the quantity of work, its quality, and the amount of responsibility involved. Those who "worked double merited being paid double," and those who "do better work, bring more profit to the enterprise, should be paid more." Consequently, the factory director and the foreman, both of whom furnished greater "intellectual work," or brought greater managerial skills to the enterprise, merited greater compensation.[184] Likewise, remuneration for the factory worker combined a base wage, or daily wage, sufficient to put bread on the table with that which, based on the piecework system, rewarded high-quality craftsmanship. By integrating a base wage with an incentive wage, not only was product quality given greater assurance, but a certain regularity of wages was guaranteed when compared to systems relying solely on the business cycle to set wage levels.[185]

Furthermore, since the family was, for Harmel, the societal unit par excellence, wages needed to be determined with its needs in mind.[186] This meant that to be adequate, wages had to support not only the single *ouvrier* or *ouvrière* but in the case of the married male worker his entire family as well.[187] Those family units that included children were paid a supplement, or *salaire familial* (family wage), proportionate to the number of children and intended principally for nourishing those children.[188] Taking into account the moderate housing costs, the pleasure and benefit of individual gardens adjacent to housing, and the advantage of country living offered at Val, Harmel calculated 4.20 francs as the weekly cost of living for each member of the family unit, which amounted to 218.4 francs per year. He determined that living at Val-des-Bois was less costly than living in the city, which according to his estimate amounted to 5.60 francs per week for each individual family member, and thus the reduced cost-of-living valuation for Val. On average, he dispensed 1,800 to 2,000 additional francs per year to cover the cost of the family supplement, which, though not nearly as generous as he would have liked, was sufficient to prevent "la misère noire."[189]

Léon Harmel became one of the original practitioners of the family wage among the *patronat* of France, thereby placing him among the foremost reformers on this matter.[190] From syndicalist militants to radical republicans to social Catholics, men across the ideological spectrum in France argued in favor of the family wage. The percent of married women in French industry was noticeably high, and as the birthrate declined, ever more women chose to work outside the home.[191] Working women concerned French men, but the reasons varied. They competed for jobs, drove down wages, and definitely went against the bourgeois ideal of womanhood.[192] Harmel's principal stated concern was the stability of the family. Yet despite the almost universal appeal of the notion, state support for the family wage was years away from Harmel's implementation of the program.

The whole point with regard to wages, Harmel reasoned, was for families to be "happy" and not that they have a "high wage," for only then would their consumer demands be moderate and the need to save for an uncertain future readily apparent.[193] Consequently, the base wage at Val-des-Bois was consistent with that at other factories in the Suippe valley, which, while sensitive to wage rates in Reims, was also adjusted to the lower cost of living that prevailed in rural areas. For example, in the 1870s a male factory worker in Reims earned 4.50 francs per day, while his counterpart at Val earned 4.0 francs. Similarly, a female factory worker earned 2.0 francs in Reims and 1.75 francs at the Harmel enterprise.[194] What is interesting to note here, moreover, is that the Harmel *ouvrières* earned 56 percent less than the Harmel *ouvriers*. If, in fact, the male-female wage differential in France was 50 percent, this suggests that Harmel underpaid his female workers not only when compared to male workers at Val but also when compared to female workers of larger cities, such as Reims. Clearly Harmel intended women's work to be supplementary to men's work at Val-des-Bois. The family wage augmented the married man's compensation in order that his wife would no longer feel compelled to work outside the home. For Léon Harmel, the family wage became an economic means to support the family unit.

To maximize these moderate wages, Harmel set out to control spending habits. For instance, the mill's tertiary personnel were paid by the month, but the less fiscally responsible factory workers were paid every two weeks so as to discourage liberal spending at the beginning of the month only to come up short at the end of the month.[195] Furthermore, remuneration was remitted to the family as a unit and personally handed to the mother or male head of the household by the *patron* himself. By remitting the family pay directly into the mother's or father's hands on Monday, market day, Harmel wanted to guarantee that wages would be spent on food and not for drinks at the local cabaret, as was frequently the case when male workers, particularly unmarried sons in the family, were paid individually at the end of the Saturday workday.[196]

Wages, however, were only one facet of the compensatory program at the Harmel factory, and this accounts in part for their meagerness. Instead of raising wages, Harmel opted to provide his workers with some degree of relief with regard to work hours, but more notably, with numerous social and economic institutions and services.

The workday at Val-des-Bois was in keeping with national law and local custom, and that was praiseworthy in itself. As Judith Stone has demonstrated, even after the national legislature passed laws restricting workday hours, there was no uniformity in implementation. The textile industry argued that having to differentiate among men, women, and children when scheduling the length of the workday was confusing and difficult. The easier thing to do was to dismiss women and children once their workdays were shortened, or to reduce wages for all workers, which as one might imagine frequently resulted in strikes.[197] Harmel's compliance was exemplary by comparison. For example, before 1893, when state law dictated a twelve-hour day, the Harmel workers had an eleven-and-a-half-hour day. After 1893 the Harmel workers were more or less in accord with state laws, so that in 1893 they worked an eleven-hour day, in 1902 a ten-and-a-half-hour day, and after 1904 a ten-hour day.[198]

Divergence from national law and local custom occurred on weekend time. Beginning in 1878, Harmel's workers were free from factory labor on Sundays. It was only in 1894 that Sunday as a day of rest became common practice in the Suippe River valley,[199] although the concept had been introduced much earlier in the century. Sunday actually became a day of rest in 1814 and coincided with the Bourbon Restoration and concomitant return of the influence of the Roman Catholic Church. However, once the Bourbon Restoration ended in 1830 and the privileged place of the Church diminished, the day had not been honored as one free from labor. Nevertheless, official reversal of Sunday as a holiday came only with the anticlerical legislation of 1880, which was unpopular among Catholics and non-Catholics alike. Throughout the intervening years, Catholics campaigned for the reintroduction of Sunday as a day of rest and were successful when, in 1906, the national assembly mandated the day to be one free of work. But while this was a popular measure—the most popular of the labor reform laws—there was no universal application after the law was enacted in 1906, and a liberal policy of exemptions was put into place.[200]

Beginning in 1907, work hours decreased at Val on Saturdays. Initially, the Saturday workday was reduced in half, but in 1913 the Conseil d'Usine granted the women at Val Saturday as another day completely free from factory labor.[201] Moreover, the reduced work hours produced no adverse effects; that is, there was no wage reduction and factory production levels were maintained.[202] After 1880 night work was the only remnant of past practices that lingered at the Harmel factory and was a source of controversy. It was, however, confined to one workroom and to a small number of male workers[203] whose work at night allowed Sunday to be honored as a day of rest.[204]

More than twenty economic and social organizations supplemented the compensation plan at Val-des-Bois and were designed to enhance the lifestyle of everyone at the factory. The workers operated these various institutions and services, with Harmel managerial presence and direction varying with the particular institution and the particular time. The tendency, by and large, was to reduce patronal control and augment worker control with the passage of years. Jacques-Joseph Harmel laid the groundwork in the early 1840s with the establishment of the savings bank, the mutual aid society, and housing for factory personnel. But Léon Harmel created the vast majority of the institutions at Val-des-Bois during his tenure as *patron*. In addition to initiating the family wage system at Val, he set up the consumer cooperative with its *boni corporatif* (corporate profit), retirement and pension plans, elementary schools, vocational training programs, and the factory council, as well as recreational facilities and organizations.

According to one account,[205] the savings bank (*caisse d'épargne*) was nearly depleted in 1861 just as the religious associations were starting up, but by all accounts, the bank surpassed expectations within a short period. It paid an interest rate of 4 percent at a time when the postal savings banks paid 2.5 percent.[206] Harmel announced in 1879 that, contrary to prevailing opinion that workers did not save money, his workers saved 10 percent of their wages.[207] As of 1900, 155 Hamel workers had a total savings of 80,000 francs and had, on average, deposited 15 percent of their wages.[208] Believing that personal economy could not start too early, the factory also established a savings bank for its children. This too was a success, for by 1900, 184 youngsters participated in the savings program.[209]

The Mutual Aid Society (Société de Secours Mutuels) was the only institution at Val-des-Bois that required participation by all Harmel workers. Monthly dues were exacted from wages, with married women and aged parents paying token amounts, in order to provide free medical care, an indemnity in case of accident or illness, and burial costs for the workers and their families. In practice, the Mutual Aid Society joined with the company to provide financial assistance during times of adversity. An injured worker received both an indemnity from the society and half-pay from the company; if permanently disabled, he received a life annuity and had his rent reduced; and if killed on the job, the society covered the cost of the funeral while the company provided his widow and children with compensation commensurate with his wage.[210] In establishing a mutual aid society at Val, the Harmel *patrons* provided their workers with a service that was fairly common at the time.

Mutual aid societies were nineteenth-century corporatist holdovers from the prerevolutionary world of guilds and confraternities. Recognizing the services they rendered in the absence of the old institutions, as well as any government-sponsored welfare program, the state permitted them to operate legally. They were voluntary insurance associations, set up under the watchful eye of the state, that collected monthly dues from members in order to provide support in times of need. Members could expect monetary assistance when facing retirement, illness, or death (the funeral was paid for). But the mutual aid societies were as much concerned with providing help in times of adversity as they were with promoting confraternity among its members; attendance at picnics and other social activities was all part of being a member.[211] Between 1881 and 1902, mutual aid societies in France doubled, claiming 131,677 societies and two million members at the turn of the century.[212]

The French state, one of the last of the Western industrialized nations to act on behalf of workers on these matters, initiated plans for accident insurance in 1898 and old-age pension in 1910, but accident insurance became nonobligatory, and old-age pensions became voluntary.[213] In short, France gave its workers nothing of substance in the years before World War I. By contrast, Germany had a health insurance program in place in 1883, a compulsory accident insurance program in 1884, and an old-age pension, beginning at the age of seventy, in 1889. Mutual aid societies, then, continued to provide a valuable service in the absence of real government reform in this area, and while the program at Val-des-Bois was not voluntary, it was the equivalent of the other societies in terms of benefits.

Léon Harmel, however, distinguished himself in emphasizing the prevention of accidents and illness. He maintained that it was the responsibility of the *patron* to create a healthy and safe environment for his workers. When hazardous work was involved, he compensated the worker with "an increase in salary and by a diminution of work hours."[214] Moreover, he equipped his workrooms with ventilators and sensing devices to monitor temperatures, as well as drinking water and shower facilities. Vigilant in his observance of the latest health regulations, Harmel was more often than not years in advance of law and custom.[215] For example, the Harmel workrooms set 75 degrees Fahrenheit (24 degrees Celsius) as the maximum temperature for health and safety, whereas other factories in the area maintained temperatures of 96.8 to 104 degrees Fahrenheit (36 degrees to 40 degrees Celsius). When a state law mandated the lowering of temperatures in the workrooms of textile factories in 1894,[216] the Harmel factory already was in compliance. Similarly, Harmel went against general practice by having the men, not the women, work in the hot and humid washing rooms and in the dyeing rooms, where workers carried skeins weighing from 66 to 88 pounds (30 to 40 kilograms).[217]

Apparently the precautions produced the desired results. Harmel proclaimed in 1907, "We rarely have a death among the men[,] . . . the last time being twelve years ago."[218] He also boasted justifiably that infant mortality rates at Val were in the 7 to 8 percent range,[219] whereas the national average was closer to 20 percent.[220] There were several contributing factors. Not only did Harmel not unduly tax the female workers at his factory, but the vast majority of married women at Val did not work, which was in stark contrast to the norm. In 1902, for example, out of 218 *ouvrières,* only 42 were married.[221] And mothers at Val, whether working outside the home or not, received material and medical assistance throughout the period surrounding childbirth. In this, Harmel kept pace with industry custom. In 1909 the state mandated paid maternity leave of one month, but this law, like so many other labor laws, was widely ignored.[222] Yet there were some one hundred fifty maternity plans functioning in France before the legalization of paid maternity leave in 1913, and many of them operated in the textile industry where high infant morality rates existed because of the concentration of female workers.[223]

An example of a somewhat less common program started during Léon Harmel's tenure as *patron* was the consumer cooperative and its adjunct, the *boni corporatif.* The cooperative society was established in 1879 with 3,325 francs in capital and seventy-two members. It enjoyed mixed success. Largely worker operated, it, like the other consumer cooperatives of the era, never attracted a majority of worker families, though it offered a savings of 5 percent on meat, 10 percent on vegetables, and 20 percent on coal when purchased in bulk quantities.[224] Members of the consumer cooperative received seven-eighths of the profits, which were automatically fed into the *boni corporatif,* a capital fund designed to encourage saving. The amount vested in the fund depended on the amount purchased at the cooperative. Funds from the individual accounts were withdrawn when the head of the family reached the age of fifty, or given to the widow if the head of the family died before reaching fifty, or when a major catastrophe struck a family, or when a worker left the employment of the factory. As in the case of the savings bank, participants in the *boni corporatif* became "capitalists" and educated in the economically responsible ways of the middle class.[225] Harmel would have preferred that all members of his worker family participate in the *boni corporatif,* but he felt it was even more important to have "fewer reserves and greater freedom."[226] His experience with lackluster worker participation appeared to be typical of other factory owners operating such a plan.

According to one contemporary study,[227] eighty-one establishments in France operated a *boni corporatif* in 1890, in which "functioning participation was more or less complete." These enterprises shared such common characteristics as business success, an extended clientele, and little unemployment. But while able to function, there were very few with "true" or enthusiastic participation. The reasons remain unspecified in the study, but more recent scholarship hints at a possible explanation. Workers did not always duplicate the lifestyle of their bourgeois employers or assimilate their values, demonstrating the resilience of working-class culture that continued to gain strength in the latter decades of the nineteenth century; contrariness was indicative of a distinct working-class ethos.[228] General lack of enthusiasm for cooperatives and their profit-sharing programs also affirmed that France at heart remained a nation of small shopkeepers.[229]

Both the savings bank and the *boni corporatif* were intended to finance partially the years of retirement. In turn-of-the-century France, fifty was the customary age for retirement, but Harmel, perhaps recalling his father's longevity and active retirement years, encouraged the elderly to work as long as possible. Even as physical strength diminished, workers continued to earn an honorable living by performing less arduous tasks in the factory or on its premises as groundskeepers and gardeners, with their pay reduced accordingly. When it became impossible to work, a special fund, completely financed by the *patron,* assured the former worker a pension of 300 francs per year.[230] Because of low life expectancy, however, few lived long enough to take advantage of retirement benefits. In 1907, for example, the Harmel factory employed twelve workers who were sixty-three to sixty-nine years old, nine workers who were seventy-one to eighty years old, and four retirees who ranged in age from eighty to eighty-four.[231]

Nor were the young neglected at the Harmel factory. This was particularly evident in the concern taken with their education at Val and perhaps reflected a generally higher regard for education in northern France. At a time when illiteracy was the norm among factory workers, as early as 1858 the literacy rate among textile workers in the Nord was 42.7 percent.[232] Primary education to age thirteen was free and compulsory at Val-des-Bois long before the national law of 1882 mandated the same for all French children. In the minds of many, the military defeat of 1870 was due in part to German educational superiority, and republicans such as Jules Ferry and Camille Sée envisioned educational reform not only as advancing pedagogy but promoting nationalism as well.[233] Since there often was considerable discrepancy between the stated national policy and what was actually practiced, Harmel's effort on behalf of education is noteworthy but not atypical among the *patronat* who perceived an educated workforce as in their best interest. Still, considering the obstacles, he probably was more successful than most mill owners in educating the next generation.

Besides the fact that state inspectors were pulled from the ranks of retired factory owners and therefore often predisposed to look the other way when underaged children were spotted in factory workrooms, parents frequently elected, for financial reasons, to have their children work rather than go to school, and factory owners continued to prefer to hire the less costly child laborer in defiance of regulations. The net result was that children continued to work illegally in the textile factories in disregard of national law.[234] The law of 1874 had set the minimum age for factory employment at twelve, but a subsequent decree reduced the age requirement to ten for certain industries, including the textile industry.

The law also mandated that children between the ages of twelve and fifteen who did not have the *certificat d'instruction primaire élémentaire* were limited to six hours' work per day instead of eight hours. Even after the law of 1882 required compulsory education to the age of thirteen, parents could petition for exemption for at least part of the school day. Teeth were finally put into national education laws for primary school children in 1892 when the state banned child labor in industry unless the child had proof he had received his *certificat d'études primaries,* which in essence became the new badge of adulthood among adolescents, replacing, at least for the less religious, the traditional rite of passage to the adult world, the first communion.[235]

Harmel, in contrast to many employers, actively encouraged education for children at Val-des-Bois. As of 1868 he permitted no child under the age of twelve to work in the factory,[236] and he not only provided free elementary education for factory children but also offered parents a choice as to where to send their offspring to school. Harmel thereby further demonstrated his belief that religion cannot be forced. In 1897, for example, nineteen boys and seven girls attended the laic school at Warmériville[237] without penalizing their future at the factory. In fact, there were some fifty workers at Val-des-Bois in 1904 who had attended the village school and were subsequently welcomed into the factory apprenticeship program and went on to became factory employees.[238]

Although education at Val was a mixture of the religious and the secular, it shared certain characteristics with the secular republican schools. Both systems taught the sexes in separate facilities and had different educational expectations for them. Nineteenth-century French society trained men to work outside the home and women to work inside the home, and school curricula were designed to meet their respective needs. Young men in the laic schools went to class two years longer than the young women, and they learned Latin, the key to passing the *baccalauréat* and entrée to higher schools and professions. Although Léon Harmel received his *baccalauréat* at the Collège Saint-Vincent de Senlis, the Catholic equivalent of the laic lycée where he studied the classic curriculum, the young men at Val, beneficiaries of Harmel's personal educational philosophy, concentrated not on the traditional liberal arts but on learning the fine points of their future lives as heads of households and factory workers. Household economy, gardening, and industrial design were cardinal to their course of study at the Harmel enterprise.

Girls in the public schools were taught a smattering of general cultural knowledge, but their education centered on the household arts.[239] Even after the Sée Law of 1880 established lycées for girls, domesticity continued to be reinforced, because the rationale behind these schools was not feminism but anticlericalism.[240] The republican government looked to its women to create an attractive home atmosphere in order to lure their men from the cabarets as alcoholism became more rampant among male workers.[241] Considering the raison d'être of Sée's lycées, it is ironic that it was in the Catholic secondary schools of France that young women first studied Latin, key to sitting for the *baccalauréat*.[242] And as for female vocational training, the state confined its efforts to the tertiary sector by setting up schools to train typists and secretaries.[243]

At Val the curriculum for young women was in accord with that of the laic school; they studied domestic hygiene, nutrition, cooking, sewing, and needlework. Even the textbooks portrayed similar personalities and role models to demonstrate the female ideal—one that was "gentle, modest, self-sacrificing, and submissive to male authority."[244] The female children at the Harmel factory, then, were educated not for the professions or service sector, or for their work as *ouvrières,* but instead for their future roles as wives and mothers. Indeed, Léon Harmel saw no need to train girls to be schoolteachers when their real vocation was in the home.[245]

Full-time training in the household arts began at age ten at Val's École Ménagère (School of Household Arts) and continued with part-time attendance (one hour daily) after the age of thirteen or fourteen, when the young woman entered the workforce, to age sixteen, when formal domestic education ended. She did, however, persist in her career formation by meeting henceforth in biweekly sessions with other young women to busy her hands with needlework while discussing religious matters under the tutelage of one of the sisters. The ceremonial culmination of this intense training in domesticity was her wedding day, at which time she was presented with a copy of *Le Bonheur domestique* (Domestic Happiness) on behalf of the factory personnel.[246]

Vocational training for the young men at Val-des-Bois took a different route, though it too was grounded in the pragmatic. The director of the boys' school, Léon Harmel, frowned on dreams of socioeconomic mobility. He counseled rather that young men follow the professions of their fathers and turn away from "brilliant careers" that were in reality "deceiving," where "the perils are numerous, the gains minimal, and the requirements terrible," for "families will be much happier if their children remain good workers instead of bureaucrats devoured by ambition."[247] This, of course, was a conservative notion, and one that did not originate with Harmel. Traditionally, sons followed fathers in vocations, no matter what their class, and there was considerable concern at this time that industrialization disrupted customary familial patterns by changing the work environment from home to factory and thereby weakening the family unit. Harmel wanted to safeguard the family unit, and in his opinion, occupational inheritance was one way to do so. Not wanting his own family to forget the Harmel legacy of hard work and intending to drive home to family members the dignity of labor, Harmel had his sons train in the factory workshops as *ouvriers* and foremen before taking up their managerial positions.

The formal apprenticeship program at Val was important to Harmel, for in his words, "he who is poorly taught in his trade will be a bad worker, nearly incorrigible."[248] The apprenticeship period for young men operated within the same time frame as that for young women: it encompassed the years from thirteen to sixteen and followed graduation from the primary school. It also consisted of one hour of daily instruction in the midst of the workday and was continued at biweekly evening sessions. The principal difference between the vocational training programs for the boys and girls at Val was their subject content.

In establishing a strong apprenticeship program, most notably the one for the boys at his factory, Léon Harmel put into practice educational views that had their inception during his own school days at the Collège Saint-Vincent de Senlis, but he also was responding to current economic reality. The pressure of international competition during the depression between the first and second phases of the industrial revolution (roughly the 1873–1895 period) in France had alerted mill owners in the textile industry to the need for well-trained workers, and the Catholic *patronat* was the first to respond.[249] In this he joined other factory owners who, before public authorities acted, pushed for what was generally acknowledged as an authentic economic demand: vocational schools.

Actually there had been an initial attempt by the state to address this problem during the Second Empire when Victor Duruy became minister of education in 1863. Duruy believed strongly in training workers and foremen in order to better meet the needs of an industrialized France, and his program of "special education" flourished in the 1870s only to be undone by 1891 when republicans diluted the vocational thrust of his curriculum by gradually incorporating academic and theoretical material.[250] The need for vocational training only seemed to become more acute with time, however. Adolescents, bereft of the discipline and pride that accompanied apprenticeship, turned to crime and gang activity for lack of anything better to do with their time; the Apaches, for instance, were a notorious gang of youths that terrorized Belleville in the 1890s. A Paris survey of 1910 confirmed what everyone suspected: 88 percent of the youth of the capital city were going without vocational training.[251]

Mill owners meanwhile recognized that on-the-job training was no longer adequate, especially after shortened work hours pressured them into having workers spend the entire workday working rather than part of the day training. Formerly employers might set aside three hours for job training, but increasingly apprenticeship programs on factory sites seemed a luxury. The Catholic *patronat* of Lille responded first to the situation by setting up a limited liability company to found a Catholic vocational school. Other communities followed the lead of the Catholic employers of the Nord, with initial efforts confined to the local level where apprentices attended the municipal vocational school during an hour break from the factory in late morning only to return for two or three additional hours in the evening, or spend part of Sunday in training.[252] Smaller firms drew from these local vocational schools, while the larger firms, such as the Harmel factory, continued to conduct apprenticeship programs on site.[253]

Self-interest played a not inconsequential role in the establishment of vocational programs whether on the factory premises or in municipal schools. In a depressed labor market and under increased pressure to compete internationally, the *patrons* were better assured of an adequate supply of workers who would be specifically trained for the production tasks of the individual enterprises if they personally took charge of the education of their workers' sons. Yet for Léon Harmel, whose educational system combined the religious with the secular, the apprenticeship program at Val had greater significance than vocational training of the young. He wanted it to be responsible for "a veritable Christian revolution in the factories."[254] By reintroducing his workers to religious practice and by providing them with sound professional training and an attractive home ambience, Harmel intended to dignify manual labor and to produce a contented and sober workforce that would join him in the re-Christianization of France.

Life at Val-des-Bois also included cultural and recreational clubs and facilities. There was a dramatic society, a symphonic society, a choral society, and a library, and the opportunity to play billiards and to bowl as well. But the principal and most costly amenity that made for agreeable living at the factory was the housing. Beginning as early as 1841, the Harmel family built homes on the factory premises with the purpose of promoting family life. These were not the "barrack"-type edifices frequently associated with mill housing but rather individual structures that assured families privacy while allowing for such practical features as vegetable gardens. In fact, the Maheude home described in Zola's *Germinal* was very like the homes of the workers at Val-des-Bois.

Rent was in keeping with that common to the area and was judged as moderate by all accounts, ranging from 70 francs to about 200 francs per year, varying with the size of the home. In 1897, for example, individual families occupied some thirty-six houses, paying an average rent of 110 francs.[255] Not everyone who worked at the factory lived in these homes. Some opted to live in the village, and others already owned property elsewhere. The only group that seemed to have no choice in their housing arrangements were the young girls who were either orphaned or living apart from their families.[256] They were housed in a *maison de famille* (family house), which was operated by the sisters and resembled the *internats,* or boardinghouses, for working-class women and children that were prevalent at the time.

By providing his workers with housing, Léon Harmel was not atypical of owners of larger textile enterprises. Indeed, as has been demonstrated by Peter Stearns,[257] Val-des-Bois was in many ways representative of what had been taking place at some enterprises throughout the nineteenth century. Savings plans, mutual aid societies, cooperatives, bonus systems, schools, pension plans, profit sharing, free medical care, and housing were the means by which factory owners attracted and retained workers. Harmel saw these benefits as a "pledge of security" in that they assured a certain "permanence in appointments," as well as guaranteeing a contented workforce.[258] Moreover, in the long run, these perquisites were less costly to the mill owners than raising wages to keep pace with the cost of living, and allowed the employer to "discipline" his workers in that he controlled their lifestyle.

But how did the workers regard the substantial benefit packages that paternalistic bosses offered them? Did they resent being "disciplined"? David Gordon argues that labor historians rarely take note of the fact that not all workers regarded company savings plans, mutual aid societies, cooperatives, profit-sharing plans, schools, pension plans, free medical care, and housing as programs merely to be suffered, especially when the state did not match in kind. Leaving aside the motives of the *patronat,* the workers might have been grateful for the concrete benefits that improved their lifestyle, judging from the absence of wide support for the socialist party.[259]

Harmel, *le bon père* of Val, appears, then, to have been an exemplar of the paternalistic system by providing his workers with every possible amenity available to the more fortunate workers in France during the nineteenth century. But he went beyond the mere provision of material benefits. In an era in which employers routinely evaded laws governing workplace hours, health and safety, and child labor, he not only consistently complied with the rules but also frequently set standards at Val that anticipated future factory regulations. Though he did not raise wages above industry or regional norms, he offered his workers and their families educational opportunities, housing, discount buying, savings and pension plans, medical benefits, and financial assistance in time of adversity that either equaled or improved on what other employers extended to their employees.

But Harmel also distinguished himself as an innovator in several areas. The *salaire familial,* or family wage, was a benefit seldom seen during this era. Unusual if not unique was the notion of including the family of the worker in the various benefit programs at the factory. And the practice of permitting the worker an increasingly effective role in administering virtually all the organizations and services at Val-des-Bois was rarely attempted by other factory owners of the time. In short, what we are seeing here is a growing ambiguity with regard to Harmel's practice of paternalism. On the one hand, he was its chief exemplar: he used it and promoted it. On the other hand, by handing over managerial responsibility to the workers at Val, he assisted in its dismantling, at least in its traditional form. Indeed, as John McManners has pointed out, Harmel perhaps was the first *patron* to realize that paternalism would never be adequate in itself if the worker was to reach his full potential.[260]

Step Three: Professional Organization

With religious, economic, and social organizations operating, Harmel organized Val-des-Bois professionally in 1875. The *syndicat professionnel* (professional union) embraced all the existing groups at the mill and, in so doing, transformed a Christian factory into a Christian corporation. Structurally, the *syndicat* was identical to other organizations at Val in that it was "mixed"; that is, it included both management and labor in its membership and its administration.

The inspirational source for the *syndicat professionnel* was the medieval guild, although Harmel recognized the need for contemporary adaptation.[261] He observed that in the old corporations, one hardly could distinguish the *patron* from the *ouvrier;* they were comrades and companions, and their roles were quite similar. In his day, by contrast, he noted, the size of enterprises meant that employers had increased power and authority over employees and their families, thereby necessitating greater protection of workers by their employers.[262] Therefore, he argued initially not only for paternalism in industry but also for an institutional structure that would accommodate such a concept.

The nineteenth-century Christian corporation departed considerably from the original medieval model. Not only were workshop size and increased mechanization factors, but so too was class stratum a consideration. While the medieval guild was hierarchical in the sense that it distinguished among the apprentices, journeymen, and masters in the guild, all were of the artisanal class and intent on owning their own workshops. Consequently, the hierarchy inherent in the medieval corporation was not based on a difference in socioeconomic background but rather was a matter of greater or lesser vocational training and experience, which theoretically at least all but disappeared with the passage of time. In stark contrast, few if any French factory workers aspired to being *patron* of their own enterprises, because they accepted—especially those in rural areas, according to Michelle Perrot—as "natural" and "legitimate" the notion of a paternalistic hierarchy in the workplace.[263] In other words, the rags-to-riches dreams and boot-strapping ambitions endemic to Anglo-American culture were simply not a serious consideration in nineteenth-century France. Therefore, the idea of a corporation of equals in *potentia,* such as existed in the medieval guild, was not written into the blueprint of the *syndicat professionnel* in 1875 when Val-des-Bois officially became a Christian corporation.

Harmel's Christian corporation subsequently was modified in two highly significant ways. First, in response to the national law of 1884 that overturned the Chapelier Law of 1791 and legalized labor unions and defined their rules of conduct, the *syndicat professionnel* divorced itself in 1885 from the religious associations at the factory. Henceforward, workers legally could join a union—or refrain from joining one—and choose which union they would become members of, although there was only one union to choose from at Val. According to Francine Soubiran-Paillet, legalization of professional unions represented a landmark step in the labor history of France, for the worker now had the capability of moving from a condition of isolation to one in which he could bargain collectively;[264] in a real sense, the anomie, which Durkheim and others had worried over, had ended. Second, and partly in response to the growth of socialism, labor's participation in the day-to-day operations at Val-des-Bois increased. The most striking example of this was the Conseil d'Usine.

The Conseil d'Usine, created in 1883, became officially codified in the statutes of the *syndicat professionnel* in 1885. Not a social or economic entity, it fell under the aegis of the professional branch of the corporation. Its purpose, according to Harmel, was "not to settle disputes but to prevent them."[265] To accomplish this goal, the council used numerous committees and subcommittees to reach into the inner core of factory life and, not incidentally, to purposely involve as many workers as possible in the process. Strictly speaking, the council was an advisory board whose recommendations were always subject to Harmel's scrutiny, but in reality he preferred that it, like other workers' councils at the factory, take care of the business at hand, for this developed "responsibility."[266]

While not suggesting a complete abrogation of patronal authority, he certainly advised constricting its exercise, as he cautioned, for example, other *patrons* to remain "discreet" by allowing a "vast field of personal initiative to the workers and their councils."[267] Yet he considered the presence of the *patron* at meetings of the council beneficial. Speaking specifically of his experience on the Conseil d'Usine, he saw it as a forum from which "we can open our hearts to them [the workers], make them understand our thoughts, and initiate them in the business and the workings of the factory, not only to interest them in it, but to make them *véritables cooperateurs,*" or real participants of the corporation.[268] Consequently, both labor and management were represented on the Conseil d'Usine.

Its members included worker-representatives from each of the eleven *salles,* or workrooms, as well as two men of the Harmel family, the chaplain, a religious brother, and a secretary. Not surprisingly, the workers elected to these administrative positions were the seasoned employees. Intentionally excluded from the board were the foreman, whose presence was thought to inhibit liberty of speech on the part of the workers, and women.

Instead the women had their own council, the Conseil d'Atelier (Workshop Council). It too consisted of representatives from each of the women's workrooms and met regularly with one of the Harmel men or with one of their wives, but its scope was more limited than the men's council. Nevertheless, the Conseil d'Atelier was effective in eradicating concerns that were peculiar to the female workers at Val. For example, the council was vigilant for any "displaced familiarity" on the part of male supervisory personnel, and its workshop representative had the authority to excuse a female worker from her work station without first seeking permission from the foreman.[269] Apparently the worker-representatives on the council were genuine advocates for the *ouvrières* at Val, because when Harmel attended their meetings from time to time, he came away impressed with the boldness with which the women defended the interests of their coworkers.[270]

The same seriousness of purpose characterized the biweekly meetings Harmel held with the Conseil d'Usine. Involving itself in just about every aspect of factory life, the council reviewed matters dealing with accident prevention, workroom hygiene and discipline, wage schedules, the bonus system, and the apprentice program. Work atmosphere and factory morale were given attention as well. For instance, in response to worker suggestions, the council agreed to provide hot coffee in each of the *salles* in time for the 8:00 A.M. break. In addition, the council assisted

Harmel in actively soliciting worker opinion on product improvement by having the workroom representatives periodically meet with him on the subject.

The role of the Conseil d'Usine continued to expand over the years, moving from a purely advisory board to one with decision-making powers. By 1893, for example, it was creating the curriculum for the apprenticeship program and by 1903 it was selecting workers to oversee that program, as well as assuming full responsibility for accident prevention measures. It never, however, became privy to the major financial and business decisions of the firm.[271]

Nevertheless, the Conseil d'Usine presents the best example of the workers at Val-des-Bois affecting, within limits, their own work environment. That the other factory organizations, with the exception of the consumer cooperative, also elicited a high degree of worker involvement only served to multiply the positive results, namely, high morale and overall job satisfaction. The Christian corporation appeared, then, to have been successful in fortifying the mutual respect between labor and management at Val-des-Bois. But was it smart business to turn a factory into a Christian corporation?

The Business

The Harmel factory specialized in the manufacture of wool thread and therefore was involved in the combing, dyeing, and spinning of wool. But to stay competitive, it diversified its product line around 1862 to include threads for fabrics such as *velours* (a fabric with a nap like velvet and made of wool, silk, linen, or cotton), *epongé* (material for Turkish towels), *noeuds* or *boucles* (notted or "bumpy" thread), *flame* (fabric with luster), and *paillettes d'or* ("straws of gold").[272] It even attempted to sell sheepskin in New York City in 1894, but that venture failed.[273] The keys to its success as a business, according to Trimouille, were several: judicious use of personnel, quality products, penetration of foreign markets, and modernization of production.[274]

Although steam power was installed at Val-des-Bois in 1849 and contractual pricing replaced piecework pricing in the early 1860s, both of which allowed the Harmel spinning mill to outstrip regional competitors in sales, the fire of September 1874 that destroyed a sizable portion of the factory provided the principal occasion for modernization. Updating capital equipment by importing the latest machines from Germany permitted Val-des-Bois not only to compete domestically and internationally but also to weather business crises without loss of production levels. Most of the factory's sales henceforward were directed at foreign markets in Germany, Austria, Italy, and Russia,[275] with brief forays into markets in the United States, Great Britain, Spain, and Argentina. Generally, the factory continued to grow and register a profit, despite difficult circumstances in 1848 and 1870 (political turmoil) and 1874 (the factory fire), until 1900 when there was a terrible crisis in the wool industry nationwide, which resulted in sales at Val dropping 50 percent in a period of several months. From 1900 to the temporary closing of the factory in 1915, the business ceased to compete globally.[276]

When there was a downturn in business, such as during the 1900–1904 period, the workforce needed to be reduced. The chief consideration then became keeping long-term families employed at Val, but if heads of these families retired, they were not replaced. Neither new families nor "debauched" single men were hired, and the number of married women and widows working at the factory diminished noticeably. The young, single woman—the least costly employee—represented the only segment of the worker population that grew during times of economic stress. Although the Germans destroyed business and personnel records at Val during World War I, Trimouille has been able to piece together the following supporting evidence. In 1899 there were 288 female workers, but in 1904 their numbers had dwindled to 192; meanwhile, the number of young female workers went from 57 in 1899 to 73 in 1904. Married women and widows were "let go," thereby giving greater security to male employees; and to protect male wage levels, the least costly employee, the young woman from thirteen to eighteen years of age, was recruited.[277] In other words, when it came to hiring and firing practices, female workers at Val-des-Bois helped to sustain job stability for male workers. But even some of the men left the factories at these times to work for less pay as groundskeepers or gardeners.[278] The raison d'être in this case, as in so much else that went on at Val, was the preservation of the family unit. In Harmel's view, widows were beneficiaries of pension and mutual aid funds, and married women were supposed to be in the home anyway where they could work as seamstresses or domestics.[279]

But despite obvious personal deprivation during economic crises, the familial spirit and benefit programs at the Harmel factory made work instability and wage victimization less traumatic in human terms than it was at other factories where periodic unemployment was routine, assistance negligible, and strikes a distinct possibility.

Aside from the personnel disturbances associated with periods of economic depression, the only other employee-related problem that surfaced during Léon Harmel's tenure at Val-des-Bois occurred around 1893. The issue corresponded to a general economic slump triggered by the McKinley Tariff of 1890 that had the effect of restricting the exportation of wool to the United States, but the incident also came at a time in Harmel's life when he was most active in events outside the factory (1883–1902) and therefore frequently absent from Val. The problem took the form of a fairly widespread "malaise," and proved its seriousness by a sudden and dramatic abstention from taking the Eucharist. Since a sizable number of those associated with the "malaise" happened to be Belgian, Harmel linked the problem to uncertainty with regard to their naturalization status and thus to their concern for job security.

A nativist campaign was under way in France at that time which demanded the limitation of nationalization as a way to curb foreign labor,[280] but in 1889 and 1893 new French laws eased the requirements for citizenship that should have relieved Harmel's Belgian workers, if in fact they were interested in becoming French citizens, since the laws in essence shortened the naturalization process from ten years to three years.[281] If, on the other hand, the Belgian workers were content to remain citizens of Belgium, they would be concerned about victimization due to nativist sentiment and consequently worried about job discrimination in an already tight employment market. Michelle Perrot says that from 1867 to 1893 there were eighty-nine incidents between French and foreign workers, and the Belgians were the first victims. The tension over foreign workers, especially likely during a depression, resulted in strikes, petitions, and demonstrations.[282] And because French workers in general were hostile to foreign workers, who were predominantly Belgian and Italian at the turn of the century, it is not inconceivable that even at Harmel's Christian corporation, xenophobia was present.

Harmel's son Felix gently reprimanded him for his extended absences as he reviewed the living and working conditions for his Belgian employees. As a result of Léon's attention to the matter and his renewed assurances of job security for the Belgians, the malaise apparently passed. But henceforward the factory relied less on Belgians in recruiting workers. Adding to the aforementioned components of the factory malaise was the suggestion that local socialists were responsible for the current discontent among the Belgian workers,[283] although there appears to be no ready documentation to support the contention. In any event, once on site again, Léon restored the congenial atmosphere characteristic of Val-des-Bois. The problem was that his numerous commitments and interests outside the factory continued to distract him from factory matters, but he never formally relinquished his duties as *patron*. As a result, a committee of Harmel men actually managed the factory.

Family management of an enterprise was quintessentially French, according to David Landes. The entrepreneur, in this case Léon Harmel, was as interested in preserving wealth as in creating it, regarded the business as a place to employ not only his immediate family but also his extended family, and knew that any business decisions would be scrutinized by the entire clan. In short, the business was but a means to an end: the preservation of the family patrimony.[284] Val-des-Bois was a perfect example of the French family enterprise, and Harmel was quick to acknowledge the importance and contribution of "la solidarité familiale" to the running of the business.

Forty members of Harmel's extended family were involved in one capacity or another at the factory, and they supplied sufficient managerial talent for the operation of the business that appropriately went by the name of Harmel Frères in brochures on the business published around 1900. Despite some crossing-over in functions, four Harmel men carved out their areas of expertise and responsibility to become major contributors to the management of Val-des-Bois during the latter half of the nineteenth century. Jules, the imaginative, artistic older brother, who had returned to the factory after helping out his father-in-law in his business, created all sorts of new and exotic threads and dyes that sustained the business in hard times and made for name recognition in the area of quality goods. Ernest, the younger brother who Léon nursed back to health in their student days, specialized in foreign business transactions, which represented the dynamic sector of the business. Albert, a first cousin and able technician, assisted Jules in product development and headed the renovation project at the factory following the 1874 fire, and the equipment he put in place at that time lasted until the destruction of the factory by the Germans in 1914.[285] Léon, of course, was the general administrator and peacemaker par excellence, as demonstrated, for example, when he was called on to settle matters between Jules, the man who had an idea a minute, and Ernest, the man who tried to rein him in. Léon also dominated by sheer longevity, for he outlived them all and was most intensively involved in factory management from 1853 to 1883 and then again from 1905 to 1911.[286]

Competent management of the factory by talented family members was a key factor in enabling the Harmel enterprise to not only survive but prosper during the turbulent free-market years from 1860 to 1892, but it was not the only component that led to its success. In February 1898 Léon Harmel addressed the "veterans"[287] of Val-des-Bois with these words:

> With you a fruitful mutual apostolate has been organized.... With you numerous councils have been founded, which have placed you at the head of institutions, and you have learned to govern your own affairs.... Thanks to your good spirit and your confidence in your leaders, we have been able to establish factory councils, which combined the efforts of the *patrons* and the *ouvriers* for industrial prosperity, at the same time giving you a real participatory role in the government and the discipline of the establishment. In my distant travels, on behalf of my social mission, it is the memory of you, your affection, which sustains my courage. It is your example that I use to demonstrate the practical application of institutions, that so many *patrons* believe impossible, because they haven't made a sufficient appeal to the generous initiatives of their personnel.... The earthly paradise is a reflection of the Christian household.[288]

Léon Harmel, building on a foundation set by his grandfather and father, came as close as anyone in nineteenth-century France to establishing an earthly paradise for factory workers. The Christian corporation at Val-des-Bois apparently produced concrete results: the reconciliation of labor and management in the *sydicat professionnel* brought social peace and economic prosperity. In the process of creating this successful Christian corporation in the Suippe valley, Harmel used all the appropriate motivational tools. Equipment and procedural modernization, along with product research and development, improved factory efficiency and performance, which in turn opened up additional markets for Harmel textile products. Business expansion and adequate profits underwrote benefit programs that attracted and kept a well-trained and satisfied workforce. The compensation system was based on fairness, and workers were encouraged to participate in decisions. As a result, though the hours were long by present standards and hard work was a matter of course, morale for the most part remained high.

Clearly, Harmel was not reluctant to experiment either with new technology or with new managerial methodology. His innate pragmatism necessarily led to social and economic reform. But what were the chances that "la méthode Harmel" could be transplanted from the rather isolated, rural setting of Val-des-Bois to the larger industrial centers of the Nord and elsewhere in France?

Figure 1. Léon Harmel, 1880. Courtesy Archives Jésuites.

Figure 2. Léon Harmel at eighty-four. Courtesy Archives Jésuites.

Figure 3. The "Bon Père" surrounded by children. Courtesy Archives Jésuites.

Figure 4. Life at Val-des-Bois. Courtesy Archives Jésuites.

Figure 5. Val-des-Bois after 1875. Courtesy Archives Jésuites.

Figure 6. The home of Jacques-Joseph Harmel and the chapel at Val-des-Bois. Courtesy Archives Jésuites.

Figure 7. The Roman Pantheon. Photo by author.

CHAPTER THREE

The World Beyond

> A simple visionary; but if all the owners acted as he did, the social problem would become insignificant.
> —*René Viviani, socialist member of the Chamber of Deputies, referring to Léon Harmel in 1913*[1]

WHILE MANY ADMIRED THE HARMEL ENTERPRISE, INCLUDING THE socialist René Viviani, the number of its religious associations and the range of its benefit programs intimidated even the best-intentioned factory owner. Moreover, Léon Harmel's apparent willingness to tamper with traditional paternalism, chiefly through the establishment of the Conseil d'Usine, set him apart not only from the average factory owner of late-nineteenth-century France but also from some of the major Catholic social thinkers of the era. Indeed, he encountered skeptics from the outset. As early as 1877, Harmel answered charges that his Christian corporation worked only because it was geographically isolated by emphatically stating that the same "moral resurrection" could be had in all industrial centers if Christians concerned with the salvation of souls participated in the corporations' governance. For those willing to follow him, he promised concrete results: profits in factories, protection of trade interests, job safety, security for the future, improvement in the moral life of bosses and workers, and social peace in France.[2]

Harmel's Christian corporation appealed in the abstract to many industrialists struggling with a surly labor force and challenging economic times, but how many were willing to abandon old ways and risk losing control of their enterprises? His experiences with other Catholic factory owners, principally through the organization known as the Patrons du Nord, demonstrated how difficult it was to live one's ideals in a concrete setting, especially if one might have to put the family patrimony on the line. Just how singular Harmel and his social experiment were becomes even clearer once one ventures beyond the world of Val-des-Bois.

Likewise, his contributions to the development of nineteenth-century social Catholicism and the social teaching of the Catholic Church become increasingly evident when placing his ideology in the context of other French theorists of the era. Just as his family profoundly shaped his values and lifestyle, so too did other nineteenth-century theorists. The Christian corporation developed in the context of nineteenth-century corporatism, and theorists such as Claude-Henri de Rouvroy, Comte de Saint-Simon, Charles Fourier, Philippe Buchez, Louis Blanc, Pierre-Joseph Proudhon, Frédéric Le Play, and Charles Périn wrote and dreamed of ways to ameliorate the social conditions of the working people of France. Val-des-Bois reflected what went on elsewhere; whether workshop or producers' cooperative or Christian corporation, numerous institutions attempted to blend individualism with collectivism by allowing the individual worker self-fulfillment while cooperating for the common good of the whole. Harmel's worker-family was but one example of what was occurring in nineteenth-century corporatism.

Harmel's notions of corporatism, as realized in the Christian corporation, affected the ideology of social Catholicism, which in the late nineteenth century centered on individuals such as Albert de Mun, René de La Tour du Pin, and others in their organization, L'Oeuvre des Cercles

Catholiques d'Ouvriers. This principal organization for Catholic workingmen in France welcomed Harmel's fresh interpretation of corporatism but also discovered they had quite a tiger by the tail as Harmel's inexhaustible energy and creativity found organizational constraints difficult to suffer.

But then a larger world soon beckoned. As Leo XIII prepared his great papal encyclical on labor, *Rerum Novarum,* he received inspiration from Val-des-Bois, which he quickly recognized as a realization of what had been up to that time mostly theory. Harmel's Christian corporation was a living model on which Leo could base his own ideas. *Rerum Novarum* united Harmel to the Vatican in a new and profound way and assured him a place in the history of Catholic social teaching.

Corporatism in Nineteenth-Century France

Léon Harmel defined the Christian corporation as an "association between bosses and workers of the same profession, or similar profession, that had for its end the reign of justice and charity."[3] He also represented it as a "community of interests" that looked to the "well-being of the workers" and the "prosperity of the enterprise."[4] He hoped the Christian corporation would replace the "disorder" and "anarchy" in fin-de-siècle society with a structure and a spirit modeled after the human family. The corporation, for him, was both hierarchical and fraternal. The *patron,* as the father figure, guided his community of labor not only in its business aspects but also in the promotion of *solidarité,* or brotherhood, among all corporate members. Harmel envisioned that the Christian corporation would provide France with a third alternative, that is, a middle way between the rampant individualism of laissez-faire liberalism and the total collectivism proposed by the more radical socialist groups.

His thoughts on the Christian corporation captured the essence of corporatism in several ways. Corporatism blends individualism with collectivism within a community of labor interested in producing a product, creating a profit, and involving workers in the management or ownership of the enterprise. Corporatism also connotes an element of spirituality by its insistence on fraternal relationships and goodwill. Not only are communal members responsible for each other's material needs, but an esprit de corps, whether religious or secular in origin, serves as a bonding agent for the corporate unit. Corporatism, under various forms, has been a constant in France since the Middle Ages, and Harmel's Christian corporation both assimilated past French notions on corporatism and contributed to the ongoing corporate heritage.

The medieval guild from which corporatism originated combined a public spirit with self-interest by creating an artificial family to nourish its members spiritually and materially through mutual aid societies, just wages, apprenticeship programs, health and safety regulations, Sunday holidays, employment of whole families, and mediation of fraternal disputes. Its ethos continued into the early modern period, which has often been portrayed as the classic era of the craft guild because of the economic vibrancy of the *ancien régime* corporation.[5] The French Revolution failed to eliminate corporatism. Despite the official ban of 1791 on workers' associations, or guilds, French labor continued to press for recognition of corporations, albeit in forms reflecting contemporary social and economic conditions, throughout the nineteenth century.

Corporate theorists of the first half of the nineteenth century adopted various forms of religious socialism as philosophical backdrops for their corporate structures. Their belief in a supernatural being and hierarchical order in the universe stood in stark contrast to later theorists who preferred a secular moral order and sought to dismantle corporate hierarchies. Because religious socialists often were more reticent to abandon the concept of hierarchy, religious socialism frequently represented a protest against what was perceived as the overly rational and overly egalitarian notions of the Enlightenment and the French Revolution. Religion, in their opinion, was an essential but missing societal component since the Revolution and therefore needed reinstatement—but without formal ties to the Roman Catholic Church. They intended "socialism" to signify opposition to the individualism associated with English economists of laissez-faire.

From the outset, then, a spiritual or moral component accompanied the concept of socialism in France. However, after the Revolution of 1848 and the Second Republic, that is, after 1852, the use of religious themes and terminology diminished among French socialists in general, especially after the appearance in 1864 of the papal encyclical *Quanta Cura,* with its *Syllabus of Errors.*[6] It was at this point that socialism split into secular and religious branches; a transcendental element remained inherent in French socialism, while more overtly religious themes characterized Christian socialist ideology of the second half of the century.

In addition to finding expression in socialist ideology, another general feature of early-nineteenth-century corporatism was its devotion to class reconciliation. Though its spokesmen talked of revolution, they actually were proponents of peaceful, as opposed to violent, institutional change. Among the first to delineate a system for such change were the Comte de Saint-Simon (1760–1825) and Charles Fourier (1772–1837).

Of the two, Saint-Simon was the more modern from an economic standpoint. He advocated a cooperative society in which industrial and managerial technocrats joined forces with a centralized government in order to control production and financial investments.[7] In an era when most French workers participated in the agricultural segment of the economy, Saint-Simon championed manufacturing. His ideas captured the attention of the notable few but failed to persuade the common man to join his program for societal cooperation, and hence never blossomed into an organized movement.

Certain aspects of Léon Harmel's philosophy and workplace endeavors resembled the social plan of Saint-Simon. One can point to the purchase of the latest capital equipment at the Harmel mill, resulting in greater factory efficiency, and the belief that government intervention could be a positive development. However, Harmel wanted the state to intervene by enacting laws that would improve factory conditions for the workers, whereas Saint-Simon restricted state intervention to groups of advisors looking to improve the efficiency of industry. But the most glaring difference between the two men was that Harmel was a populist and Saint-Simon was an elitist.

Fourier, in contrast to Saint-Simon, sought the reconciliation of capitalists and workers by stressing agriculture over manufacturing. Though less modern in its economic outlook, his social plan in some ways more accurately reflected the contemporary situation. Fourier intended, for example, to locate manufacturing enterprises in small rural communities where workers could continue to maintain vegetable gardens, and here we could be describing the factory at Val-des-Bois. However, Fourier's ideal communal association, or "phalanx," removed itself from the societal mainstream and certainly from any association with the Christian corporation by its restructuring of the traditional family unit, and in this respect he was poles apart from the Christian corporation at Val-des-Bois, where the cornerstone of the community was the traditional family. Though not an elitist in the Saint-Simonian sense, Fourier nonetheless failed to generate any kind of mass following. Instead, the significance of Saint-Simon and Fourier in the chronicle of corporatism rests in their pleas for class cooperation as a way to bridge the widening gulf between labor and management in early-nineteenth-century France. And in their desire for societal harmony, there was total concurrence among the three reformers—Saint-Simon, Fourier, and Harmel.

The most popular form of corporatism at this time did not develop from the ideas of either Saint-Simon or Fourier, however, but from the notion of the worker owned and operated consumer and producer cooperatives. The ideology of the producer cooperative in particular became part of the revolutionary rhetoric of 1830, 1848, and 1871, and was best articulated by the Christian socialist Philippe Buchez (1796–1865), the democratic constitutionalist Louis Blanc (1811–1882), and the mutualist Pierre-Joseph Proudhon (1790–1865).

Buchez's cooperative was an independent production unit that originally included only skilled workers but after 1833 welcomed the unskilled too. Rather than have the unskilled placed in *syndicats mixtes* where they would have to deal with an overbearing *patron*, he preferred to eliminate the "idle class" from his social schema by organizing all workers in producer cooperatives. What he called for was complete worker autonomy, independent of state manipulation or reliance on the "pure parasites," the factory owners. Management would be drawn from the ranks of the more able workers, and worker owned and operated enterprises would free labor from the wage system.[8] Like Saint-Simon in stressing manufacturing over agriculture, he parted company with Saint-Simon over who would control the cooperative venture; for whereas Saint-Simon looked to an elite to manage the workplace, Buchez looked to the worker.

Buchez, the Christian socialist, clearly was more progressive than Harmel on this matter, and if measured by the standards of Buchez, one would have a hard time placing Harmel within the ranks of Christian socialists. Though eager to have his workers participate in the governance of daily life at Val-des-Bois, Harmel preferred to play a role and thus supported the *syndicat mixte*. Completely turning over his factory to the workers was a move that Harmel never contemplated. Yet, in fairness, one must point out that Harmel was operating a family business and therefore had to be concerned not only about providing for the financial needs of his present family but also, in customary *patronat* fashion, for future family members. In short, he did not have the luxury of operating solely in the world of ideas. Buchez, a theorist, was not restricted by such practical considerations.

Ultimately, Blanc reached a conclusion similar to Buchez with regard to worker managed and owned enterprises, albeit by a more circuitous route. Blanc wanted the state, by supplying the workers with the "tools of labor," that is, by financing "social workshops," to initially intervene in industry. He asked the same of capitalists. Blanc invited capitalists to invest in the workshops to help them get off the ground.[9] The invitation to state and industry to subsidize a system of national workshops addressed what was the most urgent problem for producer and consumer cooperatives—undercapitalization, a factor the *patron* of Val-des-Bois never considered an arena for government involvement. For Harmel, government intervention came solely in the guise of factory reform legislation. But Blanc was optimistic that once the seed money became available the producer cooperatives would more or less run themselves, as he projected state disengagement from a managerial role after only one year. And the higher morale and motivation engendered by worker-controlled enterprises would result in production efficiency, which would result in lower prices and allow workshops to compete favorably with private industry. Once this became apparent, Blanc posited, capitalists would feel compelled to convert their factories into cooperatives. Finally, the whole system of national workshops would be directed from a central workshop.[10]

Proudhon eschewed the delineation of a precise social plan, but he identified the workshop as the most suitable place for his ideas to take root and flower. Like Blanc, Proudhon sought the assistance of the government in setting up the workshops and in helping to "proportion production to needs." And like Buchez, he welcomed both the skilled and the unskilled, as well as the bourgeoisie, whose expertise he figured would be useful. He also planned an apprenticeship program that combined educational training with instruction in civic virtue.[11] Finally,

Proudhon grounded his whole system in an ethic of *mutualité*, reminiscent of guild confraternity, in order to create a cooperative atmosphere.[12]

Despite certain similarities, Proudhon departed from Buchez and Blanc on several counts, and in so doing, he pointed the way to future developments within French socialism. In 1843 he shifted from an espousal of religion as the ethical bedrock for his corporate system and turned to a secular moral code. The change occurred as a result of an intransigent social policy on the part of the Catholic Church in the era before *Rerum Novarum* and therefore reflected his concern for the future of society more than it signified an intellectual abrogation of the divine.[13] But it represented a shift of no small consequence; Proudhon replaced Christian virtue with civic virtue, justice being the principal secular virtue for him,[14] and henceforth the majority of French socialists followed a secular path. Once he eliminated institutional religion as a guide to right living, Proudhon relied on civic education to provide guidelines for correct societal behavior while recognizing that the whole matter of virtue would be largely a self-taught phenomenon.

Another departure from the social philosophies of Buchez and Blanc was in the matter of federation. Proudhon's plan for the association of producer cooperatives called for professional and geographic unification. The latter particularly was ambitious, for federation began on the communal level, progressed to the national level, and culminated with the institution of a global confederation.[15] But once again Proudhon anticipated future events, since French *syndicalism* would take its cue from him in the matter of national unification.

In sum, Proudhon was the midcentury link between the corporatists who endorsed a religious socialism and those who outlined their corporatist ideology within the framework of secular socialism. Moving away from traditional Christian ideology, he created a secular philosophy with moral overtones. He also stood for the economic independence of the worker and the political autonomy of the region while simultaneously fostering a spirit of mutuality. Thus Proudhon created a form of secular socialism that had corporatist principles at its core, and would serve as the ideological foundation for the *syndicalist* movement that blossomed later in the century.

Léon Harmel identified with Proudhon on the need for class cooperation, the importance of confraternity, and the acknowledgment that workers should participate in factory governance. But he certainly parted ways with him on the matter of religion. Harmel ardently supported institutionalized religion in the form of the Roman Catholic Church, whereas Proudhon abandoned traditional religious affiliation for civic virtue. And though banded together in their religion and their effort to ameliorate the more egregious horrors of the industrial revolution inflicted on workers, organizations such as Notre Dame de l'Usine, the Patrons du Nord, and L'Oeuvre des Cercles Catholiques d'Ouvriers, which were either founded by Harmel or benefited from his leadership, never pretended to be part of a federation with formalized political goals, or took part in the 1848 and 1871 revolutions as did the Proudhonists.

The joint efforts of Buchez, Blanc, and Proudhon, on the other hand, gave voice to worker demands for cooperatives, which became a significant part of the political rhetoric and activity of the Second Republic, when associated workers in Paris established more than three hundred producer cooperatives, representing one hundred and twenty trades.[16] These cooperatives were democratic in structure and egalitarian in spirit. All workers in a given trade became members, officers and delegates were chosen by universal male suffrage, and important matters were voted on by assemblies of the entire association. In addition, and in this matter similar to the Christian corporation, mutual aid funds aided the sick and injured, provided pensions for the old, the widowed, or the orphaned, and in some cases had provisions for unemployment compensation.[17] That these cooperatives had political overtones was demonstrated in 1848 and again in 1871 when the Paris Commune, attempting to put into practice Proudhon's call for the restructuring of French society into small territorial units of self-governing workers, declared its autonomy from the rest of France. The idea was not to die with the end of the insurrection, as *syndicalism* appealed to a significant portion of rural and urban labor throughout *la belle époque*.[18] Although the movement recognized no single theorist or organizer as founder, Proudhon typically is considered its chief forerunner.

Whereas the producer cooperative was popular among the numerous secular socialist groups in the latter half of the nineteenth century, most Catholics intent on reform abandoned the notion of Christian socialism of the kind promoted by Buchez after 1848 and instead favored the Christian corporation as the best institutional way to bring the classes together. The Christian corporation was a form of corporatism that combined elements from the medieval guild and the consumer cooperative in which ownership of factories was to remain in the hands of the *patron* and was not to be transferred to the workers. Harmel's contribution was to move the Christian corporation closer to other expressions of French corporatism by involving the workers more intimately in the factory's governance.

Corporatism, then, was quite obviously an umbrella concept, generous in including diverse groups who, one way or another, wanted the restoration of social harmony and the correction of economic and political injustices. The Christian corporation was not created in a vacuum but was part of a heritage that had existed in France since the Middle Ages. The formulation of an ideology for the nineteenth-century Christian corporation, however, is largely attributed to the Catholic economists Frédéric Le Play (1806–1882) and Charles Périn (1815–1905), the two men who most directly influenced Harmel's social philosophy.

Frédéric Le Play

Frédéric Le Play, engineer, economist, and sociologist, was less well known than Auguste Comte (1798–1857), the so-called father of sociology, but contributed perhaps equally to the discipline. He, like Villermé, specialized in empirical sociology, the gathering of data, and organized his theories of social reform under the main headings of religion, property, family, and *patronage*. An inveterate world traveler, he used the basic scientific methodology of observation as he moved from place to place over a period of approximately twenty-five years. In his youth, he had been a follower of Saint-Simon, and like other social reformers of the nineteenth century, the events of 1830, 1848, and 1870 disturbed him greatly. He looked for ways to restore the social order and deduced that religion was central to any such program.[19]

Religion was the foundation of society for Le Play, and woman was its principal agent. Without her moralizing influence, a nation was incapable of "social progress," which, in turn, affected "national progress."[20] He condemned women who worked outside the home, for in his opinion, the entire family suffered morally and socially.[21] He believed that men benefited from the presence of women in the household because feminine charm "repaired physical strength, invigorated character, and made the men more productive in the workshop."[22] For example, since women of the Middle Ages were not *ouvrières* exposed to the demoralization attendant to factory life, their morality remained intact and both the family and society prospered as a consequence. But while he admired the religiosity of the medieval era, best exemplified in the time of Saint Louis (1226–1270) for its connection between good moral behavior and economic prosperity, he failed to endorse the guilds as an appropriate model for contemporary society. For Le Play, the guilds were long on security but short on freedom and as a result were best left in the premodern world.[23] He emphasized, however, that Christianity brought about good economic times in medieval France,[24] and this was the lesson to be learned. His conclusion was a straightforward one: in order for contemporary Europeans to preserve their preeminence, they needed to "practice known moral truths."[25]

Social research also demonstrated to Le Play that private property, like religion, was established spontaneously among all peoples who had "reached a certain degree of civilization." He therefore presented private property as a second foundation of social organization.[26] Its acquisition carried with it a plethora of middle-class values—industry and thrift, for example—and opened up the possibility of social mobility for the workers.[27]

A third foundation was the family. He was struck in his travels to the East with the fact that there families still lived "in peace." The riches and evils that had so demoralized western Europe since the Renaissance had yet to work their corrupting influence on eastern families and societies. Le Play's solution to societal breakdown was to reassert the primacy of the family. Strange as it may seem, Le Play was introducing a rather novel concept since thinkers of the early modern era preferred to rely on guilds to impose societal stability. It was only in the aftermath of the dismantling of the artisanal associations at the time of the French Revolution that reformers began to see the potential for society if the family were sound.[28] And Le Play further observed that peace within individual family units yielded something more—*la communaté familiale,* or family-like communities.[29]

That observation led directly to Le Play's major contribution to the ideology of the Christian corporation, namely, that of the worker-family under the care of a *patron*. For him, the *famille patriarcale* (patriarchal family) was the most appropriate form to preserve traditional custom[30] and bring about societal peace. *Patronage,* according to Le Play, was an especially appropriate institution for contemporary society since "the working class, in particular, showed an extreme repugnance to all change."[31] He was convinced that the workers were a conservative segment of society who would welcome the strengthening of familial forms both at home and in the workplace. And in imitation of the traditional family, social reform would necessarily be directed from the top. But then this was only in accord with the nature of things, because "all religions were based on paternal authority,"[32] and work was only an extension of the moral order.[33]

Le Play's ideas on social reform included a specific program for the worker-family. He saw as essential the creation of a stable workforce, the complete agreement between *patron* and worker on the matter of wages, an "alliance" between the work that takes place in the workshop and that in domestic industry, the practice of saving which protects family dignity, the establishment of an "indissoluble union" between family and its home, and respect and protection for women.[34] Allowing the mother of the family and her daughters to remain at home guaranteed not only their respect and protection but also the physical and psychological health of the men of the household.[35] Le Play also thought that a vegetable garden was a good idea, for it bonded the family to the earth and thereby kept ties to agriculture while permitting the head of the family and his sons to prosper with a relatively small wage.[36]

The Christian corporation at Val-des-Bois put into practice many of the ideas Le Play wrote about. Harmel made sure religion occupied a place of importance at the factory. He reinforced women's traditional role and supported the family unit. He prided himself on being able to maintain a stable workforce, encouraged savings, and provided housing that included vegetable gardens. By creating the Conseil d'Usine, workers consulted with the *patron* on matters of wages, as suggested by Le Play. And in one of his most innovative steps at Val-des-Bois, a family wage, Harmel implemented something suggested by Le Play.[37] In short, Harmel, according to Philippe Levillain, borrowed ideas on the worker-family from Le Play and used them at Val-des-Bois.[38] Harmel was equally familiar with the ideas of Charles Périn.

Charles Périn

Charles Périn, professor of economics at the University of Louvain, shared many philosophical tenets with Le Play. Like Le Play, he taught that the material world submits to the moral order,[39] that private property is good because it is a means of rapprochement and union between the classes while providing for future financial security,[40] and that prosperity is guaranteed by living the life of a good Catholic.[41] In addition, he observed that the moral energy of a people is measured by its work, its accumulation of capital, and its ability to save. Religious orders, with their proclivity for order and sobriety, functioned in society like *la force vitale,* energizing and moralizing all.[42] Still, there was to be no embarrassment over riches, according to Périn. In fact, to achieve the greatest happiness, one strove to procure "la plus grande richesse,"[43] since rather than act as a deterrent, wealth, if relegated to its proper place, actually helped one reach eternal salvation. For personal sanctification to happen, however, certain caveats needed to be heeded. Quite obviously, wealth provided one with independence and dignity but also could lead to cupidity if moral virtue did not exert its controlling influence. In other words, one was allowed to amass wealth if the accumulation thereof was accompanied by a spirit of renunciation.

Périn's philosophy of wealth was premised on the assumption that economic liberalism established a climate in which "everybody could be rich."[44] However, since humans possessed an infinite number of variables with regard to abilities and talents, there would always be the poor. But there need not be misery, because the wealthy, armed with Christian charity and a spirit of detachment from things material, possessed the resources to aid the less fortunate.

The Christian corporation was an ideal forum, according to Périn, in which all of this could be played out because it was flexible enough to allow the workers a hand in determining, within specified guidelines, their own workplace environment and simultaneously maintained the patronal presence requisite for order and efficiency. He perceived the mixed *syndicat* as the best form of association, for the separation of labor and management into distinct organizations, like the producer cooperatives seemed to suggest, preordained an atmosphere of "combat"[45] and precluded the patronal presence judged essential by Périn. Only through contact with those of proven moral vibrancy would those of lesser wealth and virtue acquire a feeling for discipline, hard work, and brotherhood.[46] In short, paternalism was the key to success.

Périn knew that what he wrote about lay in the realm of the possible because he cited Léon Harmel and the factory at Val-des-Bois as living proof of his theories.[47] Harmel, for his part, corresponded frequently with his "dear friend and teacher" and worked with him at L'Oeuvre des Cercles Catholiques d'Ouvriers. Clearly, Harmel digested much of what Périn had written about, since Périn's *Le Patron sa fonction, ses devoirs, ses résponsabilités* (1886) is similar in tone and substance to Harmel's own *Catéchisme du patron* (1889). Périn's philosophy of wealth, for example, is mirrored in Harmel's belief that factory profits and personal wealth carry a moral responsibility.

Over time, however, philosophical differences developed between Léon Harmel and the two men who most directly influenced his social philosophy. Both Le Play and Périn were lifelong monarchists who never became reconciled to the Republic and who advised in true laissez-faire fashion that the best government was that which governed least. They saw legislation to protect workers as a last resort, always a distant second to individual efforts of Catholic *patrons*. And the *patron* of Le Play and Périn, though assuredly not a slave master, was reticent to relax the reins of authority held tautly over the worker-family. Thus while Harmel had assimiliated much of the social program of both Le Play and Périn, he would in the years before 1891, that is, before the publication of *Rerum Novarum,* and most assuredly in the years after 1891 distance himself from them by modifying and developing further the notion of the Christian corporation. Two leaders of the next generation of social Catholics, Albert de Mun (1841–1914) and René de La Tour du Pin (1831–1924), recognized Harmel's innovative approach to the Christian corporation.

L' Oeuvre des Cercles Catholiques d'Ouvriers

Count Albert de Mun and Count René de La Tour du Pin founded L'Oeuvre des Cercles Catholiques d'Ouvriers in 1871. While prisoners of war at Aix-la-Chapelle (Aachen) in 1870, de Mun and La Tour du

Pin read about the social philosophy of Wilhelm Emmanuel Ketteler, Bishop of Mainz, one of the outstanding figures in social Catholicism in nineteenth-century Europe and someone who had a tremendous influence on French social Catholics.[48] Like so many Catholics of his generation, Bishop Ketteler looked disparagingly on the Enlightenment and the French Revolution for ushering in unrestrained economic liberalism and the concomitant suffering of the laboring classes. His solution was simple yet profound: he dusted off the Catholic social teaching of Thomas Aquinas and repackaged certain aspects of it for the industrial age. For example, he talked of the importance of maintaining the *juste milieu* between socialism and liberalism when it came to private property, for ownership of property was not an absolute right but rather one that came with strings attached; those individuals who received in abundance were stewards of their earthly goods and needed to take care of the poor through traditional charity. According to Ketteler, the Catholic Church, not the state, was the proper agent to address the Social Question. His chief contribution was to challenge Catholics throughout Europe to respond.[49]

On returning to France, de Mun, an army officer, was given the job of guarding Communard prisoners, one of whom, a dying man, chastised de Mun for being a part of the class of order. The verbal assault, coming shortly after his reading about Ketteler's work among the German workers, caused de Mun to redefine his life's work. Although never quite able to shed his officer's demeanor, he henceforward dedicated himself to bringing about a national regeneration through the reconciliation of the classes.[50] De Mun's aristocratic background had not prepared him for the type of Catholic action Ketteler called for, but Maurice Maignen (1823–1890), influenced by Fourierists and a member of the religious order of St. Vincent de Paul,[51] convinced de Mun that collaboration between the upper classes and workers was possible. Maignen had established a settlement in Paris on Boulevard Montparnasse where workers and upper classes mingled, and this original Montparnasse workers' club became the model for L'Oeuvre des Cercles Catholiques d'Ouvriers that was established throughout France by de Mun, La Tour du Pin, and Harmel.[52] Maignen's settlement had a chapel, with a chaplain in residence, and clubrooms where artisans could show off their craftsmanship. The settlement also set up a consumer's cooperative. The upper classes administered the Parisian club, of course, and they divided their duties into four areas of responsibility: publicity, club activities, finances, and studies.[53] The same basic facilities and organizational structure were duplicated in the other workers' clubs.

Between 1872 and 1875 the Cercles expanded geographically and numerically from the original Paris setting. The organization established clubs in the northern industrial centers of France where young men newly arrived from rural areas found camaraderie, free entertainment, and a hot meal, but it was also successful in the less urbanized regions of France, such as the Vendée and Brittany. In the mid-1870s there were some 150 clubs nationwide with a total membership of 18,000,[54] and by 1881 more than 550 clubs had been formed, with more than 50,000 members.[55] Most of the members, however, were not factory workers from large, industrial enterprises but traditional artisans and city shop assistants. Reflecting the aristocratic and military comportment of its chief organizational founder, Albert de Mun, the clubs, with their hierarchical and centralized structure, never became a true meeting ground for the classes. Instead, the upper classes and their chaplains, many of whom clung to royalist dreams, dictated policy to the lower classes in reaffirmation of traditional paternalism while continuing to adhere to antiliberal tenets of the papal encyclical of Pius IX, the *Syllabus of Errors,* which condemned rationalism, socialism, materialism, Gallicanism, liberalism, and secularism in seeming disregard for the contemporary world.[56] The result was predictable. The clubs lost the support of the urban worker and the more liberal Catholics,[57] especially after the publication of *Rerum Novarum* in 1891. The papal document on labor addressed many of the concerns of the Cercle members, thereby diminishing the need for the organization, and monarchist members became disenchanted when shortly thereafter, in 1892, Leo XIII asked them to "rally to" the Republic.[58]

After *Rerum Novarum* and the Ralliement directive, the general meetings of the Cercles increasingly turned from discussion of the worker and his problems to the Church and its problems. The presence of priests assured this, although the clergy resented not being in full control of the organization.[59] Police reports of these meetings depict a politically reactionary organization in matters of private property and anti-Semitism, for example.[60] Government officials expressed concern that L'Oeuvre des

Cercles Catholiques d'Ouvriers was merely a trompe l'oeil for what was basically a political group intent on uniting 35 million Catholic Frenchmen and forming an opposition party.[61] In reality, the fact that the organization had lost two-thirds [62] of its membership by 1912 due to doctrinal inflexibility diminished any realistic chance for such a venture. Yet in its formative years, that is, in the years before *Rerum Novarum,* it was an ideological think tank in which innovative ideas were welcomed, discussed, and sometimes acted on. Harmel joined Maignen, de Mun, and La Tour du Pin in the Cercles during its early, creative years.

Harmel gained entrée to the Cercles quite by accident. He was making a pilgrimage to Notre Dame de Liesse, near Lyon, when he encountered de Mun and La Tour du Pin's contingent along the way on August 17, 1873. According to reports, Harmel, displaying his distinctive panache, announced his presence with drums beating and trumpets sounding, forcing de Mun and La Tour du Pin to stop their own pilgrim journey to take note of the passing group. Although impressed with Harmel's energy and enthusiasm for the cause of the worker, the aristocrats apparently were less appreciative of what they judged to be Harmel's bourgeois coarseness.[63] Once he joined the Cercles, Harmel did not take a backseat to the two aristocrats, or anyone else for that matter, and soon unleashed an ideological power struggle that at once energized the movement and diffused its organizational effectiveness. The struggle was over the insertion of an idea into the workingmen's clubs, namely, the structure of the Christian corporation as it existed at Val-des-Bois. La Tour du Pin introduced the concept for consideration, Maignen opposed it in its Val-des-Bois form, and de Mun attempted to mediate the philosophical ruckus that played itself out mainly in the ideological wing of the organization, the Conseil des Études.

Le Conseil des Études

The Conseil des Études was an adjunct to the Cercles' Section IV, the teaching or education wing. In 1876 it created a monthly journal, *L'Association catholique*[64] that served as the official mouthpiece for the organization until the journal and the Cercles severed ties in 1890. The Conseil was the most significant subgroup within the Cercles because it was responsible for the organization's social doctrine, which was, according to Robert Talmy, the "only constructive doctrine that the Catholics in France presented in opposition to socialism."[65] Talmy seemingly undervalues the contribution of Philippe Buchez and other Christian socialists in the first half of the nineteenth century. He also appears to fail to recognize Le Play's and Périn's endorsement of the family as the cornerstone of societal stability in diametric opposition to Marxist notions on family but reflecting the mainstream ethos from midcentury forward. Moreover, his assessment ostensibly ignores the importance of such later developments within the social teaching of the Catholic Church as the publication of *Rerum Novarum*, the evolution of the Christian democratic movement, and the creation of organizations such as Le Sillon. Nevertheless, there is no denying the fact that the Conseil des Études produced numerous innovative ideas, and contention among its members is indicative of this point.

There were differences of opinion among the members of the Conseil over the concepts of property, wages, justice, and state intervention, but the first and major difficulty to surface concerned the Christian corporation.[66] The occasion for the discord was the adoption of a report drawn up by La Tour du Pin in November 1875 in which he sanctioned Val-des-Bois as the model for Christian corporations.[67] Maignen became Harmel's chief adversary over the issue.

Maignen refused to endorse Val-des-Bois as a model, for in his opinion Harmel was unique and so was his factory. The Harmel enterprise was larger than the typical artisanal workshop operated by most of the Cercles members, and his workers were "subservient" when compared to the "independent, nomadic, disseminated, and disaggregated" workers of large cities.[68] Re-Christianization, therefore, might best be left to outside organizations, like the Cercles, for example, because the chance of wholesale reintroduction of religious practice in factories seemed slim.[69] But rather than address the needs of these new urban workers by the introduction of more modern institutions, Maignen's plan was to reconstruct the medieval corporation and thereby satisfy the major clientele of the Cercles, the skilled artisans. By attempting to duplicate the medieval guilds, Maignen turned a blind eye to industrial capitalism; he emphasized, as did the old guilds, product quality and labor stability without equal attention to profits. Besides, Maignen could not condone a system in which the *patron* wielded greater authority than the clergy.[70]

Neither did Maignen support freedom of choice when it came to joining the corporation. In his opinion, the Christian corporation would succeed only if the state required all workers and bosses to unite in the *syndicat mixte*. This approach was of course directly the opposite of what Harmel professed. Harmel insisted that the re-Christianization of the individual workers take place first and in the context of the factory, but once that process was under way, he made it clear that religious associations were voluntary, and parents decided whether to send their children to the laic or religious schools or shop at the discount stores.

All in all, Maignen's position on the Christian corporation was "incomprehensible" to Harmel,[71] who continued to maintain that just as one could not force another to become a Christian, so one could not force membership in a Christian corporation.[72] The solution to the discord in the Conseil des Études was a relatively easy one for Harmel; in essence, he decided to "pack the court" by bringing into the organization additional industrialists. They might not be as conversant with the various theories on the Christian corporation, but this would be more than compensated for by their familiarity with the "practical science of business."[73] Maignen, for his part, saw Harmel's plan as limited to a "handful of *bon maîtres* (good masters) who would save a few lucky workers from injustice while society as a whole remained condemned to suffer."[74] And, as will be pointed out shortly, Maignen's assessment largely was correct.

In November 1878 the organization devised a compromise. In a nod to the medieval aspects of Maignen's corporation, it condemned "unlimited competition." But of more essential importance, the Conseil mandated that the Christian corporation would remain "open," that is, voluntary, and free of state regulation.[75] Léon Harmel, and the five thousand industrialists who were the mainstay of his support,[76] claimed an ideological victory in that the Conseil, at least for the moment, ruled in favor of the Val-des-Bois model.

The disagreements between Maignen and Harmel continued in the Conseil des Études, weakening the entire structure of the Cercles but providing simultaneously an intellectual stimulus to their membership, as well as to all who followed the debates in *L'Association catholique*. But whereas Harmel generated discussion principally on the matter of the Christian corporation, La Tour du Pin, the chief theorist of the organization, contributed the most to the continuing development of the ideology of corporatism by arguing for the federation of Christian factories.

René de La Tour du Pin

The social philosophy developed by La Tour du Pin, according to Talmy, was "removed from the *mentalité* of the Catholics of his era."[77] His was a form of corporatism that spanned the centuries by looking back to the Middle Ages while simultaneously anticipating the state corporatism associated with fascism and as such departed from the social philosophy of Harmel in several ways. He, like Harmel, recognized the need for a partnership between industrial capitalists and their workers, but unlike Harmel, La Tour du Pin held on to the concept of the *syndicat mixte* even when, in the aftermath of *Rerum Novarum* and Leo XIII's approval of separate trade unions (*syndicats séparés*) for workers and Harmel's endorsement of the notion, he never wavered from his commitment to trade unions composed of both labor and management. La Tour du Pin was less adventuresome than Harmel in terms of empowering the worker.

Moreover, he thought Maignen correct in insisting on an obligatory system of corporations, concurring for essentially the same reasons; re-Christianization should take place after the corporation was formed, not before, as was the case with Harmel's methodology, which insisted on total freedom of choice in religious practice. La Tour du Pin argued, as had Maignen, that Harmel's selective recruiting and diligent nurturing of faith would be hard to duplicate at other factories. Thus it was safer, according to La Tour du Pin, to reverse the procedure Harmel used at Val-des-Bois and create the corporation first and only afterward Christianize it.

In another departure from the Val-des-Bois model, La Tour du Pin maintained that his association would be Christian because the principles of justice and *solidarité*[78] were practiced therein and not because, as in the case of Val-des-Bois, religious orders were marshaled in an effort to rehabilitate lapsed Catholic workers.[79] Without the presence of Catholic missionaries on factory premises, La Tour du Pin hoped for more universal appeal and in the process advocated a Christian humanist approach that was less overtly confessional than Harmel's technique, which called for the incorporation of Catholic clergy and religious personnel in programs and organizations. La Tour du Pin mirrored the concern of Maignen: if the corporation were strictly confessional, many workers would be left out. While not ready to exchange Christian values for civic virtue, as was the case with Proudhon, La Tour du Pin argued for a less confessional corporation.[80]

Though not a political system per se, La Tour du Pin's plan to create a national network of corporations was bound to have political repercussions, much like the program of federated producer cooperatives proposed by Proudhon. A monarchist, weary of the slow machinations of the electoral process, La Tour du Pin favored representation through corporations. The actual organizing began with the individual *syndicat*, progressed to the local level by uniting all *patrons* and *ouvriers* within a single industry, and culminated by federating in a great national corporation.[81] His goal was to touch all segments of working society, not only the traditional artisans, but also those workers whose jobs had been created alongside industrialization. What La Tour du Pin intended to establish, then, was his own brand of *syndicalism*, complete with political decentralization and royal concurrence. In 1882 the Conseil des Études, moving away from its 1878 Harmelian model, adopted La Tour du Pin's notions on the Christian corporation.[82]

La Tour du Pin's corporate ideology propelled L'Oeuvre des Cercles Catholiques d'Ouvriers out of the mainstream of social Catholicism, and discord developed when he wanted to make the Cercles the base of operations for his "Christian social order."[83] As director of *L'Association catholique*, he filled its pages with controversial material on the family wage and profit sharing,[84] and even on these subjects, he distanced himself from Harmel and the Christian industrialists who were ever mindful of the practical application of theory. For instance, while Harmel was one of the original proponents of the family wage, his supplement never pretended to match need completely to wage as suggested by La Tour du Pin. To do so would result in the bankrupting of firms that preferred to employ families rather than single men and women. Similarly, the industrialists could not afford to subsidize a profit-sharing program in times of company losses.[85]

By 1890 La Tour du Pin was openly flirting with socialism, calling for a limitation to private ownership of property when the common good was at stake and inviting state intervention to facilitate his proposed social order.[86] Yet in 1908 he was philosophically attached to Charles Maurras and the Catholic reactionary political group, Action Française,[87] which has been called a precursor of twentieth-century French fascism. Indeed, the expansive social theory of La Tour du Pin illustrates how difficult it is to politically pigeonhole ideology associated with French corporatism, as well as social Catholicism, during the nineteenth century and the opening decades of the twentieth.[88]

Compared to the corporatist system envisioned by La Tour du Pin, Harmel's thoughts on the future of the Christian corporation were far less ambitious, although he implemented La Tour du Pin's notions on federating Christian corporations when he established the Patrons du Nord. Before *Rerum Novarum,* Harmel's Christian factory, which was a *syndicat mixte,* certainly remained closer to the nineteenth-century ideal as delineated by Le Play and Périn than did La Tour du Pin's, and as a result, Harmel and Val-des-Bois provided a more comfortable and therefore appealing social program for other Catholic *patrons* and other members of the Cercles than did La Tour du Pin's social program. Even after *Rerum Novarum*'s endorsement of the *syndicat séparé* and Harmel's promotion of the newer form throughout France, Harmel was seen as more in tune with the general populace than was La Tour du Pin.

As La Tour du Pin disengaged himself from administrative duties associated with the Cercles to devote his time to promoting his theories, Léon Harmel became increasingly involved in helping to run the organization. Harmel set about establishing a national network of workers' clubs, beginning with the creation of an individual religious association of workingmen on factory premises, and took on the presidency of the Cercles in the 1890s. Still, despite the obvious philosophical differences between La Tour du Pin and Harmel, there were areas of theoretical agreement and synergy, and they remained lifelong and devoted friends, closer in age and less in the spotlight than their more famous colleague, Albert de Mun.[89]

Albert de Mun

Aware of the debilitating effect the fratricidal struggle within the Conseil des Études had on the Cercles and not a theorist by nature, Albert de

Mun played the role of mediator. Publicly he stood for a "free" *syndicat mixte* that was confessional and not part of a corporate system and therefore seemingly sided with Harmel, but privately he worried that a protracted ideological battle within the organization could only "work to the advantage of Harmel and the economists."[90] De Mun recognized the revitalizing effect Harmel exerted on the Cercles but looked for ways to contain that dynamic presence. He would have preferred, for example, to limit Harmel's involvement in the Cercles to that of the less critical and less visible industrial commission but found no convenient way to exclude him from the Conseil des Études.[91] Yet by his own admission, de Mun owed much to Harmel, who had helped to shape his career in public office and formulate his social philosophy.

The heart of Léon Harmel's social theory was of course his personal interpretation of the Christian corporation, and for de Mun this represented "a profound idea . . . destined to transform in the end all of Catholic social action."[92] A frequent visitor to Val-des-Bois, de Mun credited the factory with inspiring his social legislation in the Chamber of Deputies. In his words:

> The experience of Val put the finishing touches on my conviction. From then on my ideas became more defined from year to year and this was the fruit of hard work that began in 1883 at the tribune of the Chamber in my first speech on the professional syndicats.[93]

Elected to the Chamber of Deputies in 1887, de Mun, a Catholic and a royalist, sat on the extreme right, but he and the other social Catholic deputies challenged the socialists in the sheer amount of labor legislation they sponsored. In an era when collective bargaining played a negligible role in determining working conditions and wages, the significance of these laws becomes even more apparent. De Mun's maiden speech on behalf of the *syndicat mixte* inaugurated a career devoted to labor's oppressed. He was instrumental in the passage of the law of 1884, which legalized labor unions; the laws of 1892, 1900, and 1909, which restricted female and child labor; the law of 1898, which called for accident compensation; the law of 1905, which provided for old-age assistance; the law of 1906, which designated Sunday as a holiday; and the law of 1910, which decreed old-age pensions.[94] These were the very same issues that had been raised earlier and hotly debated in the Conseil des Études, and gave de Mun, like La Tour du Pin, a philosophically colorful persona. For despite his efforts on behalf of labor, de Mun resisted being called a "Christian socialist" and preferred instead to be identified as a counterrevolutionary,[95] although he never intended to re-create the pre-1789 world.[96]

Léon Harmel initially was apprehensive about the intervention of the state in ameliorating the condition of the worker. His hesitation was not so much over the granting of additional power to the state, as was the case with most of his fellow industrialists, but over whether government officials were competent in labor matters.[97] Nevertheless, by 1891 he committed fully to state intervention. His travels throughout France convinced him solutions other than strict reliance on the Christian corporation were in order.[98] As a result, he encouraged de Mun to press for social legislation. In one letter to de Mun, Harmel specifically asked him to sponsor laws controlling the length of the workday and the ending of night work while urging him to promote *syndicats*, professional associations, and Conseils des Prud'hommes[99] in the national legislature.[100]

Involvement in the legislative process made republicans out of both Harmel and de Mun. Neither one was as tied theoretically to the notion of a monarchy as was La Tour du Pin, who saw royal restoration as inseparable from Christian social order.[101] De Mun's commitment to the monarchy began to fade in 1883 with the death of the Comte de Chambord, the pretender to the throne, but once Leo XIII encouraged him in 1892 to rally round the Republic, he abandoned the monarchy and endorsed the Republic.[102] De Mun had supported the monarchy because it represented a certain religious, social, and political tradition, one that was in his mind counterrevolutionary. Thus only the death of the Comte de Chambord "freed de Mun from a suffocating political *milieu*."[103] As for Harmel, he readily converted from monarchist to republican because, he said, "I am a democrat by instinct."[104] Vatican endorsement of French republicanism in 1892 released Harmel, an ardent champion of the papacy, from any lingering pro forma ties he had had with the monarchical form and strengthened his commitment to the Republic, especially since the parliamentary process held promise for labor reform and was not immune to the influence of pressure groups. In short, he thought his social agenda stood a better chance of a hearing in the republican arena.

Estrangement among the principals of the Cercles perhaps was inevitable given the strong personalities, but philosophical differences hastened the rupture.[105] De Mun, not particularly well read in comparison to his philosophical adversaries, the liberals and socialists, was uncomfortable with the theoretical boxing and the dynamic social program generated by the Conseil des Études and tried to cool the burgeoning friendship between Harmel and La Tour du Pin. De Mun wanted Harmel to accept the organization as it was in 1872. Harmel, while uneasy with the verbal repartee associated with the Conseil des Études, felt constrained by the organization and theories of 1872; he had moved beyond traditional paternalism, and his Christian corporation, unlike the workers' clubs of the Cercles of 1872, included women and children.[106]

De Mun and La Tour du Pin had a falling out, beginning in 1876, over de Mun's political ambitions, but they also disagreed over the role of the Conseil des Études: de Mun wanted limited theorizing and acceptance of official Church doctrine; La Tour du Pin wanted to advance Catholic social doctrine.[107] La Tour du Pin was just too intellectual for the kind of organization de Mun had in mind.[108] La Tour du Pin became military attaché in Vienna in 1877, at which time he visited Chambord in exile, and on his return to France in 1881, he spent most of his time working on his corporate theories.[109] In 1890 de Mun withdrew organizational support for *L'Association catholique,* chief vehicle for La Tour du Pin's increasingly reactionary social and political views.[110] The strained relationship became more pronounced after 1892 when de Mun joined the rallies and La Tour du Pin remained an avowed monarchist.[111]

Philosophical differences surfaced early among the three principals of the Cercles, with de Mun drawing his own line in the sand at Chartres on September 8, 1878. Here, speaking on behalf of the organization and calling himself a counterrevolutionary, he came out squarely against economic liberalism.[112] De Mun attempted to incite Cercles members in a crusade against economic liberalism but in so doing, offended not only Charles Périn, who was an economic liberal, but also the bulk of the Catholic *patronat.*

Instead de Mun made his major contribution to the Social Question in the Chamber of Deputies, where, in large measure, his social philosophy remained static. With the exception of finally accepting the concept of separate workers' unions in 1909, the man who typically gave speeches in military uniform to symbolize his enduring belief in a moral if not political counterrevolution remained tied to solutions first outlined in the 1870s. For example, in a speech given before the General Assembly of the Cercles as its president, de Mun, as late as 1912, merely reiterated a litany of familiar problems and tried solutions: the family "dislocated" by moral weakness, workshops witness to a "dispersal" of its members, trades "dying like bodies," institutions, such as the corporation with its harmony and protection, abolished, and all ties between *patrons* and workers broken. For de Mun, the contemporary world was but a "reconstruction of the pagan state," and the sole institutional solution remained the Christian corporation.[113]

De Mun founded a new organization in 1886 that was a spin-off of the Cercles and in reality a more natural fit for him than workers' clubs. The Association Catholique de la Jeunesse Française (ACJF) sought out young men in colleges and universities and organized them into study groups. Since only a few peasants and workers joined the group, and only after 1896, this was in a more comfortable social milieu for de Mun, as here he could be friend rather than master. The ACJF, consequently, was more receptive to the ideas of de Mun than the Conseil des Études had been, and it was largely through the ACJF, whose membership reached sixty thousand, that *Rerum Novarum* was brought to the youth of France.[114]

La Tour du Pin physically distanced himself from de Mun's conservatism by going off to Vienna, and when he returned, he wrote articles in *L'Association catholique* as an individual rather than as an official mouthpiece for the Cercles. For him, "the Christian corporation of Harmel must be complemented by the corporate regime in the Christian state."[115] La Tour du Pin's corporate system had moved in a different direction than de Mun's corporation of the 1870s, or the Christian corporation of Harmel for that matter, whether in the form of the *syndicat mixte* or the *syndicat séparé*. Regardless of the greater acceptability of Harmel's Christian corporation, the Conseil des Études adopted the corporate system of La Tour du Pin in 1882.[116]

Should we speak of L'Oeuvre des Cercles Catholiques d'Ouvriers, then, as an anachronistic organization that merely served as a palliative to satisfy upper-class and bourgeois sensitivities with regard to notions of noblesse oblige and Christian charity? Was its only legacy that of fratricidal dissention? While the organization effected no long-term solutions to the Social Question of the century, namely, how to right the wrongs inflicted on the laboring classes by the industrial revolution, the clubs alerted the privileged classes to the needs of the workers and alleviated some of the misery.[117] As a result, the Cercles helped to mend the deep societal wounds inflicted by the bitter class warfare associated with the Revolutions of 1830, 1848, and 1870. And while the various theories on the Christian corporation divided social Catholics in France, discussion within the Conseil des Études translated into concrete action, as indicated by the creation of organizations such as the Patrons du Nord. Ultimately, news of the Cercles and its Conseil des Études reached the ear of the Roman pontiff, who was in the process of gathering his own thoughts on the Christian corporation.

Patrons du Nord

Persuading factory owners to adopt the Christian corporation in its Harmelian form was not an easy task because *patrons* would never be convinced by ideology alone. These businessmen of northern France were always focused on the bottom line of any transaction and were wary particularly of new institutional structures and managerial styles in the uncertain post-1860 economic climate. A survey conducted in 1883, for example, indicated that only 20 percent of employers involved with the Cercles, a group already predisposed to some change in the social climate, favored Christian factories organized along the lines of the *syndicat mixte*.[118] On the other hand, and as Léon Harmel was quick to point out, reform within the factory reaped concrete results for the *patron,* providing him with a professionally trained, morally disciplined, and stable workforce. And if that was not incentive enough, there was always the escalating threat of socialism to nudge factory owners into modifying traditional ways. Consequently, though the average Catholic factory owner was a conservative, hardheaded businessman, circumstances were such that a new idea might win acceptance if the result was worth the risk. This indeed was the psychological tack Léon Harmel used to sell his Christian corporation to fellow textile manufacturers of the Nord.

Harmel initially presented Val-des-Bois as the model Christian corporation at the 1874 congress of the Cercles Catholiques d'Ouvriers at Lille. There he spoke of forming an organization of textile factory owners who would imitate him in transforming their factories into Christian corporations.[119] Father Eugene Marquigny, S. J., assisted him in the development stage of the new organization by speaking on behalf of the Christian corporation,[120] as well as by conducting research in 1876 on the feasibility of such a project. Data compiled indicated to Harmel that most of the potential membership were owners of factories smaller than Val-des-Bois, so he developed a structural plan that would maximize rather than minimize the impact of these factories. It called for the unionization of owners and workers in the "same profession" or "similar profession" into *syndicats mixtes* that were "essentially" Christian.[121] In other words, the organization would be restricted to the textile industry or those industries ancillary to it and would magnify the effect of the individual firms by construction of a federation.

This early overture to the industrialists of Lille eventually resulted in the creation of the Association Catholique des Patrons du Nord, but before certain of the Catholic industrialists agreed to organize formally in 1884, ideology needed to be worked out. Both Léon Harmel and Albert de Mun were quite excited at the prospect of bringing into their orbit these *patrons* of the Nord, since in their estimation the textile industry of the Nord was a perfect "lab" in which to realize their social program.[122] Their success was limited, however, and roadblocks were set up early. When Marquigny denounced economic liberalism and endorsed state intervention in an address in Lille in 1879, he echoed men such as the Christian socialist Philippe Buchez but also stirred up the proverbial hornet's nest among the Catholic *patronat,* who became divided over the issue. As a consequence, from 1879 to 1884 meetings were infrequent, and the goal of bringing on board the Catholic industrialists of the Nord stalled. It did not help matters that simultaneously the state ordered the Jesuits to disperse and abandon their establishments, that there were strikes throughout northern France, and that the Conseil des Études issued six *Avis,* or opinions, that caused considerable consternation among industrialists.

The Conseil des Études said that the right to work was based on natural and divine law, that coalitions and strikes were legitimate when the real interest of the workers was at stake and when violence was restrained, and that associations of employers and employees (*syndicats mixtes*) were necessary. The Conseil said too that the state needed to find the *juste milieu* when it came to intervention, maintaining a balance between liberalism and socialism, and was required to intervene in industry for the sake of assuring rest on Sunday, limiting the length of the workday, and protecting women and children. The Conseil also suggested the creation of people's banks, advocated the right to own property, and argued for a just wage.[123] This was a lot for most of the captains of the northern textile industry to swallow. But while only a limited number took the leap of faith and came together as the Patrons du Nord, the organization was the largest such group among the northern *patronat*.[124]

Formal incorporation of L'Association Catholique des Patrons du Nord occurred on September 8, 1884, and came in the wake of the 1884 law that both legalized trade unions, whether *syndicat mixte* or *syndicat séparé*, and allowed federation by regions if all the *syndicats* were of the same industry.[125] The raison d'être of the association was the social education of the factory owner, and the organization made the rather startling admission that *patrons* were partially to blame for the contemporary social crisis.[126] The only factor that the Patrons du Nord and their Christian corporations needed to be mindful of after the 1884 law was the separation of religious organizations from the *syndicat* proper, and this was precisely the issue that proved the undoing of the Patrons du Nord.

In 1892 the courts ruled that the Patrons du Nord were in noncompliance with the law and ordered it dissolved. Two representatives from the Nord brought the matter before the Chamber of Deputies in the hope of having the judgment reversed, but the government held the organization to the letter of the law, and the ruling stood.[127] The government's action galvanized the Patrons du Nord, who henceforward met and acted as legal "individuals." Perceiving themselves as victims of an anticlerical state, their hostility to the Republic increased, as did their commitment to social action. And, as in the case of the Cercles, their paternalism resulted in good works and the diminution of misery.[128] In 1888 the organization had 4,000 members in 50 enterprises,[129] but by 1895 the organization peaked with nearly 30,000 members in 177 enterprises.[130] The Christian corporations of the Patrons du Nord, including the factory at Val-des-Bois, remained *syndicats mixtes* even after Leo XIII presented the *syndicat séparé* as an option in *Rerum Novarum*.[131]

Many of the members operated reasonably successful enterprises that could afford to offer their workers benefit programs such as existed at Val-des-Bois.[132] But while quick to denigrate liberalism in the abstract, most of the *patrons* were hardened economic liberals who accepted state intrusion in their business lives only with great reluctance. In addition, many northern industrialists continued to be dedicated monarchists even after the death of the Comte de Chambord in 1883.[133] Harmel's deviation from the patronal norm was provocative. His divergence from the typical employer profile was in fact the basis of his appeal, for the other *patrons* considered him either a man "full of possibilities" or one who represented "supreme danger."[134] In either case, he challenged their traditional ways, which meant he had an uphill battle on his hands.

First, the *patrons* increasingly were guarded about their enterprises in light of recent legislation permitting government inspectors in factories to check on the ages of child laborers, for example. For although they recognized the need for traditional state protection on behalf of the "weak, women, and children," the *patrons* balked when it came to "inquisitorial inspections" and "fixing wages." Second, the Christian corporation itself proved problematic, because if it were not "Christian," it would be "socialist," and as a result the *patrons* demanded obligatory religious commitment as insurance against workers joining socialist unions. This was an area of considerable potential tension, not only because one found crucifixes in workrooms, chapels on the premises, and sisters supervising the women's ateliers, but also because socialists used the religion factor to feed an anticlerical press.[135] Third, the *patrons* opposed "forced charity," which required them to provide employees with state-designated benefits.[136]

Unwilling to pattern their factories after Harmel's Christian corporation, which precluded forced religious practice and involved reciprocity between labor and management in nearly all aspects of factory life, most northern industrialists parted ideological ways with Harmel. In refusing to accept *la méthode Harmel*, the *patrons* turned their factories into parodies of Val-des-Bois. Rather than free the worker from past abuses and limitations, the majority of factory owners used certain aspects of Harmel's plan, principally, the introduction of religion on factory premises, to further restrict worker activities. For them, the Christian corporation became a means to reinforce paternalism. The threat of socialism did not nudge average *patrons* into authentic reform but instead led them to retreat further into an authoritarian managerial style that only exacerbated tensions between labor and management. Ultimately, law, not religion, would move the vast majority of employers to introduce reform in their factories. And France lagged behind other industrialized nations in implementing labor law. De Mun's own social program in the Chamber of Deputies, for example, was less aggressive than he would have liked because he attempted to placate the Patrons du Nord.[137]

The Christian corporation at Val-des-Bois thus remained a unique phenomenon in the annals of French labor history, and therefore the earlier suspicions of Maignen and La Tour du Pin seemingly were validated—but not entirely. Harmel's principal disciples in the Nord were Bailliencourt of Douai, Camille Féron-Vrau of Lille, and Alfred Dutilleul of Armentières.[138] But there were others too. Hyppolite André and M. Marcellot, *patrons* of large metallurgy plants, dispelled the notion that the Christian corporation succeeded only in rural, textile enterprises.[139] In Saint Chamond, near Lyons, Camille Thiollière and Charles Neyrand tried to replicate Val-des-Bois at their factories, and although less successful than Harmel, they nevertheless "were given credit for defusing the hostile influence of anarchists, for pulling together the different elements of work in Saint Chamond, and for contributing to maintaining there an atmosphere of social peace."[140] At Marseille, Félix Fournier, owner of a textile factory that employed eight hundred workers, responded to Harmel's appeal.[141] There is also evidence that Harmel influenced Franz Brandts, the German industrialist, who hung a portrait of Harmel behind his desk, supported worker initiative in plant management, and attempted to organize fellow industrialists to follow in his path.[142]

Not all *patrons* accepted the Val-des-Bois model in its entirety, however, and Harmel never demanded total acceptance. It is for this reason, and for lack of thorough record keeping, that confirming discipleship is a shadowy undertaking.[143] For example, Eugène Déchelette enthusiastically enforced the Sunday holiday at his textile operation of five hundred workers but would not dream of setting up a Conseil d'Usine that handed over management responsibilities to his workers.[144] Then too there were *patrons*, like Alfred Mame, who began improving conditions for their workers at midcentury, before Harmel set out on his mission, but became recommitted to the effort later in the century through the inspiration of Harmel.[145] Finally, there were those who attempted to implement the Harmelian model but, after a few years of trying with minimal results, gave up.[146] It becomes very difficult, therefore, to quantify the success of the Christian corporation in the Harmelian format, or to even determine what was meant by "success." But clearly Léon Harmel motivated others to act on behalf of workers, although rarely were other *patrons* ready to hand over to their workers as much responsibility in the running of their factories as did Harmel at Val-des-Bois.

When it came to empowerment of the workers, as practiced at Val-des-Bois, Harmel went further in theory than either de Mun or La Tour du Pin and consequently not only rejuvenated the nineteenth-century Christian corporation as outlined by Le Play and Périn but also helped to bridge the gap between social Catholics of varying philosophical stripes.[147] Leo XIII recognized the significance of Harmel's achievement, for his experiment at Val-des-Bois was a concrete answer to the Social Question[148] and also demonstrated that religion was not necessarily alienated from an industrialized world.

The Vatican Connection

The papacy of Leo XIII (r. 1878–1903) coincided with that period when the programs of French Catholics intent on societal reform flourished. Reformers such as Harmel universally acknowledged the inspirational debt owed to Leo XIII, especially since the Vatican had responded slowly in issuing a mandate for change in response to the effects of the century's industrial and political revolutions. The tardiness stemmed from traditional caution, exacerbated when, after 1860, the papacy had to contend with its own territorial insecurities. The net result was an ideological intransigence that typically finds its most infamous example in the 1864 encyclical *Quanta Cura* and its adjoining *Syllabus,* or summary list, of modern society's chief philosophical errors. Here Pius IX (r. 1846–1878) condemned liberalism and socialism without addressing the ills that gave rise to them and without suggesting reform. In many respects, the early years of Leo XIII's papacy promised more of the same.

Leo XIII

Gioacchino Vincenzo Raffaele Luigi Pecci was born on March 2, 1810, in the Papal States. Educated by the Jesuits in the classics before going on to study law and theology, Pecci was well trained for the priesthood, which he entered in 1837. His energy, empathy for the poor and suffering, and considerable diplomatic skills were recognized early on and led to postings in the Papal States, the Kingdom of Naples, Perugia, and Belgium, where, in 1843, he was appointed nuncio, or papal representative. Before leaving for Belgium—and to give him adequate rank for an important international position—Pius IX named him archbishop of Damietta.[149]

Belgium exemplified the most egregious horrors of the industrial revolution among western European nations, worse than Great Britain or France, because the capitalists there virtually were unfettered by state regulation of any sort. The Catholic episcopacy seemingly turned a blind eye to the situation, and social Catholicism developed more slowly in Belgium than in France.[150] There is no indication that Archbishop Pecci reacted directly at that time to what he witnessed among laboring Belgians in the years from 1843 to 1846.[151] Instead he involved himself in a local political issue by supporting Catholic schools. Pecci sided with the Catholic bishops and laity on this matter, and against the government. His actions made him persona non grata with King Leopold of Belgium, and he was recalled to Italy where he was named bishop of Perugia in 1846. He remained in Perugia until elected to the papacy in 1878 on the death of Pius IX.

Physically weak, morally assertive, and a natural leader, he worked for an expanded role for the papacy in the temporal world, with mixed results. His encouragement of biblical study (*Providentissimus Deus*, November 18, 1893) and scholarly research (he opened the secret archives of the Vatican to scholars in 1883) earned him universal respect. But, above all, he is noted for reasserting the Church's role as moral leader of the modern world through its Catholic social teaching. A prolific author of encyclicals, apostolic letters, and *motu proprios*, Leo gives heart to all aging scholars, for more than fifty of his encyclicals were written after his eightieth year.[152] He did not reverse Catholic social teaching as defined by Pius IX so much as reinterpret it in light of the contemporary world. Conservative in some instances, progressive in others, he defied political classification.[153]

In *Quod Apostolici Muneris,* the papal encyclical published on December 28, 1878, Leo XIII called socialists, communists, and nihilists bold, bad men who held to "poisonous doctrines" and who permitted unlawful desires of every kind. In fact, they scheme with "horrible wickedness" and "leave nothing untouched or whole which by both human and divine laws has been wisely decreed for the health and beauty of life," including marriage and the right of property. Furthermore, they twisted the Gospel itself "so as to deceive more readily the unwary." It was for these reasons that "our glorious predecessor, Pius IX[,] . . . fought against the wicked attempts of these sects."[154] Indeed, Leo XIII never missed an opportunity to point out the insidious effects of socialism, communism, and nihilism on private and public life (*Immortale Dei,* November 1, 1885; *Exeunte Iam Anno,* December 25, 1888; *Rerum Novarum,* May 15, 1891).

Liberalism, by contrast, proved a more complex adversary. While denouncing the ideology of liberalism (*Immortale Dei,* November 1, 1885; *Libertas Praestantissimum,* June 20, 1888) for its rejection of divine guidance and law, Leo XIII concurrently conducted a foreign policy of rapprochement with contemporary European governments, liberal and parliamentary ones as well as those of a conservative and authoritarian nature. Consequently, his writings on liberalism and on government walked a finer line than those on socialism, communism, and nihilism. Leo exhorted citizens to obey their governments "constantly and faithfully," since obedience is not the servitude of man to man but submission to the will of God. "To despise legitimate authority . . . is unlawful, as a rebellion against the divine will, and whoever resists that, rushes willfully to destruction. To caste aside obedience, and by popular violence to incite to revolt, is therefore treason, not against man only, but against God."[155] As for the governments, whether parliamentary or authoritarian in form, accountability would, in the end, be made to the Almighty,[156] but it could arrive sooner. Leo XIII warned,

> If the laws of the state are manifestly at variance with divine law, containing enactments hurtful to the Church, or conveying injunctions adverse to the duties imposed by religion, or if they violate in the person of the Supreme Pontiff the authority of Jesus Christ, then, truly, to resist becomes a positive duty, to obey, a crime.[157]

In *Immortale Dei,* then, Leo XIII fully endorsed traditional Church thinking on governmental form, namely, that it was irrelevant as long as the government in question abided by a higher law, and his pronouncement strongly hinted quite early on at the Ralliement directive of 1892. Yet the papacy here hardly came across as accommodating to temporal states; governments clearly were to subject themselves to divine and Church directives. *Sapientiae Christianae* (1890) also reflected a defensive papacy, one that had lost its once great temporal holdings, and thus its writings on states and citizenship were eerily reminiscent of an earlier epoch. *Unam Sanctum* (1302), the medieval encyclical typically cast as the embodiment of a defiant papacy, exuded the same tone. Just as Boniface VIII (r. 1294–1303) warned state leaders that it was "necessary for human salvation for every creature to be subject to the Roman pontiff," so too did Leo XIII in 1890 caution those who opposed the pontiff, or his interests, that they could expect concrete repercussions, for "no man could serve two masters."[158]

Leo XIII demonstrated a certain amount of political finesse by condemning the socialism, communism, and nihilism that contemporary European governments feared while simultaneously putting them on notice that their own conduct—particularly that toward the Vatican—could be subject to scrutiny and reprisal. For this reason, his political policy and actions are characterized as conservative and pragmatic if not outright opportunistic and wily.

His strong endorsement of Thomistic theology (*Aeterni Patris,* August 4, 1879; *Rerum Novarum,* May 15, 1891) was traditional and in keeping with the nineteenth-century Romantic movement that harkened back to the medieval world for inspiration. Yet for Leo XIII, the revival of Thomism signified something more than mere reaffirmation of Church teaching and nostalgia for the Middle Ages. During the papal tenure of Leo XIII, Thomism became the principal vehicle, through its use of both faith and reason, not only to refute liberalism and socialism but also to assimilate into Catholic social teaching recent scientific discoveries. Leo XIII encouraged Church members to deepen their religious faith by studying St. Thomas Aquinas and promoted biblical and scientific study to better prepare the faithful to discuss modern issues. In short, he used medieval philosophical tools and contested the same ideological enemies as Pius IX but brought a new, more open attitude to the task.

Modernity, with its industrial growth, advances in science, and democratization, was not evil per se. Rather the fundamental error of contemporary society rested with mankind's refusal to recognize "the existence of God, of a supernatural order, and the duty to submit to it."[159] Schooled and conversant in the fields of educational theory, scientific developments, current political affairs, modern technology, and socioeconomic problems,[160] Leo XIII drew on these scholarly resources when making his greatest contribution to Catholic social teaching in *Rerum Novarum*.

Rerum Novarum

Like his other major works, Leo XIII was the principal author of *Rerum Novarum*. Who and what contributed to his thoughts on labor are relevant subjects of inquiry.

Leo XIII studied and absorbed St. Thomas Aquinas's *Summa Theologica,* but he also relied on contemporary Catholic writing and Catholic action on behalf of labor. Early in his papacy, he read with enthusiastic approval the *Manuel d'une corporation chrétienne,* the major philosophical work of Léon Harmel. In a letter written on April 21, 1879, to Cardinal Langénieux,[161] Leo XIII observed that Val-des-Bois was "well organized ... according to the laws of religion and virtue," went on to congratulate the *patrons* and the workers of the enterprise, and concluded with an invitation to all the owners of large factories to consider "the order, the peace, and the mutual charity that reigns in the workshops of Val-des-Bois and to strive to follow such a fine example."[162] He saw in Harmel the only social Catholic who could bring about concrete results on a significant scale.[163]

In addition, during the late 1870s and the 1880s, Leo XIII sanctioned the work of the Conseil des Études of L'Oeuvre des Cercles Catholiques d'Ouvriers and read its reports on justice and charity, property, the just wage, and the corporation.[164] But while he was familiar with Harmel's social philosophy and his successful Christian corporation at Val-des-Bois, as well as the work of the Conseil des Études, the Fribourg Union had the most immediate and direct impact on the preparation of *Rerum Novarum*.[165] And Harmel and his Conseil d'Usine inspired the Fribourg Union.[166]

The Fribourg Union, brainchild of René de La Tour du Pin,[167] consisted of social Catholic leaders from France, Germany, Austria, Italy, Belgium, and Switzerland who met annually at Fribourg, Switzerland, from 1884 to 1891. The weeklong meetings were chaired by Msgr. Gaspar Mermillod (1824–1892), Bishop of Fribourg, who reported back to Leo XIII on the points discussed and conclusions drawn by the group. Members of the Union included, besides La Tour du Pin and Mermillod, Stanislao Medolago Albani, Franz Kuefstein, Kaspar Decurtins, Prince Karl zu Löwenstein, Franz Schindler, Léon Collinet, Georges Helleputte, and Jean d'Ursel.[168] The idea was to synthesize ideology and gather local data for the pope for his study of the troubling European labor situation. In the course of their work, the Fribourg Union determined that the corporation, in either the *syndicat mixte* or the *syndicat séparé* form, was the ideal structure in which the rights of workers could be protected and that state intervention was beneficial in supervising and coordinating the establishment of corporations. The Union also reaffirmed the right to work and the right to a living wage and supported workers' insurance against sickness, accidents, and unemployment. To no one's surprise, the Union also formally condemned economic liberalism. In 1888 Leo XIII discussed the results of their deliberations with nine of the Union members and asked them to summarize their conclusions. The resulting memorandum became the cornerstone of *Rerum Novarum*.[169] What propelled the publication in 1891 of the encyclical on labor, however, were the worker pilgrimages to Rome, conceived and led by Harmel. Leo XIII remarked that *Rerum Novarum* was "the recompense for the workers' pilgrimages,"[170] a subject that is explored in considerable depth in chapter 4.

Although *Rerum Novarum*[171] condemned economic liberalism for permitting "a small number of very rich men ... to lay upon the teeming masses of the laboring poor a yoke little better than that of slavery itself,"[172] it endorsed certain capitalist tenets while offering concrete suggestions for reform. In short, Leo XIII assumed a conciliatory attitude toward economic liberalism. By contrast, his treatment of socialism was uniformly negative and unsophisticated. Instead of recognizing the diversity in socialist ideology, he accepted socialists at their word—and only at their most revolutionary word, Marxism—and completely ignored those with evolutionary inclinations,[173] such as Saint-Simon, Fourier, Buchez, and Proudhon. Yet one must acknowledge, with Lillian Parker Wallace, that Leo XIII had come a long way since *Quod Apostolici Muneris* and its vituperative attack on socialism.[174]

A major fault of socialism, in the opinion of the pope, was its threat to family life: it would set aside the parent and introduce state supervision, thereby "destroying the structure of the home." Yet he was willing to allow state involvement when "a family finds itself in exceeding difficulty, deprived of the counsel of friends, and without any prospect of extricating itself . . . for each family is part of the commonwealth."[175] Obviously, the seeming ambiguity finds resolution in the degree of state intervention called for by the pope. According to Leo XIII, the socialists argued for total government involvement in the lives of its citizens, whereas he proposed in *Rerum Novarum,* as he did during the French worker pilgrimage of 1887, public aid only as a last resort. Ironically, this is one of the points that caused economic liberals of the era to label *Rerum Novarum* "socialist."

Support of the family, including state intervention on its behalf, certainly was in keeping with the sentiments of Léon Harmel and confirmed by what he practiced at Val-des-Bois. Harmel hired families as worker units, paid them a wage supplement based on the number of children in the family, provided them with free medical care, schools, retirement plans, and discount stores, as well as numerous social clubs and facilities.

When it came to state intervention, not only Harmel but also de Mun endorsed the notion when the good of the workers or their families was at stake. Earlier theorists, such as Saint-Simon, Fourier, Buchez, and Proudhon, talked of state involvement to correct societal ills, as did contemporary thinkers in the Fribourg Union. By 1891 many once-intransigent laissez-faire liberals had begun to yield to the inevitable: large-scale reform might have to be undertaken by the state to be effective. The pope, by underscoring the primacy of the family and by endorsing limited state intervention, emphasized his dogmatic differences with the Marxists but at the same time concurred ideologically with many non-Marxist social reformers of the period.

Leo XIII also took issue with the socialists' notion of leveling society. For the pope, inequality existed naturally among mankind in innumerable ways, "in capacity, skill, health, strength, and unequal fortune," and therefore attempts at total equality went against natural, or divine, law. For this reason, classes exist and "each requires the other"; that is, "capital cannot do without labor nor labor without capital."[176] Consequently, Leo XIII recommended that workers abide by agreements "freely and equitably agreed upon; never to injure the property, nor to outrage the person, of an employer; never to resort to violence . . . nor to engage in riot and disorder."[177] With these words, the pope disregarded the Thomistic principle of the just war.[178] Most commentators suggest that his refusal to condone rebellion resulted from living through political upheavals and labor demonstrations that ended in death and destruction. Moreover, it would have been impolitic for him to sanction unrest at a time when he sought better relations with European governments. The peaceful strike thus became the only popular political response to unaddressed grievances that was sanctioned by *Rerum Novarum*.[179]

Given extant documents, it is difficult to pinpoint with precision just how much Léon Harmel wanted to retain natural hierarchies, or conversely, how willing he was to allow class lines to tumble. However, he recognized that natural hierarchies did exist, given differences in intelligence and birth circumstances, and was not about to countenance much in the way of boot-strapping; for although he actively promoted the social and economic well-being of workers, he counseled the young to follow in the footsteps of their fathers by opting for technical training rather than a liberal arts curriculum at school. Nevertheless, he encouraged managerial responsibilities among his workers, making sure he stopped short of turning Val-des-Bois into any kind of producer's cooperative like Proudhon had in mind. As for strikes, it was a matter in which he had no direct experience, save for the religious malaise that gripped the factory in 1893. Neither his writing nor his speeches give a hint as to whether he would condone a strike under the guise of the "just war."

Accepting the hierarchical world of St. Thomas meant that change, for Leo XIII, would begin at the top, and this clearly echoes the thoughts of Harmel as expressed in his *Manuel,* his letters, and his public speeches. The notion is, of course, paternalism, plain and simple. The pope held that not only should the state intervene at appropriate times, but employers were not to treat their employees as "slaves" but as fellow human beings and Christians. Strikes would vanish in the face of "public remedial measures," such as labor laws, and just employers. Again, however, a certain irony was at work here. As will become more apparent as this discussion progresses, the social reform desired by Leo XIII, if carried to its logical conclusion, would produce a society of greater economic and social equality, thereby weakening the rigidly constructed hierarchical society of the scholastics.

Central to this line of argument are Leo XIII's ideas on private property. In taking the socialists to task for their endorsement of communal property, he ignored their rhetoric on inherited riches, incomes of the leisure class, and the holdings of the great capitalists.[180] He reserved his only negative comments on unearned wealth for "rapacious usury [that was] still practiced by covetous and grasping men."[181] The distinction for Leo, as for Aristotle and St. Thomas, was simple: money, as opposed to property, was unproductive, and to profit financially from another's need was exploitative.[182] Furthermore, Leo XIII's solution for the accumulation of an excess of earthly goods was the Thomistic one, namely, charity. He reminded the readers of *Rerum Novarum,* as he had the participants of the 1889 French worker pilgrimage, that "when what necessity demands has been supplied, and one's standing fairly taken thought of, it becomes a duty to give to the indigent out of what remains over. . . . [N]o one ought to live unbecomingly."[183] Léon Harmel could not have agreed more: the Harmel family was frugal but dispensed from company profits as liberally as possible in order to subsidize worker programs.

As for the private ownership of goods, Leo XIII selectively incorporated Thomistic teaching on the subject into *Rerum Novarum*. For example, St. Thomas taught that "while ownership may be private, use should be common";[184] that is, it was to "promote the interest of all."[185] Fearful of appearing too socialistic,[186] Leo deliberately refrained from references to commonality. Consequently, he seemed to side with the economic liberals by stressing the benefits attached to the private ownership of goods. He used the Thomistic defense of private property, as delineated in the *Summa Theologica,* as the basis for his own words. For instance, St. Thomas contended that private property fostered initiative, led to an orderly handling of human affairs, and promoted a peaceful society.[187] Leo XIII asserted that "every man has by nature the right to possess property as his own," for not only must a father provide "food and all necessaries for those whom he has begotten," but he also must provide for their future by the "ownership of productive property."[188] By his endorsement of patrimony, Leo clearly did not preach resignation to the propertyless urban or rural worker. In fact, he, like Harmel, actually promoted the embourgeoisement of the proletariat while simultaneously talking of the fixity and naturalness of social and economic hierarchies. As has been pointed out, houses and savings plans for the workers at Val-des-Bois instilled middle-class values. *Rerum Novarum* strongly implied that ownership of property would help to bridge the chasm between capital and labor, the rich and the poor. But in order for the worker to own property, he needed decent wages so that he had enough discretionary income to invest in property for himself and his progeny.

Here Leo XIII embarked on new theological ground, as the scholastics intended remuneration for labor to meet basic "earthly needs"[189] and not systematically to provide excess from which to build a patrimony for future generations. *Rerum Novarum* called on employers to share their wealth, not only because of the principle of Christian charity, but also because decent wages meant "less revolution," the "proliferation of private property," and a diminution of migratory labor as workers would be inclined to "cling to the country in which they were born."[190]

Leo XIII assumed an ambivalent posture on the exact meaning of a just wage. For him, "wages ought not to be insufficient to support a frugal and well-behaved wage earner."[191] The question remains whether he intended his references to a "family wage" to be taken in its absolute or relative meanings; that is, whether the wage paid to the worker was to be adequate not only for the worker but also for his entire family, or whether the wage paid to the worker was a standard base wage but supplemented by marriage and family allotments at the appropriate times.[192] La Tour du Pin argued for the former, the absolute wage, while Léon Harmel and the *patrons* of the Nord held to the relative wage, claiming the absolute wage would bankrupt them. In any event, *Rerum Novarum* asked employers to look beyond the wage contract to redress contemporary injustices and presented the Christian corporation as the most appropriate institutional construct in which to facilitate these changes.

Leo XIII sanctioned the Christian corporation in *Quod Apostolici Muneris* (December 28, 1878), in *Humanum Genus* (April 20, 1884), and in the 1889 French worker pilgrimage to Rome. But in *Rerum Novarum*, he both described it in greater detail and enlarged its horizons. To begin with, the pope endorsed neither the obligatory corporation of La Tour du Pin and Maignen nor the corporate state system envisioned by La Tour du Pin and the syndicalists whose goal was the actual restructuring of society. Instead he confined his notion of corporatism to a modernized interpretation of the medieval guild in more or less Harmelian form.

The corporation's goals, according to Leo XIII, were to draw together capital and labor and to assist those in need. Like the operation at Val-des-Bois, corporations must retain their characteristic religious nature. Consequently, he asked that particular attention be paid to their "piety and morality." In addition, he recommended benefit and insurance societies and benevolent associations, such as workingmen's unions, which would combat unemployment and establish funds to assist the needy in case of an accident or sickness and in old age.[193] He also encouraged "foundations established by private persons to provide for the workman, and his widow or his orphans, in case of sudden calamity, in sickness, and in the event of death, and institutions for the welfare of boys and girls, young people, and those more advanced in years."[194] These suggestions corresponded to the numerous social and economic institutions at Val-des-Bois that assured its families cradle-to-grave care. Next, according to Leo, Christian corporations would establish committees of firmness and wisdom to settle disputes between capital and labor.[195] The Conseil d'Usine at Val-des-Bois was governed by a board composed of both workers and *patrons,* and Harmel maintained that the factory council prevented disputes rather than settled them, but it served essentially the same function as Leo XIII called for.

It was important also, the pope said, for corporations to provide their workers with a "continuous supply of work at all times and all seasons."[196] Harmel took special pride in the fact that even in adverse economic times his workers did not remain idle, if at all possible. Leo XIII also felt that the corporation, as a private institution, should be recognized legally and given encouragement by the state since its success necessarily would be beneficial to the state; and in France the law of 1884 allowed for either *syndicats mixtes* or *syndicats séparés,* if religious organizations were divorced from the corporate union. Finally, *Rerum Novarum* stated that "difference in degree or standing should not interfere with unanimity and good will" at the Christian corporation.[197] In other words, the congenial atmosphere at Val-des-Bois merited duplication.

Yet the corporation as described in *Rerum Novarum* departed from the Harmelian version in one highly significant way. Seeking to counter the influence of socialist unions, Leo XIII condoned workers' associations, or unions, "either of workmen alone, or of workmen and employers together."[198] This proposal did not place Harmel at theoretical odds with Leo XIII, but it meant that the corporation at Val-des-Bois could no longer be presented as the sole paradigm for all those interested in establishing a Christian corporation. For although Harmel increasingly turned over management responsibilities to the workers, principally through the Conseil d'Usine, Val-des-Bois remained a *syndicat mixte* during his tenure. Harmel believed that "the mixed union was an effective means of assuring social peace [because] it reconciled labor and management."[199] But he cautioned in 1893 that if employers did not set up genuine *syndicats mixtes,* in which "worker initiative was favored, we cannot blame those who take another way."[200] In sum, after *Rerum Novarum,* Harmel was not averse philosophically to workers organizing independently of employers but felt that the *syndicat mixte* continued to be appropriate for Val-des-Bois.

As for Leo XIII, he acted on the recommendation of the Fribourg Union and endorsed the *syndicat séparé,* a revolutionary principle in the annals of Catholic social teaching but one tempered considerably by his insistence that these worker unions be confessional. The establishment of Catholic workers' unions, separate from other workers' unions, not only removed Catholics from other labor activists but also meant that in France two systems of unions developed within Catholic labor, *syndicats mixtes* and *syndicats séparés.*[201] The pope thus inadvertently contributed to the fragmentation of the labor movement in France.

This was not, moreover, the only divisive point among French Catholics after the publication of *Rerum Novarum.* According to a study by Jean-Marie Mayeur and Marie Zimmermann, only thirteen out of eighty-nine dioceses published the encyclical.[202] Most of the French Catholic episcopacy considered *Rerum Novarum* too radical for consumption. And, indeed, the socialists Jean Jaurès and Paul Lafargue initially heralded it as a "manifesto socialist."[203] After publication, French Catholics became even more divided on the other controversial aspects of *Rerum Novarum:* the definition of a just wage, state intervention in economic and social matters, and the nature of the Christian corporation itself.[204] Just as these points had raised the level of polemic within the Conseil des Études and among the Patrons du Nord, they elicited strong reactions among the general public.

In his typical unequivocal fashion, Harmel reacted positively to the encyclical on the condition of labor. For him, the encyclical not only served as an affirmation of his work to date, particularly as *patron* of Val-des-Bois; it also became the point of departure for a series of new endeavors that had as their focus the independence of the French worker and generally developed in the context of the movement known as Christian democracy. *Rerum Novarum* demonstrated that the pope and the industrialist were in basic philosophical agreement, and ideological affinity led to matters of a more political nature. For example, in thanksgiving for *Rerum Novarum,* Harmel organized the spectacular 1891 worker pilgrimage to Rome.

CHAPTER FOUR

Pilgrimage to Rome

> Vive le Pape!
> —*Written at the tomb of King Victor Emmanuel in the Roman Pantheon by three French pilgrims,*
> *October 2, 1891*

PARISIAN STREETS SUDDENLY TURNED SILENT IN THE LAST WEEK OF May 1871. After defying the national government since March, the last of the Communards fell at Père Lachaise cemetery on the right bank of the Seine River, southeast of Montmartre, a hilltop neighborhood in north Paris. Montmartre, or "mont des martyrs" (mount of martyrs), was considered sacred since St. Denis, first bishop of Paris, was martyred there at the end of the third century. In the minds of many workers, the blood of the revolutionaries of 1871 resanctified hallowed ground. Badly outnumbered by government troops, at least twenty thousand Communards had been killed and thousands more arrested, exiled, or in hiding. The Revolution of 1871, the last of the nineteenth-century French revolutions, eliminated a significant segment of the worker leadership, seriously hampered the quest to rectify the ills of the industrial revolution, and intensified class division. One wondered, had Armageddon arrived?

The Paris Commune started in the aftermath of French defeat in the Franco-Prussian War. Napoléon III was captured at Sedan on September 2, 1870. On September 4 an insurrection in Paris declared the Third Republic. The Germans responded by setting up a siege of the city from September 19, 1870, to January 28, 1871, when the French surrendered. France was represented by Adolph Thiers (1797–1877), who functioned as chief executive of the Third Republic and negotiated the Treaty of Frankfurt with the German Confederation. The treaty called for a large indemnity, German military occupation until the money was paid, and the surrender of Alsace and Lorraine. The Parisian workers refused to accept the surrender and peace terms, declared Parisian independence from the rest of France, and set up the Paris Commune in spring 1871.

The Paris Commune, lasting from March 18 to May 27, was motivated by patriotism and economic hardship. Politically, it traced its lineage from the revolutions of 1789, 1830, and 1848; but in 1871 something new was added: the Communards envisioned a particularized, decentralized France, along the lines mapped out by Pierre-Joseph Proudhon. Ideologically, it covered the gamut of leftist groups; the Parisian municipal council included republican Jacobins (34), Blanquist anarchists (11), Proudhonists (25), and Marxists (2), all of whom found unity in a strong dose of anticlericalism. Noticeably absent were the Christian socialists of 1848.

The final days of warfare unleashed a bloodbath that took the life of the archbishop of Paris, who attempted to negotiate a settlement between the two sides, and included a scorched earth policy carried out by the revolutionaries that destroyed large areas of the city. Fire engulfed the Tuilleries and Hôtel de Ville, as well as shops and homes. The crowd, a potent political agent since at least 1789, had once again turned ugly and dangerous to person and property.[1] As a consequence, future demonstrations and gatherings of any sort were suspect. Strikes were outlawed, and even religious events, such as the seemingly innocuous worker pilgrimages, were viewed with suspicion.

The French worker pilgrimages to Rome began in the decade after the 1870 defeat and humiliation at Sedan and the subsequent horrors of the Paris Commune, and thus operated within a framework of national mourning and examination. For Léon Harmel, corporate evil of such magnitude demanded corporate good on a grand scale. He attempted to market the Christian corporation, as developed at Val-des-Bois, throughout France and organized and led pilgrimages to Rome that lasted, with the exception of a six-year hiatus, for twenty-five years. Harmel created the worker pilgrimages in response to the needs of French workers and the Roman pontiff. His pilgrimages advanced not only the political agenda of the pope by paying heed to a papacy devoid of its former earthly holdings but also the social teaching of the Catholic Church. The moving crowd of pilgrims focused attention on workers, dramatizing their plight and power, and produced enough emotional energy to convince Leo XIII to write *Rerum Novarum*.

Pilgrimages assumed many forms and had existed since the early days of the Church, and while pilgrimages were part of the cultural texture of Europe, French pilgrimages were distinct from those occurring in other places. Harmel's worker pilgrimages, although fitting neatly in the context of European pilgrimages in general and French pilgrimages in particular, were unique in several ways. The worker pilgrimages served the political ambitions of Leo XIII, altered relations between church and state in France and Italy, and developed the social teaching of the Catholic Church.

The Crowd Returns

The 1870s were years of national healing and reflection. The indemnity owed by France to Germany was paid off ahead of time and military occupation ended. By the end of the decade, the president of the Republic no longer was viewed as a mere understudy for a monarch waiting in the wings but rather as head of state of a people who had decided to caste their collective lot with the republican form of government rather than a monarchical one. There would be no further revolution, peace had returned, and so it looked like a propitious time to reintroduce the normal workings of parliamentary government. The Third Republic in 1880 permitted exiled Communards to return to France, and in 1881 significantly diminished press censorship for newspapers, commentaries, and placards and legalized public meetings and electoral meetings that had been suppressed during the previous decade. By 1884 unions were legalized provided that they registered with the government, that their activities remained nonpolitical, and that religious organizations be divorced from the *syndicat*.[2] In short, the crowd was allowed to return.

Strikes, anarchist terrorism, and demonstrations became part of the French political scene in the remaining years before World War I, reaching their apogee in the early 1890s. Political life revolved around not only events taking place in the Senate and the Chamber of Deputies, or the latest election, but also around what was going on in the streets. The crowd, for example, was quick to respond to the notorious scandals of the Third Republic—the Boulanger, Dreyfus, and Panama Affairs—and thereby added to the instability of the government.[3]

The "science of mass behavior" proved irresistible, and it was studied and dissected by numerous crowd psychologists, Gustave Le Bon being the most prominent.[4] Most crowd psychologists focused on *la foule*,[5] the violent, boisterous, lower-class band depicted so powerfully in Zola's *Germinal*. They did so with good reason. Between 1871 and 1879 (the quiet years), for example, there were on average 80.4 strikes throughout France each year, according to Michelle Perrot.[6] But afterward, the pace quickened. During the 1880s, there was an average of 186.5 strikes per year, and between 1890 and 1894, an average of 378.8. The nineteenth-century record in a given year was set in 1893 when there were 634 strikes.[7] There were other venues that attracted crowds after 1870 in response to the national crisis; pilgrimages, the so-called peaceful assemblies, also were on the rise.

Pilgrimage

Simply stated, pilgrimages are journeys to sacred places and public manifestations of piety,[8] but as the seminal study by Victor Turner and Edith Turner has demonstrated, they have had a long history and resonate with meaning.[9] And while sacred ground is usually thought of as religious in origin, modern usage of the term has complicated things somewhat because it has been applied to national memorials, such as cemeteries and war monuments, which have proliferated in the Western world as a result of the twentieth-century world wars or, as in the case of the Père Lachaise cemetery, revolution at home. A key element that distinguishes a pilgrimage from other journeys is its corporate nature; typically, the pilgrim travels with a moving crowd to the sacred spot to petition or to give thanks, although it is not absolutely necessary to be part of an assembly because, for Roman Catholics, the pilgrim, whether alone or in a group, is a member of the Communion of Saints. The corporate nature of the journey is crucial, because it represents the Mystical Body, a corporate body with its Communion of Saints, and a spiritual solidarity among the saints in heaven, the suffering souls in purgatory, and the living Church members on earth. Continued membership in the Communion of Saints is assured by faith, submission to ecclesiastical rule, and good works. Pilgrimage is considered by Catholics a good work, and as such, it is capable of benefiting not only the pilgrim but also his family members, whether living or dead. Corporal good works cleanse the soul of sin and include, besides pilgrimage, alms giving and visiting the sick. Protestants, less reliant on interaction with coreligionists for personal salvation, rejected pilgrimage and its attendant spiritual benefits, and as a result, pilgrimage has not been a Protestant practice.[10]

But while a decidedly Catholic ritual, the Church has not always been enthusiastic about pilgrimages. Pilgrimage, after all, is a popular vehicle, and thus the clergy cannot be assured of controlling either the crowds or the doctrine motivating the pilgrimage. It is an event that is outside of routine Church life, neither ecclesiastic nor laic in nature but organically spiritual. That pilgrims typically travel in groups only serves to multiply their power and cause concern.[11] The Council of Trent, for example, newly sensitized about the traffic in relics and pardon from sin, worried about continuing the practice of pilgrimage.[12] Official procedure requires that the local bishop legitimate the pilgrimage, but rarely has the Church interfered with popular determination to visit a site regarded as holy, and furthermore, it has been quite adept at incorporating popular religion into official orthodoxy.[13] For example, Pius IX declared the doctrine of the Immaculate Conception in 1854 in the midst of a resurgence of popular Marian devotion that rivaled only that of the Middle Ages.

France became particularly suitable for pilgrimage sites in the nineteenth and twentieth centuries as a direct result of national woes. The peak years for national pilgrimages were 1871 to 1874, quite obviously a response to the disasters of 1870 and 1871,[14] but from midcentury on France led all of Europe in the practice of pilgrimage, particularly to Our Lady.[15] Recall that it was during the 1873 pilgrimage to Notre Dame de Liesse that Léon Harmel first encountered Albert de Mun and René de La Tour du Pin.

The French Revolution, with its assault on the Roman Church, did not encourage pilgrimage, and Napoléon I forbade it during his reign, but post-Napoléonic France experienced a resurgence.[16] Marian apparitions were an expression of millenarianism, the notion that the world was spinning toward disaster if mankind remained unrepentant, as certainly seemed the case beginning with Napoléon I's defeat. The Revolutions of 1830, 1848, and 1871 spoke to political turmoil and class warfare, defeat at the hands of the Germans in 1870 confirmed military inferiority, and the industrial revolution exposed capitalist rapaciousness in the face of phenomenal human suffering. In short, economic and political stress exposed moral weakness and resulted in an increased number of Marian apparitions and pilgrimages. Between 1830 and 1933, the Blessed Virgin appeared five times in France, once in Ireland, once in Portugal, and twice in Belgium. Unlike the earlier, medieval apparitions, in which the Virgin usually instructed the seer to build a shrine in her honor, the nineteenth-century Virgin warned of catastrophe if mankind did not mend its ways.[17] The nineteenth-century French national pilgrimages were a response to the Virgin's warnings.

The Worker Pilgrimages to Rome

From their onset, the worker pilgrimages differed markedly from the other nineteenth- and twentieth-century French pilgrimages. They were extensions of the labor movement and thus political in nature. Yet by cultivating the spiritual life of the worker, they were in keeping with other pilgrimages.[18] The French worker pilgrimages to Rome began in 1885 and continued with some regularity, except for the 1891–1897 period, into the twentieth century. Initiated by Harmel and led by Harmel,

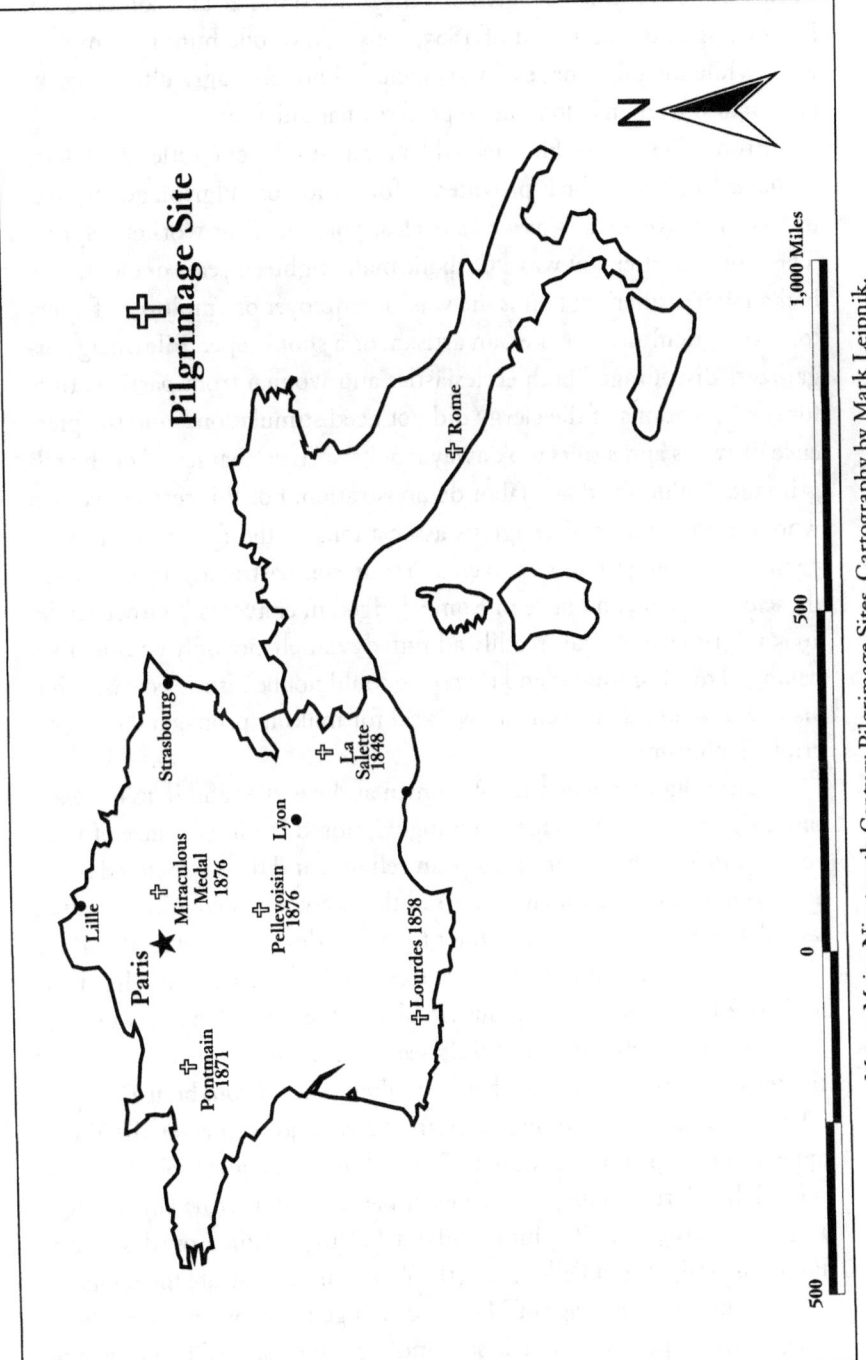

Map 2. Major Nineteenth-Century Pilgrimage Sites. Cartography by Mark Leipnik.

de Mun, and Cardinal Langénieux, they varied in size and composition. For example, the first, that of 1885, consisted of one hundred employers,[19] while the pilgrimage of 1905 included not only agricultural workers but also women belonging to professional unions.[20]

From 1888 to 1905 Harmel published a newsletter entitled *La France du travail à Rome,* which provided information on pilgrimage requirements and travel details, as well as a clear portrait of the worker-pilgrim. The typical participant was a Catholic male, eighteen years or older, who had a labor affiliation; that is, he was an employer or employee of a factory, an agricultural worker, an artisan, or a shopkeeper. Pilgrimage organizers discouraged both ecclesiastics and women from participating, for the "devotions of the clergy did not need stimulation," and the presence of wives and sisters took away from the "true character" of the pilgrimage that doubled as a labor demonstration. For this reason, women who were members of religious associations in the factories and who persisted in going to Rome traveled in train compartments separate from those of the men, and once in Rome, lodged in convents.[21] However, by 1905 pilgrimage officials readily admitted women, not only because they belonged to labor unions and therefore could not be dismissed easily, but also because of "their well-known zeal for making propaganda and recruiting pilgrims."[22]

Discouraging attendance of women at the earlier and in many ways more significant pilgrimages seemingly ignored the importance of their role in nineteenth-century European religion and their expanded social role. While European men immersed themselves in a cognitive, secular world, the women maintained their faith and those who could afford the time continued to support the organizational Church and its charitable and educational work. Religious ritual was the stronghold of women,[23] and the number of female and child seers of Marian apparitions reflected the feminization of religion that had taken place throughout Europe.[24] The seers were usually young unmarried girls, and even when the Virgin appeared to a group of children of mixed gender, a girl typically transmitted the Marian message.[25] The examples of Fatima (1917) in Portugal, Beauraing (1932) in Belgium, and La Salette (1846), Lourdes (1858), Pontmain (1871), and Pellevoisin (1876) in France illustrate the point.[26]

In addition, the image of Mary had changed. No longer the medieval Virgin who appeared to a male seer and carried no special message other than to be remembered, the modern Virgin acted independently of her Son and carried a frightening, apocalyptic, and often secret message that spelled doom for an unrepentant world.[27] In her autonomy, strength, and popularity, Mary was a potent rival to the emblematic symbol of republican France, Marianne.[28]

Not only was the modern Virgin of apparition a more commanding figure, if for no other reason than the seriousness of her mission, and the female seers and communicators given a more responsible role than earlier counterparts, but the principal pilgrimage participants were now women.[29] As Paul Seeley observes, with the possible exception of French aristocrats, "cognitively developed Catholic men had no need for visual enchantment, emotional charge, or imaginative flights."[30] Harmel's worker pilgrimages, therefore, were an anomaly: he actively recruited men and discouraged women.

The Eternal City

It was not by chance that Harmel led his pilgrims to Rome, bastion of male secular and ecclesiastical power. No sacred spring, no holy mud, no Delphic oracle to interpret life's travails, still Rome was considered a premier pilgrimage site from the early days of the Church and, like all sacred ground, a place of revelation.[31] It was a "prototypical" pilgrimage place because it was the geographic and spiritual center of one of the great religions of the world and contained shrines and relics of the founders. As such, Rome joined Jerusalem (Judaism, Christianity, Islam), Mecca (Islam), Benares and Mount Kailas (Hinduism), and Kandy (Buddhism) in that august category,[32] and the Eternal City accommodated a whole complex of sacred shrines.

The first Marian shrine in Europe was built in Rome in about 350. Santa Maria Maggiore, one of the four main basilicas in Rome, honored Mary as protectress of the city and was the special reserve of the patriarch of Antioch. The other three major basilicas were St. John Lateran, the venue for the patriarch of the West, or pope; St. Peter's, reserved for the patriarch of Constantinople; and St. Paul-outside-the-Walls, the basilica of the patriarch of Alexandria.[33] Catholic archbishops and bishops were required to visit Rome at specified intervals (once every five years for Europeans and once every ten years for those coming from greater distances) to give the Roman pontiff, as head of the institutional Church, a report on the spiritual, intellectual, social, economic, and political happenings in their dioceses. This custom was called *ad limina* (to the thresholds of the apostles), and required the episcopacy to not only visit the tombs of St. Peter and St. Paul, but pay their respects and give their report to the current representative of the Church, the pope.[34] Thus bishops were required to make periodic pilgrimages to Rome as part of their jobs, and they, along with other pilgrims, were expected to visit the four major basilicas during their Roman pilgrimage experience. Harmel and the French worker-pilgrims customarily visited these basilicas during the course of their Roman pilgrimages.

With the Reformation came diminution of the practice of pilgrimage among Protestant Christians and resurgence of the Roman pilgrimage for Catholics in the aftermath of the Counter-Reformation and Catholic Reformation. The Church triumphant intended to dazzle the world with its power and majesty. Its grandiose baroque basilica, the new St. Peter's, became the central gathering point for pilgrims, with Bernini's colonnades enclosing the vast piazza eagerly embracing them. The Church encouraged pilgrims to visit the papal capital by announcing Jubilee Years of celebration, which always concluded with Mass at St. Peter's. In 1575, 400,000 pilgrims flocked to Rome; in 1600, 500,000 visited the Eternal City, putting stress on housing and other facilities in a city that normally accommodated 100,000.[35] Leo XIII called seven Jubilee Years, with that of 1893, marking his fifteenth year as pope, being the most solemn.[36]

Jubilee Years provided the pope with the opportunity to award plenary indulgences to pilgrims, a practice that began with Urban II, who granted plenary indulgences to Crusaders going off to the Holy Land in 1095. An indulgence removed temporal, purgatorial punishment for sin, and a plenary indulgence removed all and not merely part of the punishment. Beginning in 1300, Boniface VIII, recognizing that pilgrims could no longer travel to Jerusalem to receive plenary indulgences, began the custom of granting them to pilgrims visiting Rome, the new Jerusalem and spiritual center for Christians. Rome henceforward became the premier pilgrimage site for receiving plenary indulgences, and the principal occasion on which to receive them was the Jubilee Year.[37] In order for pilgrims to receive a plenary indulgence, it was necessary to visit all four of the major Roman basilicas.[38]

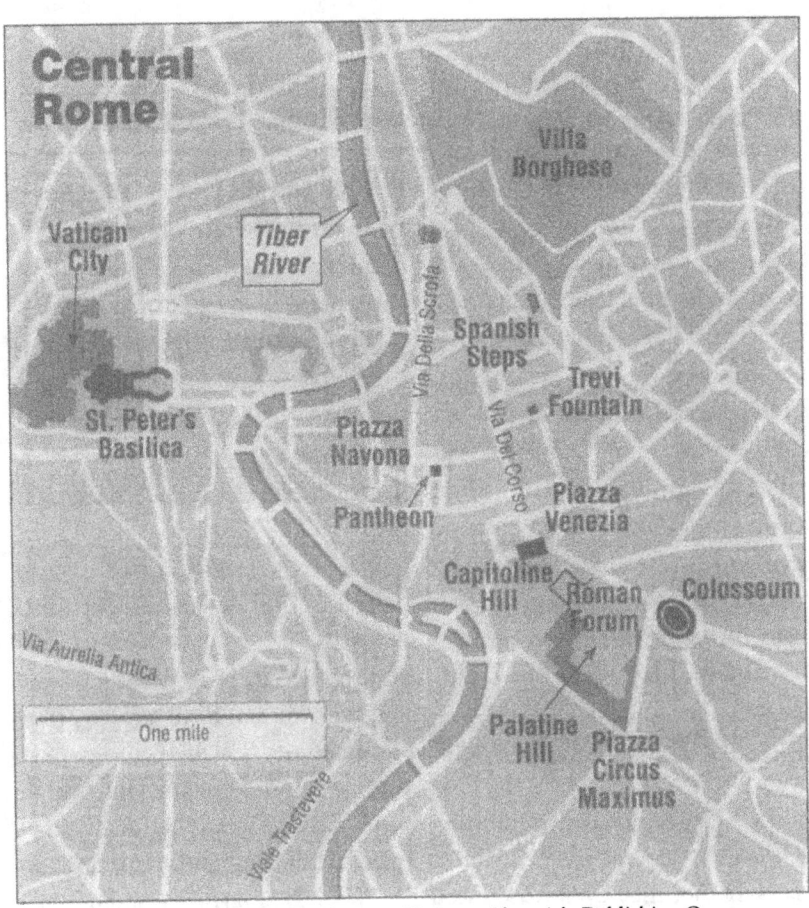

Map 3. Central Rome. Copyright 2002 Houston Chronicle Publishing Company. Reprinted with permission. All rights reserved.

The Journey

Léon Harmel initially had little trouble finding French workers to go on his pilgrimages to Rome. After all, pilgrimages were not only an occasion to spiritually walk the way of the Cross and thereby cleanse oneself of sin but also an opportunity to play the tourist. Like tourism in general, pilgrimages entailed considerable outside activity, and thus to ensure maximum comfort and enjoyment, they were planned for the most pleasant seasons of the year, spring, summer, and fall.[39] The worker pilgrimages, for example, typically took place in late summer or fall of the year. Pilgrimages also traditionally included a festive element, and the nineteenth- and twentieth-century pilgrimages were no different from the earlier ones. As Weber points out, before tourism became an active sport, there was pilgrimage to stimulate the senses with "adventure, therapy, and trade."[40] The Church, finding the mix of sacred and profane troublesome, had attempted to draw the line between pilgrimage and tourism, but it discovered the task was nearly impossible, especially since a person could arrive a tourist and depart a pilgrim, for sacred sites often have a transforming effect.[41]

Those pilgrimage sites that included sacred, healing springs surpassed in popularity the thermal springs that were, and still are, so prevalent throughout Europe. Lourdes, for example, became more popular than Vichy, especially for the lower middle class and women who might not otherwise travel.[42] Interestingly, the Harmel family annually "took the waters" at Vichy, usually during the month of May, but records do not say whether they ever visited Lourdes. That the Harmel women joined their men on the Vichy vacations and traveled to Vichy, as did Alexandrine Tranchart Harmel, Léon's mother, rather than Lourdes in times of illness signified a certain class: they were members of the middle to upper bourgeoisie.[43] Jacques-Joseph, Léon's father, did the same. Father and son stopped off in Vichy on their way home from Rome in 1860 to allow thermalism to work its wonders on the ailing Jacques-Joseph.[44]

The organizing of Harmel's worker pilgrimages began with the religious associations at the factories under the aegis of L'Oeuvre des Cercles Catholiques d'Ouvriers, progressed to the dioceses, and eventually reached the national level. Not everyone who wanted to participate in the pilgrimages could do so; therefore, lotteries, at one franc a chance, determined the list of pilgrims.[45] Workers looked forward to a holiday from factory routine, and railroad travel made the pilgrimage journey considerably easier than in the past.

Though traditionally pilgrims traveled to their holy destinations on foot, the nineteenth century introduced the railroad as the most efficient mode of travel for workers who needed to return to jobs in a reasonable time (in the case of the worker pilgrimages, about five days), and thus the French workers assembled at locations throughout France serviced by trains. During the first worker pilgrimage to Rome in 1885, for example, pilgrims boarded trains from such diverse parts as French Flanders, Picardy, Lorraine, Champagne, the Ardennes, Normandy, Forez, Lemousin, and Provence.[46] For travelers without a pilgrimage discount, train fares were high by today's standards, somewhat the equivalent of air travel in the contemporary world, and remained remarkably stable during the fifty years before 1914. For example, a nondiscounted one-way first-class ticket from Paris to Vichy cost 40.20 francs in 1864 and 40.90 francs in 1914. There was a bit of leeway in third-class fares, however: 22.55 francs in 1864 but 18.0 francs in 1914.[47] With a pilgrimage discount, the fare from Reims to Rome for the 1891 worker pilgrimage was 135 francs,[48] and the average daily expenditure for the worker while on pilgrimage was 20 francs.[49]

When on pilgrimage to Rome, Harmel and the other *patrons* initiated new rules of social conduct and customarily traveled in third class with the workers, while Cardinal Langénieux and de Mun booked seats in first class. But by the time the worker pilgrimages started in the last quarter of the nineteenth century, the French pilgrims, whether traveling in first or third class, were able to benefit from the special trains and fares offered by the railroads to capitalize on the booming tourist industry. To capture the pilgrimage market in the opening years of the twentieth century, special trains brought 300,000 to 400,000 pilgrims to Lourdes each year,[50] a clear indication of the lucrative business attendant to pilgrimages. Railroad travel allowed the middle and lower classes to imitate the upper classes and engage in a common leisure activity, at least while on pilgrimage.[51] Railroads also brought about a decline in visitation to remote pilgrimage sites not serviced by trains. But once the automobile became fairly commonplace, many tucked-away medieval pilgrimage sites experienced revivification.[52]

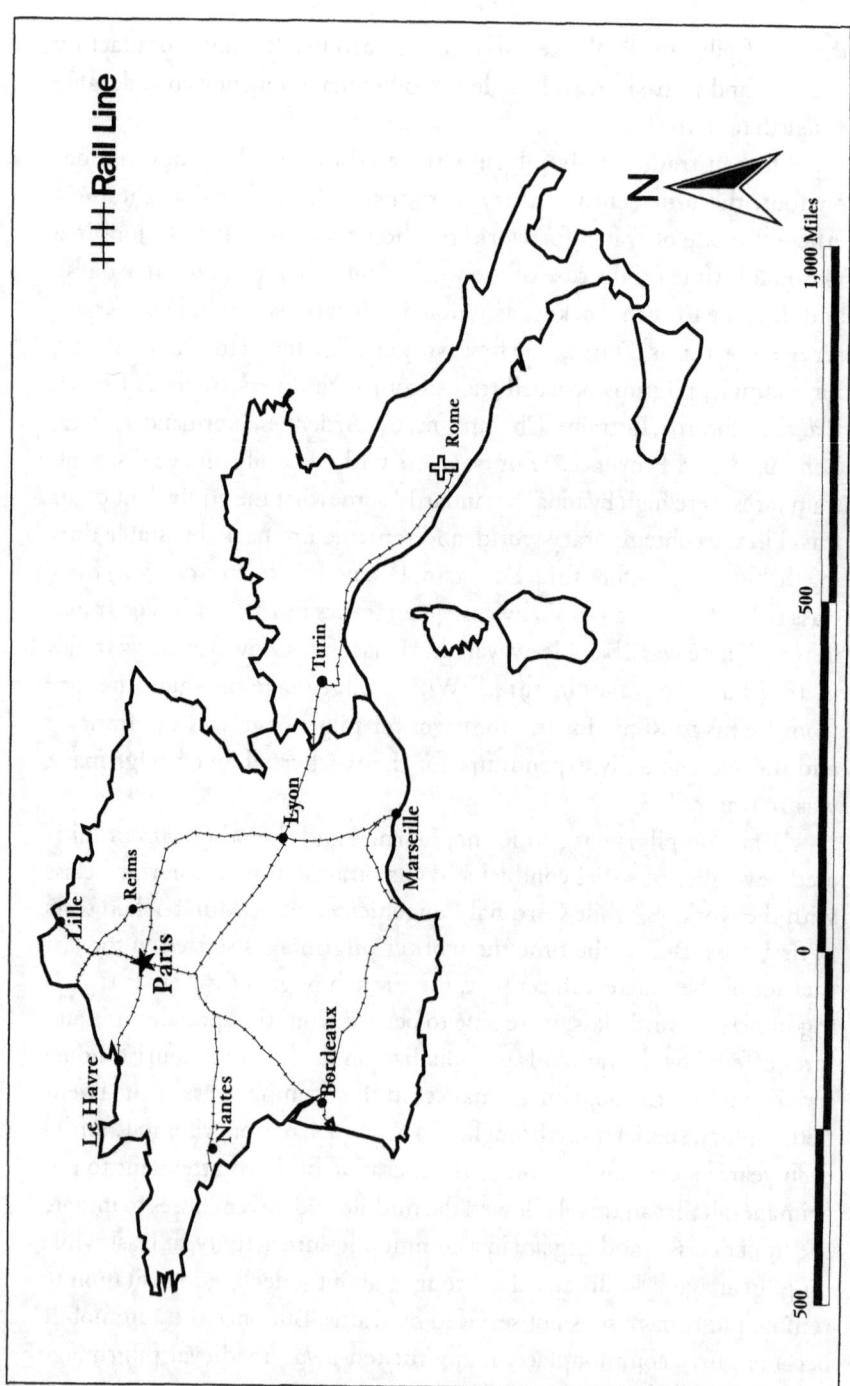

Map 4. Pilgrimage Routes to Rome. Cartography by Mark Leipnik.

Details such as providing an adequate number of trains and planning the spacing of the departures and arrivals of the French workers concerned both the French and the Italian governments.[53] The Church, wanting to encourage pilgrimage along with the states, scheduled special Masses and services in the main basilicas and went out of its way to assure maximum comfort for the French pilgrims. Once in Rome the men were housed in seminaries, as close as possible to the Vatican at the request of the pope, and ate two meals a day in refectories. There also were rooms where the workers could smoke, take refreshments, play music, and plan the next outing to a church or historical site.[54] The red carpet was rolled out for Harmel and his French workers for a reason.

Pilgrimage Goals

The goals of Harmel's pilgrimages were numerous. Clearly the pilgrimages intended to call papal attention to the plight of workingmen, if not always women. They also promised a reconciliation between the laboring and managerial classes by the rekindling of Christian charity that resulted from shared travel and, especially, from the religious benefits associated with pilgrimages. Papal masses and audiences, replete with special blessings, medals, and indulgences, guaranteed spiritual rewards for the participants.

But the pilgrimages also represented more mundane goals. These mass demonstrations, involving thousands of representatives from labor, at once replicated and countered the other mass demonstrations of the era, such as strikes and May Day parades. The crowd had been unleashed. Strikes were on the rise, notably from 1885 to 1891,[55] the very years the most important of the worker pilgrimages took place. Likewise, May 1, 1890, was the occasion of the first May Day demonstration. The crowd concerned French government officials and financiers to the extent that they closed the principal financial establishments in Paris—the Bourse du Travail, the Stock Exchange, the Banque de France, the Maison Rothschild, and Crédit Lyonnais. Important government buildings remained opened but were placed under heavy guard. And the demonstrations went beyond the capital city; sizable marches occurred in Marseille, Lille, Toulon, Lyon, Bordeaux, Calais, Saint-Quentin, Roubaix, Angers, and Vienne. The May Day demonstrations of 1890 were, apart from the occasional scuffle with police, peaceful, but violence and death blackened May Day 1891, just weeks before the publication of *Rerum Novarum*. The incident occurred at Fourmies, near the Belgian border, and it left nine dead and eighty wounded.[56] The worker-pilgrims traveled to Rome, then, in the midst of heightened social tension in the streets of France.

As public events, strikes and May Day parades necessarily carried with them political overtones. For those in French society who abhorred the violence and class division attributed to revolutionary socialism and anarchism, Harmel's worker pilgrimages became a novel and powerful means to express an alternate view. An expanding newspaper readership and electorate encouraged the creation of a public image for every cause that might have political repercussions. The pilgrimages became a major media event, alongside strikes and May Day demonstrations, and were duly reported in the press. The newspapers published papal and pilgrim addresses, as well as the daily comings and goings of the French visitors to Rome. Léon Harmel intended to use the publicity to his advantage. On the occasion of the 1889 pilgrimage, for example, he expressed the hope that the pilgrimage would enhance the public image of the pope and thereby turn public opinion, the "sole power in our nations without principles," to the papal cause.[57] Though remaining obscure in its exact program, documents mentioning the "cause" consistently pointed in the direction of the pope's political ambitions.[58] The pope considered the worker pilgrimages useful and in accord with his political agenda.[59]

The Pilgrimage of 1885

In autumn 1884 Harmel sent out eight hundred circulars advertising the 1885 pilgrimage to the Catholic *patronat* of France. He simultaneously began an active correspondence with the Vatican to arrange a papal audience, scheduled religious ceremonies, and gathered maps and guides for the Roman sojourn.[60] This initial worker pilgrimage was restricted to French employers who spoke on behalf of their employees.

The one hundred *patrons* who gathered in Rome in 1885 represented every region of France; for instance, Monsieur Dutilleul came from the north, Monsieur Mennesson from the east, Monsieur Nheyrand from the center, and Monsieur Fournier from the south. The organizing committee comprised the Messieurs André, Chagot, Blanzy, Féron-Vrau, Thiollière, and Harmel. This inaugural meeting between the papal entourage and their French visitors was somewhat awkward as cardinals and Roman nobles were unaccustomed to socializing with factory owners.[61] It did not help matters that Leo XIII spoke little, but reportedly he nevertheless absorbed much.[62] The first of three papal audiences took place on February 23,[63] and during it and the two subsequent audiences, the pope expressed an interest in learning about the world of factories and workshops.[64] The *patrons* brought with them an address, signed by one thousand French employers, which said, in part, that "the Church alone can reestablish in the industrial family the practice of justice and charity."[65] They were in essence asking Leo to become directly involved in their effort to better conditions for the laboring masses. The pope advised them to "resuscitate the wise institutions of the past" and urged them to return to Rome, but the next time, to bring workers.[66] He clearly was interested in pursuing the dialogue. Apart from the Catholic press, French newspapers virtually ignored the event, except for *Cri du peuple*. This socialist Parisian daily noted that Léon Harmel, "the apostle of the factory," promoted the visit to Rome but dismissed the 1885 pilgrimage "with a scornful laugh," since it was held to discuss the labor situation and its only representatives were from management.[67] That criticism was no longer valid once the 1887 pilgrimage was under way.

The Pilgrimage of 1887

The 1887 pilgrimage led by Harmel consisted of one hundred industrialists, three hundred clergy, and fourteen hundred workers.[68] Three trains, taking about sixty hours to reach Rome, transported the pilgrims. On the way, they stopped briefly in Turin, where they were greeted by Dom Bosco, the old saint who pioneered technical education for young Italian workers.[69] And once in the Eternal City, the French ambassador, the Comte Lefèbvre de Béhaine, invited the pilgrimage leaders, Cardinal Langénieux, Albert de Mun, and Léon Harmel, to dinner.[70]

While traveling to Rome, Langénieux and de Mun typically distanced themselves from associating directly with the workers, while Harmel preferred riding whenever possible in the third-class section with his beloved workers. Still, there is no doubt that their presence and interest helped to put the pilgrimages in the French national spotlight. Harmel, not quite the dignitary and a lesser-known commodity than the cardinal from Reims and the deputy who was the chief spokesman for the social Catholics in the Chamber of Deputies, stood at the back of St. Peter's on October 16 as de Mun presented the workers to the pope and Langénieux delivered the opening address before the assembled. Yet this capitalist, with the rotund outlines of a well-fed bourgeois and a metallic speaking voice, enjoyed a certain confidence because Leo XIII "approved and encouraged his work."[71]

The French pilgrims attended four papal audiences while in Rome,[72] the first of which was on October 16. And as would become customary, Harmel stood at the side of the pope and introduced the workers to him.[73] During his formal address, Cardinal Langénieux asked the pope to bless their endeavors on behalf of the workers of France who hoped for dignified lives for themselves and their families. Leo responded, in fluent French, to the pleas of the visitors by reminding them that the Church had always been concerned with the worker and his problems.[74] He endorsed their goals and talked of the necessity for state intervention in order to assure the workers a life of morality, justice, and human dignity. Personal interaction with the French workers encouraged the pope to become more intimately involved in the Social Question.[75] Each pilgrim saw Leo XIII at one of the papal audiences and received a medal from him.[76]

The significance of the 1887 pilgrimage was twofold: it was the first pilgrimage attended by workers, and it served as the occasion for Leo XIII to endorse qualified state intervention in industrial life. The novelty of workers going on pilgrimage with their bosses and receiving VIP treatment from the Vatican was quite a newsworthy event, for it had just the right dose of the sensational to catch the notice of the general public. Not only did employers and employees share third-class compartments on the trains, but the Vatican granted special allowances for attire. Leo XIII granted permission to male workers to forgo the customary formal dress for papal audiences and instead appear "en blouse," or in overalls.[77] Women in attendance, however, remained bound by the traditional dress code that stipulated a black silk or wool dress and a veil to cover the head,[78] which no doubt meant that female pilgrims were family members of the *patrons* rather than *ouvrières*, who would have been hard pressed to come up with such a distinctive and costly outfit. As to state intervention, the pope saw the involvement of government as an "indispensable necessity," and when doing so in "just measure, it carrie[d] out a work of societal salvation."[79] In the words of Harmel, who received this official directive with the "docility of a child," the state thereby received papal license to intervene in the workplace to "protect and safeguard the true interests of its dependent citizens."[80]

Newspaper coverage was more extensive, going beyond the religious press and the occasional dismissive remark by the radical press to penetrate the more centrist Parisian dailies. Newspapers noted the important shift in the Church's social teaching.[81] In a not so subtle manner, the pope moved the Church away from the "hands-off" policy of liberalism and on to turf typically associated with nineteenth-century socialism. Those papers representing the right and center of the political spectrum reported the news in a straightforward fashion, hinting at times of a papal nod in the direction of socialism. The left, caustic and skeptical in its commentary, acknowledged that early in its history the Church experimented with socialism but that after several centuries power and wealth became concentrated in papal hands. The only solution the contemporary Church offered the workers was the Christian corporation, something, according to the left, to which the workers would never be drawn. Furthermore, those who participated in the pilgrimage were only "occasional" workers who no doubt were enticed in part by the reduced railroad fares.[82]

La Croix, the chief vehicle of the religious press,[83] without naming names, alluded to accolades received by the papal address in the foreign press and reported that the pope received congratulatory messages saluting his solicitude on behalf of the workers from certain foreign governments.[84] France's representative to the Vatican, the Comte Lefèbvre de Béhaine, invited Harmel, de Mun, and Langénieux to dinner in a show of cooperation if not outright support between church and state for the Roman pilgrimages, while Leo XIII repeatedly declared his affection for France, its glorious role in Church history and in civilization. Indeed, it appeared in fall 1887 that papal fortunes were on the rise in continental governmental circles, including republican France.

Even the Italian public seemed enthralled with the French visitors. Romans invited them to a concert near the Forum of Trajan and in other ways welcomed them as their presence helped to boost the sagging local economy. The striking cab drivers of Rome, for example, gave Harmel the title "honorary driver" after observing his splendid rapport with the French workers. No wonder that the next pilgrimage to Rome attracted more workers and warranted greater press coverage—and encouraged hopes for the realization of social and political dreams held by pilgrimage leaders and the papacy.

The Pilgrimage of 1889

Since Leo XIII requested at his farewell meeting with Harmel in 1887 to see even greater numbers of workers assemble in Rome, Harmel had his work cut out for him, but nevertheless he promised the pope ten thousand workers. And in his usual energetic fashion, he promptly got to work. By the end of November 1888, he had mailed over more than two hundred thousand circulars, with his recruitment campaign focused on dioceses throughout France. The religious press, as well as some of the papers oriented toward the right, aided him by advertising the papal invitation to join in the pilgrimage of 1889. Along with the major papers of the religious press, such as *La Croix* and *L'Univers, Les Semaines religieuses,* the diocesan newspaper that penetrated the large cities as well as the small towns, became one of the principal agents of dissemination.[85] The pilgrimage was presented as "an enterprise of atonement."[86] During Lent, Harmel crisscrossed France doing a bit of campaigning himself and used the slogan of dubious rhythmic value, "Pagan Rome, Christian Rome, the Pope Imprisoned," to drum up business.[87] The Patrons du Nord met, and Monsieur Cheneslong gave an impassioned speech advocating the "sovereign independence of the papacy," for that "safeguarded the liberty of the world." The assembled agreed and sent Leo XIII assurances of their complete "filial attachment."[88]

Harmel twice visited Rome in advance of the pilgrimage to work out the myriad details that needed attention for so large a group. One of the most critical tasks was to find adequate housing, and thus he devoted considerable time on both his April 1888 visit and his January 1889 visit to looking into lodging; contemporary Rome was geared for 2,500 visitors, not 10,000. Cost of room and board would be a factor for the workers, of course, and so, along with lotteries, French seminaries and schools began a campaign to raise funds for the worker-pilgrims. Still, it would not be easy for workers to come up with the 115 francs needed for five days in Rome.[89] This led to the socialist charge that Harmel's pilgrims were not bona fide workers, and although the claim was disputed vigorously by boosters of the pilgrimages, extant records disclose neither how many of the workers received subsidies to defray their travel expenses nor the socioeconomic profile of the participants. But Harmel successfully assembled 10,000 pilgrims to journey to Rome in 1889, all of them claiming a labor affiliation, despite the fact that there was competition for their time and money: France was celebrating its centennial with an exposition and national elections.[90]

Ten thousand workers, representing all industries, necessitated a total of seventeen trains moving back and forth between serviceable sections of France and Rome for more than a month.[91] As had become customary from the time of the previous pilgrimage, the route was lined with Italians who welcomed their French visitors to Italy. Signor Scolastri, president of the Italian railroad syndicate, was also on hand. His practice of greeting the worker-pilgrims from France began in 1887 and continued for the next twenty years,[92] and was indicative of the fanfare and novelty attached to mostly male workers on pilgrimage, as well as an endorsement and tribute to the pilgrimages as labor demonstrations.

Because there had been train delays along the way, the travelers arrived in Rome exhausted from their journey but eager to see the sites. They were welcomed, perhaps somewhat disingenuously, by merchants who were more than eager to sell them rosaries and other religious souvenirs. The drivers of Rome took Harmel out to lunch and said wistfully, "If only our Roman princes devoted themselves to popular causes[,] . . . how much better things would go."[93]

A solemn papal Mass celebrated at eight o'clock on the morning of October 20 marked the official opening of the pilgrimage, at which time Cardinal Langénieux thanked the pope for his support of the workers.[94] Leo XIII remained with the French workers until one o'clock in the afternoon but read his address instead of delivering it, leading observers to comment on the frail pope's physical health.[95] And on this pilgrimage, in stark contrast to the rather stilted atmosphere of the 1885 pilgrimage, Italian notables and French bishops made the rounds of the workers' tables at the evening meal. Harmel had an eye for every detail, and in addition to looking over the next day's schedule, at the end of each day he dictated letters, sent off telegrams, and issued press releases.[96]

In gratitude for the enormous time and energy he expended on the pilgrimage, Leo XIII granted Harmel and his family (Harmel's son Felix was a big help to him)[97] a personal audience on November 3 and warmly thanked Harmel for all his work, which the pope admitted he followed closely. Then the pope went on to say, alluding to the current temporal status of the papacy, that in the unhappy circumstances in which he presently found himself, with his liberty jeopardized, he was pleased to see so many workers who, having the vote, would enable the "good cause" to triumph.[98]

The pilgrimage yielded four additional papal audiences.[99] St. Peter's basilica could not accommodate all of the pilgrims at one time, so 2,500 to 3,000 gathered at each of the papal audiences, with the remaining pilgrims attending religious services at one of the other major basilicas in Rome. At St. Peter's, Leo had his papal throne centrally placed in order that he might be surrounded by workers. The workers reportedly were "transformed" by the opportunity to be so close to the pope,[100] which would be in keeping with the spiritual purpose of the pilgrimage.

During the five audiences, Leo XIII talked of labor as a natural condition, and said that man, by accepting work with "courage," brought dignity to that work. He also spoke of the family of man as bound together through religion yet inherently unequal. Thus, he maintained, its need for charity to create social ties amid the "inevitable inequality of the human condition." The coming together of the classes was best realized, according to the pope, in the Christian corporation, an institution that responded to the spiritual and material needs of the workers. Harmel's factory at Val-des-Bois, of course, was the perfect example of the type of factory the pope had in mind. But for factories to be converted successfully into Christian corporations, employers had to "[h]ave a heart for those who earn bread by the sweat of their brow, [to] curtail their insatiable desires for riches, [and to] guarantee the interests of the laboring classes . . . by protecting the young, the weak, the domestic mission of women, and Sunday as a day of rest."[101] By so doing, the employer would be considering his employee "as a brother," thereby softening, within possible limits, the inevitable inequalities. That brotherhood held responsibilities for the worker too. The pope exhorted the French workers always to show respect for their employers by the quality of their work and by abstaining from all acts that disturbed societal order and tranquillity.[102] He also repeated a now-familiar admonition. The workers were asked to find consolation in religion, for it would see them through trials and tribulations; the Christianization of society would solve the Social Question.[103] The distinction between social Catholicism and revolutionary socialism was defined clearly: while the pope was prepared to nudge the Church away from laissez-faire capitalism by condoning state intervention on behalf of the workers, he wanted no part of class warfare or abandonment of religion. Leo's words were transmitted to the French public through the prism of the press and consequently received various interpretations.

Papal pronouncements naturally prompted retorts from some of the French socialist press. *La Lanterne,* the most vitriolic, scolded Leo XIII for ignoring the fruits of 1789. In its view, the pope wanted the workers to submit to the managing classes who would, in turn, yield to the wishes of the Church. This scheme meant the workers remained without rights, weakened by ignorance, and resigned to their lot.[104] *L'Intransigeant* focused its commentary on the French workers themselves. How strange were these pilgrims who made up such a small portion of the proletariat and yet claimed to speak for all workers. Stranger still that they directed their pleas to someone who had no influence in the debate between capital and labor, for "all the encyclicals in the world won't change a thing."[105] Most of the socialist press, however, merely reported the daily comings and goings of the pilgrims, reserving their editorial columns for other matters.

The same was true for the republican press. *Le Temps* and *Le Voltaire,* for example, gave detailed and frequently front-page coverage to the pilgrimage but with little commentary. Yet *L'Estafette* described the pope's message as "socialist" but of a type that looked to the past for inspiration, that is, to the Christian corporation.[106]

Not surprisingly, the religious press extolled and detailed the events of the 1889 pilgrimage year. It also countered charges that the pilgrims were not genuine members of the labor force. *L'Univers* quoted from an

Italian newspaper that described the pilgrims as authentic workers with "callused hands and suntanned faces, fatigued from difficult labor."[107] *La Croix* elaborated by saying that the workers of Rome reacted positively to the presence of the French workers. In fact, the cab drivers of Rome scheduled a strike, but because Harmel discussed the matter with them and because they witnessed firsthand the harmony between the French workers and their bosses, they abandoned the plan.

Even the nonreligious press of the right, newspapers such as *Le Figaro*, seemed enthusiastic about Harmel's growing celebrity, the amount of conversation generated by the "famous" worker pilgrimage to Rome, and the well-behaved pilgrims with their "admirable discipline."[108]

Still there were warnings in 1889 of future troubles. *La Riforma,* the organ (it cost him 100,000 lire a year) of Francesco Crispi, Liberal prime minister of the Italian government,[109] complained that the worker pilgrimage was an affront against the Italian state. This Italian newspaper, according to *La Croix,* declared the 1889 pilgrimage a "provocation" by France against Italy, an outrage against its institutions. Because of these sentiments, *La Croix* continued, the French government again dismissed allegations that it sent a congratulatory telegram to Cardinal Langénieux and the pilgrimage committee.[110]

Meanwhile, Italians were asking if all of France had descended on Rome.[111] *Le Monde* reported that the pilgrimage caused tension between the Italians and the French. Police escorted the French workers from the moment they disembarked from the trains through all their visits to holy places and historic sites. These safety measures were necessary, *Le Monde* observed, because the pilgrims came to give homage to the pope, and the Italian government feared the restoration of his temporal power.[112] When members of the French Embassy attended Mass with the pilgrims at St. Peter's and when Gabriel Harmel, son of Léon, lingered in Rome after the official end of the pilgrimage to consult the Vatican Archives on the subject of the temporal power of the pope, Italian fears seemed justified.[113] In sum, not only were the worker pilgrimages turning glaringly political, but the French government, despite its anticlerical rhetoric, appeared to be an accomplice in papal scheming. Because relations between France and Italy were strained already, in the minds of Italian officials, Harmel's worker pilgrimages were adding fuel to the fire.

Franco-Italian Relations

Francesco Crispi became president of the Italian council and minister of the interior and foreign affairs in 1887. He held these posts until his ouster from his first ministry in January 1891 and reappeared as prime minister off and on until 1893. Democrat and hero of the Risorgimento, he fancied himself an Italian Bismarck.[114] An ardent Italian nationalist, he was suspected of harboring anti-French feelings because of statements such as "France must forget the days of her influence beyond the Alps and recognize that Italy is her equal."[115] But despite claims of nationalists like Crispi, Italy was not yet the equal of France economically or politically. French investors and financiers provided Italy with the wherewithall for building railroads and establishing credit institutions. The era of free trade, inaugurated by the 1860 Cobden-Chevalier Treaty, had a positive ripple effect on commercial relations between France and Italy, at least during the 1860s; France and Italy became active trading partners. After 1870, however, protectionism prevailed, and for the most part, Italy was the loser. The situation worsened during the 1880s, with a resulting trade war that became so intense that the two nations were on the brink of war. The French occupation of Tunis and Italy's joining the Triple Alliance with Germany and Austria sent Franco-Italian relations spiraling downward.[116]

Crispi intended to free Italy from the Gallic grasp that had prevailed culturally and politically since, some would argue, the time of Charles VIII and certainly since the time of Napoléon Bonaparte by forming close ties with Germany. Italian nationalists had never forgiven France for forsaking the Italian cause in 1859 by pulling out of the war against Austria and thereby delaying Italian unification. French worker-pilgrims on Italian soil reopened old wounds.

The Italian people reacted ambivalently to Crispi's pro-German foreign policy, for despite memories of French military and political domination, they had an affinity for the French and their culture.[117] Nevertheless, Crispi backed Germany in 1870 and saw the German colossus as just the right partner for the ongoing struggle with France over hegemony in the Mediterranean.[118]

The result was a marked deterioration of Franco-Italian relations, particularly during Crispi's first ministry. The tariff war had reached its most dangerous point in 1887, and after the signing of the Italo-German military convention in 1888, essentially a reenforcement of the 1882 Triple Alliance, the French saw Crispi as Bismarck's "agent provocateur."[119] The continuation of Italian participation in the Triple Alliance only served as confirmation that French and Italian relations were troubled. In addition, the papacy made no secret of the fact that it did not consider the diminution of its temporal power, as a direct result of events surrounding the Franco-Prussian War of 1870, a fait accompli. As partner in the Triple Alliance, albeit the junior one, Italy had received assurance from alliance members that papal lands would not be restored,[120] and this understanding further strained church-state relations in Italy. Moreover, what to do about the pope and his lost land aggravated the already bad blood between France and Italy.

Not all Italians supported Crispi's rash manner and aggressive foreign policy. The right in particular took exception to his tariff war with France and his excessive dependency on Germany. This led directly to Crispi's fall from power in January 1891 when Marquis Antonio di Rudinì succeeded him as prime minister of Italy. Rudinì possessed a more temperate manner and opted for a policy of détente with France and the Church while simultaneously loosening ties with Germany.[121] Nevertheless, the Triple Alliance remained and was the obvious focal point of French foreign policy in the closing years of the nineteenth century. Of all the opportunities for escaping from the diplomatic Gordian knot, tied so tightly by Bismarck, rapprochement with Russia held the most promise for France, and the papacy, angling for its own place in the sun, decided to try to facilitate the escape. If successful, the Roman Question might, at long last, be resolved in favor of the pope.

The Roman Question

The Roman Question concerned papal lands taken during the nineteenth century first by Napoléon I and after 1860 by Italian nationalists. Legitimacy was on the side of the papacy, but the Italians had the principle of nationalism working in their favor.[122]

After the collapse of the Napoleonic Empire, the Roman Question again began in earnest when the pope, disguised and disgraced, fled Rome for Gaeta in 1848, as Mazzini and other Italian nationalists took over the city and established the Roman Republic. The pope became a refugee from his lands, but since the papal lands were ill managed and rarely the beneficiary of reform, his absence was not missed in 1848 or in 1870 when the French removed their protective troops, allowing Rome once again to come under the control of Italian nationalists. The French, traditional supporters of the papacy in Italy, despite the treatment of the pope by Napoléon I, saw to the reinstatement of the Roman pontiff in Rome on April 12, 1850,[123] but not in 1870.

Events surrounding the Franco-Prussian War of 1870 only exasperated the delicate situation when Italian troops of Victor Emmanuel II marched into Rome on September 20 to take what they considered legally theirs. The action effectively ended the temporal power of the pope and furthered the inclination of Pius IX to centralize the Church organizationally and dogmatically. The calling of the First Vatican Council and the declaration of papal infallibility were direct results. The papal dogma of infallibility displeased enormously European secular leaders who were already agitated over the earlier *Syllabus of Errors*. Indeed, 1870 marked the nadir of European church-state relations.[124] The French, who had occupied the ancient capital since the time of Louis-Napoléon (later Napoléon III) departed Rome in 1870 to wage an all-out though futile effort against the Germans in places like Sedan and Metz. To many, the subsequent arrangement between Italy and the Holy See seemed like a half measure. The Italian state allowed the pope to occupy a portion of the Eternal City, and there was neither a formal concordat nor a return to regalism whereby the Church would submit to the state.[125] The Roman Question lasted until the 1929 Lateran Accord clarified the situation and gave the papacy a morsel of Italian territory within Rome, henceforth known as Vatican City, and with it, geographic independence and, as interpreted by some, greater moral respect. Until 1929, the pope, according to the papal view, was at the mercy of the Italian government.[126]

Italy formalized the rather awkward situation that existed on the Italian peninsula from 1870 to 1929 in the Italian Law of Guarantees of May 1871, which the papacy refused to recognize. It gave the pope rights of extraterritoriality over the palaces of the Vatican, the Lateran, and the summer residence of Castel Gandolfo and immunity against criminal investigation. The pope at the time, Pius IX, rejected financial compensation offered him. He, and subsequent occupants of the papal throne during these troubled years, also refused to recognize the Italian occupation of Rome, forbade Catholics from participating in Italian national politics, and made sure that no ruler of a Catholic country accepted the hospitality of the king of Italy at the Quirinal.[127] There was no official communication between the two sides, although informally there was contact between church and state in Italy, since Catholicism was the state religion and Church appointments were made by the state.[128] Predictable squabbles over religious orders, charitable institutions, public education, and civil marriages continued to disrupt relations throughout these years.[129] Still, despite appearances to the contrary, the papacy hoped ultimately for better relations with Italy.[130] While waiting for that day, the pope became by his own doing, as well as that of the Italian state, the "prisoner of the Vatican."

Responsible for sixty-two formal protests against the Italian usurpation, no pope was as preoccupied with the Roman Question as was Leo XIII.[131] While willing to recognize nationalism elsewhere and as a legitimate principle, he was disinclined to disavow the position of his predecessor, Pius IX, on this matter.[132] With the secularization of Italian society, the Roman pontiff's distress increased, as geographic proximity meant that the papacy and the Italian state had, for better or worse, an "intimate alliance."[133] It was difficult for Leo XIII to accept the loss of papal land and prestige, as well as to witness the removal of religion from everyday Italian life and institutions, and he said so in no uncertain terms in *Etsi Nos,* his encyclical of February 15, 1882, on "conditions in Italy." Therein he objected to

> [r]eligious houses suppressed, the goods of the Church confiscated, marriages contracted in despite of the laws and without the rites of the Church, the position of the religious authorities as to the education of the young utterly ignored—in fine, a cruel and deplorable war without limit and without measure declared against the Apostolic See, a war on account of which the Church is weighed down by inexpressible suffering, and the Roman Pontiff finds himself reduced to exteme anguish. For, despoiled of his Civil Princedom, he has of necessity fallen into the hands of another Power. More than this; Rome, the most august of Christian cities, is now a place laid

open to all the enemies of the Church; profane novelties defile it; here and there, temples and schools devoted to heresy are to be found.

But the pope was not about to capitulate without a fight:

> It is of supreme importance to Christian interests that the Roman Pontiff should be, and should be clearly seen to be, free from all danger, from all vexations, and from all hindrance in the government of the Church, it is necessary, to attain this end, that action be taken, petitions, and every possible means within the limits of the law should be adopted, and that none should rest until We have restored to Us, in reality and not in appearance only, that liberty on which, not only the welfare of the Church, but the prosperity of Italy and the peace of Christian nations depend by a necessary connection.[134]

Papal losses in Italy help to explain Leo's desire to retain the Concordat with the French government. Though the effort ultimately would be as unsuccessful in France as it had been in Italy, he, more than his papal successor, who would actually oversee the dismantling of the agreement between church and state that had lasted from 1802 to 1905, made a valiant attempt. The Concordat provided for a French ambassador to the Holy See, as well as a papal nuncio to France who was accorded the highest honor among the diplomatic corps and led them in official processions.[135] All this might be lost should papal fortunes continue to plummet and the Concordat abrogated. As early as 1884, Leo XIII officially reminded the French state of promises made:

> When, therefore, a solemn public compact has been made between the sacred and the civil power, then it is as much the interest of the State as it is just that the compact should remain inviolate; because, as each power has services to render to the other, a certain and reciprocal advantage is enjoyed and conferred by each.[136]

And the pope fully intended to play the game of give-and-take with France.

Leo XIII knew what the modern world demanded in order for a reversal of fortune to take place. A scholar of some note, he now immersed himself in politics and current events. He observed that the spectacle caught the eye of the press and its male readers, who, newly enfranchised, influenced governments. In this context, the worker pilgrimages indeed might prove useful since they attracted attention, and the attendant publicity would surely keep the Roman Question in the spotlight. He warmed to Harmel's grand gesture and enthusiastically encouraged Harmel to bring workers to Rome for the pilgrimages of 1887, 1889, and 1891. As will become evident shortly, political considerations compelled him to be more reticent in welcoming Harmel's pilgrims to Rome in the years after the 1891 pilgrimage, however.

The pope also studied diplomacy and calculated that, if used adroitly, it could extricate the papacy from the Italian conundrum. Lacking the normal accoutrements of nation-states, such as land and an army, he would be forced to enlist the aid of others. Opportunity looked most promising in France, diplomatically isolated since 1870, but Leo XIII tested German waters too.

Papal Diplomacy

Relations between the Holy See and the German Empire had improved significantly since the 1870s when Bismarck waged war on the Church in Germany. The Kulturkampf had not been politically successful for the Iron Chancellor, and therefore he was ready to make peace with the papacy after a decade of cultural warfare. Leo XIII, assuming the papal throne in 1878, also was interested in fence mending. Diplomatic relations, severed during the tenure of Pius IX, were reestablished, and Bismarckian anticlericalism abated. Leo XIII, an able diplomat, decided to capitalize on the thaw and, with the encouragement of the Catholic royal family in Austria, courted the Germans until the closing years of the 1880s. It is in this context that Emperor William II of Germany decided to visit Rome in 1888. No sovereign had dared to stop in the politically sensitive city since 1870. Instead heads of state played a masquerade of sorts, inviting the king of Italy to visit them at their official homes, or at some neutral site, but avoiding Rome and the Quirinal at all cost. But this German emperor frequently defied convention, and indeed announcement of his planned visit initially caused considerable anxiety to the Italian government, especially when he consented to visit Leo XIII before appearing at a public reception at the Quirinal.[137] The brief diplomatic exchange between William II and the pope, however, did not result in significant change: the Triple Alliance held fast, and papal dreams went unrealized.

Leo XIII, encouraged by Cardinal Rampolla, his Francophile secretary of state as of 1887, courted instead a more realistic prospect for a diplomatic partnership, France. Pursuit of the French lasted from 1887 to the death of Leo in 1903.[138] Papal diplomatic skills would be put to the test, as perhaps nowhere else in Europe were the clashes between propapal and anticlerical elements so intense as in France.[139] The papacy was aided, however, by the outbreak in March 1888 of a bitter tariff war between France and Italy, which precipitated an international crisis. Soon anticlerical Third Republicans and the papacy detected they had a common foe, Italy.[140] To win French favor, the pope decided to play the Russian card. Not only would it impress the French and thereby generate better relations with the Third Republic, but it would weaken Italy and the Triple Alliance should France and Russia move toward an alliance. To this end, Leo XIII conducted secret communications with Alexander III at the end of 1890.[141] Part of the papal strategy consisted of convincing Russia that the studied atheism of the Third Republic was just that, more for public consumption than from deep conviction.[142]

Alexandre Ribot, foreign minister of France, was the real architect of the Franco-Russian thaw, but fate played a role too. Bismarck's retirement from office in 1890 meant that the Reinsurance Treaty between Russia and Germany would not be renewed, and Russia, once again in the diplomatic marriage market, settled on France as the most attractive partner.[143] Initial contacts occurred in summer 1890 between the two war ministries, leading to the military convention of 1892 and ultimately to the alliance of 1894.[144] In spring 1891 relations had warmed to the point that the French fleet visited Kronstadt and the tsar awarded a decoration to President Carnot. France, greatly encouraged, celebrated the end of diplomatic isolation.[145]

In recognition of efforts made by Leo XIII on behalf of the French, Ribot attempted to facilitate a reconciliation between the papacy and the republican government of France. He pleased Leo XIII by moderating the anticlerical legislation of the early 1880s and by working with the Church in appointing higher clergy (see chap. 5) and setting education policy. For example, republican officials routinely looked the other way while religious orders continued to teach in the primary schools and unauthorized religious orders, such as the Jesuits, pursued their ministries until legislation in 1903 curtailed their activities.[146] The papacy benefited in another way too: relations with Russia, severed since the time of Pius IX, as had been the case with Germany, were normalized.[147]

The last of the three great worker pilgrimages, that of 1891, occurred at a time, then, when the fortunes of the papacy indeed looked promising. Antonio di Rudinì had replaced Francesco Crispi as head of the Italian government, and Rudinì pressed for a policy of détente with France and the Church. Alexandre Ribot, foreign minister of France, sought improved relations between the Third Republic and the Church. And Leo XIII, increasingly confident of a successful resolution to the Roman Question, welcomed to Rome the largest of Harmel's worker pilgrimages.

The Pilgrimage of 1891

The pilgrimage of 1891 occurred in the immediate aftermath of the publication of *Rerum Novarum,* and Léon Harmel wanted it to be a massive demonstration of thanksgiving and support for the encyclical on labor. Not only did he enlist twenty thousand French workers, but he encouraged Catholic workers throughout Europe to join in giving thanks for the papal encyclical on the condition of labor. In February he gave the opening address for the pilgrimage in Paris in which he called for a peaceful crusade. Harmel's audience consisted of members of the diocesan committees who would assist him in organizing the pilgrimage,[148] and he intended all dioceses of France to be represented in it.[149] He spent the next weeks and months immersed in the details that would assure a successful pilgrimage to Rome. For instance, when Cardinal Rampolla rebuffed his request for a three-hundred-day indulgence for each of the pilgrims, Harmel boldly wrote the pope directly. But Leo XIII held to past custom and issued the one-hundred-day indulgence, as had been the case in 1887 and 1889.[150] Toward the end of July bulletins advertising the pilgrimage started to appear on the doors of all the churches in France, and letters, distributed by French bishops, arrived in homes.[151] The pope expressed his satisfaction and gratitude to Harmel for his efforts in preparing the 1891 pilgrimage[152] and as a symbol of his appreciation, proposed making him a Roman count. But Harmel recoiled in horror at the idea and had his son Felix politely decline for him.[153]

The pope joined Harmel and other pilgrimage leaders in trying to assure a successful pilgrimage. In mid-August, accompanied by Langénieux and Harmel, Leo personally toured the dormitories and refectories set aside for the French pilgrims.[154] He also asked the papal nuncio in Paris to send him an accurate report on the "present situation of religious matters in France, indicating the main points the Holy Father should treat in his speech before the pilgrims." Leo XIII wanted Cardinal Langénieux to know the contents of his formal address so that Langénieux's own speech could be prepared accordingly.[155] Cardinal Richard, Archbishop of Paris, assisted the papal nuncio in collecting information for the pope by providing him with news concerning the present state of the working classes in France and especially about practical ways to improve their moral, religious, and material conditions.[156] Advance word on the papal theme for the 1891 pilgrimage indicated the pope would emphasize cooperation between labor and management, a point that would illuminate the stark contrast between Catholic social teaching and the ideology of revolutionary socialism.[157]

In advance of the arrival of the French pilgrims, Harmel and his family attended a pontifical Mass and private audience on September 13.[158] A few days earlier, Harmel had taken a tumble, and although he was not seriously hurt, the pope had sent his personal physician to tend to him.[159] He was ready then to greet the first of the French pilgrims, who, coming from Toulouse, Amiens, and Lille and pausing in Turin to visit the grave of Dom Bosco, arrived in Rome on September 16. Later trains carried pilgrims from Bordeaux, Agen, Roubaix, Arras, Lyon, Grenoble, Chambéry, Marseilles, Nantes, Reims, Versailles, and Paris.[160] Comte Lefèbvre de Béhaine, the French representative to the Vatican, declared that all details were in place, and hoped that the pilgrims would not provoke any ugly incident that would undermine the hearty welcome they had received from the Italian people.[161] He no doubt had heard that Italians had started to complain about all the attention accorded the French visitors.[162]

In sheer numbers, the 1891 pilgrimage represented the apex of the French worker pilgrimages: twenty thousand workers[163] filled nine trains from France and attended six papal audiences.[164] In keeping with the wishes of the pope, the poorest pilgrims gathered around the Vatican as often as possible, even taking their meals there,[165] sometimes under a vast tent set up in the Belvédere Court, dining heartily on meat, potatoes, vegetables, fruit, and cheese and drinking wine and coffee. The more well-to-do had to content themselves at the local hotels.[166] Refectories and apartments of the Vatican flew the French flag,[167] and medals, with the pope's image on one side and the inscription "pèlerinage ouvrier français" on the other, awaited the arriving pilgrims,[168] who once again were permitted to abandon traditional dress etiquette and wear their work clothes to all the functions.[169]

Leo XIII judged it appropriate that he receive French workers on September 19 as the first representatives of labor after the publication of "our encyclical," for "you have understood, dear sons, these teachings of the Church and its leader."[170] In fact, according to the pope, *Rerum Novarum* was the "recompense for the workers' pilgrimages."[171] The worker pilgrimages were visible proof of the union between pope and people,[172] and Leo, standing for his delivery and speaking in French, offered them some fatherly advice. The pope encouraged the French workers to look to the Church to help with their labor problems, for solutions could never be found totally in civil law; to be successful, labor needed an "apostolic benediction." The ideal way to handle the Social Question, Leo continued, was for church and state to work together, as partners combining efforts and resources. Finally, the pope exhorted the French workers to show diligence in their work and respect and obedience to their bosses, for which he promised them concrete blessings from heaven.[173]

Worker-pilgrims from other European countries arrived in Rome toward the end of September to join in the pilgrimage of thanksgiving and attend some of the Masses and audiences with the French pilgrims. The European workers decorated St. Peter's with banners and flags from their diverse groups.[174] Communicants at the Masses numbered about 1,000 (the average attendance at the Masses at St. Peter's was 2,500 to 3,000),[175] evidence of outward religiosity among a considerable percentage of the worker-pilgrims.

As for Léon Harmel, the pope paid homage to the character and work of the man when he told him, "You are among those who give me the greatest consolation."[176] Harmel and his children and grandchildren attended a second private papal audience at which time Leo wanted to know all the details of the 1891 pilgrimage, such as how many trains had arrived and what kind of press coverage the pilgrimage was receiving.[177] Clearly, the mood of the pilgrimage was triumphant and euphoric.

Papal recognition of the French workers and Harmel did not go unnoticed in the press. *La Croix* reported that the Italians complained about the special attention given to the French pilgrims,[178] while the Italian newspaper, *Il Secolo,* posited that the pope's underlying intentions were political.[179] *Le Voltaire* concurred. Not only did all the attention showered on the pilgrims by the French and Italian governments diminish confidence in those governments, but it ultimately risked the peace of Europe. According to *Le Voltaire,* the Italians were persuaded that France remained inherently clerical, that it conspired with the pope against the unity of Italy, and that once victorious in a European war it would reestablish the temporal power of the pope. Even though the newspaper acknowledged that these observations were fantastical, it nevertheless cautioned the French government to bend over backward to correct such impressions.[180] Events of October 2, 1891, only exacerbated these existing perceptions and fears.

The Pantheon Incident

Shortly after noon on Friday, October 2, 1891, three young men, part of a group of fifty French pilgrims visiting the Pantheon in Rome,[181] walked over to the tomb of King Victor Emmanuel[182] and proceeded to write in the guest register, "Vive le pape!" Italian policemen and a lawyer reportedly followed the young men into the Pantheon and promptly arrested them. The timing of the incident could not have been more inopportune, for all of Italy, but especially Rome, had celebrated on September 4 the anniversary of the entrance of Italian troops into Rome, which completed the unification of the Italian peninsula in 1870 (ironically, the very day when Prussian troops entered Paris), and anticipated celebrating on October 20 the twentieth anniversary of the plebiscite of 1871 that invited Victor Emmanuel II to incorporate Rome into the Kingdom of Italy.

Demonstrations erupted almost immediately, as a hostile crowd gathered to shout at the French pilgrims when they were led from the Pantheon. Within hours the entire city of Rome rocked with turbulence.

Crowds clustered around Roman hotels occupied by French pilgrims, causing hotel proprietors to display Italian flags in their windows and Italian police to surround the premises with guards. Unfriendly Roman crowds likewise assembled at the Piazza Colonna and under the windows of the French Embassy on Piazza Farnese, as well as at French consulates throughout Italy. Anti-French protests of equal intensity spread across Italy during the next days as Italians staged demonstrations in Turin, Milan, Pisa, Florence, Palermo, Bari, Livorno, Bologna, Arezzo, and other cities. There were isolated demonstrations against the Russians too, as Russia was judged close to France and home to a tsar who was the symbol of despotism and ignorance.[183] In a remarkable demonstration of solidarity, Italians met throughout Italy, from small villages to large cities, to discuss the incident and plan their next course of action.[184]

In keeping with the growing xenophobia at the end of the nineteenth century, Italian crowds greeted French pilgrims arriving in Rome on the second wave of trains from France with curses and stones and shouts of "Long live Italy, long live the king!"[185] Violence against foreigners typically mirrored international political events in the closing decades of the nineteenth century, but it also resulted from a tight job market amid downturns in the economy, as was the case when French workers directed their hostility against immigrant workers from Belgium and increasingly against those coming from Italy.[186] Recent ugly incidents fed Italian memories and contributed to demonstrations against the worker-pilgrims from France: memories of past French military and political domination of the Italian peninsula, abusive treatment of Italian workers in France, humiliation in colonial North Africa, and support of the papal cause by the ultramontane party in France and perhaps even by the Third Republic itself. The demonstrations against the French visitors in Rome were a bit of tit for tat, but they also were testament to the success of the pilgrimages and their political agenda. Judging the pilgrimages too successful to allow their continuation, the Italians staged nationwide demonstrations and, in the aftermath, saw the worker pilgrimages stopped for six years.[187] There was, moreover, speculation that the demonstrations were preplanned.[188]

King Humbert,[189] son of Victor Emmanuel, declared the Italian demonstrations an honor to the mortal remains of his father: "These mortal remains have been insulted, you [Italians] have chastised the insulter, you have done well. As a son and as a citizen, I thank you."[190] As a precautionary measure, the French positioned their Mediterranean fleet, and the Italians countered by putting their reserves on alert.[191] The incident at the Pantheon also activated diplomatic channels in France, Italy, and the Vatican, as well as in other principal European nations. Quite obviously something more was at work than initially met the eye, and Leo XIII knew that the political implications for the papacy were not good. He received Léon Harmel with visible emotion and commented, "I was a prisoner, now I am a hostage."[192]

The three offending visitors were members of the worker pilgrimage, but technically they were not workers, and that fact apparently offered some consolation to Leo XIII.[193] Michel Dreuze was a seminarian, Maurice Grégoire was a lawyer, and Eugène Choncray was a correspondent for the *Nouvelliste de Morvan*.[194] Grégoire and Choncray were released in a matter of hours, but the Italian authorities detained Dreuze for several days before quietly hustling him to the northern border since it was understood he had been the one who penned the vexatious inscription on the guest register beside the tomb of the first king of Italy. The three were among the group of twelve hundred members of the Association Catholique de Jeunesse Française, coming from forty-eight seats of the association in France, in Rome to celebrate the three hundredth anniversary of St. Louis de Gonzagua and to join the French workers in honoring the publication of *Rerum Novarum*. Fifty of the twelve hundred youths were not bona fide members of the ACJF, and among those fifty were Dreuze, Grégoire, and Choncray.[195] Once released, the three and the ACJF were quickly forgotten as attention focused on the French workers and their cause.

On the day of the incident, Harmel, director of the French pilgrimage, met with Signor Luca, Italian Undersecretary of State for the Interior. Harmel expressed regret about the actions of the three young men. Luca said he was touched by Harmel's words and regretted that he had to make his acquaintance under these circumstances. He also expressed the hope that the pilgrims would exercise prudence by not going out at night. Later the French ambassador thanked the Italian government for protecting his embassy and the pilgrims.[196] The president of the French Chamber of Commerce also expressed his regrets to the Italian government.[197]

In Paris, Fallières, Minister of Religious Affairs, met with Ribot, Minister of Foreign Affairs, concerning the occurrence at the Pantheon. After reviewing the details of the incident, they instructed Lefèbvre de Béhaine to approach Cardinal Langénieux with the suggestion that the 1891 worker pilgrimage to Rome be suspended forthwith.[198] The request entailed taking immediate measures to stop the second group of pilgrims due to arrive in Rome on October 15. Thus the 1891 French worker pilgrimage to Rome officially and abruptly ended on October 4, with trains carrying the departing pilgrims leaving Rome quietly and under military escort.[199] The pope granted one last papal audience to workers who had just arrived from France and were disappointed at having to end their Roman sojourn before it began.[200] According to the Italian press, Italians in large measure applauded the suspension of the pilgrimage[201] and in a parting salvo and visible sign of their sentiments, threw stones at the trains returning to France.[202]

Harmel departed Rome on October 14 but not before commenting that the accusations against the French worker pilgrimage were "most slanderous."[203] Langénieux stayed on a few more days to meet with the pope, who reportedly was despondent over the thought that he might never see another worker pilgrimage.[204]

Ribot assured his colleagues that the pope continued to disavow all political intentions and that Italy was in direct communication with France over the matter, including King Humbert who wanted to prevent the situation from becoming "plus grave." Nevertheless, as precautionary measures, the foreign affairs minister planned to monitor the movements and statements of the pope and keep a close eye on what the Italian newspapers were writing on the matter.[205]

The episode at the Pantheon obviously brought to the surface feelings and suppositions long held in check by an activity that operated ostensibly as a religious journey to a holy place. But no longer could the worker pilgrimages to Rome masquerade as strictly religious events.

The organizers of the 1891 pilgrimage—Harmel, de Mun, and Langénieux—had come to Rome to celebrate past success. The pilgrimages of 1885, 1887, and 1889 convinced Leo XIII that the workers needed assistance in redressing social ills. The pope responded by issuing *Rerum Novarum,* arguably the most important encyclical of the modern era. The pilgrimage leaders had an additional agenda, however. Since 1870 the pope was "imprisoned" in the Vatican and anxious to retrieve lost land. The French pilgrimages to Rome intended to make his cause a public one. Harmel, for example, wrote in 1889 of his hope that "our popular demonstrations will be favorable to the freedom of the Holy Father by influencing public opinion" and that future pilgrimages would be "large and solemn demonstrations by France in favor of the Holy See."[206] Indeed, Leo XIII was ready to press on despite the unfortunate occurrence at the Pantheon. According to an article that appeared in *La Croix,* he wrote Harmel that the incident did not diminish the pilgrimage, that the pilgrimages were "good for those who look at us." "We will go forward with even more zeal."[207] The pope wanted the pilgrimages to continue.[208]

Social Catholics, like Léon Harmel, believed the worker pilgrimages were beneficial to the papacy but also to France. Throughout its history France experienced troubled times when it abandoned the papacy and happy times when it returned to the papacy. If France as a nation wished a reversal in fortune, it needed to return to the papal fold.[209] Thus, the logic went, by aiding the papacy in its political ambitions, French workers simultaneously aided France. In 1891 even the Catholic youth joined the workers in what was perceived as a patriotic effort. De Mun welcomed the linking of the workers with these young men "from the best of families." He noted in his welcoming address to the members of ACJF that the "children of the rich and the children of the poor are but a single family that makes up Christian France" and urged them "to break the division of caste and only look to bringing about the triumph of papal doctrine in France."[210]

Reaction of the French Press

For the Catholic press, the events surrounding October 2 provided an opportunity to reverse the anticlericalism of the Third Republic by convincing the reading public that the papal cause and the French cause were one and the same. *La Croix,* for example, portrayed the pilgrims and France as common victims of Italian chauvinism. Were not, *La Croix* asked, the Italians shouting "A bas la France! Vive Sedan!" in their streets?[211] And did not the Pantheon affair represent a blow against France at the expense of the pilgrims?[212] Moreover, by keeping its pages filled with inflammatory commentary, *La Croix* no doubt believed it was a participant in the Leonine strategy of using publicity to further the papal cause.[213]

The religious press readily acknowledged the political motives of the worker pilgrimages,[214] as had long been charged by their adversaries, but accused others of using the Pantheon incident to advantage too. It suggested that the demonstrations were staged to shore up a weak Italian government, for example.[215] And *L'Univers,* no doubt guilty of promulgating gossip, published an account of a meeting that allegedly took place on October 2, 1891, at 3:00 P.M. at a café on the Corso. Here, employing dramatic narrative, the paper related that Luca, the organizer of the anti-French demonstrations, met with General Pelloux, the Italian minister of war. Pelloux, arriving breathless from the demonstrations, declared that the riots would lead to a rupture with France. Luca responded by saying that these demonstrations against the pope and for the king were necessary in light of the demonstrations (i.e., pilgrimages) for the pope. Pelloux, nervous, said that this could lead to war and that he was not ready for war. To calm his fears, *L'Univers* continued, Luca sent a man to Billot, the French ambassador to Italy, to test him. Billot responded to the probe, "It's an affair that I don't take note of." When the messenger reported the ambassador's response to the two men at the café, both men smiled, according to *L'Univers,* and Luca announced, "We have won!"[216] In sum, there were those among the religious press that were convinced the Pantheon incident was a precooked plot, and when the French government failed to take Italy to task, it worked to the advantage of the antipapal party in Italy.

The nonreligious press saw this latest worker pilgrimage as political and dangerous. For example, *La Patrie,* seen as a guardian of patriotic and rightist interests, disapproved of the worker pilgrimage of 1891. Not only was the inscription written on the visitors' register at the Pantheon provocative, but so too was the very presence in Italy of these pilgrims. Harmel's formal account of the events of October 2 was also a provocation, *La Patrie* said, because he ended by hoping "recent events will result in the triumph of the Church." So much for the patriotism of the clerical party! *La Patrie* concluded.[217]

After the incident of October 2, the moderate republican press also criticized the pilgrimages. *L'Estafette* noted that these pilgrimages, by supporting the pope, served as political statements and consequently irritated the Italians.[218] It further pointed out that the three "workers" involved in the Pantheon incident were in reality a seminarian, a lawyer, and a journalist.[219] While *Le Figaro*, before October 2, sang the praises of the well-behaved French workers, it also warned that their presence did not please all the Italians and predicted that some unfortunate incident could result.[220] After the Pantheon incident, *Le Figaro* claimed that everyone realized the Italian state did not start the demonstrations, but what message, the paper asked, was sent to the Italians when Count Lefèvbre de Béhaine welcomed his compatriots while they were in Italy? Actions spoke for themselves: the pilgrims came to Rome to acclaim the pope "king," were led by a cardinal (Langénieux), an employee of the state, and the French ambassador to the Vatican received them. This led the Italians to conclude, *Le Figaro* declared, that the French government was involved "somewhat" in the affair.[221] The French and Italian governments knew the truth, that is, that their governments were not involved directly, but the misperception came from the "frequency and the importance of the pilgrimages."[222] *Le Figaro*, unlike the religious press, distinguished between demonstrations that were directed against France and those directed against "la France cléricale," believing that those taking place in fall 1891 were anticlerical in nature.[223] The right-wing press, departing from past sentiment, distanced itself from the religious press once the Pantheon incident occurred.

The republican press of the center and center-left generally did not fault the concept of the French pilgrimages to Rome, but after October 2 most of them expressed reservations. *Le Voltaire* did not deny the Catholics the dream of reestablishing the temporal power of the pope but cautioned against "displaced demonstrations."[224] *Le Radical* suggested that because of all the ensuing trouble the clergy ought to cease giving an "official character" to the pilgrimages, since for them Church interests always would take precedence over those of the state.[225] *Le Temps*, however, remained sympathetic throughout the events of fall 1891. It pointed out that the pilgrims were in Rome as Catholics and not for political reasons, and above all, they did not intend to jeopardize the foreign affairs of France.[226] In fact, the workers, coming to Rome in such numbers to demonstrate for the pope, were welcomed for two reasons: they limited their official functions to the Vatican proper, and they brought tourist money to the hotels and cab drivers.[227] The youthful prank of October 2 merely was ill timed and became exaggerated, leading to deplorable scenes.[228]

Not surprisingly, the most caustic commentary during fall 1891 came from the socialist press. Its newspapers gave extensive coverage to the pilgrimage, before but especially after October 2. Articles appeared on a daily basis, frequently on front pages. Before the Pantheon incident, *La Petite république* spoke of the worker pilgrimages as "stage productions" for Christian socialism[229] and of the French pilgrims as "pseudo-workers."[230] After October 2, it blamed the French pilgrims for causing the demonstrations and advocated that the French government disengage from any association with pilgrimages.

La Lanterne shifted blame from the three young men and placed it instead on the three pilgrimage leaders. Albert de Mun was declared guilty because he excited the pilgrims with his "ridiculous speeches"; Cardinal Langénieux was guilty because he "preached civil war"; and Léon Harmel was guilty because he was an industrialist "looking for paradise."[231] Moreover, *La Lanterne* pointed out, the French talked of "appeasement" and "conciliation" with the Church, but the Italians knew better. There could be no appeasement because the Catholics "translate[d] that into a power play for control."[232]

As to the patriotic intentions of these pilgrims, the paper offered, they brought a French flag to Rome only to compromise it by an adventure to advance the temporal power of the pope, all the while attempting to portray the demonstrations in Rome as solely anti-French in nature.[233] This merely played into the hands of the Italian government, *La Lanterne* speculated, as Italy needed a grievance, more or less serious, against France to justify the Triple Alliance. The French pilgrims, crying "Vive le pape!" conveniently provided the excuse.[234] Thus, while not denying that Italian actions were politically motivated, *La Laterne* refused to acknowledge the French and papal causes as common or mutually beneficial.

What effect did the Pantheon incident have on the public image of the pilgrimages as portrayed in the French press? The religious and socialist newspapers were consistent in their portrayal of the worker pilgrimages to Rome. The religious press viewed them in a positive light, beneficial to labor relations, the papacy, and France. The socialist press mocked them as theatrical productions and concluded that they did not represent French labor. After the Pantheon incident, the attacks broadened to suggest the pilgrimages were unpatriotic.[235]

The public image of the pilgrimages shifted most dramatically in the other newspapers of the right, but change occurred among those of the center and center-left too. Before the Pantheon incident, these papers generally devoted considerable space to the daily events and major addresses of the pilgrimages. Commentary was limited but when offered, it was often favorable, though occasionally foreboding. After October 2, 1891, commentary became negative, with the political and unpatriotic nature of the pilgrimages a common theme. Seemingly the pilgrims could not support simultaneously the papacy and France. The exception was *Le Temps*. This republican newspaper of the center and center-left distanced itself from the rest of the nonreligious press after October 2 by refusing to condemn the worker pilgrimages or rigorously examine their motives.

In sum, the Pantheon incident revivified earlier societal and political emotions, and the press, as a prism of French society, presaged the deterioration of political accord between Catholics and moderate republicans. But the unraveling of goodwill was not immediately apparent.

The French government, acting through its Vatican representative, seemingly endorsed the worker pilgrimages by attendance at pilgrimage functions and hosting receptions for pilgrimage leaders. Likewise, the French government responded quickly to the turmoil surrounding the Pantheon incident, thereby preventing any further deterioration in Franco-Italian relations. This leads one to conclude that indeed the republican government of France sought to improve relations with both the Church and Italy in the closing years of the 1880s and the opening years of the 1890s. But how long could governmental officials ignore the shift in press commentary, and presumably public opinion, that resulted from events surrounding the Pantheon incident? And would government policy, both foreign and domestic, change as a result?

Debate in the Chamber of Deputies reflected heightened emotions and concerns. Witness the session of October 26, 1891. De Mun accused Ribot of not protecting adequately French citizens abroad. He charged that France did not respond fast enough; for four days the pilgrims suffered. Ribot defended his actions, assuring de Mun that France did not have two classifications of citizens; it protected all Frenchmen. Moreover, the French ambassador to the Quirinal, Billot, engaged the Italian government from the first moments after the incident occurred. That evening Rudinì sent a telegram to Ribot that expressed "la plus grande cordialité," wishing to acknowledge again the friendship between the two countries. As for the Pantheon incident, it produced a reaction out of proportion to the actual deed, but as small as the event was, it had become an international incident.

Ribot went on to quote *L'Osservatore romano,* known for its close ties to the Vatican, which recognized the French government's need to halt the pilgrimage, a decision that the Holy Father himself said in a conversation with Cardinal Langénieux was "justified" by events. (Langénieux disclaimed this interpretation.)[236] Furthermore, the French and Italian governments continued to meet in order to restore relations to the state that existed before the Pantheon incident. Italian officials, Ribot explained to the deputies, told him that the demonstrations were the work of a minority, that the majority of Italians did not share their sentiments. He also disclosed that Rudinì promised an inquiry into the physical abuse suffered by the French pilgrims and that he would, should it be necessary, carry out disciplinary measures.[237] Comte Lefèbvre de Béhaine had kept Ribot apprised of events taking place in Rome. Sensitive to press commentary, he regularly sent reports of it, as well as actual clippings from the newspapers, to the foreign minister. Of interest, for example, was the notion portrayed in *Popolo romano* that the French worker pilgrimages were principally political in nature.[238] Indeed, the mere presence of French pilgrims in Rome caused "some apprehension" in diplomatic circles.[239]

After October 2, Ribot and Béhaine exchanged confidential letters that reflected the tense days and weeks following the incident. From their correspondence, it appears that Cardinal Langénieux asked Béhaine to convey to Ribot that he was taking steps to halt the second group of pilgrims due to arrive the second week of October.[240] Just who initiated the suspension of the 1891 pilgrimage is not clear, but it became a point of contention between the French government and some of the French episcopacy. The French government claimed to have approached Cardinal Langéniex with the proposal. Langénieux asserted that he stopped them,[241] thereby making unnecessary the Fallières Circulaire (see chap. 5), and this contention appears to be verified in a letter from Billot to Ribot.[242]

In any event, the Fallières Circulaire, issued on October 4, officially ended the pilgrimages for the indefinite future. According to Béhaine, the pope approved of this measure, though he regretted the impassioned polemics after such pleasant experiences of 1887 and 1889. Béhaine opined that the successes of 1887 and 1889 were irritants to those who saw them as part of the Roman Question[243] and questioned, based on reports in Roman newspapers, whether the demonstrations were indeed spontaneous.[244] The papal nuncio in Paris shared the same sentiments.[245]

Apparently the Italian government satisfied the French officials that measures had been taken to prevent as much as possible "serious disorders." Police were at their stations, and the undersecretary of the interior personally directed the movements of the police.[246] Within a matter of days, all traces of agitation had disappeared,[247] save for the sporadic outbreaks in Rome.[248] Officials of the two governments continued to view Franco-Italian relations generally in a favorable light. The Italian press, however, presented a contrary view, causing lingering apprehension among French government leaders.[249] Rudinì worked to dispel French anxiety. When he received the diplomatic corps on October 15, the first time since the Pantheon incident, he uttered "kind words and assurances" to Billot, again implying that the demonstrations were an excessive response to the words penned on the guest register on October 2.[250]

Moreover, at a reception ushering in the New Year, King Humbert remarked to Billot how pleased he was to note the improvement in relations between France and Italy since October 2.[251] Rudinì echoed the monarch's sentiment when he told the French ambassador, "We are all disposed to accord with France."[252]

Of greater concern to Italy than its relationship with France, which stabilized after a few uncertain days, was what the Pantheon incident meant for the pope's political agenda. French relations with the Vatican continued to be followed in Italy with "extreme solicitude."[253] Italian officials also had monitored closely for several years the rapprochement between the Vatican and the empires of the European center, and felt that the papacy profited from its improved relations with Austria and Germany.[254] Austria and Germany saw the Pantheon incident as an opportunity to create tension between France and the Vatican and thereby further isolate France diplomatically. As evidence of this attempt to dislodge the papacy from the French orbit, the two empires now concluded, to Vatican satisfaction, negotiations over the naming of bishops. Emperor William II of Germany, after long resistance, ceded to papal preferences, and Emperor Francis Joseph of Austria simultaneously yielded.[255]

Austria was of particular concern to the Italians, for the ruling family[256] was Catholic and seemed more inclined than the Germans to be sympathetic to the pope's political plight. For example, they alarmed the Italians by alluding to the temporal power of the pope, an issue that for Italians was strictly an internal one.[257] And Prince Karl zu Löwenstein confidently suggested to the pope that Austria would act boldly on the papal behalf if only Germany would support initiatives to that end that were now being planned.[258]

The Vatican felt that the Pantheon incident spoke to the desperation of Italian patriots who viewed the number of French pilgrims journeying to Rome as testament to the popularity of the pope and his cause.[259] If, in fact, the French worker pilgrimages to Rome were achieving their political goal, those who supported the papal cause took heart and acted. Some, as will become apparent, risked dangerous encounters with the Third Republic by challenging, on theoretical grounds, the directives of the Fallières Circulaire of October 4, which temporarily forbade pilgrimages to Rome. Others attempted to circumvent the Fallières notice. For example, Léon Harmel, always irrepressible, schemed for ways to get French workers to Rome without declaring a formal pilgrimage. His "project" consisted of sending ten to twenty men from each diocese to Rome. They would stay near St. Peter's and visit with the Holy Father.[260] Initially, the idea found favor with Leo XIII,[261] but within weeks the Vatican felt compelled to abandon the "project," for the "situation in Rome was far from tranquil and it feared a renewal of troubles."[262]

Dénouement

Unquestionably, 1891 had been a significant and disquieting year for the industrialist and the pope. *Rerum Novarum* at once validated and questioned Léon Harmel's experiment at Val-des-Bois. No longer was the *syndicat mixte* the sole format for French labor; henceforth, the *syndicat séparé* also was a viable way for workers to organize. After May 15, 1891, the Christian corporation, as interpreted by Harmel, ceased to be the paragon it once was. The worker pilgrimages, however, reenergized both Harmel and his workers. *Le bon père* brought workers from all over France to Rome, where the pope warmly embraced them. Thousands of workers attended papal Masses and received communion, thereby dispelling the notion that French labor had abandoned the Catholic faith. While the national Marian pilgrimages appealed to women, Rome, center of male power, lured the French *ouvrier*. And as an extension of the labor movement, the worker pilgrimages gave a new and different voice to the workers of France. They came to Rome in impressive numbers, and this crowd, in contrast to the less predictable crowds of strikers and May Day marchers, threatened no violence. They did vote, however, and as a consequence pilgrimage goals became suitable subjects for newspaper commentary and parliamentary debate.

The pilgrimages of 1885, 1887, and 1889, and the opening days of the 1891 pilgrimage helped to advance Harmel's twin objectives of serving his beloved workers and the papacy. The 1885 pilgrimage focused Leo XIII's attention on the Social Question plaguing workers throughout Europe. The 1887 pilgrimage personalized the Social Question for the pope by introducing him to workers, and was the occasion when Leo broached the notion of state intervention in industry on behalf of the workers; the timing of this pilgrimage also corresponded to his decision to write an encyclical on labor. During the 1889 pilgrimage, the pope delineated the respective duties of employers and employees, principles that would be incorporated in *Rerum Novarum*. The 1891 pilgrimage was, of course, Harmel's thanksgiving journey to Rome for the encyclical on labor[263] and spotlighted, particularly after October 2, the political nature of his worker pilgrimages.

Each successive pilgrimage grew in size and notoriety, but the Pantheon incident of October 2, 1891, ended the momentum and was a major turning point for both pope and industrialist. Subsequent pilgrimages never recaptured the interest or enthusiasm of these initial journeys to Rome, which had demonstrated dramatically Harmel's commitment to workers and given workers a voice outside the voting booth.[264] Instead Léon Harmel redirected his considerable energy toward the movement known as Christian democracy, which at least initially received the full endorsement of Leo XIII.

Leo XIII suffered a reversal in political fortunes as a result of the Pantheon incident. Relations with Italy became, if anything, even more precarious. Because of the ill will between church and state in Italy, the Catholic social program there was stunted,[265] while the Church, by mandating an electoral boycott, significantly undermined its political clout.[266] Simultaneous with railing against socialism in his papal encyclicals, Leo XIII unintentionally oversaw the growth of radicalism in Italy by not cultivating a conservative countermeasure to its growth. When Catholic laymen, in defiance of the electoral boycott, or the *non expedit,* as it was known, went to the polls despite papal protestations, the pope lost credibility as Catholic leader in Italy, especially after the 1900 election.[267]

In France, the Fallières directive provoked the episcopate to issue fresh challenges to the Third Republic in the wake of the Pantheon incident and in the process managed to sour much of the goodwill that had existed between church and state during the previous few years. None of this, quite obviously, promised to resolve the Roman Question, which was, according to Wallace, "the gravest weakness of Leo's pontificate."[268] Yet Leo XIII tried to salvage what he could through adroit diplomacy, and at least until the politically explosive French scandals associated with the Boulanger, Panama, and Dreyfus Affairs sabotaged his efforts, he pursued a French policy.

Leo's greatest legacy rests not in his political actions but rather in his important contribution to Catholic social teaching. With the proclamation of *Rerum Novarum,* the social teaching of the Catholic Church entered the modern age. Léon Harmel's factory demonstrated to Leo that a Christian corporation indeed was possible, and Harmel's worker pilgrimages personalized the Social Question for the pope and gave him the emotional energy to issue his great document on the condition of labor. But while many in France rejoiced over the papal encyclical, numerous Catholics did not, and the fact that the worker pilgrimages were rather unceremoniously halted only added to their bitterness and feeling of betrayal. Indeed, some were spoiling for a good Gallic fight.

CHAPTER FIVE

New Directions

> But I have promises to keep,
> And miles to go before I sleep,
> And miles to go before I sleep.
> —*Robert Frost,*
> *"Stopping by Woods on a Snowy Evening"*

LÉON HARMEL WAS SIXTY-TWO YEARS OLD WHEN THE PANTHEON incident effectively ended his dream of serving workers and pope through his pilgrimages to Rome. Instead of easing into retirement, Harmel launched new projects to achieve the goals that had been thwarted by events of October 2, 1891. But while the directions were fresh, his basic orientation remained the same, focused always on the workers and the pope. Inspiration came initially from *Rerum Novarum*. Subsequent doctrinal interpretation of *Rerum Novarum* aligned Catholic social teaching more closely to the needs of the most neglected segment of society, the laboring poor. Harmel now harvested additional fruit for his workers and the Roman Church largely by means of the movement known as Christian democracy, which received its impetus from *Rerum Novarum* as well as from a pope who intended the Church to play a role in political matters.

Christian democracy was an outgrowth of Leo's willingness to have the Church and its members become involved in the modern world; it called French Catholics to the voting booth and to political office and asked its priests to be schooled in practical subjects and acquainted with life outside the seminary. Though the movement did not result in an organized political party, as it did elsewhere in Europe in the prewar years, Christian democrats operated as a political pressure group in fin-de-siècle France.

That the pope and the industrialist had a political agenda had become readily apparent in the initial worker pilgrimages to Rome, and other events quickly underscored that reality. The shifting tactics of Léon Harmel and Leo XIII, as they sought to continue the development of social Catholic teaching on behalf of the worker while simultaneously trying to recapture the momentum established by the worker pilgrimages of 1885, 1887, 1889, and 1891 to aid the papacy in its quest for temporal power, displayed how intimately the Church was immersed in the politics of the era. The French episcopacy's response to the Fallières Circulaire, which officially shut down the worker pilgrimages for six years and set the stage for a renewal of church-state warfare in France, culminating in the 1905 separation of church and state, is a case in point. Political struggles between church and state dramatically altered the role of the Roman Catholic Church in French society.

But while understandably resistant to accepting a diminished position, the Church profited in numerous ways. The mobilization of the French priesthood, particularly its younger members, into the secular world through seminars organized to study *Rerum Novarum,* working vacations at Val-des-Bois, and initially repugnant but ultimately beneficial military service allowed the message of *Rerum Novarum* to be experienced by French clergy in ways not possible if it were restricted to the Christian corporation alone. Harmel understood this and was in the forefront in encouraging continual study, interpretation, and expansion of Leo's message on labor.

Along with the press, the Christian democratic congresses became forums through which to explicate the major issues and personalities that shaped Christian democracy in its formative years in prewar France. Not only did Christian democrats respond to papal doctrine and to contemporary issues such as anti-Semitism and the challenge from the Masons, but they also found themselves caught up in the polemic surrounding controversial notions such as Modernism and Americanism. The perception that Christian democrats endorsed Modernism and Americanism ultimately led to the movement's suspension at the dawn of the twentieth century but not before groundwork had been laid for the rebirth of the movement in the years after World War I. Though Harmel always preferred to be known simply as the *patron* of Val-des-Bois, his instrumental role in the formative years of Christian democracy assured him a place in the history of Catholic social teaching after 1891.

THE FALLIÈRES CIRCULAIRE, OR THE SO-CALLED AIX AFFAIR

The Aix Affair started with a letter from Armand Fallières, Minister of Religious Affairs, to the bishops of France, which asked the eighty-seven prelates to suspend the worker pilgrimages.[1] The circular produced responses from fifteen of the hierarchy. Five deferred to its mandates, nine disputed the terms, and one, Monsignor Gouthe-Soulard, the affable seventy-two-year-old archbishop of Aix, was outraged.[2]

In a letter of October 8, 1891, Gouthe-Soulard disputed the minister's contention that the pilgrimages "easily lost their religious character," citing the proper behavior and good relations between the French pilgrims and Italians on all previous occasions.[3] Besides, the archbishop pointed out to Fallières, "your letter is useless," for the organizing committee had already suspended the pilgrimages.[4] Gouthe-Soulard's letter was, perhaps not without reason, insolent and confrontational, for as Adrian Dansette posits, the Fallières Circulaire was poorly worded and seemed indeed to place blame on the bishops.[5]

Both the Fallières Circulaire and the Gouthe-Soulard response invited reaction from many quarters. The papal nuncio in Paris, Domenico Cardinal Ferrata, archbishop of Thessalonica, met with Fallières a few days after the minister had received the Gouthe-Soulard letter. According to the papal nuncio, Fallières heatedly pointed out that the tone of his circular was

> [r]estrained and courteous; that it was a matter of a simple appeal to the patriotic sentiments of the bishops and not a recourse to the Organic Articles to which, in the circumstances, he had not at all alluded; that there was not the slightest intention of forbidding the journey *ad limina apostolorum* for diocesan matters, but intended only to invite the bishops, in view of the Roman disturbances, to abstain for the time being from participating in other pilgrimages until the Pantheon incident was determined to be a rash act committed by a private individual and one not even remotely attributable to authoritative French citizens.

Fallières went on to say that it was hard to account for Gouthe-Soulard's "provocative and offensive style" and expressed concern that his political friends would demand retribution. The budget designated for the French ministry to the Holy See possibly could be eliminated, and a call for the separation of church and state surely would be renewed. The minister also pointed out to the papal nuncio that the text of the archbishop's letter made available to the press contained words that were "harsher than those in the letter to the minister, thereby showing himself disloyal and almost desirous of provoking the government."[6] Newspaper accounts certainly focused on the more inflammatory comments of the archbishop, for example: "Peace is sometimes on your lips, hatred and persecution are always in your actions, since that daughter of Satan, Freemasonry, directs and commands you."[7]

The papal nuncio sensed serious trouble ahead for church-state relations in France. "I am convinced that Monsieur Fallières would be inclined, as far as he is personally concerned, to forget Monsignor Gouthe-Soulard's letter, but the radical press, as well as part of the moderate republican press, are fanning the flames and they demand that this prelate, together with others who exceeded the limits, be taken to task."[8]

The Vatican found news of the exchange between the papal nuncio and the minister of religious affairs "most unpleasant," and instructed the papal nuncio "to make every effort to avoid adding yet another regrettable incident to the many that have already resulted from the deplorable events that took place in this city during the first days of the month."⁹ Unfortunately for the papacy, church-state relations continued to deteriorate, and this distressed Ribot, the foreign minister,[10] who claimed that he had nothing to do with the preparation and dissemination of the Fallières Circulaire[11] and who increasingly seemed driven by criticism from the radical political parties and press.[12]

The most immediate result was the decision by the government to prosecute Gouthe-Soulard in the Paris Court of Appeals. Leo XIII instructed the papal nuncio to try directly or indirectly to prevent the trial from going forward,[13] but the pope did not consider it "convenient that the authority of the Holy See intervene in any way."[14] In the charged atmosphere that prevailed, the nuncio's attempts to prevent the trial were unsuccessful, especially when Gouthe-Soulard was disinclined to write an explanatory letter to the minister of religious affairs on the grounds that it would be "contrary to French pride."[15] Once the trial was under way, Leo XIII instructed his papal nuncio in Paris to do his "utmost to see that this disgusting incident has no unfavorable consequences for Catholics." [Y]ou will more easily succeed," he continued, "if you argue that the suit brought against the archbishop of Aix is not in the best interests of the government."[16]

The Aix trial brought to the surface many issues. One of them was the matter of the Organic Articles (July 15, 1801; published April 8, 1802), which in turn were intrinsically tied to the Concordat (signed September 10, 1801; published April 8, 1802). Both documents were the product of Napoleonic hegemony and governed church-state relations in France from 1802 to 1905, when a formal separation occurred. Pius VII signed the Concordat, which recognized Catholicism as the "religion of the great majority of French citizens," restored regular pastoral life, and paid the clergy a living wage. But the Organic Articles, presented in the form of an imperial *diktat,* were another matter indeed. The papacy steadfastly refused to accept the document, although equally careful not to flagrantly abuse its mandates. The Organic Articles stipulated, for example, that no papal bull or other official communication could be published, no seminaries established, and no religious holidays celebrated without government approval. The document also mandated that civil marriage would precede religious ceremony, a single catechism would prevail throughout France, and bishops would need government permission when visiting Rome to fulfill the *ad limina apostolorum* requirement. Nevertheless, French bishops routinely and quietly traveled back and forth to Rome without government permission or censure, as was the case with Cardinal Langénieux when he participated in the worker pilgrimages.

But "sassy" bishops required disciplining by the state and discouragement by the Roman Church if church-state relations were to get back on track. Ribot cautioned that the spirit of the Concordat asked that bishops act not only as "simple citizens but as public servants[,] ... in things political to take the part of the government, and not form a Catholic party that in essence would be a political party." He also acknowledged to the Vatican that the Concordat currently was under attack and "if the bishops didn't show good will, it [would] be hard for the government to defend the Concordat."[17]

Retention of the Concordat mattered a great deal to the Vatican, for of all the nations it counted as friends—Austria, Spain, France, and Portugal—France was the most crucial to its political ambitions. The pope's unease stemmed not only from the resurgence of anticlericalism brought on by the incident of October 2 but also from conservative Catholics in France who welcomed a separation of church and state because they believed the Concordat enslaved the French church by reserving the right to appoint bishops and to approve or to disapprove the choice of curates. In short, in contrast to papal wishes, there were those in France who readily embraced the prospect of a split between church and state, and Monsignor Gouthe-Soulard's letter and subsequent trial advanced their cause.

Had Gouthe-Soulard been the only bishop to voice his opinion, the matter might not have reached the proportions it did, but as it was, the French bishops used the press to present their interpretation of events. Before, during, and after the trial, bishops from all parts of France sent letters to newspapers, mainly in support of the archbishop. The press, ever on the lookout for sensational material to tantalize their readers, fanned the embers of discord by publishing and commenting on the more inflammatory clerical letters. The situation pleased neither the foreign minister of France nor the pope. Ribot felt the matter only gave "power to the radical party which plans shortly to reopen the discussion on the separation of church and state."[18] Fallières even suggested to him that the Vatican was behind the letter-writing campaign.[19] Quite to the contrary, the bishops' actions concerned Leo XIII, but he felt "powerless" in trying to get them to be "more prudent and more reserved."[20]

The trial of the archbishop of Aix took place on November 24, 1891, before the Court of Appeals in Paris. The government charged Gouthe-Soulard with violating Article 22 of the Penal Code, which stipulated two weeks' to two years' imprisonment for words of outrage spoken against a minister performing his duties.[21] The government further argued that the worker pilgrimages were "dangerous given the current political situation" and that they had provoked the Italian demonstrations.[22] Gouthe-Soulard responded that the demonstrations in Rome were against France, not the pope, and that the circular was useless, since the pilgrimages had been suspended already. The archbishop further charged that "your circular," rhetorically addressing Fallières, "was a speech in favor of the Italian revolutionaries." For good measure, Gouthe-Soulard baited the government by declaring that he had never asked the state's permission when traveling to Rome.[23]

Cooler heads prevailed when it came to the judicial decision, and both sides felt vindicated. The state technically won since the archbishop was found guilty and fined 3,000 francs. The Church noted that Gouthe-Soulard had not been imprisoned, which it viewed as a bow to its status, but the state obviously considered the matter important since the archbishop received a respectable fine.[24] In seeking to offset the cost of his courtroom defense, Gouthe-Soulard stated his own version of the trial in *Mon procès, mes avocats,* in which he published letters of support that he had received during the ordeal. Among the letters were those from Cardinal Langénieux, Albert de Mun, and Léon Harmel. Since the worker pilgrimages indirectly had been impugned along with the archbishop of Aix in the French court, it was not surprising to find the three principals of the pilgrimages lined up in support of Gouthe-Soulard.

The Vatican hoped to salvage its damaged policy of rapprochement with the Third Republic. Roman newspapers representing the papal point of view were careful not to mistake French policy for that of Italy and its allies, and the Vatican continued to look upon France as "friend."[25] Still, Cardinal Rampolla reportedly was in a state of "profound sadness," concerned "for the future of the Vatican and the politics of accord with France." The pope, perhaps more optimistic, or at least more proactive, began steps to encourage conservative Catholics to get involved in politics and hinted at a national Catholic party.[26] When Ribot learned that the bishops planned to gather in Paris on November 18, he notified the Vatican that the cabinet was alarmed by the news. Taking a position against the government and organizing a Catholic party would overstep the bounds of appropriate behavior, according to Ribot.[27] Ultimately, the Vatican and the bishops would back down on the matter of a Catholic political party in France.

Though Leo XIII was upset over the trial of Gouthe-Soulard, he wanted to put it behind him as soon as possible. He did not reply to the archbishop's announcement of his sentence,[28] and the archbishop's name was "not even mentioned at the Vatican."[29] Intent that the Aix trial remain an isolated incident, the pope asked that French bishops write no more letters to the editors of newspapers and that they "use moderation, remain calm, and avoid compromising the Holy See."[30] Leo XIII kept close watch on the debates in the Chamber of Deputies in order to monitor the French political pulse, especially on the subject of church-state relations.[31] "Rest assured that all other preoccupations cease to exist here," the French representative to the Vatican wrote the foreign minister.[32]

That his name was used in the French parliamentary arena in connection with the Fallières Circulaire and the Gouthe-Soulard letter pained Leo XIII.[33] Nevertheless, he advised those responsible for producing a favorable press that the Gouthe-Soulard controversy was a way to "hold the attention of Catholics and stimulate them."[34] During these crucial weeks of fall 1891, the Vatican press redoubled its efforts to keep its commentary "prudent and moderate."[35] Although the pope never was able to exert similar control over the French conservative press, Ribot expressed his appreciation for the Vatican's policy of "pacification."[36]

When the Chamber of Deputies defeated the motion calling for the separation of church and state, the Vatican moved to ensure that its victory would not be merely a temporary one. The conservative monarchist party in the chamber countered papal policy, however, by using "sharp, violent language in order to prevent a reconciliation of the conservatives [Catholics] and the government of the Republic."[37] Because of the inflammatory tactics used in the chamber, the papal nuncio felt that despite the favorable vote in the parliament, the notion of separation of church and state had "made great progress" during fall 1891. "It seems quite unlikely to me," he wrote, "that in this country, at least for the time being, the idea of reconciliation will prevail when it is so bitterly opposed by the radicals, the conservative monarchists, and also by a good number of Catholics who, without reflecting too much on the serious, and perhaps irreparable, harm that could be done to the Church, opt for an open, violent conflict."[38]

Leo XIII, understandably, was "distressed" by the turn of events and apparently disillusioned when old animosities checkmated his efforts to increase goodwill between church and state in France.[39] As a consequence, he asked the papal nuncio to "avoid as much as possible situations that might lead to further conflicts,"[40] and on February 16, 1892, he made a further gesture toward reconciliation with the French state.

On that date, Leo XIII sent French bishops his famous Ralliement letter (*Au Milieu des Sollicitudes*) asking them to "disregard all germs of political strife in order to devote their efforts solely to the pacification of their country."[41] He referred, of course, to the past hundred years of French history during which revolution had damaged social cohesiveness and had produced an assortment of political forms, with practicing Catholics typically lined up in support of the monarchy or the empire and all others favorably disposed to the republic. Leo XIII now attempted to bridge the political chasm that separated the French nation. He wrote that "each of them [forms of government] is good, provided it leads straight to its end—that is to say, to the common good for which social authority is constituted." Moreover, "Catholics, like all other citizens, are free to prefer one form of government to another precisely because no one of these social forms is, in itself, opposed to the principles of sound reason nor to the maxims of Christian doctrine."[42]

But while directing French Catholics to give their full allegiance to—or to "rally to"—the Third Republic, the pope also gave them moral permission to oppose laws at odds with divine law or Church teaching. This directive, then, employed traditional Catholic social teaching and applied it directly to the contemporary French political situation. The Vatican sought rapprochement with the French Third Republic but opposed such state initiatives as the removal of religious instruction from public schools, restrictions on religious orders, removal of patois from regional catechisms, induction of priests into military service, and the separation of church and state.

The results of the Ralliement letter were similar in many respects to those that followed the death of the Comte de Chambord, the Bourbon pretender, in 1883: the pope's encyclical, *Au Milieu des Sollicitudes,* freed French Catholics from adherence to traditional political forms, made them less oppositional vis-à-vis the contemporary political scene, and encouraged their political involvement. But the pope's blessings for Catholic involvement in politics represented something more. In acknowledging the Republic as an admissible political form, the Church henceforth recognized the political as well as the moral equality of each French citizen.[43] Thus politics now existed alongside the Christian corporation as a suitable forum in which aspirations for the worker could be played out.

Not all French Catholics rallied to the pope's encyclical on church and state, since, like *Rerum Novarum,* the Ralliement letter proved divisive. For example, only thirteen out of eighty-nine dioceses published *Rerum Novarum,*[44] and the Ralliement letter elicited the same sentiment among the French episcopacy. To endorse *Rerum Novarum* or the Ralliement letter implied approval of political and social revolution, and few bishops were suited temperamentally for societal change of that magnitude.[45] Reaction among leaders of social Catholicism was mixed too. René de La Tour du Pin refused reconciliation with the Republic and remained a monarchist, but Albert de Mun rallied to the Republic while boycotting the political congresses of the Catholic reformers because he considered the assemblies too radical. Léon Harmel, on the other hand, embraced the Ralliement and declared that "we ought to clearly affirm ourselves as republicans, as democrats, and as Christians, in order to serve God, the people, and the country."[46]

The Ralliement letter made a difference in French political life. Catholics abandoned monarchist candidates for moderate republicans in the elections of 1893, and Christian democracy sprang to life. Throughout the 1890s moderate republicans and moderate Catholics, or *ralliés,* worked together effectively to block the left. Their coalition existed despite the continued reluctance of much of the Catholic leadership to support the Third Republic and despite the intractable anticlericalism of the republican radicals.[47] By 1899, however, the Dreyfus Affair had reunited the moderate and radical republicans, and many of the *ralliés* had joined their coreligionists in endorsing anti-Semitism and assuming an anti-Dreyfusard position. With the elections of 1898, the separation of church and state had become acceptable to the majority of voters and to the government. The separation occurred when the successor to Leo XIII, Pius X (r. 1903–1914), and his secretary of state, Monsignor Merry del Val, challenged French nationalism in spring 1904.

Pius X and Merry del Val refused to endorse one of two proposed candidates for vacant bishoprics, and that inaction was an aberration from the ritualistic pas de deux practiced by the Vatican and the Third Republic when it came to the appointment of French bishops. Customarily, the state selected candidates from a running list of men who were perceived as sympathetic to the Republic—although once appointed, they frequently became staunch conservatives. The papal nuncio in Paris next reviewed the candidates and indicated his approval or disapproval before the names were submitted formally to the pope.[48] In 1904 these preliminaries had been ignored, and consequently when the Vatican received the names of the unapproved candidates, it balked. Simultaneously, and without government approval, the papacy censored two other bishops for misbehavior. Then when President Loubet visited Rome and met with the Italian king in an effort to improve Franco-Italian relations, Merry del Val sent a letter of protest to all the European governments; the letter, which was provocative, quickly appeared in the press. The French were outraged, and the government responded promptly and severely.[49] On July 30, 1904, France severed relations with the Holy See, and on December 11, 1905, the state declared that "the French Republic assures liberty of conscience" and "does not recognize, subsidize, or pay wages to any creed."[50] The Concordat and the Organic Articles no longer governed church-state relations in France.

Despite the best efforts of individuals such as Leo XIII and Alexandre Ribot, the Aix Affair demonstrated the difficulty of reversing traditional sentiments at both ends of the French political spectrum during the waning years of the nineteenth century. Given the intent of a politically oriented press to sell newspapers and given the intent of radical and conservative political parties to hold their ground against rapprochement between church and state, brief periods of goodwill and accommodation, such as were experienced during the worker pilgrimages of 1885, 1887, and 1889 and the opening days of the 1891 pilgrimage, could not be sustained. While moderates in the republican and Catholic camps were willing to cooperate in the domestic political arena, events realigned groups along more traditional lines. As a result, resolution of the Roman Question was not advanced and Christian democracy waited until after World War I to reach full fruition in France.

Throughout his papacy Leo XIII remained consistent in his policy of reconciliation with the Third Republic, which, of course, made Harmel's acceptance of the Ralliement quite effortless. But however imaginative Leo's policy might have been, it was premature; the opposition of a significant number of the French clergy and laity, as well as of the conservative press, doomed it for the time being. Documents related to the Aix Affair indicate that Church accord with government officials often came more easily than with its own bishops. The absence of unified support from the French Church weakened the Vatican's policy of reconciliation with the Third Republic and failed to settle the Roman Question in the pope's favor.

Italy continued to monitor closely relations between France and the Vatican throughout this period, as the Italian government attempted to restore stability to its relationship with the Third Republic and simultaneously prevent the papacy from realizing its territorial dream. After the Pantheon incident, Prime Minister Rudinì extended a welcome to French men and women wishing to visit the pope in Rome and promised that there would not be a "single act of violence against them."[51] His policy of reconciliation and moderation received a vote of confidence in the Italian Chamber of Deputies later that fall.[52] Italians intensely followed the debates in the French parliament with regard to the Aix trial and the matter of separation of church and state. In fact, anything that might alter the relations between France and the Vatican interested them immensely, especially since they had their own church-state problems to work out.

Resumption of the Worker Pilgrimages

A definitive answer as to whom — church or state — was the initial and responsible agent for shutting down the pilgrimages for six years remains elusive, and there appears to be no readily apparent reason or formal announcement accompanying their resumption after a six-year hiatus. Perhaps Leo XIII and Léon Harmel hatched plans to restart them as early as 1892. Harmel visited the pope at the beginning of the year and would have been encouraged to take up the pilgrimages once more when the pope declared before several witnesses, "Harmel, you are the man of France who has given me the most pleasure."[53] Clearly the pilgrimages were on Harmel's mind later that year as he hosted an anniversary Mass and luncheon in Paris on September 22, 1892, for workers who had attended the pilgrimages of 1887, 1889, and 1891. The mood did not appear to be in the least bit gloomy, despite the Pantheon incident, for the participants dined on such playfully named fare as "potage pontifical" and "fruits du Vatican."[54]

The purpose of the resumption of the worker pilgrimages, however, was direct and well defined, to renew contact between the French workers and the pope, and they asked for papal benediction on endeavors inspired by *Rerum Novarum*.[55]

But the next pilgrimage to Rome, that of 1897, clearly was anticlimactic when compared to the previous pilgrimages, most notably the one of 1891. In 1897 neither de Mun nor Cardinal Langénieux accompanied Harmel, who no longer was overshadowed by his more famous countrymen and instead became the chief spokesman for the worker-pilgrims. Harmel arrived in Rome ahead of the workers in order to meet with Leo XIII on August 5. The pope warmly greeted Harmel and his family and expressed delight that workers were again coming to Rome to seek his blessing. He told Harmel that "when the workers are with the pope, they are *chez eux*," or at home. He also recalled fondly, "I was called in 1891 the pope of the workers, and truly I love the workers with a special affection."[56]

Italian officials had taken every precaution to assure the safety of the French visitors, who began to arrive in Rome on August 6. Only three trains were needed to bring the 1,100 pilgrims to Rome, where they remained for the customary five days and were lodged close to the Vatican. In addition to visiting the major basilicas and historical sites, the pilgrims attended two papal audiences. Harmel addressed the assembly, calling to mind *Rerum Novarum* and beseeching the pope to bless the worker-pilgrims and Christian democracy. The pope replied by saying, "If in a word, democracy will be Christian, it will give to your country a future of peace, prosperity and happiness," and asked for "respect for Christian democracy and for union and harmony between workers and all honest people who are interested in the common good."[57] But the more inclusive tone of the papal words were modified by a final warning to be "careful of dangerous men who seek to overturn family, property, and all humanity."[58] Socialism remained a forbidden ideology, and contact with socialists was to be avoided.

The pilgrimage of 1897 merited attention in the French newspapers, and editorial commentary fell along traditional political lines. The socialist press mocked the worker-pilgrims, describing them as theatrical figures and "pseudo-workers," and charged that they were only in Rome because Harmel had pressured them. In short, the socialist press characterized the worker-pilgrim as a sad and passive figure and not a bona fide worker.[59] Republican newspapers challenged the patriotism of Harmel and his "amateur workers." By opting to support the Vatican, they argued, Harmel assumed a position incompatible with being a citizen of France, and one cannot pardon "a religious mask which profits the pope." Furthermore, by undertaking a Roman pilgrimage, the worker-pilgrims risked placing France in a very difficult situation, which could lead to "une conflagration generale" in Europe.[60] Thus, according to this point of view, the worker pilgrimages to Rome were political and dangerous, and the events of October 2, 1891, clearly had not been forgotten. Newspapers whose political alignment was viewed as more conservative and more representative of government views preferred to emphasize the Christian democratic message delivered during the 1897 pilgrimage rather than question the authenticity of the workers or the patriotism of Léon Harmel. On this matter, certain of the secular papers, such as *Le Temps*, shared common ground with the religious press in concentrating on the new message of the worker pilgrimages—Christian democracy.

The 1897 pilgrimage reflected changes that had occurred within Catholic social teaching since the publication of *Rerum Novarum*. Rather than stress reform in the workplace by transforming factories into Christian corporations, the pilgrimage speeches and addresses concentrated on Christian democracy, the movement inspired by *Rerum Novarum* but ignited by the 1892 Ralliement letter of Leo XIII. The theme of Christian democracy dominated subsequent pilgrimages too, and symbolized a new alliance between the Church and democracy.[61] Henceforward Leo XIII addressed small businessmen, farmers, and working women, along with the traditional male worker of past pilgrimages, as he welcomed the latest worker-pilgrims and warned of the dangers of "Americanism" and "Modernism," new concerns that joined the old bêtes noires, liberalism and socialism.[62] The last of the worker pilgrimages took place during the pontificate of Pius X, with whom Harmel celebrated in September 1912 the twenty-fifth anniversary of the pilgrimages. Harmel again visited with Pius X on April 4, 1914, to defend his worker *syndicats,* then under threat by conservative Catholics. It was his last visit to Rome.[63]

DEVELOPMENT OF CHRISTIAN DEMOCRACY

When the momentum of past pilgrimages became unsustainable, Harmel continued his pilgrimages to Rome but also embarked on a campaign to inform the workers of the latest developments in Catholic social teaching in other venues. Energized by the papal encyclicals of 1891 and 1892, he decided to serve the workers and the pope by becoming one of the principal leaders of the Christian democratic movement in France. Harmel's new mission was a natural extension of his earlier efforts on behalf of the Christian corporation and can best be summed up in his own words: "The reign of justice . . . cannot exist without the ascension of the popular classes, without the effective and permanent participation of government personnel[,] . . . in order to propagate above all the teachings of Leo XIII, whose words are infallible . . . and who is particularly the liberator of France."[64]

Harmel symbolically launched the new movement by traveling to Reims to explain *Rerum Novarum* to a group of workers.[65] This question-and-answer session was the first Cercle Chrétien d'Étude Sociales of the future Christian democracy, and its organizational base was L'Oeuvre des Cercles Catholiques d'Ouvriers, the workingmen's circles created by Maignen, de Mun, La Tour du Pin, and Harmel in the 1870s. The objective of the study circles was to deliberate the principles of *Rerum Novarum* with the hope that Cercle members would be inspired to act out its message in their daily lives. The Cercles were significant in several ways: the workers announced their readiness to abandon paternalism, Harmel became "the first *patron* to recognize publicly the legitimacy of that desire,"[66] and Cercle members who took to heart the words of *Rerum Novarum* now began to be called "Christian socialists"[67] along with other reform-minded Catholics. Without abandoning L'Oeuvre—in fact, he was to become its president in 1896—Harmel separated the two workers' groups organizationally when it became apparent that they were not meant for marriage; while Harmel and de Mun approved of their merger, La Tour du Pin dissented. Thereafter Harmel devoted more time and emotional energy to the Cercles Chrétiens d'Études Sociales than to L'Oeuvre.[68]

Harmel led a personal campaign in northern France to create additional Cercles, visiting individual factories to encourage their establishment while at the same time using the opportunity to promote the family wage. Attendance at these forays into the workers' world typically consisted of twenty to forty workers and one *patron*, many of whom now at least were persuaded to read *Rerum Novarum*. To entice workers to join the study groups, Harmel dropped the previous requirement to join a religious association, such as Notre Dame de l'Usine, as had been the case with participation in Christian corporations.[69] *Patrons* increasingly distanced themselves from the study groups—and indeed from Christian democracy in general—and priests took over as discussion facilitators, with at least one priest ingeniously opting to move the locus of discussion to the local cabaret.[70] But the best sessions were those at which Harmel was in attendance, because he not only answered questions on the current social teachings of the Catholic Church but also addressed concerns about workplace conditions.[71] Harmel's ultimate dream was to create a federation of all the Cercles Chrétiens d'Études Sociales in France, which coincided with the goal of the *ralliés* by providing a base on which to build a Christian democratic political party. But since the membership of the Christian democratic movement included both republicans and monarchists and the state discouraged the formation of a Catholic party in France, the notion was an illusive one. As a result, Christian democracy remained a political pressure group with principally a social itinerary.[72]

In spring 1893 Harmel traveled to Rome to confer with Leo XIII on the subject of Christian democracy. From his experience as *patron* at Val-des-Bois, he knew that workers were intelligent, interested, and easy to work with, and these impressions were confirmed and amplified in the Cercles Chrétiens d'Études Sociales. Whether or not Harmel was conscious of it, he in fact was moving away from paternalism as a modus operandi and toward an even more worker-oriented program.[73]

Concurrently, Harmel presented the idea of holding congresses to match and counter the socialist congresses then in vogue, and since socialist parades and other events typically focused on May 1, he decided that at least the initial Christian democratic congress should be held in May. As with the worker pilgrimages, which intentionally vied with the parades and mass demonstrations of the socialists, he again attempted a bit of *tant pour tant,* or tit for tat, in calling for Christian democratic congresses. An additional benefit of the congresses, according to Harmel, was the opportunity to bring together members of the Cercles Chrétiens d'Études Sociales from throughout France. Starting with the first Cercle in Reims, the Cercles had expanded in the city of Reims, as well as throughout the North and Northeast, before becoming a national phenomenon with membership centered predominantly in the North and Northeast regions of France as well as in Lyon. Its regional bias was apparent from the start; Christian democratic congresses convened at Reims in 1893, 1894, and 1896, and at Lyon, the other regional bastion of Christian democracy, in 1896, 1897, and 1898. Harmel served in executive positions at the congresses,[74] and like other Harmelian activities, Leo XIII enthusiastically endorsed the Cercles Chrétiens d'Études Sociales and the congresses.[75]

Involvement in Christian democracy necessitated that Léon Harmel become more active politically than in the past. He preferred, however, not to affiliate himself with any particular political party as he wished to preserve his "freedom on the social terrain."[76] He was too much of a realist to attempt founding an authentic workers' party because that would have required considerable participation of men with more "education" and "place" than that possessed by the average fin-de-siècle worker. In other words, Harmel determined that workers were not yet ready to organize a political party on their own. Instead he envisioned a federation of Christian workers whose goal would be the protection of "popular interests."[77] Harmel wanted the Cercles Chrétiens d'Études Sociales to become the core of a new political pressure group. To this end, he actively campaigned for suitable candidates for political office during the 1889 election. Though Harmel never ran for political office himself, judging by the universally positive response he elicited from workers as he visited with them on their own turf, including cabarets, he no doubt could have been elected had he tried.[78]

His electoral tactics were simple and direct. He advised the selection of "new men," men who had "rendered service to the people" and who were "honest workers and courageous peasants."[79] Thus Harmel endorsed not only the bourgeois populist but also the industrial and agricultural worker for elected office.

As for a political platform, he purposely made it broad so that "everyone would be at ease with it."[80] His platform asked for (1) freedom for the individual with guarantees similar to those in England and the United States; (2) freedom for the family; (3) freedom for schools and instruction on all levels; (4) decentralization, which would lead to communal autonomy, similar to that of the Middle Ages; (5) and freedom of association for all. This was not a terribly complex or sophisticated political tract, but he wanted it to include rather than exclude potential backers.

Harmel's Christian democratic message and tactics, then, began simply enough, but in time the movement adopted a more detailed political agenda and became more exclusionary. Principal newspapers for the dissemination of its message included *La Croix, L'Univers, Le Peuple français, La Justice sociale, La France libre,* and *La Voix de la France.*[81]

THE CHRISTIAN DEMOCRATIC CONGRESSES

The congresses began in 1893 and ended in 1900.[82] They occurred at least once a year, some regional gatherings and others national; they met frequently in Reims and Lyon. And although Harmel "wished to see in our ranks large representations from the building trades," as well as "other professions,"[83] priests and journalists, that is, the bourgeoisie, dominated the assemblies, and early social Catholics and priests comprised most of its leadership.[84] That the middle classes led the movement was nothing new, but now rather than social Catholic laymen, the principal spokesmen for reform were priests, such as Paul Naudet, Pierre Dabry, Théodore Garnier, Léon Dehon, Paul Six, and Jules Lemire. These were the so-called *abbés democrats* who specialized in oratory, journalism, and good works[85] and who interpreted literally Leo XIII's wish that priests become more involved in the secular world.[86] Harmel was, of course, an exception to this general rule; though no longer young in years, he remained young in spirit, and was a mentor to many of the new generation of reformers. Hundreds of parish priests, especially those of the younger generation, idolized the *abbés democrats* and Léon Harmel.[87] Women also attended the congresses, though in token numbers. Factory workers, as a specific category of worker, do not appear in descriptive accounts of the meetings. For example, at the November 30 session of a 1895 congress, there were five hundred in attendance, with some two hundred priests and ten women.[88] Furthermore, the number of participants varied considerably from eight thousand at one 1896 gathering[89] to a mere forty at a 1900 congress.[90] The dwindling numbers reflected the ill fortunes of the Christian democratic movement and, in general, the Roman Church in France in the years before World War I.

The minutes and platforms from the congresses explain much about the rise and fall of the movement and its contribution to the state of affairs of the Church in France during these critical years. In keeping with the message of *Rerum Novarum,* the congresses routinely insisted on the sanctity of religion, family, and private property but found the pope's admonition on the matter of wages more difficult to accept, since he had cautioned employers that a living wage—with or without the family wage adjustment—must not be tied to booms and busts in the economy.[91] In addition, delegates at the congresses argued for laws that conformed to the Ten Commandments and to the Gospels, that allowed professional *syndicats* greater autonomy, and that protected small workshops and businesses against monopolies. They petitioned for Sunday holidays, for ten-hour workdays, for suppression of both night work for women and piecework, and for limitation of work for young women. They also demanded accident and unemployment insurance as well as retirement funds for workers.[92] Using the factory at Val-des-Bois as a standard, none of these demands was particularly innovative. Others issues, however, marked a departure from the Harmelian paradigm, and became sources of controversy within the Christian democratic movement.

Members attending the 1896 and 1897 congresses, for example, pressed for the establishment of a system of parallel unions for Catholic labor. Only instead of *syndicats séparés* and *syndicats mixtes,* proposals now called for separate workers' unions and separate employers' unions, operating side by side in the same trade, with a *conseil de métier* (professional council), or labor-management board, to iron out differences.[93] Catholic industrialists, for the most part, repudiated the proposal for the new *syndicat* form both in theory and in practice, preferring to remain in the *syndicat mixte*.[94] Harmel retained the *syndicat mixte* at Val-des-Bois too, but he had a ready explanation: for him, it still remained the ideal format for bringing together labor and management. Yet his preference came with a caveat. If workers genuinely were not served by the *syndicat mixte,* that is, if *patrons* ignored their duties as Christians and employers, then separate workers' unions became the preferred alternative.[95] And the majority of employers, even those within the ranks of the Patrons du Nord, resisted workplace reform. He therefore regretted the "forgetting of the *syndicat mixte*" but encouraged participation in the new system since it would be "an opportunity to get ourselves involved in the professional unions and on the work councils."[96] Harmel promoted both forms of association because that would maximize contact with workers.[97] But the preference of workers increasingly was obvious; in 1893 only six unions out of 163 were *syndicats mixtes*.[98]

Despite encouragement from individuals like Harmel and government support for parallel unionization throughout French labor, the system failed to be effective, for although workers joined the *syndicats séparés,* weak employers' unions diminished chances of conducting meaningful negotiations within the *conseil de métier.* And since the 1884 law that legalized unions withheld from them the right to bargain, the only institutional structure designed for collective bargaining at the time was the work council.[99] The net result for the labor movement in general was continued dependence on the state to settle differences between labor and management and reliance on laws to determine working conditions and wages. Given that employers refused to support the *conseil de métier* in significant numbers, Harmel's Conseil d'Usine at Val-des-Bois takes on added importance, even in the face of diminishing interest in the Christian corporation. Here at least labor and management met to discuss workplace problems and to attempt solutions; dialogue between the *patron* and the workers was ongoing and took place in a nonconfrontational atmosphere.

Harmel also was at loggerheads with the Patrons du Nord over the matter of inserting the Harmelian wage package into the congressional platforms. Northern employers generally refused to implement the family wage, retirement plans, and cooperatives, claiming that the current depression made these benefits economically unsound. They argued that they were in compliance with *Rerum Novarum* because it called for the honoring of a "just wage," which was not necessarily commensurate with a family allowance or other benefits advocated by Harmel.

The fratricidal rift included Léon Harmel and Camille Féron-Vrau, vintage social Catholics and associates of long standing. In 1895 Féron-Vrau visited Harmel at Val-des-Bois, and later in that year, Harmel proposed they go to Rome to patch up differences. Though the meeting resulted in a declaration of peace, with Leo XIII basically endorsing the Harmelian viewpoint, the Patrons du Nord never went along with the agreement and hostilities persisted.[100] Nevertheless, when discord erupted over congressional platforms, typically pitting labor's interests against management's, Harmel attempted to emphasize the positive; he advised downplaying the importance of the platforms and concentrating instead on the real mission of the Christian democratic congresses, namely, the empowerment of the workers. On this matter, the congresses were successful; they gave the workers responsibility and encouraged their initiative.[101] But once a policy detailing labor-management relations and worker benefits was reduced to a standoff at the Christian democratic congresses, anti-Semitism became one of the chief drawing cards for the largest congressional turnouts of the decade and the unifying theme of the congresses.

ANTI-SEMITISM AND FREEMASONRY

Anti-Semitism first appeared as an organized movement in France during the 1880s. The 1882 crash of the Union Générale Bank, in which many small savers suffered severe losses, triggered the general business recession known as the "great depression." The Union Générale was a Catholic bank, and according to the contemporary French press, its failure came as a direct result of action taken against it by its Jewish rivals, particularly the Rothschilds.[102]

Associating Jews with high finance, with shady business deals like the 1892 Panama Scandal, and with economic hard times remained a common practice throughout the waning years of the nineteenth century, and fanned the flames of anti-Semitic fires.[103] Edouard Drumont (1844–1917), ardent Catholic and anti-Semite, did his best to keep the embers blazing by blaming all that was wrong with France after 1870 on finance capitalism and the Jews.[104] Even the Franco-Prussian War resulted from the manipulations of finance capitalism and the Jews, according to Drumont.[105] But Drumont did not confine his xenophobic bombast to the Jews. Since Italian immigrants frequently were targets of French nationalistic violence,[106] he played that card brilliantly; in the preface of *France juive* (1886), his best-selling book, he reminded his audience that Léon Gambetta, legislative leader of the Third Republic, was the son of an Italian.[107]

It was Drumont who blew the whistle on the financially shaky project to build a Panama canal through inhospitable terrain in Central America. The resulting scandal presaged the later Dreyfus debacle in its disregard of reality and by the complicity of government officials and newspaper editors who, in the case of the Panama Canal, accepted bribes to bolster the myth of financial soundness and engineering feasibility.[108] Ominous news of the impending scandal was whispered earlier, but the publication of Drumont's second best-seller, *La Grande enterprise* (1890) exposed the false advertising perpetuated by the Panama Canal Company, headed by Ferdinand de Lesseps of Suez Canal fame, and government and newspaper acquiescence in the scam. Newpapers with a rightist tilt, such as *La Gaulois* and *La Cocarde,* joined in Drumont's unsuccessful quest to topple the Third Republic.[109] Because of duplicity on the part of government and press personnel, the average hardworking Frenchman was sold a colossal bill of goods; eight hundred thousand people bought stock in the underfinanced company on margin and came away with their life savings wiped out.[110] Furthermore, the Third Republic once again suffered dishonor. Not a single government official or newspaper editor of any stature was ever convicted, while young French engineers went off to the jungles of Central America hoping to recoup French honor lost on the battlefields of Sedan and Metz but instead died in astounding numbers from malaria and other tropical diseases. The scandal, moreover, succeeded in turning anti-Semitism into a popular, national phenomenon.

Jews were a minority in French society, and except for a few cities, such as Paris where 45,000 lived,[111] they were dispersed throughout the French state. In the late nineteenth century, for example, Jews numbered

70,000 to 80,000 out of a general population of 39 million, or about 0.18 percent, the smallest Jewish population of any major European country.[112] But although relatively unobtrusive in numbers, the Jewish population of France became more visible after 1870. After the Franco-Prussian War (1870-1871), Jews from Alsace relocated in France, only to be followed in the next three decades by 10,000 Jews from eastern Europe. Most of the newcomers settled in certain *quartiers* in Paris where their Yiddish speech and orthodox customs and dress reconfirmed the anti-Semitic stereotype.[113] In the minds of many Frenchmen, the influence of Jews on French business and culture belied their relatively insignificant numbers.[114] But then there was something to that perception since they were often among the intellectual leaders: Henri Bergson, the philosopher, Émile Durkheim, the positivist, Marcel Proust, the writer, Jacques Offenbach, the composer, were all Jews, not to mention the so-called court Jews, the Rothschild family of international bankers. Turn-of-the century Jews entered the École Normale Supérieure and the École Polytechnique, the grandest of the *grande écoles,* in record numbers and reached the highest echelons of government.[115] But unlike older communities of French Jews who strove to become assimilated, the recent immigrants appeared "foreign." The quantum leap from the particular to the general occurred during the Dreyfus Affair of the mid-1890s: all Jews became characterized by their antagonists as foreigners, enemies, and traitors.[116]

The Dreyfus Affair[117] began when Captain Alfred Dreyfus, a French Jew whose family fled from Alsace when the Germans moved in after the 1870 military fiasco, was charged with treason. A spy war flourished after the Franco-Prussian War, and Dreyfus became a victim when convicted on the basis of flimsy evidence (a note found in the trash and the author's handwriting never positively identified). That Dreyfus was a Jew mattered; most of the press, and indeed the country, regarded him as guilty until disclosures brought about reconsideration. The government convicted Dreyfus and sentenced him to Devil's Island for four years and three days despite the fact that Ferdinand Walsin-Esterhazy, a Hungarian-born French citizen serving as an officer in the French army, seemed to be the real culprit. Gradually, the sordid truth surfaced, but not before a suicide and military and government cover-ups damaged the already tarnished integrity of the Third Republic. Ultimately,

Dreyfus was released from imprisonment, reinstated in the army, and served honorably in World War I. The nation, however, never fully recovered from the affair. It polarized France perhaps more than any other political incident in recent history, and still is a source of controversy and emotional discussion.

Not surprisingly, there were winners and losers when the dust settled. Since Alfred Dreyfus was vindicated, those who championed his cause, as most of the radical republicans and socialists eventually did, reaped political benefits. Henceforward, the left forged a new coalition in the national assembly, cemented by anticlericalism, which made the Catholic *ralliés* politically expendable.[118] It ended any chance the Church had of permanent political accommodation with the republican state at the turn of the century when French Catholics used the Dreyfus Affair to justify further their anti-Semitic inclinations. Lines had been drawn, and *ralliés* and Catholics in general suddenly found themselves outside the political mainstream.

That the Christian democratic congresses of the 1890s picked up on the anti-Semitic theme and used it to unify their membership was not unique. Before and during the Dreyfus Affair, and despite shifting political alliances, socialists maintained their anticapitalist and anti-Semitic views. Ideologically, capitalism was the enemy of socialism, and since common perceptions associated Jews with the evils of capitalism, individual socialist leaders used anti-Semitic rhetoric to attract popular support. Jules Guesde, for instance, raged against the "evil Jew."[119]

Nevertheless, Catholics as a group stood in the forefront when it came to anti-Semitic diatribe. For example, the 1896 Christian democratic congress at Lyon welcomed Karl Luger,[120] the Christian democratic mayor of Vienna who ran on an anti-Semitic platform, and applauded France's chief spokesman for anti-Semitism, Edouard Drumont, who suggested "taking away citizenship from Jews and excluding them from jobs in public education, law, civil service, and in the army."[121] Drumont successfully linked anti-Semitism with patriotism, a dangerous nexus hinted at earlier by General Boulanger,[122] while simultaneously lashing out at the French Revolution and heralding a new order reminiscent of medieval society.[123] Drumont knew his audience.

Léon Harmel linked Jews and Freemasons[124] in some sort of common conspiracy against France and against the people. After all, he offered, the

Freemasons "borrowed their rites from the Jews,"[125] and both "increasingly ally with the socialists."[126] Together, according to Harmel, they "control newspapers, theaters, and books [and] they have become instructors of public education." Soon the result would be the "denationalization" of France, as the younger generation would despise "our past, our traditions, and our beliefs."[127] Furthermore, he attributed to Jews and Freemasons the delay of the national assembly in passing laws that would improve conditions for the workers. Legislation calling for the suppression of night work, limiting work hours, and creating consumer and producer cooperatives "do not leave the parliaments." To the contrary, he continued, the only laws that move "more quickly," such as the 1884 one on unions, are "against the people and for the Jews."[128] That the 1884 law required unions to disassociate themselves from religious affiliation convinced Harmel of a common conspiracy against the welfare of the worker since Jews and Freemasons "wish to return workers to their old slavery."[129]

Harmel's perception of a government dominated by anti-Catholic forces was not total fabrication. Masonry in France grew significantly in the prewar years; in 1903, for example, there were 24,000 Masons, but by 1908 the number had climbed to 32,000. And many government officials and functionaries were Masons because it was professionally advantageous. In the 1902 Chamber of Deputies, there were between 170 and 250 Masons, and the Senate counted between 90 and 150 members. The numbers varied simply because the average length of membership in the organization was five years—just long enough to get one established in a professional career. Membership in the organization assured consideration by fellow members when it came time for job promotion, election to political office, or selection for cabinet position. That the ideology of Masonry corresponded to the notions inherent in a secular society made membership in the association easy for many French republicans. Its rituals and language, however, were incidental in attracting membership and consequently were not taken very seriously.[130]

Léon Harmel's assessment of the role played by Freemasons in late-nineteenth-century French society was consonant with the message delivered in Leo XIII's encyclical *Humanum Genus* (April 20, 1884), in which he denounced Freemasonry as an organization that "now boldly rises up against God Himself." The pope was convinced that politically

France remained in the grip of the Freemasons, and therefore he blamed the disintegration of the working relationship between moderate Catholics and moderate republicans after the 1898 elections on the Freemasons in the national parliament.[131] Leo XIII spoke frequently and directly on the subject of Freemasonry and its deleterious effects on Catholic interests.[132]

One can only speculate, however, that in condemning "rapacious usury" in *Rerum Novarum* Leo XIII attempted to impugn the Jews. But there were those who interpreted the papal attack on usury to justify a campaign against Jewry. Had not, asked Abbé Gayraud at a 1895 congress, Leo XIII condemned "Jewish usury, voracious usury" in *Rerum Novarum*?[133] No matter that the pope never specifically mentioned "Jewish usury" in his encyclical on the condition of labor, many French Catholics mentally supplied the missing word, especially since the pope seemingly did nothing to discourage the anti-Semitic tone of the congresses.[134] Harmel shared the anti-Semitism of his coreligionists. Never content to allow words to substitute for action, he organized the Union Fraternelle and promoted the Third Order of St. Francis in order to combat the influence of Jews and Freemasons.

L'Union Fraternelle and the Third Order of St. Francis

L'Union Fraternelle, founded in 1891,[135] wanted to safeguard Catholic enterprises against Jewish competition.[136] The organization attracted mostly Parisians who, by consulting the *annuaire,* or yearly directory, could lend support to businesses of fellow members.[137] The several thousand members[138] took their stand against monopolies, credit houses, and "false" cooperatives[139] by boycotting department stores and other enterprises they identified as Jewish. In so doing, L'Union Fraternelle, under the presidency of Harmel, earned the dubious distinction of being possibly the first organization in modern French history to direct a boycott of Jewish business.[140] Certain details eluded the fraternal union, however. For example, Jews neither founded nor operated large Parisian department stores such as the Bon Marché, the Louvre, the Belle Jardinère, the Printemps, and the Samaritaine that became targets of the boycott.[141] Yet Harmel remained convinced not only of the "facts" but of the moral correctness of the cause.

After all, he argued, the Church fought "Jewish usury" from the "first centuries of Christianity," and Leo XIII stood "against monopolies of capital and merchandise."[142] Consequently, in planning the 1897 worker pilgrimage to Rome, Harmel informed Cardinal Rampolla that "a certain number of *petits commerçants* [small shopkeepers] would be among the pilgrims," and expressed concern that these *petits commerçants* would "disappear in ruin" if more Catholics "didn't get involved" in the boycott. The boycott apparently did not meet expectations. Harmel complained, "There are Catholics who continue to buy from Freemasons and Jews because of a slight advantage.... [But] they don't consider that money carries a moral message."[143]

Yet Harmel remained optimistic about ultimate success because "*Rerum Novarum* begins to bear fruit." He also hoped for the continued "abundant intervention of the papacy in these vital questions for contemporary society."[144] In fact, Leo XIII solicited information on the group's activities and in general encouraged them.[145] Harmel considered his anti-Semitic actions in perfect harmony with contemporary social Catholic teaching, as well as with papal directive, for the Vatican approved of the Union Fraternelle.

Leo XIII also encouraged membership in the Third Order of St. Francis. The pope mentioned the Third Order in the encyclical *Auspicato Concessum* (September 17, 1882) and promoted participation in the organization in his encyclical *Humanum Genus* (April 20, 1884). He did so because "it ought to be of great influence in suppressing the contagion of wicked societies [by] drawing the minds of men to liberty, fraternity, and equality of right; not such as the Freemasons absurdly imagine, but such as Jesus Christ obtained for the human race and St. Francis aspired to."[146] In other words, Leo XIII intended that the Third Order of St. Francis combat the influence of the Freemasons.

Harmel joined the Third Order in 1860 as a road to personal sanctification and as an additional opportunity to show his personal devotion to the workers. When the pope charged the Third Order with a new mission, Harmel responded by hosting a meeting on July 20, 1893, at Val-des-Bois to encourage membership in the organization.[147] Harmel anticipated that the Third Order would be the "salvation of the nineteenth century as it had been for the thirteenth century."[148] No longer an association satisfied with performing corporal works of mercy among the nation's poor, it now actively campaigned against capitalism, Freemasonry, and the Jews. Moreover, it became part of the Christian democratic movement when its "peoples' congresses" met annually from 1893 to 1897. But whereas Harmel wanted to avoid the polemic associated with the anticapitalism presentations at the congresses[149] and whereas Leo XIII advised "peace, harmony, and calm"[150] over the same issue, neither man registered a formal complaint about the anti-Masonic and anti-Semitic sentiments expressed at the congresses.

Still, there is some evidence that perhaps both men wanted to tone down the anti-Semitic rhetoric. Certain unnamed "ecclesiastical authorities" requested that anti-Semitic remarks be deleted from the program of the 1897 Christian democratic congress, because anti-Semitism was "too lively" a topic given the "current circumstances." And, indeed, Edouard Drumont was not invited to attend.[151] What role Leo XIII played in this directive remains unclear. One can only speculate that in this matter, as with much of what went on at the other congresses, communication with the Vatican occurred. The French police, careful to monitor all groups with political implications, continued in their conviction that "Christian democracy responded, with the most perfect precision, to the instructions of the Sovereign Pontiff."[152] As for Harmel, he wrote in 1910 that he was tired of listening to "maledictions against adversaries [especially since, in reality] ideas lead the world [and] they [the "conservatives"] always attack persons and not their errors."[153] He preferred henceforth to concentrate his efforts on fighting socialism rather than the Jews and Freemasons, and one way to do that was to educate Catholic clergy on the Social Question in order that they might minister to workers who increasingly were attracted to socialist ideology.

THE FACTORY CHAPLAINS AND THE SEMAINES SOCIALES

Beginning in 1891, Harmel inaugurated the *aumôniers d'usine* (chaplains of the factory) project at Val-des-Bois in order to acquaint seminarians and young priests with the Social Question in an authentic setting. He intended to form a corps of chaplains for the workplace. The idea for creating what was in essence an army of worker-priests came from Belgium where a similar program was operating in Seraing. Father Dehon, of the Oblates of the Sacred Heart religious order, directed the sessions at Val, and the religious associations at the factory underwrote the cost of hosting the annual meetings. The group assembled at Val-des-Bois until 1895, when it became too large to be accommodated on the factory premises. The classroom sessions then relocated to Saint-Quentin, while students continued to visit Val in smaller groups to experience firsthand factory life. The program called for young clergy to spend two weeks of their summer vacation learning how to become effective factory chaplains. They studied Harmel's *Manuel d'une corporation chrétienne* and Father Dehon's *Manuel social chrétien* in the classroom before going out into the factories to minister to workers.[154]

Léon Harmel initiated a complementary program for young clergy at Val-des-Bois, beginning in 1892,[155] the same year in which a similar program was inaugurated in Germany. The project, known as the Semaines Sociales, or Social Weeks, targeted young clergy who were not necessarily preparing to minister full time in the factories of France but rather viewed instruction on the Social Question as fulfillment of their priestly education. Seminarians and young priests of the Social Weeks program, in imitation of the factory chaplain corps, met at Val until their growing numbers sent them to classrooms at Saint-Quentin in 1895. This group was under the direction of Father Dehon and Canon Perriot,[156] and many of the young men came from the Seminary of Saint-Sulpice in Paris or from the Nord. The students spent two weeks of their summer vacation alternating living with the workers and touring the factory at Val with studying history, the scriptures, and *Rerum Novarum* and discovering how to reconcile paternalism with worker initiative.[157]

Actually Harmel's project of acquainting the clergy of France with subjects outside the traditional curriculum of seminary education began sooner than the early 1890s. In 1876 the superior general of the most influential seminary in France, Saint-Sulpice,[158] invited Harmel to Issy, one of the two campuses of the seminary in the vicinity of Paris, to talk to his students about social action.

The event was remarkable for the time. Not only was the "bon père" a relative unknown in 1876, but most seminaries did not encourage contact with the secular world while their charges were in their formative years. However, that Saint-Sulpice took the lead in this matter was indicative of a pattern that prevailed throughout the 1870–1914 period at the seminary. For example, when the Third Republic mandated in 1889 that seminarians join their secular counterparts and serve in the military, the superior general of Saint-Sulpice, while not endorsing the government directive, encouraged his young men to serve with distinction and with continued commitment to the spiritual life. Sending young clergy to the barracks in 1889 helped to repair the damage incurred by the Church, because of such past episodes as the Aix Affair and the Dreyfus Affair, long before the Union Sacrée of World War I pursued a fence-mending program to reconcile differences between church and state. But barrack life also masculinized the French clergy at a time when religion routinely was viewed as a feminine domain. The Military Law and the Sulpician response to it advanced the mission of the Church by giving its young clergy a more vigorous and worldly education than that offered by contemporary seminaries, thereby preparing clergy to serve more convincingly in their ministries.[159]

Harmel's mission to educate French clergy on the matter of the Social Question, and the appropriate response to it as called for in *Rerum Novarum* at the sessions for the Aumôniers d'Usines and the Semaines Sociales, was a continuation of his earlier program with the seminarians of Saint-Sulpice. His work on behalf of the young clergy of France complemented the Military Law of 1889 by exposing seminarians and priests to contemporary secular society.

Beginning in 1887 and continuing for fourteen years, superiors general of seminaries sent their young men to Val-des-Bois during their summer vacations before the formal inauguration of the Semaines Sociales program in 1892. Harmel was the master teacher, explaining methods, debating their pros and cons, and promoting his *syndicat* and Conseil d'Usine as institutions worthy of duplication. Because his delivery was passionate and uncompromising, he invited and received from time to time lively rebuttals. But on the whole what he had to say made eminent good sense to the participants, who received lasting impressions and memories from their weeks spent with *le bon père* and his numerous guest speakers. Besides young clergy, there were "lay" seminarians, such as Marc Sangnier, who attended sessions so as to learn how to put *Rerum Novarum* into practice in their ministries.

In sum, Harmel contributed perhaps as much or more than any other individual at the time to the education of the clergy,[160] as well as the next generation of Christian democratic leaders, both clerical and lay. But desiring peace amid a growing furor over Christian democracy by the more conservative members of the Church, Harmel abruptly suspended both the factory chaplain and the Social Weeks projects at Val-des-Bois at the beginning of the twentieth century.[161]

While his programs for the clergy of France functioned, Harmel kept the Vatican informed of their activities and results. He wrote to tell Leo XIII that his papal blessings for Christian democracy have "borne fruit.... [P]riests have become involved and are studying *Rerum Novarum*.... [T]hey have organized an army of workers in order to know the teachings of the Holy Father and to combat socialism in the work *milieu*."[162] But he also wrote of his problems. Presaging future developments, Harmel complained to the Vatican, "A certain number of bishops showed themselves to be adversaries of democracy. They blame the priests who wish to go to the people, often punishing them by a disgrace, and bring about discouragement among the most zealous."[163]

A few months later, in an attempt to quell a rising tide, Leo XIII sent *Depuis Le Jour* (September 8, 1899), his encyclical on the education of the clergy, to the archbishops, bishops, and clergy of France.[164] The letter asked that French seminaries "remain faithful to the traditional methods of past ages"[165] in instructing their young men. The pope specifically advised that seminarians in the junior and senior seminaries study the *Summa Theologica* of St. Thomas Aquinas, the Catechism of the Council of Trent (the Roman Catechism), Holy Scripture, and Canon Law. But he cautioned against individual interpretation of Holy Scripture, adoption of doctrinal skepticism as a result of reading non-Catholic philosophy, and compromising priestly vocations by intermingling with the laity to the point where their faith and purity were jeopardized. Nevertheless, Leo also recognized the enthusiastic response of the French to *Rerum Novarum*:

> Docile to the counsels we gave you in the Encyclical *Rerum Novarum*, you go to the people, to the workers, to the poor. You endeavor by all means in your power to help them, raise them in the moral scale, render their lot less hard. To this end you form reunions and congresses; you establish homes, clubs, rural banks, aid and employment offices for the toilers. You labor to introduce reforms into economic

and social life, and in the difficult enterprises you do not hesitate to make serious sacrifices of time and money; and with the same scope you write books and articles in the newspapers and reviews. All these are, in themselves, highly praiseworthy, and in them you give no equivocal proofs of good will and of intelligent and generous devotedness to relieve the most pressing needs of contemporary society and of souls.[166]

And he asked that young priests continue to take part in social action if their zeal is accompanied by "discretion, rectitude, and purity."[167] The pope encouraged them, moreover, to become familiar with the physical and natural sciences, "so as to be able to solve the objections which infidels draw from these sciences against the teachings of Revelation."[168] Leo XIII added a final warning, however, before concluding his letter to the French clergy; he reminded young clergy who were actively involved in Christian democracy that they were to "take care to conform to ecclesiastical discipline"[169] and to obey their superiors, for to fail to do so would only strengthen the enemies of the Church. "[And] so priests, do nothing without your bishop."[170] The pope had begun to respond to conservative clerical pressure, and decided that the multiplicity of groups that had sprouted in the aftermath of *Rerum Novarum* needed to be reined in.

When Harmel ended his programs for educating clergy, he said publicly that it was for "purely material reasons," but privately he admitted that a "coalition of bishops" halted the sessions.[171] Conservative clergy reacted negatively against other challenges to traditional Catholic teaching too and pressured Leo XIII to respond accordingly.

Modernism and Americanism

Harmel's experience with the coalition of bishops indicated a growing concern among the episcopacy that the period of openness and experimentation that accompanied the publication of *Rerum Novarum* had gotten out of hand. A group of Jesuits, associated with the Roman review *Civiltà cattolica,* piloted the drive against the innovations of the decade[172] and found many adherents in France, where doctrinal retrenchment took place along with mounting anti-Catholic sentiment at the time of the Dreyfus Affair.[173] They, and all who sympathized with their point of view, became known as "integral Catholics" for their defense of traditional Church dogma and social vision.[174] Specifically, the Integrists identified with the neo-scholasticism of the period, which reaffirmed doctrinal immutability and the hierarchical order of Church and society.[175] Therefore, they resolutely opposed Modernism and Americanism.

Modernism applied scientific methods to the study of religion, thereby insinuating that Catholic dogma evolved and changed as much as nature.[176] In other words, the scholarship of the Modernists led them to a relativism that was the antithesis of the doctrinal absolutism characteristic of the Vatican since the declaration of papal infallibility in 1870.

Americanism, as the name suggests, was associated with the American Church, which enjoyed amicable relations with its government despite the official separation of church and state.[177] Leo XIII recognized the advantages of being unencumbered by state rules and regulations and applauded the fruits produced by the American Church in *Longinqua* (January 6, 1895), his encyclical to the archbishops and bishops of the United States. In his words:

> You were enabled to erect unnumbered religious and useful institutions, sacred edifices, schools for the instruction of youth, colleges for higher branches, homes for the poor, hospitals for the sick, and convents and monasteries.... [And] the numbers of the secular and regular clergy are steadily augmenting.[178]

But the democratic values of American culture predisposed certain of its clergy to press for greater democracy in the Church, and this trend was dangerous to the welfare of the universal Church and was not to be emulated. He asked for American clergy to preserve a submissive spirit and reverence for bishops, and for American bishops to "work together with combined energies to promote the glory of the American Church and the general welfare."[179] Leo "ardently desired that this truth should sink day by day more deeply into the minds of Catholics—namely, that they can in no better way safeguard their own individual interests and common good than by yielding a hearty submission and obedience to the Church."[180] He cautioned them further:

> [It would be] very erroneous to draw the conclusion that in America is to be sought the type of the most desirable status of the Church, or that it would be universally lawful or expedient for State and Church to be, as in America, dissevered and divorced. The fact that Catholicity with you is in good condition, nay, is even enjoying a prosperous growth, is by all means to be attributed to the fecundity with which God has endowed His Church.... [S]he spontaneously expands and propagates herself; but she would bring forth more abundant fruits if, in addition to liberty, she enjoyed the favor of the laws and patronage of the public authority.[181]

In short, Leo XIII wanted to have his cake and eat it too. He welcomed a state that left the Roman Church free to carry out its mission in schools and hospitals but preferred to have the state favor the Church in its laws and monetary support. Since he staunchly resisted the separation of church and state in France and Italy throughout his papacy, one can conclude with assurance that Americanism posed a greater menace to his principles than did the persistent church-state troubles he encountered in Europe.

Americanism also threatened to carry out what the conciliar movement of the Middle Ages had attempted—the dismantling of the hierarchical structure of the Catholic Church.[182] For this reason, when a coalition of bishops indicted the Christian democratic movement in France for its Americanism, Leo XIII supported them.

Neither Leo XIII nor Léon Harmel fit neatly into the ideological camps of the period. For while the pope read of recent scientific discoveries, encouraged biblical scholarship, and opened the doors of the Vatican libraries to researchers, he also disapproved of doctrinal impurity, as well as such American notions as endorsement of nonconfessional *syndicats* like the Knights of Labor by certain of its clergy and the introduction of democratic procedures into the Church's hierarchical structure. Thus, though responsible for creating the climate for change by issuing *Rerum Novarum* and the Ralliement letter, Leo XIII was not prepared to sanction unauthorized interpretations of Catholic social teaching, which included tampering with the institutional format of the Roman Church. Consequently, he sent *Testem Benevolentiae* (January 22, 1899) to Cardinal Gibbons, Archbishop of Baltimore, cautioning, "We cannot approve the opinions which some comprise under the head of Americanism[,] ... for it raises the suspicion that there are some among you who conceive of and desire a Church in America different from that which is in the rest of the world."[183] When Cardinal Gibbons assured the pope of American submission to papal directives, Leo XIII expressed his gratitude to the clergy of the United States in the encyclical *In Amplissimo* (April 15, 1902).

But papal retreat from earlier positions had begun and would continue in the years leading up to World War I. In condemning Americanism, Leo XIII directed concern at democratic tendencies within the European Church too[184] but withheld official commentary until the publication of *Graves de Communi Re* (January 18, 1901). In this last major encyclical before his death, Leo XIII distinguished between social Catholicism and Christian democracy. Because he perceived social Catholicism as less threatening than Christian democracy to existing societal structures, *Graves de Communi Re* discouraged zealous support of popular governments and encouraged the liberal use of justice and charity, traditional methods for dealing with societal woes. But even in his support of social Catholicism, Leo XIII seemed to retreat in 1901 from positions taken in 1891 in *Rerum Novarum*. For example, when speaking of "the necessity to elevate the mass of the people" by appeals to "those whose rank, worldly wealth, and culture gave them a certain standing in the community,"[185] he reinforced the type of social Catholicism that held fast to paternalistic practices rather than that which gave way to worker independence. And whereas in 1891 he scolded the privileged classes for neglecting the working poor, in 1901 he cautioned against forgetting "the upper classes of society, for they also are of the greatest use in preserving and perfecting the commonwealth."[186]

Discussion of Christian democracy in *Graves de Communi Re* was somewhat more forthright. By choosing to present commonly held criticisms of Christian democracy without simultaneously issuing a strongly worded refutation, the encyclical suggests that the pope was more or less in accord with the movement's critics. Objections raised were basically three. First, Christian democracy seemed to "covertly favor popular governments ... [and therefore] there might easily lurk a design to attack all legitimate power either civil or sacred." Second, "it appear[ed] to belittle religion by restricting its scope to the case of the poor, as if other sections of society were not of concern." And third, it imprudently tolerated aspects of socialism that had the potential to threaten class structure and property. In short, Leo XIII's defense of Christian democracy was tentative. The pope's advice for future activity within the Christian democratic movement, moreover, served as further admonishment for past conduct.

Leo XIII warned Catholics against joining political parties, undertaking projects without episcopal guidance, and neglecting family while counseling them to show proper respect to superiors, to perform their work willingly, to guard the rights of others, to keep religious practices, and in hardships and trials to seek out the Church for advice.[187] In sum, the pope sought to preserve traditional Church teaching and societal structures that must have appeared to him more threatened in 1901 than in 1891, for indeed the workers' flirtation with socialism continued and Catholic reformers had taken *Rerum Novarum* to heart and sometimes interpreted its message in a way that the Holy Father deemed inappropriate. Consequently, commentators see *Graves de Communi Re* as an attempt by the papacy to fortify the spiritual life of Catholics while simultaneously putting into motion a series of intellectual setbacks for the forces of change and modernity. It essentially ended for the time being the Christian democratic movement in France.[188] After 1900 the Christian democratic congresses and the congresses of the Third Order of St. Francis no longer met; groups such as the Aumôniers d'Usines and the Semaines Sociales ceased to function; Modernism was condemned in 1907, the Sillon in 1910; and in 1909 Pius X removed his support of the Ralliement.[189]

Harmel's response to *Graves de Communi Re* was somewhat predictable but not entirely. Like Leo XIII he saluted those who studied recent scientific and technological advances. Witness, for example, the factory modernization and innovative managerial style at Val-des-Bois. Yet, given the opportunity, Harmel seemed at times more eager than the pope to embrace change. For although there is no specific evidence to suggest that Harmel approved of doctrinal scholarship outside Church auspices, such as the Modernists carried out, he was nevertheless prepared to continue schooling clerical students in subjects outside the traditional seminary curriculum until the coalition of bishops convinced Leo XIII to limit the worldly education of seminarians.

Subtle nuances also separated the pope and the industrialist over the issue of Americanism. During the 1899 worker pilgrimage to Rome,

Harmel heard numerous discussions regarding *Testem Benevolentiae*. On one occasion, an American clergyman bluntly suggested to Harmel that "[w]e [French] are too timid with regard to personal initiative. There remained in France a fetishism for authority that crushes the personality."[190] We do not learn whether Harmel debated the clergyman on the pointed comment, but it raises an important issue. If this is an accurate rendering of the French character, it would certainly explain in part Harmel's utter devotion to the papacy and its causes, as well as his complete submission to the papal will. But Harmel's analysis of Americanism yields something more here too, for while he admired American individualism— à la Andrew Carnegie, for example—he associated individualism on his side of the Atlantic with the French Revolution and all its pernicious side effects, which indeed were more devastating to traditional societal structures in France than that which resulted in the American colonies from the less radical American Revolution. Thus Harmel reasoned that it was necessary in France to "form again in the population the spirit of association and the ideas of brotherhood [*solidarité*],"[191] which had been destroyed by the revolutionaries of the First Republic. In other words, Harmel's condemnation of Americanism was not based solely on its threat to papal authority, as was the case with Leo XIII, but rather on its challenge to something peculiar and integral to the French nation if not to Europe in general, corporatism.

When it came to his personal criticism of the Christian democratic movement, Harmel tended to focus on the discord rather than the issues,[192] and his response to *Graves de Communi Re* was consistent with his previous accord with Vatican wishes. On September 14, 1901, he wrote to Leo XIII in praise of the "admirable encyclical on Christian democracy which completes your teaching on the necessary action of the people of our epoch."[193] Although he could speak disparagingly of a "coalition of bishops," Harmel remained submissive before the Chair of St. Peter in all matters.

Post-Leonine Relations

After the death of Leo XIII in 1903, Harmel continued to travel to Rome to pay homage to the new pope, Pius X, for he wanted the Holy Father to "illuminate the cold obscurities of the moment."[194] When the Vatican issued a reprimand to the Third Republic over the separation of church and state in 1905, Harmel likewise stood in opposition to French policy. But his relationship with the papacy after 1903 seemed decidedly more perfunctory than earlier. Perhaps the years finally were catching up with him. More likely, the change in tone reflected not only the loss of a lengthy relationship between men committed to a similar ideal but also the further retrenchment of Catholic social teaching. For once the French cardinals failed in their efforts to have elected the moderates' papal candidate, Cardinal Rampolla, Christian democracy in France underwent additional curtailment.

Pius X, the candidate of the conservatives, lacked Leo XIII's expertise in foreign affairs and his understanding of modern culture, and was particularly intent on maintaining doctrinal purity. For example, in response to the Integrists' charge that the Christian democratic organization, the Sillon,[195] was guilty of Modernism, the pope in 1910 condemned it, since "they do not work for the Church but for humanity."[196] Marc Sangnier, the organization's founder and a young disciple of Léon Harmel, learned his master's lessons well for he promptly bowed to the wishes of the Vatican and disbanded the Sillon. In a letter to Sangnier, Harmel acknowledged the difficulty of this action but commended him in characteristic hyperbole on his decision: "[B]y this magnanimous gesture you have advanced the triumph of the cause of Jesus Christ more than if you had converted the entire world. A time that bestows such events is a time when one is proud to be alive."[197]

Although the next pope, Benedict XV (r. 1914–1922), was more of the Leonine school than his predecessor, Harmel was by then in semiretirement and a year from death. Thus the Vatican connection for Harmel largely was confined to the papacy of Leo XIII, and indeed events following the Pantheon incident on October 2, 1891, resulted in important changes for the men personally, as well as for church-state relations in France and Catholic social teaching.

The ebb and flow of events in the years from 1891 to 1903 produced a prolific and varied slate of social teaching emanating from Rome. The decade opened with the publication of *Rerum Novarum,* arguably the most important papal encyclical of modern times, and closed with the cautionary messages of *Testem Benevolentiae* and *Graves de Communi Re.* Events in France both inspired and reflected the contents of these papal directives. The Pantheon incident and the Aix trial signaled an abrupt downturn in papal political fortunes vis-à-vis the Third Republic, thereby prompting Leo XIII to issue the Ralliement letter so as to recoup lost favor with the French government. Papal approval of the *syndicats séparés* and the republican form of government, as well as the Fallières Circulaire issued by the French government in the wake of the Pantheon incident, had immediate consequences for Léon Harmel. The experiment at Val-des-Bois ceased to be the sole paradigm for reformers desirous of improving workplace conditions, and the worker pilgrimages to Rome were suspended for six years, giving Harmel the time and incentive to begin his involvement with the Christian democratic movement. Thus, while the Christian corporation at Val-des-Bois slipped increasingly into the past with the publication of *Rerum Novarum* and the development of Christian democracy, organizations created by Harmel after 1891 matched in importance his earlier contributions to social Catholicism. The Cercles Chrétiens d'Études Sociales, the Christian democratic congresses, the Aumôniers d'Usines, the Semaines Sociales, and even the founding of L'Union Fraternelle and the refashioning of the Third Order of St. Francis, along with all the anti-Semitic and anti-Masonic rhetoric, have been woven permanently into the fabric of the prewar years in France.

CONCLUSION

Made weak by time and fate, but strong in will
To strive, to seek, to find, and not to yield.
—*Alfred Lord Tennyson,* Ulysses

LÉON HARMEL MARSHALED WHAT LITTLE ENERGY REMAINED IN HIS eighty-five-year-old body on August 3, 1914, the day Germany declared war on France, to devote himself to doing all he could for his country and his beloved workers at Val-des-Bois. As early as 1911, he accurately read the signs of war between the two continental neighbors and stockpiled enough wool to carry the factory through the opening phase of World War I without having to lay off any of his workers. Once the fighting began, he exhorted the young men from Val who headed for the front to serve "nobly" and to read Léon Bourgeois's *Declaration des droits de l'homme,* which addressed not only the rights of French citizens but also their duties.[1] For those who remained at the factory, Harmel staged

Le Bois de la Coudrette for Mardi Gras 1914. The play was set in 1871 and developed the theme of patriotism amid defeat. In harkening back to the earlier war for a timely play to entertain his Val-des-Bois family, Harmel reminded his audience that the enemy was again Germany, but he was quick to point out on other occasions in 1914 that there were certain differences in the two wars. In noticeable contrast with the national response in 1870, he observed that the people in 1914 rose up with pride and faith, and with an enthusiasm that portended victory.[2] Indeed, much had changed in France between the two wars, and Harmel had every right to look back with pride on a lifetime of work that had contributed substantially to the transformation of France during the early Third Republic.

The idée fixe of a public career that spanned five decades was most assuredly devotion to the workers and to the pope. Possessed with a deep religious faith and a seemingly inexhaustible supply of energy and ideas, Harmel impressed all who came in contact with him with the scope of his accomplishments. Yet he remained quintessentially human. Refused sainthood by the Church because of his impatience and temper, he preferred not to wait for others to mend society in the aftermath of 1870 but instead put to use his extraordinary organizational skills and promotional ability to correct what he perceived as evil. His many achievements demonstrated his reverence for the past and his hope for the future.

Social Catholicism and Christian democracy were principal beneficiaries of Léon Harmel's time and talents, but so too were myriad other movements and crosscurrents of the times. Directly or indirectly he also was involved with the formalization of a labor-management accord, the challenge of scientific socialism, the creation of Solidarism, and changes in paternalism, as well as the reconfiguration of perhaps the most characteristic expression of popular religiosity of the era, pilgrimage. In the process, he contributed significantly to the social teaching of the Roman Catholic Church and became one of the notables of fin-de-siècle France. His legacy is impressive.

The Christian Corporation

In an era in which employers in large industry and small workshops alike opposed reform legislation governing the workplace, Harmel was a paragon of legal compliance and innovation. Notwithstanding the state mandate of 1900 for a ten-and-a-half-hour workday, for example, workers in the textile factories of the Nord routinely put in twelve-hour days and six- or seven-day weeks.[3] The workers at the Harmel factory complied with the ten-and-a-half-hour regulation and, in addition, from 1878 observed Sunday as a day of rest and Saturday afternoons as holidays. By contrast, only in 1894 was Sunday typically a holiday for other factory workers, and a Saturday afternoon holiday did not become commonplace until 1907. As early as 1913, Harmel workers observed all of Saturday as a holiday.

Harmel also was either in strict compliance with the law or in advance of it when it came to health and safety regulations, as well as medical care, accident or illness indemnities, and pension funds. His workroom temperatures, for instance, were lower than the accepted maximums, and the Harmel *ouvrières* did not labor in the washing and dyeing rooms as was customary in the industry.

Furthermore, beginning in 1842, Val-des-Bois offered its families free medical care and made special financial contributions and arrangements for those who were ill, suffered an accident, were widowed, orphaned, or pregnant, or chose to retire after the age of fifty. The state, on the other hand, did not look seriously to health and safety regulations until 1893, initiated a noncompulsory accident insurance only in 1898,[4] and waited until 1910 to devise plans for old-age pensions, which were to go into effect only after age sixty-five and only became available to all French wage earners in the 1960s. The state, moreover, delayed approval of maternity leaves until 1913.[5]

Harmel also provided free and compulsory elementary education, either religious or laic, for the children at Val-des-Bois and established apprenticeship programs for young people between the ages of thirteen to sixteen that prepared them for adulthood. The state mandated free and compulsory elementary education for French children beginning in 1882 but continued to lag behind Catholic efforts in the professional training of the young at the turn of the century. And whereas the family wage was part of the compensation program at Val-des-Bois during Harmel's tenure, its facsimile, the family allowance, first appeared among government workers during World War I as an incentive to produce larger families but was not extended to the private sphere until 1932 and did not become a universal benefit until 1962.[6]

Most employers did not emulate Harmel in improving living and working conditions for their employees. Nor were they interested in negotiating with organized labor. Consequently, collective bargaining did not become an effective means to settle labor-management discord, with the exception of the mining and printing industries, until after 1936.[7]

This was the case despite the fact that union membership, though low relative to numbers in the workforce, continued to grow. In 1890, for example, some 139,000 workers belonged to a union; by 1914 the number reached one million, or 12 percent of the workforce.[8] Membership in Catholic unions during this period paled by comparision. Harmel calculated that there were some 30,000 to 32,000 men and women in Catholic unions in 1914, with the largest areas of concentration in the Nord (8,000) and Lyon (11,000).[9] The problem, according to Carl Strikwerda, was the paternalistic image of the confessional unions.[10] Harmel suggested that the reason was procrastination in organizing Catholic labor unions after the 1884 law gave them legal recognition. He speculated that if Catholics had organized sooner, much of the "destructive work of socialism" would have been prevented. This was particularly painful to Harmel since he remained convinced in 1914 that the worker *syndicat* at Val-des-Bois, with its 727 members, had established social peace.[11]

In the absence of an environment conducive to collective bargaining, whether because of employer intransigence or employee abstention from union membership, French workers relied on state intervention or worker councils. State intervention in the form of forced arbitration began in the 1880s and 1890s when the local state agents, the *préfets,* intervened in serious conflicts (a practice that continues into the present).[12] The worker councils handled the less serious, or smaller, conflicts. The worker representatives elected to these councils, over which *patrons* presided, were the only workers legally recognized as bargaining agents until 1968.[13] For although unions were recognized in 1884, they were acknowledged for their right to associate but not for the right to bargain. Despite the absence of legalized bargaining power, however, unions received de facto bargaining rights, especially after 1936.[14]

But at the turn of the century, the only practical recourse open to factory workers who did not have access to a worker council, such as the Conseil d'Usine at Val-des-Bois, was either the strike or the local Conseil des Prud'hommes. By making effective use of the Conseil d'Usine, the

Harmel factory avoided not only strikes but the Conseil des Prud'hommes as well. Harmel, writing in 1914, prided himself on the fact that for a ten-year period there was not a single complaint registered by any of his workers at the Tribunal of the Conseil des Prud'hommes. This record was especially gratifying to him because the initiation of a complaint procedure by a worker was free of charge, and the Conseil des Prud'hommes was "very partial to the workers."[15]

Scientific (Revolutionary) Socialism

Harmel clearly was a serious labor reformer. He not only stood out from other employers of the era in his compliance with factory regulations, but he was often in advance of republican lawmakers in correcting workplace ills. Harmel put into practice many of the demands of contemporary socialists, but this was not as extraordinary as it might initially seem since Christianity and socialism shared many common traits.

Both addressed their messages to an oppressed people, promised salvation, suffered persecution by the prevailing society, gave assurance of ultimate victory, and created organizations that were hierarchical in structure and universal in scope.[16] Karl Marx (1818–1883) commented in the *Communist Manifesto* that "Nothing is easier than to give Christian asceticism a socialist tinge." But Marx believed that the two creeds could never be reconciled because socialism was a materialist ideology while Christianity was a metaphysical one, and besides religion was an instrument of class rule.[17] Thus he vigorously opposed socialists who found inspiration in Christianity.

Yet certain French socialists contemplated political partnership with Christians. Witness an exchange that took place in the Chamber of Deputies on December 8, 1891. On this date, just months after the publication of *Rerum Novarum*, Paul Lafargue, who happened to be Marx's son-in-law, appealed to Christian socialists to join revolutionary socialists in an alliance to overcome the bloc of bourgeois republicans and enact a social program. He asked for "the cooperation of all who desire labor reforms, of all who wish to alleviate human sufferings." "[W]e address ourselves as much to this side of the Chamber [the right] as to that [the left]," he said. De Mun responded by disclaiming the socialist label while admitting that he was "separated by an equally profound disagreement [with the republicans] touching social reforms, in principle and in application."[18] And indeed the labor legislation sponsored by de Mun and other social Catholics in the Chamber of Deputies rivaled that of the socialists in the closing decades of the nineteenth century.

Shared values and parliamentary cooperation did not go unnoticed by the republican majority. Eugene Spuller, a republican deputy, commented:

> It is certain, in fact, that at the present hour the general principles of the Revolution are being battered down with redoubled vigor by all the socialists. Whether it be the pretendedly scientific socialism of Karl Marx or the Christian socialism of men who claim to draw inspiration from the teachings of the Church, little matters. There is evident a movement against the liberty of labor and even against the principle of property, as these principles were understood and comprehended by the Revolution, and the social evolution of the Church can only give new force to this movement.[19]

Christian socialists and scientific socialists took note of one another outside the Chamber of Deputies as well (and both groups were monitored by the republicans). Revolutionary socialists frequently attended the Christian congresses of the 1890s, for example. At one such congress, thirty members of the Parti Ouvrier (Worker Party) were present, and three of their contingent spoke before the congress. Monsieur Geronin chastised Christians for not supporting socialists at the polls when many of the Catholic reformist programs, like those for day care, benefits for the ill and injured, and family savings banks, were identical to those of the scientific socialists. Monsieur Guerin talked of their common ground in that both Christians and revolutionary socialists were against "the capitalists who are symbolized in the Jew." And Monsieur Gons declared that he was in agreement with most of the Christians' program but could not endorse their proposal enabling clergy to head a government, for the clergy will "never have the confidence of the worker."[20]

Christians also sensed possible cohabitation with socialists. Despite evidence to the contrary in the socialist press, Etienne Lamy, in his "Report on the Situation of the Catholics in France" to the Vatican, asserted that the "socialists are the least passionate against the Church."[21] But because of the Pantheon incident, the Aix Affair, and, above all, the Dreyfus Affair, dialogue between Christian democrats and socialists broke down in the late 1890s. Christians stepped up their anti-Semitic campaign, while socialists placed themselves squarely in the anticlerical and pro-republican camp. The result was renewed polarization. Jules Guesde represented the new socialist attitude when he baited de Mun in the Chamber on June 15–16, 1896, by saying, "Your only solution to the social problem is the good *patron*.... [T]hat is in essence what you call Christian social-ism[,] ... but the good *patron* has a corollary, an underside, the bad *patron*." Moreover, de Mun and his collaborators were, for Guesde, "our lost children of socialism who were not even worth taking the trouble to combat."[22]

Léon Harmel saw things somewhat differently. Like many of his coreligionists who were intent on societal reform, he maintained an ambiguous position with regard to socialism. To begin with, he, unlike de Mun, was comfortable with the term "Christian socialism,"[23] and he wanted to study socialist theory.[24] Apparently, he followed through on this matter because he was able to refer to the theories of Proudhon, Marx, and Lassalle, as well as to express a certain familiarity with contemporary socialist groups like the "possibilistes," the "radical collectivists" (Marxists), and the anarchists.[25]

From his studies, Harmel determined that socialist theory by and large erred. For not only had socialism developed from liberalism,[26] but it represented materialism in all its "coarseness" by wishing to undermine "God, family, and property."[27] Besides, he felt that the revolutionary socialists were primarily focused on the strike, and once the strike ended, so did their work.[28] Harmel took particular exception to socialist theory in its disregard for religion, its objective of creating a classless society and of transforming private property into public property,[29] and its desire to eliminate the wage system.[30]

Still, he acknowledged that the socialists upheld two "correct" ideas, that of justice and that of brotherhood (*solidarité*). Harmel also believed that dialogue with the revolutionary socialists was crucial to the Christian mission because "there is but a fine line between saint and sinner."[31] With this as his working premise, he conceived the confrontation with socialists as primarily a "battle of ideas" in which truth ultimately would prevail. Consequently, he advised Christian socialists:

[Be] indulgent and nice towards adversaries. They are your brothers. Their errors come from prejudices, from ignorance, and from the *milieux* in which they live. They are often sincere.... [Y]our adversaries of today will be your best friends tomorrow. Tomorrow they will be the most intrepid defenders of your cause; be then nice towards them, and in combating their errors, don't ever wound their hearts.[32]

Little did Harmel know how prescient his words were. Recently socialist parties in Europe have become conciliatory toward religion and its representatives, while the Catholic Church has softened its rhetoric against scientific socialism. Though still opposed to the concept of class warfare, John XXIII, writing in *Pacem in Terris* (April 11, 1963), could say about his philosophical opponents and their social and economic goals: "Who can deny the possible existence of good and commendable elements in these programs, elements which do indeed conform to the dictates of right reason, and are the expression of men's lawful aspirations."[33] And while John Paul II (r. 1978–) discourages the practice of liberation theology with its tint of socialism and its implied endorsement of class warfare, and while he remains adamant on the right to private ownership of property,[34] he simultaneously negotiates globally with socialist governments.

During the 1890s, social Catholics and Christian democrats, like Harmel, joined formally and informally with socialists to act as a pressure group to encourage republican reform, thereby presaging what later would become accepted political behavior between doctrinal enemies. Indeed, police records of both the Christian democratic congresses and the socialist congresses indicate the extent to which the government of the Third Republic monitored the activities and pronouncements of their assemblies, while the party platforms of the congresses,[35] as well as the other activities of the groups, provided the impetus for republican legislative labor reform. The ideological synthesis that resulted from the amalgamation of numerous philosophical components was known as Solidarism, and it became the ideology of Third Republicans at the turn of the century.[36]

Solidarism

Solidarism called for the extension of rights first delineated during the French Revolution. But instead of emphasizing the civil rights of French citizens, as had been the case throughout the nineteenth century, Léon Bourgeois and other proponents of the ideology wanted contemporary society also to pay attention to political and social rights implied in the Revolution's cornerstone document, *The Declaration of Man and Citizen*. In addition, Bourgeois introduced to Third Republicans the complement to civil, political, and social rights, duty. But it was a duty intended to reach beyond traditional Christian charity, and consequently Solidarists viewed the Roman Church's emphasis on charity as inadequate for contemporary obligations. Likewise, they viewed with a critical eye the shortcomings of republicanism as it had been practiced since 1789, that is, to the distinct advantage of the bourgeoisie, who considered its duty fulfilled by educating its citizenry. Bourgeois summoned his fellow republicans to do more; it was necessary not only to educate French men and women but also to share with fellow citizens the material benefits of social progress. He dismissed scientific socialism as well, for he wanted no part of a monolithic state that made little allowance for the pluralistic nature of society; in his opinion, the state was to operate solely as a *primus inter pares*. In short, Solidarism marked the transition from a society characterized by individualism to one of more statist inclination, and it guided French republicans toward the modern welfare state.[37] In steering republicans on a road between individualism and statism, Bourgeois emulated Léon Harmel and other Catholic reformers who also sought the middle way between republican individualism and socialist statism but who attempted to do so as early as the mid-nineteenth century.

Unlike socialist theorists who gave priority to the proletariat and refused all collaboration with the bourgeoisie, Harmel espoused a corporatist point of view that envisioned all classes as functional components of the whole and worked toward class cooperation rather than warfare. By holding to this notion, Harmel was more in tune with republicans, who heralded Solidarism as the answer to the Social Question, than were socialists and anarchists, who still favored revolution as the remedy. In sum, at a time when the balance of industrial power was entirely on the side of the employers, Harmel gave his workers a certain status and recognition unparalleled for the time. But he and his factory were unique, for ultimately legislation, under the banner of republican Solidarism, was necessary to assure all workers dignity and justice.

Paternalism

The paternalistic order that Harmel represented changed between 1870 and 1914. During the early years of Harmel's factory, paternalism assured the workers considerable protection against the numerous social and economic ills associated with industrialization under a laissez-faire economic system. From the initial establishment by Jacques-Joseph Harmel in the 1840s of a savings bank and a relief fund for the workers to the organization of more than twenty economic and social institutions, largely under the aegis of Léon Harmel, the factory at Val-des-Bois symbolized the best of nineteenth-century paternalism.

The advent of social legislation in the 1890s and the concurrent rise in wages, however, made the Christian corporation at Val-des-Bois an anachronism. Many of the benefits attendant to this form of paternalism faded as the public sector assumed greater responsibility for the individual. Nevertheless, paternalism as practiced within Harmel's Christian corporation served as a link to the paternalistic management style of the present.

Some assert that modern paternalism is what accounts for the absence of "worker mobilization,"[38] while Michelle Perrot claims that paternalism persists simply because it is accepted by the French worker.[39] In a nation oriented to familial values, a paternalistic relationship between employer and employee is normal, and in an economic environment characterized by small enterprises, the inclination intensifies. In short, paternalism is quintessentially French.

Harmel anticipated twentieth-century changes to the paternalistic system principally by giving increased managerial responsibility to workers elected to the Conseil d'Usine, but he never surrendered the fundamental elements of paternalism. These are, according to Perrot's definition, (1) the physical presence of the *patron* at the place of production; (2) the use of language and practices "of a familial type" between the employer and employee (witness Harmel's sobriquet, *le bon père*); and (3) the emotional bonding of the worker to the enterprise.[40] The historical record demonstrates that both in his lifetime and by contemporary standards, Harmel was a model of paternalistic behavior, for the ethos of fin-de-siècle paternalism, such as existed at Val-des-Bois, prevails in many European enterprises today. Even after the dynamic tenure of Léon Harmel, the

Harmel factory functioned like most other French factories that assimilated sound managerial methods, namely, with overtones of paternalism.

Harmel's son and nephew oversaw the reconstruction of Val-des-Bois in 1922, more or less duplicating institutions and associations from the prewar era. But although the factory remained in family hands until it closed in the early 1970s, the atmosphere of the Leonine era was never fully re-created. By 1945 the Conseil d'Usine had become a mere factory committee as more and more of the workers became involved with outside unions; the communal spirit had diminished as workers and their families increasingly lived off site and commuted to the factory; and the religious atmosphere became less pervasive when the factory chaplaincy closed down in 1957 and the religious orders left in 1958. Though economic conditions and outdated technology ultimately brought about the closure of the Harmel enterprise, Trimouille detected perceptible change between the older and younger workers when he interviewed them in 1967: the younger men and women regarded Val-des-Bois with a noticeable indifference when compared to the older workers.[41]

Worker Pilgrimages

Though involved in numerous projects generated by social Catholicism and Christian democracy, the venture that propelled Léon Harmel into the national and international spotlight almost overnight was the worker pilgrimages to Rome. His collaboration with Leo XIII on this project joined pope and industrialist in an enterprise that promised to call attention not only to the misfortunes of the worker but also to the temporal situation of the Vatican. Because of the so-called Roman Question, the Italian capital was supercharged politically. By arranging to bring thousands of French workers to Rome, in part to call attention to the beleaguered papacy, Harmel reached well beyond the comfort and familiarity of Val-des-Bois. The pilgrimages of 1887 and 1889 and the opening weeks of the 1891 pilgrimage instilled confidence in the grand project. The number of pilgrims grew steadily, and newspapers, with the exception of the socialist press, tolerated and, in some cases, celebrated the pilgrimages.

It was only a matter of time, however, before the Italian government, adamant about retaining former papal land, reacted to the French pilgrims and their political agenda. The Pantheon incident halted the pilgrimages, thereby somewhat discrediting Léon Harmel personally and certainly deflating papal political ambitions. The repercussions of the Pantheon incident were most pronounced in France, long divided as to the role of the Roman Church on French soil but particularly so in the years following 1870. Consequently, the government of the Third Republic did not appreciate outspoken bishops who voiced displeasure with the Fallières Circulaire. The trial of the archbishop of Aix exhibited that goodwill between Throne and Altar was a fragile commodity and anticipated what many endorsed, especially after the Dreyfus Affair, the separation of church and state in France.

The worker pilgrimages to Rome would appear at first glance to be a failure. But Léon Harmel and Leo XIII, gambling at considerable odds, received a payoff in numerous ways. The Church maintained its moral leadership as Leo XIII welcomed the worker-pilgrims to Rome, listened to their grievances, and issued *Rerum Novarum* on their behalf. The great encyclical on labor received praise from all quarters, the socialist applause being the most noteworthy. The encyclical on labor, as well as the worker pilgrimages, announced to the world that the Roman Catholic Church intended to respond to the demands of the age. The worker pilgrimages to Rome also demonstrated that pilgrimage was not a female reserve and that male workers, in contrast to the prevailing view and in impressive numbers, were indeed active, practicing Catholics. Moreover, the worker pilgrimages allowed Léon Harmel to use his increased notoriety to advantage by launching a fresh round of projects, referred to collectively as Christian democracy. Leo XIII, meanwhile, relentlessly pursued his dream of recouping lost land and supported until his death in 1903 a pro-French foreign policy, as well as Harmel's post-1891 endeavors.

Christian Democracy

Harmel's relevance is readily apparent in the development of twentieth-century Christian democracy. The flourishing of the Christian democratic movement after World War II in Europe testifies to the durability of organizations first formulated in the closing decade of the nineteenth century. With the demise of the Christian corporation, Harmel immersed himself in Christian democracy, and one of its activities was the formation of Catholic trade unions. The growth of confessional unions in the twentieth century owes much to early organizers such as Harmel. At the onset of World War II, Catholic unions represented a hefty one-fifth of the strength of the Confédération Générale du Travail,[42] while they claimed even greater success after the war[43] only to become "deconfessionalized" in 1964 when the Confédération Français du Travail Chrétien became the Confédération Français Démocratique du Travail.[44] Harmel predicted in 1914 the eventual numerical breakthrough of the Catholic *syndicats* whose "slow but effective and sure growth increased their influence in the legislature and economic spheres."[45] The breakthrough, however, did not occur in the de-Christianized Champagne district, locus of the Harmel factory, but rather in the Nord during the interwar period.[46] The Nord, although the geographic domain of Marxist socialism, was both highly industrialized and noted for its adherence to traditional religious practice. Consequently, it was a propitious site for the expansion of both confessional and nonconfessional syndicalism.

Christian democracy prospered politically as well in the twentieth century. For example, the postwar French Christian democratic party, the Mouvement Républicain Populaire (MRP), was tangible fruit of the turn-of-the-century movement spearheaded by Léon Harmel. Early Christian democracy in France generated considerable political activism in the 1890s only to be undermined by its anti-Semitic rhetoric. The MRP enjoyed substantial electoral success, as did the socialists, after World War II but nevertheless capitulated in the wake of military defeat in the French Indo-China War to the Parti du Rassemblement du Peuple Français, the personal political organization of Charles de Gaulle.

Catholic Social Teaching

Léon Harmel's social program was consonant with the development of Catholic social teaching. The Christian corporation received official papal endorsement in 1891 with the publication of *Rerum Novarum*. And Pius XI

(r. 1922–1939), in his encyclical *Quadragesimo Anno* (May 15, 1931), used the opportunity of the fortieth anniversary of *Rerum Novarum* not only to reiterate the validity of the earlier message but also to enlarge on it. *Quadragesimo Anno* sanctioned the Harmelian family wage and also asked that workers share in the management, profits, or ownership of an enterprise.[47] The workers at Val-des-Bois participated in company management through the Conseil d'Usine and benefited from company profits when they shopped at the factory cooperative, but Harmel did not entertain the notion of coownership with the workers.

Besides endorsing corporatism in the workplace, *Quadragesimo Anno* offered the corporate structure as a political solution for the societal turbulence in the years immediately preceding World War II. But papal sanction of political corporatism led to disillusionment when the corporate regimes set up in Italy, Austria, Portugal, Spain, and Vichy France betrayed Catholic corporate ideals; corporatism became a mere facade for centralized power and departed from the principles of such earlier corporate theorists as La Tour du Pin who advocated decentralized governments.[48] Fascist governments also departed from *Quadragesimo Anno*'s insistence on the principle of subsidiarity which stipulated that "one should not withdraw from individuals and commit to community what they can accomplish by their own enterprise and industry."[49] Pius wanted the associations, or corporations, to retain autonomous power vis-à-vis the state and not be absorbed by it.

Even though corporatism as a political structure was discredited after World War II because of its Fascist connections, the ideals associated with Christian corporatism persisted both in the Roman Church and in European society. The publication of *Mater et Magistra* (May 15, 1961) by Pope John XXIII (r. 1958–1963) demonstrates this point. Marking the seventieth anniversary of *Rerum Novarum,* John XXIII spoke out on contemporary social and labor problems by repeating the basic message of *Rerum Novarum* but with appropriate updating to reflect the times. For example, whereas John, like Leo XIII, called for wages to be just and equitable, the ownership of private property to be expanded, and worker associations to be created, he also said that merely increasing wages did not satisfy justice, the primary role of private property was no longer patrimonial, and worker associations henceforth could be not only confessional but nonconfessional and international as well.[50]

In redefining *Rerum Novarum*'s message to reflect contemporary conditions, *Mater et Magistra* also illustrates the enduring nature of the values of Christian corporatism as practiced at Val-des-Bois. For here John XXIII taught that in addition to paying workers a just wage, employers must allow employees to participate in the ownership, the profits, or the management of a company in order that they might exercise control over their workplace environment. The concept of a stock option plan was not part of Harmel's world, but he offered his workers the *boni corportif,* as well as considerable opportunity to control their work environment.

John XXIII acknowledged in *Mater et Magistra* that the welfare state had replaced patrimony as a hedge against future adversity. But by establishing a cradle-to-grave benefit system, Harmel furnished his workers with not inconsiderable security disassociated from traditional patrimony far in advance of a formal welfare state in France. By encouraging saving for an uncertain future, Léon Harmel kept the option of a worker patrimony intact.

Finally, Harmel's leadership in the development of Catholic syndicalism outside the framework of the Christian corporation demonstrates his foresight and his willingness to entertain new ways to advance associational institutions. For as John XXIII emphasized in *Mater et Magistra,* intermediary bodies, such as labor unions, were more important than ever as governments become increasingly intrusive in the daily lives of their citizens with the near-constant barrage of rules and regulations.[51]

Pope Paul VI (r. 1963–1978) and Pope John Paul II have reiterated and enlarged on the earlier messages of Leo XIII, Pius XI, and John XXIII on the Labor Question. In *Populorum Progressio* (March 26, 1967), Paul VI addressed not only "the whole Catholic world" but also "all men of good will" in his encyclical that applied the message of *Rerum Novarum* to the world at large; nations blessed with abundance needed to feed hungry nations.[52] Paul intended wealthy nations to do more than feed the hungry of the world, however. His mandate provided for a full range of social and economic structures so as to allow the underprivileged countries to develop more fully in the framework of the modern world. Reminiscent of traditional Catholic social teaching, Léon Harmel's thoughts on the rights and duties of employers and employees, and Solidarist ideology, Paul cautioned in *Populorum Progressio* that human solidarity had obligations as well as benefits, because each man belongs to the community of men. He warned further that if the current reign of technology was not tempered with a concomitant service to man rather than to profits, modern technology could inflict as much damage on today's world as liberalism did in an earlier era. Paul's solutions included providing basic education, support of the family, a just wage, and encouraging world peace. Though the promotion of world peace was never a specific project of Harmel, other mandates of *Populorum Progressio* clearly were. Paul VI appropriated earlier Catholic social teaching on labor and applied it globally.

Pope John Paul II, writing on the occasion of the ninetieth anniversary of *Rerum Novarum*, followed in the footsteps of Leo XIII and his other papal predecessors by issuing *Laborem Exercens* (September 14, 1981), his own encyclical on the subject of labor, for "the social question has not ceased to engage the Church's attention."[53] In *Laborem Exercens*, John Paul II glorified human work but acknowledged that in the contemporary world labor encounters hazards that were not present or fully developed in 1891 when the context for the Social Question was more or less limited to the relationship among the socioeconomic classes rather than between the industrialized and nonindustrialized world. Widespread automation in factories, the high cost of energy and raw materials, pollution, and the constant need to retrain workers because of rapidly advancing technology are some of the challenges people currently face in a world that is increasingly interdependent due to the proliferation of multinational companies that dominate the global economy. Given this situation, John Paul saw the gap between rich and poor countries continuing to widen, taking its heaviest toll on the youth of undeveloped countries.

Thus there remained a need for new movements of solidarity among workers, according to John Paul II, especially since the Church has always endorsed "the principle of the priority of labor over capital."[54] Likewise, strikes have their place in the modern world, as long as the right to strike is not abused, leading to the "paralysis of the whole socioeconomic life."[55] In sum, in *Laborem Exercens,* the Church responded to the needs of laborers, whether manual or intellectual, by calling attention to the dignity and rights of those who work.

But responsibility to address specific material needs of the workers rested with the state, according to John Paul II, for along with a world of increased economic complexity, the Church no longer can rely on the goodwill of *patrons*. Today the state alone has the means to guarantee unemployment benefits, vocational training, and a just wage. Adequate remuneration for work should take into consideration the entire family of the worker, so as to allow mothers the option of remaining at home with children rather than being forced into the workplace. The pope therefore expressed the same values and concerns regarding the critical role of the mother of the family that Léon Harmel did earlier. But to respond to current conditions, the pope, unlike Harmel, made allowances for women who preferred to work outside the home, regardless of family circumstances. If for whatever reason a woman prefers to work outside the home, then John Paul advocates nondiscriminatory remuneration. But ideally, according to the pope, the wage package should be structured in such a way that women will have every incentive to remain at home. Just as Harmel initiated the family wage, medical assistance, housing, a consumer cooperative, and retirement plans to encourage mothers to be full-time homemakers, so too did *Laborem Exercens* suggest that employers devise wage packages to include health and accident benefits, as well as insurance and retirement programs, in order that mothers who preferred to stay at home and care for families would have financial security. As for women in the workplace, the pope urged employers to provide a salutary work environment, a weekly day of rest, and a yearly vacation, proposals that he also recommended for workingmen, of course, and were in place at Harmel's factory.

Laborem Exercens reasserted that although the Church has always been concerned with human labor, the teaching on the Social Question really began with *Rerum Novarum*, and "human work is a key, probably the essential key, to the whole social question."[56] John Paul II reaffirmed, then, the crucial role played by Léon Harmel and Leo XIII in the development of Catholic social teaching during the early Third Republic.

Final Days

On September 2, 1915, as the war closed in on them, the civilian population of Warmériville, including the personnel of Val-des-Bois, evacuated to Reims. Circumstances dictated that the Harmel family separate. Some of the younger men returned for a time to the factory in a last-ditch effort to keep it running, while Léon Harmel, heeding the advice of his family, had retired to Nice in August. By November he was suffering from pneumonia and had limited mobility, venturing from his sickbed only to visit a small chapel on the premises where the Blessed Sacrament was contained. Progressively weaker with each passing day, visits to the chapel where he prayed before the Blessed Sacrament were his only solace. He visited the chapel for the last time on November 19, at which time he broke down and sobbed over the situation at Val-des-Bois. Confined now to his bedroom, his physical condition continued to deteriorate and he increasingly retreated into the spiritual world. On November 21 he received the Last Sacraments, and three days later he donned the scapular and cords of the Third Order of St. Francis. After blessing his family and all the workers at the factory, Léon Harmel died peacefully on November 25, 1915, surrounded by family members and Marie, a former worker at Val-des-Bois.[57]

NOTES

Introduction

1. Georges Guitton, S.J., *Léon Harmel, 1829–1915*, 2 vols. (Paris: Action Populaire, 1927), 1:74.
2. Gérard Noiriel, *Les Ouvriers dans la société française XIX–XX siècle* (Paris: Éditions du Seuil, 1986), 112.
3. Eugen Weber, *France Fin de Siècle* (Cambridge, Mass.: Harvard University Press, 1986), 23.
4. Pierre Nora, "Between Memory and History," in *Realms of Memory*, under the direction of Pierre Nora (New York: Columbia University Press, 1996), 1:5.
5. Allen Mitchell, *The Divided Path* (Chapel Hill: University of North Carolina Press, 1991). See especially chapter 3 (pp. 44–67) for the German model for French social reform. For military reform, see Mitchell's *Victors and Vanquished: The German Influence on Army and Church in France after 1870* (Chapel Hill: University of North Carolina Press, 1984); chapters 2 through 5 (pp. 29–117) focus on the importance of the German factor in French military reform. On German influence in French intellectual life and higher education, see Martha Hanna, *The Mobilization of the Intellect* (Cambridge, Mass.: Harvard University Press, 1996), especially pp. 27–32.

6. For a closer look at this subject, see Joan L. Coffey, "Of Catechisms and Sermons: Church-State Relations in France, 1890–1905," *Church History* 66 (1997): 54–66.

7. Pius IX (r. 1846–1878), Leo XIII (r. 1878–1903), Pius X (r. 1903–1914), and Benedict XIV (r. 1914–1922).

8. Gérard Cholvy, *Être chrétien en France au XIXe siècle, 1790–1914* (Paris: Éditions du Seuil, 1997), 121.

9. See, for example, Gérard Cholvy and Yves-Marie Hilaire, *Histoire religieuse de la France contemporaine, 1880–1930* (Toulouse: Bibliothèque Historique Privat, 1986); Adrien Dansette, *Histoire religieuse de la France contemporaine, 1880–1930*, 2 vols. (Paris: Flammarion, 1951); Jean-Marie Mayeur, *Catholicisme social et démocratie chrétienne: Principes, romains, experiences français* (Paris: Éditions du Cerf, 1986); John McManners, *Church and State in France, 1870–1914* (New York: Harper & Row, 1972), see especially pp. 84–86, 88–95; Paul Misner, *Social Catholicism in Europe* (New York: Crossroad, 1991), especially pp. 111–112, 132–135, 227–231, 320–321; Parker Thomas Moon, *The Labor Problem and the Social Catholic Movement in France* (New York: Macmillan, 1921); Pierre Pierrard, *L'Église et les ouvriers en France (1840–1940)* (Paris: Hachette, 1984); Henri Rollet, *L'Action sociale des catholiques en France, 1871–1914* (Paris: Desclée de Bronwer, 1958); Robert Talmy, *L'Association catholique des patrons de Nord, 1884–1895* (Lille: Facultés Catholique, 1962); Robert Talmy, *Aux Sources de catholicisme social* (Tournai: Desclée & Co., 1963); Robert Talmy, *Le Syndicalisme chrétien en France (1871–1930)* (Paris: Éditions Bloud & Gay, 1965); Alec R. Vidler, *A Century of Social Catholicism, 1820–1920* (London: SPCK, 1964), especially pp. 123–125; L'Abbé Emmanuel Barbier, *Le Progrès du liberalism catholique en France sous le pape Léon XIII*, 2 vols. (Paris: P. Lethielleux, 1907), 2:217.

10. Misner, *Social Catholicism in Europe*, 192; L'Abbé Emmanuel Barbier, *Le Progrès du liberalism catholique en France*, 2:124.

11. Talmy, *Le Syndicalisme chrétien en France*, 16.

12. Rollet, *L'Action sociale des catholiques en France*, 223.

13. Dansette, *Histoire religieuse*, 193.

14. Guitton, *Léon Harmel, 1829–1915;* and Pierre Trimouille, *Léon Harmel et l'usine chrétienne du Val des Bois* (Lyon: Centre d'Histoire du Catholicisme de Lyon, 1974).

CHAPTER ONE Family History and Legacy

1. Gloria K. Fiero, Wendy Pfeffer, and Mathé Allain, *Three Medieval Views of Women* (New Haven: Yale University Press, 1989), 109 (verse 45).

2. Georges Guitton, S.J., *Léon Harmel, 1829–1915*, 2 vols. (Paris: Action Populaire, 1927), 1:1.

3. Guitton, *Léon Harmel, 1829–1915*, 3–6; Pierre Trimouille, *Léon Harmel et l'usine chrétienne du Val des Bois* (Lyon: Centre d'Histoire du Catholicisme de Lyon, 1974), 15.

4. Guitton, *Léon Harmel, 1829–1915*, 1:6.

5. Guitton, *Léon Harmel, 1829–1915*, 1:6–7.

6. Trimouille, *Léon Harmel et l'usine chrétienne*, 16.

7. Guitton, *Léon Harmel, 1829–1915*, 1:9.

8. Guitton, *Léon Harmel, 1829–1915*, 1:15.

9. Guitton, *Léon Harmel, 1829–1915*, 1:10–17.

10. Bonnie G. Smith, *Ladies of the Leisure Class* (Princeton: Princeton University Press, 1981), 35–36.

11. Trimouille, *Léon Harmel et l'usine chrétienne*, 65.

12. Guitton, *Léon Harmel, 1829–1915*, 1:19, 40–41; Trimouille, *Léon Harmel et l'usine chrétienne*, 16–19.

13. Alec R. Vidler, *A Century of Social Catholicism, 1820–1920* (London: SPCK, 1964), x.

14. Vidler, *A Century of Social Catholicism*, x.

15. After the final defeat of Napoléon Bonaparte at Waterloo in 1815, Louis XVIII (r. 1814–1824) returned to Paris to claim the Bourbon crown for a second time. He was the second of the Bourbon brothers to rule France; he followed Louis XVI, who was executed by revolutionaries on January 21, 1793. The young son of Louis XVI and Marie Antoinette never ascended the throne (he died in a Parisian prison on June 8, 1795, when he was ten years old), but out of respect for the Bourbon heir, he was known as Louis XVII. After the death of Louis XVIII in 1824, the third of the brothers became king of France. Charles X (r. 1824–1830) ruled until the Revolution of 1830 sent him into exile in Great Britain where he died.

16. The July Monarchy was the name given to the reign of Louis-Philippe (r. 1830–1848) because it was on July 27, 28, and 29 that revolution in Paris ended the reign of Charles X and installed Louis-Philippe, Duc d'Orléans, as king of France. As a youth, he was a republican before the Reign of Terror sent him into exile. On returning to Paris after 1815, he was known as a liberal and thus seemed to be the perfect candidate to replace Charles X in 1830. Because of his plebeian sympathies he was called the "citizen-king," but when he disappointed political groups intent on greater change, he went into exile once again in 1848.

17. Vidler, *A Century of Social Catholicism*, 3–7; Paul Misner, *Social Catholicism in Europe* (New York: Crossroad, 1991), 44–45.

18. Vidler, *A Century of Social Catholicism*, 9–19; Misner, *Social Catholicism in Europe*, 46–63.

19. As a result of revolution in Paris, beginning in February and ending in June 1848, France abandoned the monarchical form and replaced it with a republic from 1848 to 1852.

20. On this subject, see, for example, Edward Berenson, *Populist Religion and Left-Wing Politics in France, 1830–1852* (Princeton: Princeton University Press, 1984).

21. Napoléon III, born Charles Louis Napoléon Bonaparte in 1808, was the third son of Louis Bonaparte and Hortense de Beauharnais (respectively, the brother and stepdaughter of Napoléon I). He was the president of the Second Republic from 1848 to 1851. After staging a coup in 1851, he became emperor of the French from December 2, 1852, to September 4, 1870, when he surrendered to Prussian forces. He married a Spanish countess, Eugenia Maria de Montijo de Guzman (1826–1920), known to history as Eugénie, and undertook numerous public works projects in Paris, encouraged agriculture, industry, and economics, and founded several charitable institutions. He died in exile in England in 1873.

22. Vidler, *A Century of Social Catholicism*, 25.

23. Guitton, *Léon Harmel, 1829–1915*, 1:60–62.

24. For a discussion of sacred places and their significance, see Roger Lipsey, *Have You Been to Delphi?* (Albany: State University of New York Press, 2001).

25. The Bourbon grandson of Charles X, Count of Chambord, lived in exile in Frohsdorf, Austria, where he died without an heir in 1883. Misner, *Social Catholicism in Europe*, 117.

26. Régine Pernoud and Marie-Véronique Clin, *Joan of Arc* (New York: St. Martin's Press, 1999), 65.

27. Pernoud and Clin, *Joan of Arc*, 28.

28. Raymond Jonas, *France and the Cult of the Sacred Heart* (Berkeley: University of California Press, 2000), 89.

29. Jonas, *France and the Cult of the Sacred Heart*, 8, 141, 148.

30. Jonas, *France and the Cult of the Sacred Heart*, 182–184.

31. Trimouille, *Léon Harmel et l'usine chrétienne*, 33–34.

32. Trimouille, *Léon Harmel et l'usine chrétienne*, 34.

33. Guitton, *Léon Harmel, 1829–1915*, 1:73.

34. Guitton, *Léon Harmel, 1829–1915*, 2:394; Trimouille, *Léon Harmel et l'usine chrétienne*, 34.

35. Guitton, *Léon Harmel, 1829–1915*, 1:192.

36. The Catholic *collège* is the equivalent of the laic *lycée*. Lycées are secondary schools where pupils study for their *baccalauréat* after leaving *collège*. In

both the Catholic and laic systems, if students pass the "bac," they may then go on to study at a university or one of the *grandes écoles,* which are professional schools. Léon Harmel successfully passed "the *bac.*"

37. Guitton, *Léon Harmel, 1829–1915,* 1:13.
38. Trimouille, *Léon Harmel et l'usine chrétienne,* 23.
39. Guitton, *Léon Harmel, 1829–1915,* 1:117.
40. Léon Harmel to La Tour du Pin, 13 March 1879, 59 J 72, Archives de la Marne, Châlons-sur-Marne, France (hereafter cited as AM).
41. Address by Léon Harmel to the Congrès Ouvrier de Tours, 5 June 1897, Ch. 982, AM.
42. Trimouille, *Léon Harmel et l'usine chrétienne,* 21–23, 197.
43. Trimouille, *Léon Harmel et l'usine chrétienne,* 26.
44. Guitton, *Léon Harmel, 1829–1915,* 1:40.
45. Léon Harmel to P. Delaporte, n.d., 59 J 18, AM.
46. Trimouille, *Léon Harmel et l'usine chrétienne,* 28.
47. Smith, *Ladies of the Leisure Class,* 35.
48. Guitton, *Léon Harmel, 1829–1915,* 1:8.
49. Guitton, *Léon Harmel, 1829–1915,* 1:13–16.
50. Guitton, *Léon Harmel, 1829–1915,* 1:10.
51. Guitton, *Léon Harmel, 1829–1915,* 1:2–11.
52. Guitton, *Léon Harmel, 1829–1915,* 1:23.
53. Guitton, *Léon Harmel, 1829–1915,* 1:24; Trimouille, *Léon Harmel et l'usine chrétienne,* 28.
54. Guitton, *Léon Harmel, 1829–1915,* 1:68.
55. Guitton, *Léon Harmel, 1829–1915,* 1:18.
56. Guitton, *Léon Harmel, 1829–1915,* 1:2–17.
57. Smith's book in its entirety verifies Alexandrine Harmel's qualification as a *vrai bourgeoise,* as she indeed held center stage in the Harmel household (Smith, *Ladies of the Leisure Class,* 63).
58. Guitton, *Léon Harmel, 1829–1914,* 1:17.
59. Guitton, *Léon Harmel, 1829–1915,* 1:52.
60. Guitton, *Léon Harmel, 1829–1915,* 1:3.
61. Léon Harmel, *Souvenir de Felix Harmel* (Blois, 1900), n.p.
62. Smith, *Ladies of the Leisure Class,* 57, 61.
63. Smith, *Ladies of the Leisure Class,* 63.
64. Guitton, *Léon Harmel, 1829–1915,* 1:49–66.
65. Peritonitis is an inflammation of the peritoneum produced by bacteria or irritating substances introduced into the abdominal cavity by a penetrating wound or perforation of an organ in the GI or reproductive tract.
66. Guitton, *Léon Harmel, 1829–1915,* 1:34, 72.

67. Guitton, *Léon Harmel, 1829–1915*, 1:170–173.
68. Trimouille, *Léon Harmel et l'usine chrétienne*, 86.
69. Léon Harmel, "Souvenirs de Famille," gathering of 9 September 1907, Ch. 982, AM.
70. Guitton, *Léon Harmel, 1829–1915*, 1:173.
71. Harmel, "Souvenirs de Famille," Ch. 982, AM.
72. Trimouille, *Léon Harmel et l'usine chrétienne*, 86.
73. Léon Harmel, n.d., 59 J 15, AM.
74. Léon Harmel, *Catéchisme du patron* (Paris, 1889), 20.
75. Anthony Black, *Guilds and Civil Society in European Political Thought from the Twelfth Century to the Present* (Ithaca: Cornell University Press, 1984), 226.
76. Léon Harmel, speech given at the Cercle de Vaugirard, 27 April 1890, Ch. 982, AM.
77. Léon Harmel, speech given at the Cercle de Vaugirard, 27 April 1890, Ch. 982, AM.
78. Léon Harmel, *Manuel d'une corporation chrétienne* (Tours, 1876), 247.
79. Harmel, *Manuel*, 391.
80. Harmel, *Manuel*, 42, 363.
81. Trimouille, *Léon Harmel et l'usine chrétienne*, 28.
82. Harmel, *Manuel*, 391.
83. Marilyn J. Boxer and Jean H. Quataert, "Women in Industrializing and Liberalizing Europe," in *Connecting Spheres*, ed. Marilyn J. Boxer and Jean H. Quataert (New York: Oxford University Press, 1987), 100–101.
84. For treatment of these issues in general texts, see, for example, Gordan Wright, *France in Modern Times* (New York: W. W. Norton, 1995); Jeremy D. Popkin, *A History of Modern France* (Englewood Cliffs, N. J.: Prentice Hall, 1994); André Jardin and André-Jean Tudesq, *Restoration and Reaction 1815–1848* (New York: Cambridge University Press, 1988); Alain Plessis, *The Rise and Fall of the Second Empire, 1852–1871* (New York: Cambridge University Press, 1987); Jean-Marie Mayeur and Madeleine Rebérioux, *The Third Republic from Its Origins to the Great War, 1871–1914* (New York: Cambridge University Press, 1987). For more detailed accounts of problems associated with the industrial revolution, see Gérard Noiriel, *Les Ouvriers dans la société française XIX–XX siècle* (Paris: Éditions du Seuil, 1986); Laura L. Frader, "Doing Capitalism's Work: Women in the Western European Industrial Economy," in *Becoming Visible*, ed. Renate Bridenthal, Susan Mosher Stuard, and Merry E. Wiesner (New York: Houghton Mifflin, 1998), 295–325; Elinor A. Accampo, Rachel G. Fuchs, and Mary Lynn Stewart, *Gender and the Politics of Social Reform in France, 1870–1914* (Baltimore: Johns Hopkins University Press, 1995); Mary Lynn Stewart, *Women, Work and the French State* (Montreal: McGill-Queen's University Press, 1989);

Rachel G. Fuchs, *Poor and Pregnant in Paris* (New Brunswick: Rutgers University Press, 1992).

85. Harmel, *Manuel,* 17.
86. Léon Harmel writing in 1879, 59 J 72, AM.
87. Harmel, *Manuel,* 24.
88. Léon Harmel, writing in 1879, 59 J 72, AM.
89. See, for example, Guitton, *Léon Harmel, 1829–1915,* 1:188; Trimouille, *Léon Harmel et l'usine chrétienne,* 26.
90. Léon Harmel, *Souvenir de Felix Harmel* (Blois, 1900), letter of 17 February 1898, n.p.
91. Trimouille, *Léon Harmel et l'usine chrétienne,* 27.
92. Léon Harmel à ses petits-enfants, 17 February 1906, Ch. 982, AM.
93. See David McCullough, *The Path between the Seas* (New York: Simon and Schuster, 1977), for a detailed account of the building of the Panama Canal.
94. Léon Harmel, 55 J 72, AM.
95. Léon Harmel, address before the Congrès des Directeurs des Associations Ouvrières Catholiques, 1881, Ch. 982, AM.
96. Harmel, *Manuel,* 190.
97. Claude Langlois, "Catholics and Seculars," in *Realms of Memory,* Vol. 1 (Conflicts and Divisions), edited by Pierre Nora (New York: Columbia University Press, 1996), 111.
98. Léon Harmel, Ch. 982, AM.
99. Léon Harmel, address before the Congrès des Directeurs des Associations Ouvrières Catholiques, Ch. 982, AM.
100. Harmel, *Catéchisme du patron,* 260.
101. Léon Harmel, address before the Congrès National de la Démocratie Chrétienne at Lyon, 27 November 1896, AM.
102. Léon Harmel, address before the Conférence sur le Capitalisme, le Travail, et la Prosperité at Macon, 3 December 1896, Ch. 982, AM.
103. Harmel, *Manuel,* 25.
104. Léon Harmel to R. P. Bailly, 19 March 1892, Ch. 982, AM.
105. Léon Harmel, speech given on 28 June 1898 at the Congrès de l'Union Fraternelle (Paris: Rondelet et Cie, Editeurs), n.p.
106. Léon Harmel, speech given on 28 June 1898 at the Congrès de l'Union Fraternelle, n.p.
107. Harmel, *Manuel,* 205–206; Léon Harmel, "Le Commerce et l'Église," speech given on 28 June 1898 at the Congrès de l'Union Fraternelle (Paris: Rondelet et Cie, Editeurs), 12.
108. Léon Harmel, address before the Congrès des Directeurs des Associations Ouvrières Catholiques, 1879, Ch. 982, AM.

109. Trimouille, *Léon Harmel et l'usine chrétienne*, 23.

110. Léon Harmel, address before the Congrès des Directeurs des Associations Ouvrières Catholiques, 1879, Ch. 982, AM.

111. Léon Harmel to "Très révérend père," n.d., 59 J 17, AM.

112. Langlois, "Catholics and Seculars," 122-123.

113. Harmel, *Manuel*, 213.

114. Harmel, *Catéchisme du patron*, 120.

115. Harmel, *Manuel*, 303.

116. Léon Harmel to La Tour du Pin, 17 February 1882, 59 J 18, AM.

117. Léon Harmel to M. Robert Welles, 14 September 1882, 59 J 18, AM. My emphasis.

118. Gloria K. Fiero, "The *Dits:* The Historical Context," in *Three Medieval Views of Women,* ed. Gloria K. Fiero, Wendy Pfeffer, and Mathé Allain, 28-83 (New Haven: Yale University Press, 1989), 76, 68. See also David Herlihy, *Women in Medieval Society* (Houston: University of St. Thomas Press, 1971), 4.

119. Fiero, "The *Dits:* The Historical Context," 61, 68, 69.

120. Fiero, "The *Dits:* The Historical Context," 69.

121. Gerda Lerner, *The Creation of Feminist Consciousness* (New York: Oxford University Press, 1993), 116.

122. Lerner, *The Creation of Feminist Consciousness,* 121.

123. See, for example, Mary Lynn McDougall, "Protecting Infants: The French Campaign for Maternity Leaves, 1890s-1913," *French Historical Studies* 13 (Spring 1983): 79-105.

124. Average family size peaked in the years from 1869 to 1878, with 7.3 live births among the bourgeoisie of the Nord. Smith, *Ladies of the Leisure Class,* 225.

125. See, for example, Fiero, "The *Dits:* The Historical Context," 35, 62; Lerner, *The Creation of Feminist Consciousness,* 124; Olwen Hufton, *The Prospect before Her* (New York: Vintage Books, 1995), 62; Thomas Aquinas, *Summa Theologica* (Chicago: Encyclopedia Britannica, 1952), 606-700. Until the Gregorian reform, Catholic women were prominent in the hierarchy of the Church too, but once clerical celibacy began to be enforced rigorously, the Church cultivated an exaggerated fear of women, which some have characterized as antifeminine. Herlihy, *Women in Medieval Society,* 8-9.

126. Harmel, *Manuel,* 120.

127. Harmel, *Manuel,* 137.

128. See, for example, Timothy (I Timothy 2:15) when he says that women are saved through motherhood.

129. For an account of how patriarchy skewed not only gender relations but human relations in general, see Gerda Lerner, *The Creation of Patriarchy*

(New York: Oxford University Press, 1986) and *The Creation of Feminist Consciousness*.

130. Harmel, *Manuel,* 300.
131. Harmel, *Manuel,* 183.
132. See, for example, Fuchs, *Poor and Pregnant in Paris*.
133. Harmel, *Manuel,* 302.
134. Léon Harmel, *Organisation chrétienne de l'usine, par un industriel* (Paris, 1874), 47.
135. Harmel, *Catéchisme du patron,* 86; *Organisation chrétienne de l'usine, par un industriel,* 47.
136. Karen Offen, "Feminism, Antifeminism, and National Politics in Early Third Republic France," in *Connecting Spheres,* 183.
137. Louise A. Tilly and Joan W. Scott, *Women, Work, and Family* (San Francisco: Holt, Rinehart and Winston, 1978), 49.
138. Léon Harmel to _____, 1891, 59 J 21, AM.
139. Harmel, *Manuel,* 190.
140. Harmel, *Manuel,* 298–299.
141. Harmel, *Manuel,* 120.
142. Harmel, *Manuel,* 120.
143. Léon Harmel to _____, 27 October 1882, 59 J 18, AM.
144. Léon Harmel to M. Herve-Bazin, 3 December 1882, Ch. 982, AM.
145. Harmel, *Catéchisme du patron,* 163.
146. Harmel, *Catéchisme du patron,* 37, 20.
147. Harmel, *Manuel,* 157.
148. Black, *Guilds and Civil Society,* 233.
149. Black, *Guilds and Civil Society,* 233.
150. Léon Harmel, address before the Conférence du Cercle Catholique de Seéz, 17 October 1881 (Seéz, 1881), 3; Harmel, *Catéchisme du patron,* 25; Léon Harmel, to "Excellence," 13 August 1883, 59 J 19, AM.
151. Harmel, *Catéchisme du patron,* 23.
152. Léon Harmel, address before the Conférence du Cercle Catholique de Seéz, 17 October 1881, 4.
153. Léon Harmel, address before the Conférence du Cercle Catholique de Seéz, 17 October 1881, 4.
154. Harmel, *Manuel,* 36.
155. Harmel, *Manuel,* 248.
156. Léon Harmel, address before the Conférence sur le Capitalisme, le Travail et la Prosperité at Macon, 3 December 1896, Ch. 982, AM.
157. Harmel, *Catéchisme du patron,* 118.
158. Harmel, *Catéchisme du patron,* 58.

159. Harmel, *Manuel*, 248.
160. Harmel, *Catéchisme du patron*, 41.
161. Harmel, *Catéchisme du patron*, 45, 77.
162. Harmel, *Catéchisme du patron*, 70.
163. Harmel, *Catéchisme du patron*, 32–33.
164. Harmel, *Catéchisme du patron*, 47–48.
165. Harmel, *Manuel*, 60.
166. Harmel, *Catéchisme du patron*, 91–92.
167. Harmel, *Manuel*, 51.
168. Harmel, *Catéchisme du patron*, 98–102.
169. Harmel, *Catéchisme du patron*, 98–102.
170. Harmel, *Catéchisme du patron*, 68.
171. Harmel, *Catéchisme du patron*, 66.
172. Harmel, *Catéchisme du patron*, 76.
173. Harmel, *Catéchisme du patron*, 76.
174. Harmel, *Catéchisme du patron*, 108.
175. Harmel, *Catéchisme du patron*, 117.
176. Harmel, *Catéchisme du patron*, 68.
177. Harmel, *Catéchisme du patron*, 88.
178. Harmel, *Manuel*, 37.
179. Harmel, *Manuel*, 37.
180. When referring to the workers in general, Harmel routinely used the male gender, and for the sake of simplicity and accurate rendering, I will do the same.
181. Léon Harmel, 59 J 15, AM.
182. Harmel, *Catéchisme du patron*, 33.
183. Léon Harmel to R. P. Bailly, 19 March 1892, Ch. 982, AM.
184. Léon Harmel to R. P. Bailly, 19 March 1892, Ch. 982, AM.
185. Harmel, *Catéchisme du patron*, 7. I found no evidence to suggest that this definition of 1889 was ever formally modified to take into account the expanding size of French businesses and the concurrent growth of the unskilled segment of the French labor force.
186. Léon Harmel, 59 J 72, AM.
187. Léon Harmel, report before the Conférence sur le Capitalisme, le Travail et la Prosperité at Macon, 3 December 1896, Ch. 982, AM.
188. For more on this subject, see Michèle Sàcquin, *Entre Bossuet et Maurras: L'Antiprotestantisme en France de 1814 à 1870* (Paris: École des Chartes, 1998).
189. See, for example, Y.-M. Hilaire, "Les Missions intèrieurers face à la dechristianisation pendant la seconde moitie du XIXe siècle dans le region du Nord," *Revue du Nord* 46 (1964): 51–68.

190. Léon Harmel, speech before the Cercle Vaugirard de Paris, 9 January 1898 (Reims: Nestor Moncie, 1898), 2; Léon Harmel, speech before the Congrès de Tour, 5 June 1897, Ch. 982, AM; Léon Harmel, report before the Congrès National de la Démocratie Chrétienne at Lyon, 27 November 1896, in Léon Harmel, *Le Val des Bois (exposition de l'organisation)*, Ch. B. M1837, Bibliothèque Carnegie, Reims, France.

191. Léon Harmel, address of 9 January 1898, Ch. 982, AM.

192. Léon Harmel, speech before the Cercle Vaugirard de Paris, 9 January 1898, AM, 3, 4.

193. Trimouille, *Léon Harmel et l'usine chrétienne*, 33.

194. For further detail, see Thomas A. Kselman, *Miracles and Prophecies in Nineteenth-Century France* (New Brunswick: Rutgers University Press, 1983).

195. The Cercles Catholiques d'Ouvriers were founded by Albert de Mun and La Tour du Pin in the aftermath of the Paris Commune. Their purpose was the reconciliation of the classes. The organization and Harmel's contribution to it are discussed in chapter 3.

196. Les Cercles d'Études were founded by Harmel in 1892 after the publication of the papal encyclical *Rerum Novarum* (15 May 1891). Their purpose was the study of the encyclical with the intent of applying its principles to contemporary social problems. The organization and Harmel's contribution to it are discussed in chapter 5.

197. Léon Harmel, speech before the Cercle Vaugirard de Paris, 9 January 1898, Ch. 982, AM.

198. Harmel, *Manuel*, 23.

199. Léon Harmel to his children, 17 February 1898, in Harmel, *Souvenir de Felix Harmel*, n.p.

200. Léon Harmel, address before the Conférence du Cercle Catholique de Seéz, 17 October 1881, 59 J 72, AM.

201. Harmel, *Catéchisme du patron*, 35.

202. Léon Harmel, speech at the distribution des prix de l'institution St. Vincent à Senlis, 27 July 1889, Ch. 982, AM.

203. Harmel, *Manuel*, 190.

204. Léon Harmel, address at the 1879 Congrès, Ch. 982, AM.

205. Léon Harmel to _____, 8 October 1882, 59 J 18, AM.

206. Léon Harmel, 59 J 15, AM.

207. Léon Harmel, address before the 1879 Congrès, Ch. 982, AM.

208. Trimouille, *Léon Harmel et l'usine chrétienne*, 31.

209. Guitton, *Léon Harmel, 1829–1915*, 1:79–84.

210. Guitton, *Léon Harmel, 1829–1915*, 2:326.

211. Guitton, *Léon Harmel, 1829–1915*, 2:326.

212. Guitton, *Léon Harmel, 1829–1915,* 1:78.
213. Léon Harmel to Jules (his brother), 11 June 1889, 59 J 20, AM.
214. Harmel, *Manuel,* 49.
215. Léon Harmel, address before the Conférence du Cercle Catholique de Seéz, 17 October 1881, 59 J 19, AM.
216. Léon Harmel to _____, 6 December 1880, 59 J 72, AM.
217. Aquinas, *Summa Theologica,* 2:606–700.
218. Léon Harmel to "Mademoiselle," 19 March 1890, 59 J 21, AM.
219. Léon Harmel to M. Lebreton, 12 September 1882, 59 J 18, AM.
220. Léon Harmel to "Très vénéré Père Bailly," June 1881, 59 J 16, AM.

CHAPTER TWO The Corporation at Val-des-Bois

An earlier version of this chapter appeared under the title "Labor Law and the Christian Corporation at Val des Bois, 1840–1914," in *Historical Reflections/ Reflexions Historique* 20 (1994): 125–140.

1. Louis Bergeron, *L'Industrialisation de la France au XIXe siècle* (Paris: Hatier, 1979), 6.
2. Gérard Noiriel, *Les Ouvriers dans la société française XIX-XX siècle* (Paris: Éditions du Seuil, 1986), 112.
3. Gordon Wright, *France in Modern Times* (New York: W.W. Norton, 1995), 152.
4. Wright, *France in Modern Times,* 265–266.
5. Jeremy D. Popkin, *A History of Modern France* (Englewood Cliffs, N.J.: Prentice Hall, 1994), 201.
6. François Caron, *An Economic History of Modern France* (New York: Columbia University Press, 1979), 107.
7. Wright, *France in Modern Times,* 259–260.
8. Popkin, *A History of Modern France,* 200.
9. Richard F. Kuisel, "The French Search for Modernity," in *The Transformation of Modern France,* ed. William B. Cohen (New York: Houghton Mifflin, 1997), 35; Wright, *France in Modern Times,* 148, 265.
10. Popkin, *A History of Modern France,* 200.
11. Caron, *An Economic History of Modern France,* 108.
12. Noiriel, *Les Ouvriers dans la société française,* 18.
13. Noiriel, *Les Ouvriers dans la société française,* 60.
14. Noiriel, *Les Ouvriers dans la société française,* 143.
15. Peter N. Stearns, "Early Strike Activity in France," in *The Working Class in Modern Europe,* ed. Mary Lynn McDougall (Lexington, Mass.: D.C. Heath, 1975), 24.

16. Wright, *France in Modern Times*, 263.
17. Noiriel, *Les Ouvriers dans la société française*, 12–13.
18. Kuisel, "The French Search for Modernity," 35.
19. Noiriel, *Les Ouvriers dans la société française*, 87.
20. Noiriel, *Les Ouvriers dans la société française*, 19–21.
21. Noiriel, *Les Ouvriers dans la société française*, 13.
22. Noiriel, *Les Ouvriers dans la société française*, 22; Wright, *France in Modern Times*, 161, 275.
23. Noiriel, *Les Ouvriers dans la société française*, 23, 88.
24. Noiriel, *Les Ouvriers dans la société française*, 39.
25. Noiriel, *Les Ouvriers dans la société française*, 39–40.
26. Noiriel, *Les Ouvriers dans la société française*, 23.
27. Kathryn E. Amdur, "The Making of the French Working Class," in *The Transformation of Modern France*, 73.
28. Caron, *An Economic History of Modern France*, 150; see also William M. Reddy, *The Rise of Market Culture* (New York: Cambridge University Press, 1984), for a discussion of the French textile industry from 1750 to 1900.
29. Noiriel, *Les Ouvriers dans la société française*, 14–15.
30. Wright, *France in Modern Times*, 274.
31. Noiriel, *Les Ouvriers dans la société française*, 143.
32. Madeleine Guilbert, *Les Functions des femmes dans l'industrie* (Paris: Mouton, 1966), 43.
33. Noiriel, *Les Ouvriers dans la société française*, 23.
34. Caron, *An Economic History of Modern France*, 107, 149.
35. François Sellier, "France," in *Labor in the Twentieth Century*, ed. John T. Dunlap and Walter Galenson (New York: Academic Press, 1978), 203.
36. Wright, *France in Modern Times*, 154; J. Houdoy, *La Filature de coton dans le Nord de France* (Paris: Librarie Nouvelle de Droit et de Jurisprudence, 1903), 74, 135. This initial treaty with Great Britain was terminated on 1872, but a new commercial treaty was signed in 1873 for an undetermined amount of time.
37. Caron, *An Economic History of Modern France*, 101.
38. Wright, *France in Modern Times*, 154.
39. Caron, *An Economic History of Modern France*, 100.
40. Houdoy, *La Filature de coton*, 89–97; Caron, *An Economic History of Modern France*, 151.
41. Patricia Hilden, *Working Women and Socialist Politics in France: 1880–1914* (Oxford: Clarendon Press, 1986), 70.
42. Houdoy, *La Filature de coton*, 160.
43. Wright, *France in Modern Times*, 261.
44. Hilden, *Working Women and Socialist Politics*, 70.

45. Patricia Hilden, *Working Women and Socialist Politics*, 65-66; Houdoy, *La Filature de coton*, 217, 219; Caron, *An Economic History of Modern France*, 152-153.

46. Hilden, *Working Women and Socialist Politics*, 65; Caron, *An Economic History of Modern France*, 99-100, 153.

47. Houdoy, *La Filature de coton*, 58.

48. Hilden, *Working Women and Socialist Politics*, 67, 72.

49. Hilden, *Working Women and Socialist Politics*, 73.

50. Houdoy, *La Filature de coton*, 174-175.

51. Houdoy, *La Filature de coton*, 176.

52. Gérard Noiriel, "French and Foreigners," in *Realms of Memory*, Vol. 1, under the direction of Pierre Nora, English-language edition edited by Lawrence D. Kritzmen, translated by Arthur Goldhammer (New York: Columbia University Press, 1996), 152; Hilden, *Working Women and Socialist Politics*, 65; Carl Strikwerda, "France and the Belgian Immigration of the Nineteenth Century," in *The Politics of Immigrant Workers: Essays on Labor Activism and the World Economy since 1830*, ed. Camille Guerin-Gonzales and Carl Strikwerda (New York: Holmes and Meier, 1991), 101.

53. Noiriel, *Les Ouvriers dans la société française*, 89.

54. David M. Gordon, *Liberalism and Social Reform* (Westport, Conn.: Greenwood Press, 1996), 40.

55. Noiriel, *Les Ouvriers dans la société française*, 36.

56. Stearns, "Early Strike Activity in France," 29.

57. Guilbert, *Les Functions des femmes dans l'industrie*, 44; Noiriel, *Les Ouvriers dans la société française*, 113, cites 31 percent of the workforce in 1866.

58. Noiriel, *Les Ouvriers dans la société française*, 113; James F. McMillan, *Housewife or Harlot: The Place of Women in French Society, 1870-1940* (New York: St. Martin's Press, 1981), 38, cites 55.2 percent in the textile industry at this time.

59. Noiriel, *Les Ouvriers dans la société française*, 17.

60. Noiriel, *Les Ouvriers dans la société française*, 94.

61. Noiriel, *Les Ouvriers dans la société française*, 94; McMillan, *Housewife or Harlot*, 65.

62. Amdur, "The Making of the French Working Class," 70.

63. Stearns, "Early Strike Activity in France," 31; Amdur, "The Making of the French Working Class," 79; McMillan, *Housewife or Harlot*, 66.

64. Peter Stearns, *Paths to Authority* (Chicago: University of Illinois Press, 1978), 63; Houdoy, *La Filature de coton*, 344.

65. Reddy, *The Rise of Market Culture*, 27.

66. Houdoy, *La Filature de coton*, 348.

67. Noiriel, *Les Ouvriers dans la société française*, 38.

68. Noiriel, *Les Ouvriers dans la société française*, 25–26.
69. Sellier, "France," 232.
70. Pierre Pierrard, *L'Église et les ouvriers en France (1840–1940)* (Paris: Hachette, 1984), 49; but also see Houdoy, *La Filature de coton*, 345.
71. McMillan, *Housewife or Harlot*, 38.
72. Houdoy, *La Filature de coton*, 361–362.
73. Noiriel, *Les Ouvriers dans la société française*, 28.
74. Wright, *France in Modern Times*, 162.
75. Hilden, *Working Women and Socialist Politics*, 22; David S. Landes, "French Entrepreneurship and Industrial Growth in the Nineteenth Century," *Journal of Economic History* 9 (1949): 45–61.
76. For example, in 1960 *un nouveau franc* or *franc lourd*, worth 100 *ancien francs*, was instituted.
77. Roger Magraw, *A History of the French Working Class*, 2 vols. (Cambridge, Mass.: Blackwell Publishers, 1992), 1:4.
78. Noiriel, *Les Ouvriers dans la société française*, 28.
79. Wright, *France in Modern Times*, 162.
80. Stearns, "Early Strike Activity in France," 28.
81. Noiriel, *Les Ouvriers dans la société française*, 150.
82. Noiriel, *Les Ouvriers dans la société française*, 28–29.
83. Bergeron, *L'Industrialisation de la France*, 21; Houdoy, *La Filature de coton*, 366.
84. Pierrard, *L'Église et les ouvriers*, 229.
85. Sellier, "France," 233.
86. Noiriel, *Les Ouvriers dans la société française*, 110–112.
87. Houdoy, *La Filature de coton*, 370.
88. Noiriel, *Les Ouvriers dans la société française*, 17.
89. Wright, *France in Modern Times*, 163; Magraw, *A History of the French Working Class*, 1:5.
90. Wright, *France in Modern Times*, 274, says the 10-hour day came in 1900, but McMillan, *Housewife or Harlot*, 58–59, states that the 10-hour day arrived in 1904, with significant numbers adhering to the 11-hour day.
91. Noiriel, *Les Ouvriers dans la société française*, 45.
92. Amdur, "The Making of the French Working Class," 73; for a vivid, though moralistic, account of the negative impact on family life, see Jules Simon, *L'Ouvrière* (Paris: Hachette, 1861).
93. Elinor Accampo, *Industrialization, Family Life, and Class Relations* (Berkeley: University of California Press, 1989), 8.
94. Hilden, *Working Women and Socialist Politics*, 37, 42.
95. Wright, *France in Modern Times*, 162.

96. For a thorough discussion of Parisian life among the workers during the early Third Republic, see Lenard R. Berlanstein, *The Working People of Paris, 1871–1914* (Baltimore: Johns Hopkins University Press, 1984).

97. Noiriel, *Les Ouvriers dans la société française*, 26.

98. William B. Cohen, "The Development of an Urban Society," in *The Transformation of Modern France*, ed. William B. Cohen (New York: Houghton Mifflin, 1997), 52.

99. Noiriel, *Les Ouvriers dans la société française*, 26–27.

100. Noiriel, *Les Ouvriers dans la société française*, 29.

101. Wright, *France in Modern Times*, 162.

102. Noiriel, *Les Ouvriers dans la société française*, 45.

103. Noiriel, *Les Ouvriers dans la société française*, 29.

104. John McManners, *Church and State in France, 1870–1914* (New York: Harper & Row, 1972), 5; Claude Langlois, "Catholics and Seculars," in *Realms of Memory*, 1:114–115. McManners says that 35 million, or 87.5 percent, were Catholic out of 40 million, while Langlois claims more than 95 percent were Catholic.

105. Langlois, "Catholics and Seculars," 115.

106. Thomas A. Kselman, *Death and the Afterlife in Modern France* (Princeton: Princeton University Press, 1993), 106, states that by the end of the nineteenth century, 20 percent of Parisians had civil burials; Noiriel, *Les Ouvriers dans la société française*, 101, notes that in St. Denis, a working-class suburb of Paris, 50 percent of burials in 1911 were civil.

107. Y.-M. Hilaire, "Les Missions intérieures face à la dechristianisation pendant la seconde moitié du XIXe siècle, dans la region du Nord," *Revue du Nord* 46 (1964): 58. Hilaire's study disclosed that onanism, the principal method of birth control at the time, was the major reason that men stayed away from religious observance; the men avoided confession and were not in a state to receive Holy Communion.

108. Pierrard, *L'Église et les ouvriers en France*, 58.

109. Patricia E. Prestwich, "Food and Drink in France," in *The Transformation of Modern France*, 177.

110. McMillan, *Housewife or Harlot*, 45.

111. Houdoy, *La Filature de coton*, 353; Hilden, *Working Women and Socialist Politics*, 47.

112. One gallon is equal to 3.785 liters.

113. Houdoy, *La Filature de coton*, 354, footnote 2.

114. Eugen Weber, *France Fin de Siècle* (Cambridge, Mass.: Harvard University Press, 1986), 28.

115. Prestwich, "Food and Drink in France," 177.

116. Noiriel, *Les Ouvriers dans la société française*, 98.

117. Noiriel, *Les Ouvriers dans la société française*, 98.

118. Absinthe is a green, bitter liquor originally flavored with wormwood and anise. Once distillation costs were lowered by using sugar beets in its production, it became a popular drink, especially among the workers of Paris and Marseille. It is a potent drink, with an alcoholic content of 55 to 75 percent. The government outlawed the sale of absinthe in 1914. Prestwich, "Food and Drink in France," 176.

119. Weber, *France Fin de Siècle*, 28.

120. Houdoy, *La Filature de coton*, 370.

121. Noiriel, *Les Ouvriers dans la société française*, 99.

122. Popkin, *A History of Modern France*, 191.

123. Fernand Boulard, *Essor ou déclin du clergé français?* (Paris: Éditions du Cerf, 1950), 76, 103, 105; Fernand Boulard, *Premiers itineraries en sociologie religieuse* (Paris: Éditions Ouvrières Economie et Humanisme, 1954), 67–70.

124. Ralph Gibson, *A Social History of French Catholicism, 1789–1914* (New York: Routledge, 1989), 67.

125. Eugen Weber, *Peasants into Frenchmen* (Stanford: Stanford University Press, 1976), 371.

126. Weber, *Peasants into Frenchmen*, 372; Wright, *France in Modern Times*, 251; Gérard Cholvy and Yves-Marie Hilaire, *Histoire religieuse de la France contemporaine, 1880–1930* (Toulouse: Bibliothèque Historique Privat, 1986), 117.

127. Boulard, *Essor ou déclin du clergé français?* 104–105; Jean-Marie Mayeur, *La Séparation de l'église et de l'état* (Paris: René Juillard, 1966), 193; Cholvy and Hilaire, *Histoire religieuse de la France contemporaine*, 117; Weber, *Peasants into Frenchmen*, 371.

128. Mayeur, *La Séparation de l'église et de l'état*, 193; Boulard, *Essor ou déclin du clergé français?* 104–105; Gibson, *A Social History of French Catholicism*, 65.

129. Y.-M. Hilaire, "Les Ouvriers de la region du Nord devant l'église catholique (XIXe–XX siècle)," *Le Mouvement Social* 57 (October–December 1966): 184–190.

130. Pierrard, *L'Église et les ouvriers en France*, 235.

131. Hilaire, "Les missions intérieurers," 65; Pierrard, *L'Église et les ouvriers en France*, 432.

132. For a discussion of the relationship between Catholicism and socialism in Belgium, see Carl Strikwerda, *A House Divided: Catholics, Socialists, and Flemish Nationalists in Nineteenth-Century Belgium* (Lanham, Md.: Rowman & Littlefield, 1997).

133. Pierrard, *L'Église et les ouvriers en France*, 54.

134. Pierrard, *L'Église et les ouvriers en France*, 493.

135. Hilaire, "Les missions intérieurers," 60.

136. Joseph N. Moody, "The Dechristianization of the French Working Class," *Review of Politics* 20 (January 1958): 59.

137. Moody, "Dechristianization of the French Working Class," 58.

138. Suzanne Desan, "Redefining Revolutionary Liberty: The Rhetoric of Religious Revival during the French Revolution," *Journal of Modern History* 60 (March 1988): 27.

139. Michèle Sàcquin, *Entre Bossuet et Maurras: L'Antiprotestantisme en France de 1814 à 1870* (Paris: École des Chartes, 1998), 9.

140. Sàcquin, *Entre Bossuet et Maurras,* XVI.

141. Sàcquin, *Entre Bossuet et Maurras,* XV.

142. Sàcquin, *Entre Bossuet et Maurras,* 134.

143. Sàcquin, *Entre Bossuet et Maurras,* VII.

144. See Sàcquin, *Entre Bossuet et Maurras.*

145. Hilaire, "Les Missions intérieurers," 59.

146. Hilaire, "Les Missions intérieurers," 60–64.

147. Hilaire, "Les Missions intérieurers," 51–68; Wright, *France in Modern Times,* 118.

148. David M. Gordon, "Industrialization and Republican Politics: The Bourgeois of Reims and Saint-Étienne under the Second Empire," in *French Cities in the Nineteenth Century,* ed. John M. Merriman (New York, Holmes & Meier, 1981), 117–138; David Landes, *The Unbound Prometheus* (New York: Cambridge University Press, 1969), 213.

149. Noiriel, *Les Ouvriers dans la société française,* 33, 35, 36, 50.

150. Popkin, *A History of Modern France,* 176.

151. Noiriel, *Les Ouvriers dans la société française,* 26.

152. Leslie Page Moch, *Paths to the City* (Beverly Hills, Calif.: Sage, 1983).

153. Noiriel, *Les Ouvriers dans la société française,* 38.

154. For a more complete discussion of this point, see Accampo, *Industrialization, Family Life, and Class Relations;* and Tamara K. Hareven, *Family Time and Industrial Time* (New York: Cambridge University Press, 1982).

155. Pierre Trimouille, *Léon Harmel et l'usine chrétienne du Val des Bois* (Lyon: Centre d'Histoire du Catholicisme de Lyon, 1974), 77.

156. Noiriel, *Les Ouvriers dans la société française,* 85.

157. Trimouille, *Léon Harmel et l'usine chrétienne,* 58–73.

158. Trimouille, *Léon Harmel et l'usine chrétienne,* 77, 82.

159. Léon Harmel to M. Gabriel Ardant, 3 July 1889, 59 J 20, AM.

160. Trimouille, *Léon Harmel et l'usine chrétienne,* 79–80.

161. Noiriel, *Les Ouvriers dans la société française,* 110.

162. Léon Harmel to the Congrès of Autun, 18 August 1882, Ch. 982, AM.

163. Léon Harmel, *Manuel d'une corporation chrétienne* (Tours, 1876), 169.

164. Léon Harmel's speech to the assembly of the Catholiques du Nord on the rapport between *patrons* and *ouvriers,* June 1885, Ch. 982, AM.

165. Harmel, *Manuel,* 7.

166. Harmel, *Manuel,* 72.

167. Léon Harmel, report to the Congrès National de la Démocratie Chrétienne at Lyon, 27 November 1896, Ch. 982 bis, AM.

168. Trimouille, *Léon Harmel et l'usine chrétienne,* 42.

169. See, for example, Jaubert, *L'Organisation actuelle du Val des Bois* (Blois: Imprimeries Reunies du Centre, 1904), 24, Ch. 982, AM.

170. Georges Guitton, *Léon Harmel, 1829–1915,* 2 vols. (Paris: Action Populaire, 1927), 1:46.

171. Trimouille, *Léon Harmel et l'usine chrétienne,* 38.

172. Trimouille, *Léon Harmel et l'usine chrétienne,* 37, 43.

173. Trimouille, *Léon Harmel et l'usine chrétienne,* 43.

174. Léon Harmel to "Excellence," 13 August 1883, 59 J 19, AM.

175. Trimouille, *Léon Harmel et l'usine chrétienne,* 42–43.

176. Trimouille, *Léon Harmel et l'usine chrétienne,* 44.

177. Trimouille, *Léon Harmel et l'usine chrétienne,* 42.

178. Léon Harmel, *Mémoire sur le Val des Bois, 31 March 1897* (Reims: Imprimerie Cooperative), Ch. 982, AM.

179. *Le Val des Bois, situation actuelle, March 1895,* Ch. 982 bis, AM.

180. Léon Harmel, speech at the conference of Cercle Catholique of Seéz, 17 October 1881, 7, 8R. Piece 2284, Bibliothèque Nationale (hereafter cited as BN).

181. See Bonnie G. Smith, *Ladies of the Leisure Class* (Princeton: Princeton University Press, 1981).

182. Wright, *France in Modern Times,* 149; Popkin, *The History of Modern France,* 116.

183. Léon Harmel, *Catéchisme du patron* (Paris, 1889), 147–148.

184. Léon Harmel, address before the Congrès des Directeurs des Associations Ouvrières Catholiques, 1881, Ch. 982, AM.

185. Harmel, *Manuel,* 253.

186. Léon Harmel, to the editors of *La Croix de Reims* on the question of wages, 25 October 1893, Ch. 982, AM.

187. Léon Harmel, address before the Congrès des Directeurs des Associations Ouvrières Catholiques, 1881, Ch. 982, AM.

188. Léon Harmel, address before the Conférence sur le Capitalisme, le Travail et la Prosperité at Macon, 3 December 1896, Ch. 982, AM.

189. Trimouille, *Léon Harmel et l'usine chrétienne,* 95–96.

190. The Creusot Firm was the only other example of a company offering the family wage that I could find. Roger Magraw, *A History of the French*

Working Class, vol. 2, *Workers and the Bourgeois Republic* (Cambridge, Mass.: Blackwell Publishers, 1992), 37.

191. McMillan, *Housewife or Harlot,* 39.
192. McMillan, *Housewife or Harlot,* 13–14, 37.
193. Harmel, *Manuel,* 253.
194. Trimouille, *Léon Harmel et l'usine chrétienne,* 91.
195. Trimouille, *Léon Harmel et l'usine chrétienne,* 97.
196. Léon Harmel, *Mémoire sur le Val des Bois,* 31 March 1897, Ch. 982 bis, AM.
197. Judith F. Stone, *The Search for Social Peace* (Albany: State University of New York Press, 1985), 127, 131–132.
198. Trimouille, *Léon Harmel et l'usine chrétienne,* 98.
199. Trimouille, *Léon Harmel et l'usine chrétienne,* 98.
200. Stone, *The Search for Social Peace,* 134–139.
201. Trimouille, *Léon Harmel et l'usine chrétienne,* 98–99.
202. Emile Lefevre, *Le Val des Bois: Étude économique* (Paris: Charles Amat, 1911), 20–21, Ch. 982 bis, AM.
203. *Le Val des Bois, situation actuelle,* March 1895, Ch. 982 bis, AM.
204. Trimouille, *Léon Harmel et l'usine chrétienne,* 100.
205. *Le Val des Bois, situation actuelle,* March 1895, Ch. 982 bis, AM.
206. Trimouille, *Léon Harmel et l'usine chrétienne,* 102.
207. Léon Harmel, address before the Congrès des Directeurs des Associations Ouvrières Catholiques, 1881, Ch. 982, AM.
208. Lefevre, *Le Val des Bois,* 12–13.
209. *Exposition universelle de 1900—Harmel Frères* (Reims: Imprimerie Co-operative), 57, Ch. 982 bis, AM.
210. Trimouille, *Léon Harmel et l'usine chrétienne,* 93.
211. William H. Sewell Jr., *Work and Revolution in France: The Language of Labor from the Old Regime to 1848* (London: Cambridge University Press, 1980), 163–164.
212. Magraw, *A History of the French Working Class,* 2:24.
213. Stone, *The Search for Social Peace,* 102–103, 173.
214. Harmel, *Catéchisme du patron,* 81.
215. Léon Harmel to an Industrialist of the Nord on the Conseil d'Usine, 2 April 1894, Ch. 982, AM.
216. McMillan, *Housewife or Harlot,* 60.
217. Trimouille, *Léon Harmel et l'usine chrétienne,* 97, 109.
218. Léon Harmel, *La Démocratie dans l'usine,* 1907, Ch. 982 bis, AM.
219. Harmel, *La Démocratie dans l'usine,* 1907.
220. Jaubert, *L'Organisation actuelle du Val des Bois,* 22.

221. Eugene Standaert, *Chez le bon père* (Bruges: Verbeke-Loys & Fils, 1902), 5, Ch. 982 bis, AM.

222. Hilden, *Working Women and Socialist Politics*, 37.

223. Mary Lynn McDougall, "Protecting Infants: The French Campaign for Maternity Leaves, 1890s–1913," *French Historical Studies* 13 (Spring 1983): 83.

224. Parker Thomas Moon, *The Labor Problem and the Social Catholic Movement in France* (New York: Macmillan, 1921), 114–115.

225. *Exposition universelle de 1900—Harmel Frères*, 42–44.

226. Léon Harmel, *Mémoire sur le Val des Bois*, 31 March 1897, Ch. 982 bis, AM.

227. Henri Beaune, *La Participation aux benefices dans l'industrie et le commerce* (Lyon: Auguste Cote, 1893), 8–14, 8R Piece 7711, BN; while not giving additional detail, Magraw, *A History of the French Working Class*, 2:24, says that 120 firms offered profit-sharing plans at this time.

228. Elinor Accampo discusses this point throughout *Industrialization, Family Life, and Class Relations*, but see pp. 9, 10, and 174 for specific references.

229. Theodore Zeldin, *France, 1848–1945*, vol. 1 (Oxford: Clarendon Press, 1973), 664–665.

230. *Exposition universelle de 1900—Harmel Frères*, 54.

231. Léon Harmel, *La Démocratie dans l'usine*, 1907, Ch. 982 bis, AM.

232. Robert Gildea, *Education in Provincial France, 1800 to 1914* (New York: Oxford University Press, 1983), 230.

233. McMillan, *Housewife or Harlot*, 48.

234. Gildea, *Education in Provincial France*, 230.

235. Gildea, *Education in Provincial France*, 257–259.

236. Trimouille, *Léon Harmel et l'usine chrétienne*, 99.

237. Léon Harmel, *Mémoire sur le Val des Bois*, 31 March 1897, Ch. 982 bis, AM.

238. Jaubert, *L'Organisation actuelle du Val des Bois*, 25.

239. Linda L. Clark, *Schooling the Daughters of Marianne* (Albany: State University of New York Press, 1984), 16.

240. McMillan, *Housewife or Harlot*, 50–51.

241. Gildea, *Education in Provincial France*, 268–269, 351.

242. McMillan, *Housewife or Harlot*, 52–53.

243. McMillan, *Housewife or Harlot*, 57.

244. Clark, *Schooling the Daughters of Marianne*, 40, 57.

245. Léon Harmel, letter on the question of wages to the editors of *La Croix* of Reims, 1893, Ch. 982, AM.

246. Léon Harmel, report to the Congrès National de la Démocratie Chrétienne at Lyon, 27 November 1896, Ch. 982 bis, AM.

247. Harmel, *Manuel*, 226.
248. *Exposition universelle de 1900—Harmel Frères*, 4.
249. Gildea, *Education in Provincial France*, 332, 336.
250. See Sandra Horvath-Peterson, *Victor Duruy and French Education* (Baton Rouge: Louisiana State University Press, 1984).
251. Magraw, *A History of the French Working Class*, 2:11.
252. Gildea, *Education in Provincial France*, 237, 336–337, 342–344, 350–351.
253. Gildea, *Education in Provincial France*, 346.
254. Harmel, *Manuel*, 227–228.
255. Trimouille, *Léon Harmel et l'usine chrétienne*, 102.
256. Trimouille, *Léon Harmel et l'usine chrétienne*, 66.
257. Stearns, *Paths to Authority*.
258. Léon Harmel, speech before the assembly of the Catholiques du Nord on the rapports between *patrons* and *ouvriers*, June 1885, Ch. 982, AM.
259. Gordon, *Liberalism and Social Reform*, 15; Peter Stearns makes the same point in "Early Strike Activity in France," 25.
260. McManners, *Church and State in France*, 84.
261. Léon Harmel, speech before the assembly of the Catholiques du Nord on the rapports between *patrons* and *ouvriers*, June 1885, Ch. 982, AM.
262. Harmel, *Manuel*, 274.
263. Michelle Perrot, *The Three Ages of Industrial Discipline in Nineteenth-Century France* as cited by Gérard Noiriel, "Du 'patronage' au 'paternalisme': La restructuration des formes de domination de la main-d'oeuvre ouvrière dans l'industrie metallurgique française," *Le Mouvement Social* 144 (July–September 1988): 18.
264. Francine Soubiran-Paillet, *L'Invention du syndicat (1791–1884)* (Paris: Le Réseau Européen Droit et Société à La Maison des Sciences de L'Homme, 1999), 169.
265. Léon Harmel, "Le Val des Bois," a report to the Congrès National de la Démocratie Chrétienne at Lyon, 27 November 1896, Ch. 982 bis, AM.
266. Léon Harmel to Robert Welles, 14 September 1882, 59 J 18, AM.
267. Léon Harmel, *Conférence du Cercle Catholique de Seéz*, October 1881, 6, 8R. Piece 2284, BN.
268. Léon Harmel, *La Démocratie dans l'usine—le Conseil d'usine du Val des Bois*, 1907 (Reims: Imprimerie Cooperatives, 1907), Ch. 982 bis, AM.
269. *Exposition universelle de 1900—Harmel Frères*, Ch. 982 bis, AM.
270. Léon Harmel, *La Démocratie dans l'usine—le Conseil d'usine*, conference made to Rome, 12 March 1903 (Roubaix: Imprimerie A. Reboux, 1903), 6, Ch. 983 bis, AM.
271. Trimouille, *Léon Harmel et l'usine chrétienne*, 112–115.

272. Guitton, *Léon Harmel, 1829–1915,* 1:56.
273. Trimouille, *Léon Harmel et l'usine chrétienne,* 78.
274. Trimouille, *Léon Harmel et l'usine chrétienne,* 75–86.
275. *Le Val des Bois, situation actuelle,* March 1895, Ch. 982, AM; Trimouille, *Léon Harmel et l'usine chrétienne,* 79.
276. Trimouille, *Léon Harmel et l'usine chrétienne,* 79–80.
277. Trimouille, *Léon Harmel et l'usine chrétienne,* 80-81.
278. Trimouille, *Léon Harmel et l'usine chrétienne,* 93.
279. Trimouille, *Léon Harmel et l'usine chrétienne,* 93.
280. Stephen Wilson, *Ideology and Experience* (East Brunswick, N.J.: Associated University Presses, 1982), 291–294.
281. Strikwerda, "France and the Belgian Immigration of the Nineteenth Century," in *The Politics of Immigrant Workers: Essays on Labor Activism and the World Economy since 1830,* ed. Camille Guerin-Gonzales and Carl Strikwerda (New York: Holmes and Meier, 1991), 107.
282. As cited in Noiriel, "French and Foreigners," 152.
283. Trimouille, *Léon Harmel et l'usine chrétienne,* 124–127.
284. David Landes, "French Entrepreneurship and Industrial Growth in the Nineteenth Century," *Journal of Economic History* 9 (1949): 52–53.
285. Trimouille, *Léon Harmel et l'usine chrétienne,* 77.
286. Trimouille, *Léon Harmel et l'usine chrétienne,* 82–86.
287. The "veterans" were those workers with at least twenty-five years of service at Val des Bois.
288. Léon Harmel to his children, 17 February 1898, *Souvenir de Felix Harmel* (Blois, 1900), 8 LN27, 47546, BN.

CHAPTER THREE   The World Beyond

1. Henri Rollet, *L'Action sociale des catholiques en France, 1871–1914* (Paris: Desclée de Brouwer, 1958), 227; John McManners, *Church and State in France, 1870–1914* (New York: Harper & Row, 1972), 84.
2. Léon Harmel speaking before the Congress of the Directeurs des Associations Ouvrières Catholiques, 1879, Ch. 982, AM.
3. Léon Harmel, *Catéchisme du patron* (Paris, 1889), 163.
4. Harmel, *Catéchisme du patron,* 37.
5. See William Sewell Jr., *Work and Revolution in France: The Language of Labor from the Old Regime to 1848* (London: Cambridge University Press, 1980); Steven L. Kaplan, "Social Classification and Representation in the Corporate World of Eighteenth-Century France: Turgot's 'Carnival,'" in *Work in France:*

Representations, Meaning, Organization and Practices, ed. Steven L. Kaplan and Cynthia J. Koepp (Ithaca: Cornell University Press, 1986), 176–228; Gail Bossenga, "Protecting Merchants: Guilds and Commercial Capitalism in Eighteenth-Century France," *French Historical Studies* 15, no. 4 (Fall 1988): 693–703.

6. K. Steven Vincent, *Pierre-Joseph Proudhon and the Rise of French Republican Socialism* (New York: Oxford University Press, 1984), 75–79.

7. Vincent, *Pierre-Joseph Proudhon*, 135–139.

8. Vincent, *Pierre-Joseph Proudhon*, 135–138.

9. Vincent, *Pierre-Joseph Proudhon*, 139.

10. Vincent, *Pierre-Joseph Proudhon*, 139.

11. Vincent, *Pierre-Joseph Proudhon*, 144–147.

12. Anthony Black, *Guilds and Civil Society in European Political Thought from the Twelfth Century to the Present* (Ithaca: Cornell University Press, 1984), 184–185.

13. Vincent, *Pierre-Joseph Proudhon*, 12, 26, 110.

14. Edward Hyams, *Pierre-Joseph Proudhon* (New York: Taplinger, 1979), 213–217.

15. Vincent, *Pierre-Joseph Proudhon*, 166.

16. Edward Berenson, *Populist Religion and Left-Wing Politics in France, 1830–1852* (Princeton: Princeton University Press, 1984), 120.

17. Sewell, *Work and Revolution in France*, 255–256.

18. Black, *Guilds and Civil Society*, 189–191.

19. Frédéric Le Play, *On Family, Work, and Social Change*, ed., trans., and intro. Catherine Bodard Silver (Chicago: University of Chicago Press, 1982), 5–12.

20. Fédéric Le Play, *La Réforme sociale in France*, 2 vols. (Paris: H. Plon, 1864) 1:47, 181.

21. Le Play, *On Family, Work, and Social Change*, 83.

22. Le Play, *L'Organisation du travail* (Paris: Alfred Mame et Fils, 1870), 165.

23. Le Play, *On Family, Work, and Social Change*, 34.

24. Le Play, *L'Organisation du travail*, 77–83.

25. Le Play, *La Réforme sociale en France*, 1:10–11.

26. Le Play, *La Réforme sociale en France*, 1:97.

27. Le Play, *On Family, Work, and Social Change*, 29, 81.

28. Le Play, *On Family, Work, and Social Change*, 34.

29. Frédéric Le Play, *L'École de la paix sociale* (Tours: Alfred Mame et Fils, 1881), 1–39.

30. Le Play, *L'Organisation du travail*, 1:22.

31. Le Play, *L'Organisation du travail*, 1:5.

32. Le Play, *La Réform sociale en France*, 1:200.

33. Le Play, *La Réform sociale en France*, 1:237.

34. Le Play, *La Réforme sociale en France*, 1:136–137.
35. Le Play, *La Réforme sociale en France*, 1:164–165.
36. Le Play, *La Réforme sociale en France*, 1:148.
37. Alec R. Vidler, *A Century of Social Catholicism, 1820–1920* (London: SPCK, 1964), 124.
38. Philippe Levillain, *Albert de Mun* (Paris: École Française de Rome, 1983), 415.
39. Charles Périn, *Premiers principes d'économie politique* (Paris: Librairie Victor Le Coffre, 1896), 3.
40. Charles Périn, *La Richesse dans les sociétés chrétiennes*, 2 vols. (Paris: Jacques Le Coffre, 1861), 2:540; *Premiers principes d'économie politique*, 125.
41. Périn, *La Richesse dans les sociétés chrétiennes*, 1:624.
42. Périn, *La Richesse dans les sociétés chrétiennes*, 1:271–272.
43. Périn, *Premiers principes d'économie politique*, 3.
44. Périn, *La Richesse dans les sociétés chrétiennes*, 1:2.
45. Périn, *Premiers principes d'économie politique*, 49.
46. Périn, *La Richesse dans les sociétés chrétiennes*, 2:306.
47. Charles Périn, *Le Patron, sa fonction, ses devoirs, ses résponsabilités* (Lille: Desclée de Brouwer, 1886), 106.
48. See Lillian Parker Wallace, *Leo XIII and the Rise of Socialism* (Durham: Duke University Press, 1966), 182–186; Vidler, *A Century of Social Catholicism*, 101–109, 113; Paul Misner, *Social Catholicism in Europe* (New York: Crossroad, 1991), 90, 126, 148; McManners, *Church and State in France*, 81.
49. Misner, *Social Catholicism in Europe*, 90–92, 126.
50. McManners, *Church and State in France*, 81.
51. Vidler, *A Century of Social Catholicism*, 67.
52. Steven D. Kale, *Legitimism and the Reconstruction of French Society, 1852–1883* (Baton Rouge: Louisiana State University Press, 1992), 192; McManners, *Church and State in France*, 81–82.
53. Misner, *Social Catholicism in Europe*, 154; Vidler, *A Century of Social Catholicism*, 67.
54. Benjamin F. Martin, *Count Albert de Mun* (Chapel Hill: University of North Carolina Press, 1978), 19.
55. Martin, *Count Albert de Mun*, 46; Vidler, *A Century of Social Catholicism*, 120.
56. Vidler, *A Century of Social Catholicism*, 114.
57. Vidler, *A Century of Social Catholicism*, 121.
58. McManners, *Church and State in France*, 88.
59. Police reports, F7 12483, Archives Nationales (hereafter cited as AN); Vidler, *A Century of Social Catholicism*, 121.

60. Police reports, F7 12482, AN.

61. Police reports, F7 12478, AN.

62. Henri de Boissieu speaking before the Assemblée Générale de l'Oeuvre des Cercles Catholiques, 25–27 January 1912, 8OR 25690, 71, Bibliothèque Nationale (hereafter cited as BN).

63. Georges Guitton, *Léon Harmel, 1829–1915* (Paris: Action Populaire, 1927), 1:9.

64. Later renamed *Le Mouvement social revue catholique internationale*.

65. Robert Talmy, *Aux Sources de catholicisme social* (Tournai: Desclée & Co., 1963), 29.

66. Talmy, *Aux Sources de catholicisme social*, 18–23.

67. Kale, *Legitimism and the Reconstruction of French Society*, 197.

68. Kale, *Legitimism and the Reconstruction of French Society*, 198.

69. Misner, *Social Catholicism in Europe*, 160.

70. Kale, *Legitimism and the Reconstruction of French Society*, 198–202.

71. Levillain, *Albert de Mun*, 597.

72. Léon Harmel to Albert de Mun, 1 February 1882, 59 J 17, AM.

73. Léon Harmel to "Très chèr confrère," 2 December 1880, 59 J 15, AM.

74. Steven D. Kale, "Architects of Tradition: Legitimism and the Reconstruction of French Society, 1852–1883" (Ph.D. diss., University of Wisconsin–Madison, 1987), 336.

75. Kale, "Architects of Tradition," 331.

76. Kale, *Legitimism and the Reconstruction of French Society*, 200.

77. Talmy, *Aux Sources de catholicisme social*, 228.

78. Contemporary usage for *fraternité*, or brotherhood.

79. Talmy, *Aux Sources de catholicisme social*, 280.

80. Talmy, *Aux Sources de catholicisme social*, 220, 259.

81. McManners, *Church and State in France*, 85.

82. Misner, *Social Catholicism in Europe*, 177.

83. Levillain, *Albert de Mun*, 1018.

84. Martin, *Count Albert de Mun*, 92.

85. McManners, *Church and State in France*, 88.

86. Jean-Marie Mayeur, "Le Catholicism social en France à la fin du XIXe siècle," *Le Mouvement Social*, no. 57 (October–December 1966): 212.

87. Martin, *Count Albert de Mun*, 212.

88. For a lively discussion of this point, see John F. Sweets, "Hold That Pendulum! Redefining Fascism, Collaborationism, and Resistance in France," *French Historical Studies* 15 (Fall 1988): 731–758; Paul M. Cohen, "Heroes and Dilettantes: The Action Française, Le Sillon, and the Generation of 1905–14," *French Historical Studies* (Fall 1988): 673–687.

89. Guitton, *Léon Harmel, 1829–1915*, 1:367.
90. Kale, "Architects of Tradition," 332.
91. Levillain, *Albert de Mun*, 650.
92. Albert de Mun, *Ma vocation sociale* (Paris: P. Lethielleux, 1908), 217.
93. de Mun, *Ma vocation sociale*, 219.
94. Parker Thomas Moon, *The Labor Problem and the Social Catholic Movement in France* (New York: MacMillan, 1921), 108.
95. Léon Gregoire (Georges Goyau), *Le Pape, les catholiques et la question sociale* (Paris: Perrin et Cie, 1893), 244; and Albert de Mun speaking before the Assemblée Générale de L'Oeuvre des Cercles Catholiques d'Ouvriers, Paris, 25, 26, 27 January 1912, 80R 25690, 46, BN.
96. de Mun, *Ma vocation sociale*, 185.
97. Léon Harmel speaking before the Directors of the Associations Ouvrières Catholiques, 1881, Ch. 982, AM.
98. Guitton, *Léon Harmel, 1829–1915*, 2:51–55.
99. Labor-management arbitration boards.
100. Léon Harmel to Albert de Mun, n.d., 59 J 17, AM.
101. Levillain, *Albert de Mun*, 648.
102. Misner, *Social Catholicism in Europe*, 163, 166.
103. Levillain, *Albert de Mun*, 747–748.
104. Léon Harmel, *La Démocratie dans l'usine—Le Conseil d'Usine du Val des Bois, 1907* (Reims: Imprimerie Cooperative, 1907), Ch. 982, AM; see also Jean Bruhat, "Anticlericalisme et mouvement ouvrier en France avant 1914," in *Christianisme et monde ouvrier*, ed. François Bédarida and Jean Maitron (Paris: Éditions Ouvrières, 1975), 86.
105. See, for example, Talmy, *Aux Sources du catholicisme social*, 15, 238; Levillain, *Albert de Mun*, 422, 428–429, 436, 569, 576–577, 648, 672–673, 877; Kale, "Architects of Tradition," 317, 332, 334.
106. Georges Jarlot, S. J., *Le Régime corporatif et les catholiques sociaux* (Paris: Flammarion, 1938), 54, 81; Martin, *Count Albert de Mun*, 47; Misner, *Social Catholicism in Europe*, 158; Levillain, *Albert de Mun*, 435.
107. Misner, *Social Catholicism in Europe*, 176–177.
108. Martin, *Count Albert de Mun*, 92. See also Talmy *Aux Sources du catholicisme social*, 15, 238.
109. Misner, *Social Catholicism in Europe*, 163.
110. McManners, *Church and State in France*, 88–89.
111. Levellain, *Albert de Mun*, 216, 219; Misner, *Social Catholicism in Europe*, 158.
112. Misner, *Social Catholicism in Europe*, 163–166; Talmy, *Aux Sources du catholicisme social*, 296–297.

113. Albert de Mun before the Assemblée Générale de l'Oeuvre des Cercles Catholiques, 25, 26, 27 January 1912, 80R 25690, BN.
114. McManners, *Church and State in France*, 90–91.
115. Misner, *Social Catholicism in Europe*, 177.
116. Misner, *Social Catholicism in Europe*, 177.
117. McManners, *Church and State in France*, 83.
118. Martin, *Count Albert de Mun*, 53.
119. Levillain, *Albert de Mun*, 425.
120. Eugene Marquigny, S.J., "La Réforme des ateliers," speaking before the Congress of Bordeaux, 22 August 1876 (Lyon: P. Trat Aîné, 1876), 3–6.
121. Robert Talmy, *L'Association catholique des patrons du Nord, 1884–1895* (Lille: Facultés Catholiques, 1961), 18.
122. Talmy, *L'Association catholique des patrons du Nord*, 168.
123. Talmy, *L'Association catholique des patrons du Nord*, 26–29, 35–36.
124. Rollet, *L'Action sociale des catholiques en France*, 292.
125. Talmy, *L'Association catholique des patrons du Nord*, 98.
126. Rollet, *L'Action sociale des catholiques en France*, 295.
127. Michael P. Fogarty, *Christian Democracy in Western Europe, 1820–1953* (Notre Dame: University of Notre Dame Press, 1957), 251; Rollet, *L'Action sociale des catholiques en France*, 299–301.
128. Rollet, *L'Action sociale des catholiques en France*, 300–301, 322.
129. Pierre Trimouille, *Léon Harmel et l'usine chrétienne du Val des Bois* (Lyon: Centre d'Histoire du Catholicisme de Lyon, 1974), 145.
130. McManners, *Church and State in France*, 89.
131. Talmy, *L'Association catholique des patrons du Nord*, 51, 74, 96.
132. Talmy, *Aux Sources de catholicisme social*, 50.
133. Talmy, *L'Association catholique des patrons du Nord*, 27–28.
134. Levillain, *Albert de Mun*, 606.
135. Talmy, *L'Association catholique des patrons du Nord*, 106–117; Claude Willard, "Les Attaques contre Notre-Dame dans l'usine," in *Christianisme et monde ouvrier*, ed. François Bédarida and Jean Maitron (Paris: Éditions Ouvrières, 1975), 246–249.
136. For a detailed discussion of this subject, see Talmy, *L'Association catholique des patrons du Nord*.
137. Talmy, *L'Association catholique des patrons du Nord*, 62, 65.
138. Talmy, *L'Association catholique des patrons du Nord*, 67.
139. Rollet, *L'Action sociale des catholiques en France*, 269–274.
140. Elinor Accampo, *Industrialization, Family Life, and Class Relations* (Berkeley: University of California Press, 1989), 171; Rollet, *L'Action sociale des catholiques en France*, 286.

141. Rollet, *L'Action sociale des catholiques en France*, 275–276.
142. Misner, *Social Catholicism in Europe*, 182–184.
143. Rollet, *L'Action sociale des catholiques en France*, 268–269.
144. Rollet, *L'Action sociale des catholiques en France*, 276–278.
145. Rollet, *L'Action sociale des catholiques en France*, 278–279.
146. Rollet, *L'Action sociale des catholiques en France*, 279.
147. Vidler, *A Century of Social Catholicism*, 123–124; Jarlet, *Le Régime corporatif et les catholiques sociaux*, 43–44.
148. Vidler, *A Century of Social Catholicism*, 125.
149. Wallace, *Leo XIII and the Rise of Socialism*, 8.
150. Vidler, *A Century of Social Catholicism*, 80–83.
151. McManners, *The Church and State in France*, 86; Wallace, *Leo XIII and the Rise of Socialism*, 8.
152. Claudia Carlen, I.H.M., *The Papal Encyclicals, 1878–1903*, vol. 2 (Raleigh: Pierian Press, 1981), 3–4.
153. McManners, *Church and State in France*, 68–69.
154. Leo XIII, *Quod Apostolici Muneris*, Carlen, *The Papal Encyclicals, 1878–1903*, 2:11–12.
155. Leo XIII, *Immortale Dei*, Carlen, *The Papal Encyclicals, 1878–1903*, 2:108.
156. Leo XIII, *Immortale Dei*, Carlen, *The Papal Encyclicals, 1878–1903*, 2:108.
157. Leo XIII, *Sapientiae Christianae*, Carlen, *The Papal Encyclicals, 1878–1903*, 2:213.
158. Leo XIII, *Sapientiae Christianae*, Carlen, *The Papal Encyclicals, 1878–1903*, 2:213.
159. Etienne Gilson, *The Church Speaks to the Modern World* (Garden City, N.Y.: Image Books, 1954), 7.
160. Richard L. Camp, *The Papal Ideology of Social Reform* (Leiden: E.J. Brill, 1969), 11.
161. Cardinal Langénieux was bishop of Reims from 1875 to 1905. He was, according to Pierre Pierrard in *L'Église et les ouvriers en France (1840–1940)* (Paris: Hachette, 1984), 379, the most "social" of the bishops of France. He introduced Leo XIII to the Harmelian social experiment at Val des Bois.
162. Léon Harmel, *Le Cardinal Langénieux et le Val des Bois, 1875–1905* (n.p.: Valan-Sedan O. Prin., 1910), 80L7K. 37396, BN.
163. Rollet, *L'Action sociale des catholiques en France*, 251.
164. Talmy, *Aux Sources de catholicisme social*, 2; Rollet, *L'Action sociale des catholiques en France*, 258.
165. Vidler, *A Century of Social Catholicism*, 125.

166. Misner, *Social Catholicism in Europe*, 207.
167. Misner, *Social Catholicism in Europe*, 202.
168. Misner, *Social Catholicism in Europe*, 202–205.
169. Vidler, *A Century of Social Catholicism*, 125–127; McManners, *Church and State in France*, 85.
170. McManners, *Church and State in France*, 86; Rollet, *L'Action sociale des catholiques in France*, 262.
171. All citations of *Rerum Novarum* are from Carlen, *The Papal Encyclicals, 1878–1903*, 2:241–261.
172. Leo XIII, *Rerum Novarum*, Carlen, *The Papal Encyclicals, 1878–1903*, 2: 242.
173. Camp, *The Papal Ideology of Social Reform*, 50, 57.
174. Wallace, *Leo XIII and the Rise of Socialism*, 271.
175. Leo XIII, *Rerum Novarum*, in Carlen, *The Papal Encyclicals, 1878–1903*, 2:244.
176. Leo XIII, *Rerum Novarum*, Carlen, *The Papal Encyclicals, 1878–1903*, 2:245.
177. Leo XIII, *Rerum Novarum*, Carlen, *The Papal Encyclicals, 1878–1903*, 2:246.
178. Donal Dorr, *Option for the Poor* (Maryknoll, N.Y.: Orbis Books, 1983), 48.
179. Dorr, *Option for the Poor*, 23.
180. Camp, *The Papal Ideology of Social Reform*, 56.
181. Leo XIII, *Rerum Novarum*, Carlen, *The Papal Encyclicals, 1878–1903*, 2: 242.
182. John F. Cronin, *Social Principles and Economic Life* (Milwaukee: Bruce Publishing Company, 1959), 12.
183. Leo XIII, *Rerum Novarum*, Carlen, *The Papal Encyclicals, 1878–1903*, 2:247.
184. Cronin, *Social Principles and Economic Life*, 262.
185. Cronin, *Social Principles and Economic Life*, 12.
186. Dorr, *Option for the Poor*, 48.
187. Cronin, *Social Principles and Economic Life*, 259.
188. Leo XIII, *Rerum Novarum*, Carlen, *The Papal Encyclicals, 1878–1903*, 2:244.
189. Camp, *The Papal Ideology of Social Reform*, 54.
190. Leo XIII, *Rerum Novarum*, Carlen, *The Papal Encyclicals, 1878–1903*, 2:251–253.
191. Leo XIII, *Rerum Novarum*, Carlen, *The Papal Encyclicals, 1878–1903*, 2:253.
192. For a discussion of the Catholic Church's position on the subject, see James G. Murtagh, "Theory of the Family Wage," in *The Church and Social*

Progress, ed. Benjamin L. Masse, S.J. (Milwaukee: Bruce Publishing Company, 1966), 87–90.

193. Leo XIII, *Rerum Novarum*, Carlen, *The Papal Encyclicals, 1878–1903*, 2:256.

194. Leo XIII, *Rerum Novarum*, Carlen, *The Papal Encyclicals, 1878–1903*, 2:253.

195. Leo XIII, *Rerum Novarum*, Carlen, *The Papal Encyclicals, 1878–1903*, 2:255.

196. Leo XIII, *Rerum Novarum*, Carlen, *The Papal Encyclicals, 1878–1903*, 2:256.

197. Leo XIII, *Rerum Novarum*, Carlen, *The Papal Encyclicals, 1878–1903*, 2:256.

198. Leo XIII, *Rerum Novarum*, Carlen, *The Papal Encyclicals, 1878–1903*, 2:254.

199. Léon Harmel speaking before the Assembly of Catholics of the Nord, June 1885, Ch. 982, AM.

200. Léon Harmel to M. Tiberghien, April 19, 1893, as cited in Guitton, *Léon Harmel, 1829–1915*, 2:28.

201. Dorr, *Option for the Poor*, 27.

202. Jean-Marie Mayeur and Marie Zimmermann in *Lettres de carême des évêques de France de 1861–1959*, as cited in Pierre Pierrard, *L'Église et les ouvriers en France (1840–1940)* (Paris: Hachette, 1984), 395.

203. Pierrard, *L'Église et les ouvriers en France*, 427.

204. Talmy, *L'Association catholique des patrons du Nord*, 117.

CHAPTER FOUR   Pilgrimage to Rome

An earlier version of this chapter appeared as "The Worker Pilgrimage: Religious Experience or Media Event?" in *Proceedings* (of the Western Society for French History) 20 (1993): 337–349.

1. Two classic studies of the period, useful for their rich detail, are Émile Zola's *The Debacle*, which is Zola's only purely historical work and tells the story of the Franco-Prussian War, and Alistair Horne's *The Fall of Paris*, which chronicles the siege and the Commune. Émile Zola, *The Debacle* (New York: Penguin Group, 1972); Alistair Horne, *The Fall of Paris* (New York: Penguin Books, 1966).

2. Susanna Barrows, *Distorting Mirrors* (New Haven: Yale University Press, 1981), 9–10.

3. Barrows, *Distorting Mirrors*, 8, 40.

4. Barrows, *Distorting Mirrors*, 4.

5. Barrows, *Distorting Mirrors*, 24.

6. Michelle Perrot, *Les Ouvriers en grève*, Tome I (Paris: Mouton and École Pratique des Hautes Études, 1974).

7. Barrows, *Distorting Mirrors*, 18–23.

8. Jean Chelini and Henry Branthomme, *Les Chemins de dieu* (Paris: Hachette, 1982), 132.

9. Victor Turner and Edith Turner, *Image and Pilgrimage in Christian Culture* (New York: Columbia University Press, 1978).

10. Turner and Turner, *Image and Pilgrimage in Christian Culture*, 17, 30, 203, 205, 206; Chelini and Branthomme, *Les Chemins de dieu*, 237–239.

11. Alphonse Dupront, *Du Sacré* (Paris: Éditions Gallimard, 1987), 366, 412.

12. Turner and Turner, *Image and Pilgrimage in Christian Culture*, 49.

13. Turner and Turner, *Image and Pilgrimage in Christian Culture*, 192. Tom Kselman makes the additional point that there is greater institutional control as one moved up the ecclesiastical ladder. Thomas A. Kselman, *Miracles and Prophecies in Nineteenth-Century France* (New Brunswick: Rutgers University Press, 1983), 35.

14. Chelini and Branthomme, *Les Chemins de dieu*, 319; Kselman, *Miracles and Prophecies in Nineteenth-Century France*, 114.

15. Chelini and Branthomme, *Les Chemins de dieu*, 308; Mary Lee Nolan and Sidney Nolan, *Christian Pilgrimage in Modern Western Europe* (Chapel Hill: University of North Carolina Press, 1989), 3; Kselman, *Miracles and Prophecies in Nineteenth-Century France*, 33, 89.

16. Chelini and Branthomme, *Les Chemins de dieu*, 291–295; Kselman, *Miracles and Prophecies in Nineteenth-Century France*, 12.

17. Turner and Turner, *Image and Pilgrimage in Christian Culture*, 172, 203, 209, 212; Nolan and Nolan, *Christian Pilgrimage in Modern Western Europe*, 3; Chelini and Branthomme, *Les Chemins de dieu*, 308.

18. Lilian Parker Wallace, *Leo XIII and the Rise of Socialism* (Durham: Duke University Press, 1966), 190.

19. Parker Thomas Moon, *The Labor Problem and the Social Catholic Movement in France* (New York: Macmillan, 1921), 158.

20. *La France du travail à Rome*, May 1905 (Paris: Commission Industrielle), A 241 AM.

21. *La France du travail à Rome*, September–October 1891, A 241 AM.

22. *La France du travail à Rome*, May 1905, A 241 AM.

23. Paul Seeley, "O Sainte Mère: Liberalism and the Socialization of Catholic Men in Nineteenth-Century France," *Journal of Modern History* 70 (December 1998): 879.

24. Nolan and Nolan, *Christian Pilgrimage in Modern Western Europe*, 288–289; Caroline Ford, "Religion and Popular Culture in Modern Europe,"

Journal of Modern History 65 (March 1993): 167–169; Seeley, "O Sainte Mère," 862–891.

25. Nolan and Nolan, *Christian Pilgrimage in Modern Western Europe*, 273.

26. For detail on these individual apparitions, see Turner and Turner, *Image and Pilgrimage in Christian Culture;* Nolan and Nolan, *Christian Pilgrimage in Modern Western Europe;* Dupront, *Du Sacré;* and for La Salette, Lourdes, and Pontmain, John Beevers, *The Sun Her Mantle* (Westminster, Md.: Newman Press, 1953).

27. Turner and Turner, *Image and Pilgrimage in Christian Culture,* 203; Nolan and Nolan, *Christian Pilgrimage in Modern Western Europe,* 273–274; Kselman, *Miracles and Prophecies in Nineteenth-Century France.*

28. Ford, "Religion and Popular Culture in Modern Europe," 167.

29. Ford, "Religion and Popular Culture in Modern Europe," 164.

30. Seeley, "O Sainte Mère," 879–880.

31. Roger Lipsey, *Have You Been to Delphi?* (Albany: State University of New York Press, 2001), 15.

32. Turner and Turner, *Image and Pilgrimage in Christian Culture,* 17.

33. Turner and Turner, *Image and Pilgrimage in Christian Culture,* 166.

34. Turner and Turner, *Image and Pilgrimage in Christian Culture,* 168, 192.

35. Chelini and Branthomme, *Les Chemins de dieu,* 245.

36. Chelini and Branthomme, *Les Chemins de dieu,* 337.

37. Turner and Turner, *Image and Pilgrimage in Christian Culture,* 194.

38. Chelini and Branthomme, *Les Chemins de dieu,* 245.

39. Nolan and Nolan, *Christian Pilgrimage in Modern Western Europe,* 55.

40. Eugen Weber, *France Fin de Siècle* (Cambridge, Mass.: Harvard University Press, 1986), 189.

41. Nolan and Nolan, *Christian Pilgrimage in Modern Western Europe,* 43, 46.

42. Weber, *France Fin de Siècle,* 189.

43. Georges Guitton, S.J., *Léon Harmel, 1829–1915,* 2 vols. (Paris: Action Populaire, 1927), 1:62, 81.

44. Guitton, *Léon Harmel, 1829–1915,* 1:62.

45. *La Croix,* 14 September 1889.

46. Guitton, *Léon Harmel, 1829–1915,* 1:207.

47. Weber, *France Fin de Siècle,* 188.

48. *La Croix,* 16 September 1891.

49. *La Croix,* 3 October 1891.

50. Weber, *France Fin de Siècle,* 189.

51. Weber, *France Fin de Siècle,* 190.

52. Nolan and Nolan, *Christian Pilgrimage in Modern Western Europe,* 65–66.

53. Protocollo 82597, Rubrica 1, Anno 1890, Segreteria di Stato, Archivo Vaticano (hereafter cited as ASV).

54. *L'Univers,* 12 November 1889.

55. Barrows, *Distorting Mirrors,* 18.

56. Barrows, *Distorting Mirrors,* 23–29.

57. Léon Harmel to "Eminence," 26 August 1889, Protocollo 82781, Rubrica 1, Anno 1890, ASV.

58. Léon Harmel to "Eminence," 26 August 1889, Protocollo 82781, Rubrica 1, Anno 1890, ASV; but also see Léon Harmel to "Eminentissime Seigneur," 7 September 1897, Protocollo 39743, Fascicolo 4, Rubrica 220, Anno 1897, ASV; Léon Harmel to "Eminentissime Seigneur," 17 August 1899, Protocollo 51716, Fascicolo 1, Rubrica 17, Anno 1899, ASV; Léon Harmel to "Très Saint-Père," 14 September 1901, Protocollo 65520, Fascicolo 7, Rubrica 17, Anno 1901, ASV; and Léon Harmel, *Lettres de Léon Harmel à ses enfants, voyage à Rome, février 1899,* 80K4650, BN.

59. Wallace, *Leo XIII and the Rise of Socialism,* 200; Henri Rollet, *L'Action sociale des catholiques en France, 1871–1914* (Paris: Desclée de Brouwer, 1958), 255.

60. Rollet, *L'Action sociale des catholiques en France,* 255–256.

61. Guitton, *Léon Harmel, 1829–1915,* 1:209.

62. Guitton, *Léon Harmel, 1829–1915,* 1:211.

63. M. L'Abbé Laumonier, *Guide du pèlerin à Rome* (Val des Bois, 1898), n.p.

64. Guitton, *Léon Harmel, 1829–1915,* 1:218.

65. Moon, *The Labor Problem and the Social Catholic Movement in France,* 158.

66. Guitton, *Léon Harmel, 1829–1915,* 1:210–211.

67. *Le Cri du Peuple,* 30 August 1885.

68. Robert Talmy, *L'Association catholique des patrons du nord, 1884–1895* (Lille: Facultés Catholiques, 1961), 49.

69. Laumonier, *Guide du pèlerin à Rome,* n.p.

70. *La Croix,* 21 October 1887.

71. Léon Harmel, *Exposé sommaire de l'oeuvre pronounce à Lyon le 27 novembre 1887* (Paris, 1888), 80R. Piece 4020, BN.

72. Laumonier, *Guide du pèlerin à Rome,* n.p.

73. *La Croix,* 22 October 1887.

74. *La Croix,* 18 and 20 October 1887.

75. Rollet, *L'Action sociale des catholiques en France,* 257–259.

76. *La Croix,* 21 October 1887.

77. *Le Figaro,* 13 November 1889.

78. Report from the Prefecture de Vaucluse on October 1887 to the Minister of the Interior, F7 12477, Archives Nationales (hereafter cited as AN).

79. Address of Leo XIII to the French workers on 12 October 1887, Protocollo 85875, Fascicolo 1, Rubrica 12, Anno 1892, ASV.

80. Harmel, *Exposé sommaire de l'oeuvre pronounce à Lyon le 27 novembre 1887*, 80R, Piece 4120, BN.

81. See, for example, editions of *Le Figaro, La Croix,* and *La Laterne* for October 1887.

82. *La Laterne,* 21 October 1887.

83. According to Kselman, *La Croix* was about to overtake *L'Univers* as the principal Catholic newspaper in France. Kselman, *Miracles and Prophecies in Nineteenth-Century France,* 138.

84. *La Croix,* 21 October 1887.

85. Guitton, *Léon Harmel, 1829–1915,* 1:217–218.

86. *La Croix,* 3 October 1889.

87. Rollet, *L'Action sociale des catholiques en France,* 259.

88. F7 124 82, AN.

89. Guitton, *Léon Harmel, 1829–1915,* 1:218–219; Rollet, *L'Action sociale des catholiques en France,* 259.

90. *La Croix,* 16 October 1889.

91. Guitton, *Léon Harmel, 1829–1915,* 1:220, 221.

92. Guitton, *Léon Harmel, 1829–1915,* 1:224–225.

93. *Le Figaro,* 30 October 1889 and 13 November 1889.

94. *Le Figaro,* 21 October 1889.

95. *Le Figaro,* 30 October 1889.

96. Guitton, *Léon Harmel, 1829–1915,* 1:222–224.

97. *La Croix,* 16 October 1889.

98. Rollet, *L'Action sociale des catholiques en France,* 260–261.

99. Laumonier, *Guide du pèlerin à Rome,* n.p.

100. *La Croix,* 17 October and 25 October 1889.

101. Address of Leo XIII before the French workers, 1889 pilgrimage, Protocollo 83397, Rubrica 1, Anno 1890, ASV; and *La Croix,* 24 October 1889.

102. Address of Leo XIII before the French workers, 1889 pilgrimage, Protocollo 83397, Rubrica 1, Anno 1890, ASV.

103. *La Croix,* 24 October 1889.

104. *La Laterne,* 22 and 23 October 1889.

105. *L'Intransigeant,* 16 October 1889.

106. *L'Estafette,* 28 October 1889.

107. *L'Univers,* 12 November 1889.

108. *Le Figaro,* 13 November 1889.

109. Martin Clark, *Modern Italy, 1871–1982* (New York: Longman, 1984), 40.

110. *La Croix,* 30 October, 4 and 23 November 1889.

111. *La Croix,* 8 November 1889.

112. *Le Monde,* 22 October 1889.

113. *L'Univers,* 12 November 1889.

114. Clark, *Modern Italy, 1871–1982,* 89–92.

115. C. J. Lowe and F. Marzari, *Italian Foreign Policy, 1870–1940* (Boston: Routledge & Kegan Paul, 1975), 47.

116. Rondo Cameron, *France and the Economic Development of Europe, 1800–1914* (Princeton: Princeton University Press, 1961), 431, 456.

117. Federico Chabod, *Italian Foreign Policy* (Princeton: Princeton University Press, 1996).

118. Lowe and Marzari, *Italian Foreign Policy, 1870–1940,* 48.

119. Lowe and Marzari, *Italian Foreign Policy, 1870–1940,* 48.

120. Albert Billot, *La France et l'Italie* (Paris: Librairie Plon, 1905), 35.

121. Edward R. Tannenbaum and Emiliana P. Noether, *Modern Italy* (New York: New York University Press, 1974), 37–38.

122. S. William Halperin, "Leo XIII and the Roman Question," in *Leo XIII and the Modern World,* ed. Edward T. Gargan (New York, Sheed and Ward, 1961), 117–118.

123. For additional background on the papal travails, see Kselman, *Miracles and Prophecies in Nineteenth-Century France,* 130; Claudia Carlen, I. H. M., *The Papal Encyclicals, vol. 1, 1740–1878* (Raleigh: Pierian Press, 1981), 275–276; Cameron, *France and the Economic Development of Europe, 1800–1914,* 427; and Wallace, *Leo XIII and the Rise of Socialism,* 17, 310–311.

124. Wallace, *Leo XIII and the Rise of Socialism,* 22.

125. Wallace, *Leo XIII and the Rise of Socialism,* 89–90, 310.

126. Maurice Larkin, *Church and State after the Dreyfus Affair* (New York: Harper & Row, 1973), 33.

127. Larkin, *Church and State after the Dreyfus Affair,* 38–39. The Quirinal Palace in Rome today is the official home of the president of Italy. Formerly it was the summer retreat of the popes and the official residence of the Italian kings. The palace, built on the highest of the seven hills of ancient Rome, was begun in 1573 by Gregory VIII to serve as the summer residence of the popes. Over the years the palace grew both in size and in the wealth of its collections. It was finished under Clement XII (r. 1730–1740), but as early as 1587, Sixtus V began living there during the hot Roman summer months. The palace remained a summer residence of the popes until 1870; it then became the home of the Savoy kings, a role it served until 1946, when the republican constitution designated the president of the Republic its new resident.

128. Wallace, *Leo XIII and the Rise of Socialism,* 93.

129. Wallace, *Leo XIII and the Rise of Socialism,* 94.

130. Billot, *La France et l'Italie,* 264; and Halperin, "Leo XIII and the Roman Question," 109.

131. S. William Halperin disagrees with this contention, positing instead that because of other diplomatic considerations, Leo XIII operated with more finesse than his predecessor, Pius IX, on the matter of the Roman Question, but I think this may have been more the result of different personalities than anything else. See Halperin, "Leo XIII and the Roman Question," 101–124.

132. Wallace, *Leo XIII and the Rise of Socialism*, 16; Halperin, "Leo XIII and the Roman Question," 108–110.

133. Leo XIII, "Etsi Nos," 15 February 1882, Carlen, *The Papal Encylicals, vol. 2, 1878–1903* (Raleigh: Pierian Press, 1981), 63.

134. Leo XIII, "Etsi Nos," 15 February 1882, Carlen, *The Papal Encyclicals*, 2:64, 66.

135. Larkin, *Church and State after the Dreyfus Affair*, 33, 35.

136. Leo XIII, "Nobilissima Gallorum Gens," 8 February 1884, Carlen, *The Papal Encyclicals, 1878–1903*, 2:87.

137. Humphrey Johnson, *The Papacy and the Kingdom of Italy* (London: Sheed and Ward, 1926), 52.

138. Halperin, "Leo XIII and the Roman Question," 117.

139. Wallace, *Leo XIII and the Rise of Socialism*, 102–103.

140. Halperin, "Leo XIII and the Roman Question," 116.

141. Jacques Piou, *Questions religieuses et socials* (Paris: Librairie Plon, 1910), 16.

142. William L. Langer, *The Franco-Russian Alliance, 1890–1894*, (New York: Octagon Books, 1967), 236.

143. Otto von Bismarck succeeded in weaving a tight web of diplomatic alliances following the Franco-Prussian War with the purpose of keeping France isolated and therefore weak. Above all else, he wanted to prevent an alliance between France and Russia, for should they get together, it could mean a two-front war for Germany sometime in the future. Therefore, he organized the Three Emperors' League (Germany, Austria-Hungary, Russia) in 1873, the Dual Alliance (Germany and Austria-Hungary) in 1879, the Triple Alliance (Germany, Austria-Hungary, Italy) in 1882, and the Reinsurance Treaty with Russia (which was upset after Bismarck overturned its gains in the Russo-Turkish War at the Conference of Berlin in 1878) in 1887. The system worked amazingly well until Bismarck's retirement in 1890.

144. Martin E. Schmidt, *Alexandre Ribot: Odyssey of a Liberal in the Third Republic* (The Hague: Martinus Nijhoff, 1974), 51.

145. Schmidt, *Alexandre Ribot: Odyssey of a Liberal in the Third Republic*, 51–54.

146. Theodore Zeldin, *France, 1848–1945* (Oxford: Oxford University Press, 1973), 646. See also Gordon Wright, *France in Modern Times* (New York: W. W. Norton, 1981), 229–230.

147. Halperin, "Leo XIII and the Roman Question," 116.

148. *L'Univers,* 20 February 1891.

149. Léon Harmel to Cardinal Rampolla, 27 March 1891, Protocollo 1210, Fascicolo 1, Rubrica 12, Anno 1892, ASV.

150. Léon Harmel to Leo XIII, 24 March 1891, Protocollo 1210, Fascicolo 1, Rubrica 12, Anno 1892, ASV.

151. *Le Temps,* 8 October 1891.

152. Rampolla to Harmel, 30 December 1890 and 2 April 1891, Protocollos 89465 and 1210, Fascicolo 1, Rubrica 12, Anno 1892, ASV.

153. Guitton, *Léon Harmel, 1829–1915,* 1:302.

154. *La Croix,* 12 September 1891.

155. Rampolla to Harmel, 5 August 1891, Protocollo 2990, ASV.

156. Domenico, Archbishop of Thessalonica, Papal Nuncio, to His Very Reverend Eminence Cardinal Rampolla, Paris, 29 August 1891, Protocollo 3390, Fascicolo 1, Rubrica 12, Anno 1892, ASV.

157. *La Croix,* 17 September 1891.

158. *La Croix,* 15 September 1891.

159. *La Croix,* 8, 9, and 15 September 1891.

160. *La Croix,* 24 and 28 September 1891.

161. Vol. 1106, August–October 1891, CP Rome, Ministère des Affaires Etrangères, Archives du Ministère des Affaires Etrangères, Paris (hereafter cited as AAE).

162. *La Croix,* 8 September 1891.

163. Max Turmann, *Le Développement du catholicisme social depuis l'encyclique "Rerum Novarum"* (Paris: Libraires Félix Alcan et Guillamin Réunis, 1909), 188.

164. Laumonier, *Guide du pèlerin à Rome,* n.p.

165. *La France du travail à Rome,* July–September 1891, A. 241, AM.

166. *Le Temps,* 8 October 1891; *La Croix,* 19 September 1891.

167. *La Croix,* 19 September 1891.

168. *La Croix,* 14 September 1891.

169. Guitton, *Léon Harmel, 1829–1915,* 1:317–318.

170. Address of Leo XIII to French workers during the 1891 pilgrimage, Protocollo 4186, Fascicolo 1, Rubrica 12, Anno 1892, ASV; *La Croix,* 22 September 1891.

171. John McManners, *Church and State in France, 1870–1914* (New York: Harper & Row, 1972), 86.

172. *La Croix,* 22 September 1891.

173. *La Croix,* 22 September 1891.

174. *La Croix,* 29 and 30 September 1891.

175. *La Croix*, 29 September 1891.
176. *La Croix*, 15 September 1891.
177. *La Croix*, 18 September 1891.
178. *La Croix*, 17 September 1891.
179. *La Croix*, 24 September 1891.
180. *Le Voltaire*, 1 October 1891.
181. The Pantheon is the most famous and best preserved monument of ancient Rome. First constructed by Agrippa in 27 B.C.E., it was restored by Domitian after the fire of 80 and reconstructed once again in its present rotunda shape by Emperor Hadrian. In 609 it was dedicated by Boniface IV as a Christian church (Santa Maria and Martyres). In the Middle Ages, it served as a fortress. Later it was despoiled by popes, especially by Urban VIII who melted down the bronze roof for the construction of the baldacchino in St. Peter's and for eighty cannons of Castel Sant'Angelo. It contains the tombs of Raphael and the kings of Italy. Since it was a church, the Italian royal family attended yearly Mass at the Pantheon on the anniversary of the death of Victor Emmanuel II. *Le Figaro*, 14 October 1891.
182. King of Italy (r. 1849–1878). Victor Emmanuel died in the Quirinal, after a short illness, on January 9, 1878. Pius IX, despite his bitter political contestation with Italy's first king, allowed him the last rites on his deathbed. Wallace, *Leo XIII and the Rise of Socialism*, 83. Cavour used "Victory Emmanuel II," but because he was first king of Italy, most dropped the "II." Johnson, *The Papacy and the Kingdom of Italy*, 38.
183. *La Croix*, 5 October 1891.
184. Telegram from Rome to Quai d'Orsay, Affaires Diverses Politiques, Saint-Siège, Vol. 21, 1891, AAE.
185. *La Croix*, 5 October 1891.
186. Gérard Noiriel, "French and Foreigners," in *Realms of Memory*, under the direction of Pierre Nora, vol. 1 (New York: Columbia University Press, 1996), 154.
187. Rollet, *L'Action sociale des catholiques en France*, 261.
188. *Le Figaro*, 1 October 1891.
189. His accession to the throne saddened Pius IX for it meant the entrenchment of the dynasty and lessened the chance that the temporal power of the papacy would be restored. Humbert, aware of the political implications of his every move, never set foot in St. Peter's. Wallace, *Leo XIII and the Rise of Socialism*, 83, 318.
190. *La Laterne*, 18 October 1891.
191. Telegram, 10 October 1891, Affaires Diverses Politiques, Saint-Siège, Vol. 21, 1891, AAE.

192. Rollet, *L'Action sociale des catholiques en France*, 261.

193. Telegram, 4 October 1891, Affaires Diverses Politiques, Saint-Siège, Vol. 21, 1891, AAE.

194. *La Croix*, 5 October 1891.

195. *Le Figaro*, 6 October 1891.

196. *La Croix*, 5 October 1891.

197. *La Croix*, 16 October 1891.

198. F19 5563, AN.

199. *La Croix*, 6 October 1891.

200. *La Croix*, 5 October 1891.

201. Telegram, n.d., Affaires Diverses Politiques, Saint-Siège, Vol. 21, 1891, AAE.

202. *La Croix*, 10 October 1891.

203. *La Croix*, 15 October 1891.

204. *Le Figaro*, 1 November 1891.

205. F19 5563, AN.

206. Léon Harmel to "Eminence," 26 August 1889, Protocollo 82781, Rubrica 1, Anno 1890, ASV; but also see Léon Harmel to "Eminentissime Seigneur," 7 September 1897, Protocollo 39743, Fascicolo 4, Rubrica 220, Anno 1897, ASV; Léon Harmel to "Eminentissime Seigneur," 17 August 1899, Protocollo 51716, Fascicolo 1, Rubrica 17, Anno 1899, ASV; Léon Harmel to "Très Saint-Père," 14 September 1901, Protocollo 65520, Fascicolo 7, Rubrica 17, Anno 1901, ASV; and Léon Harmel, *Lettres de Léon Harmel à ses enfants, voyage à Rome, février 1899*, 80K4650, BN.

207. *La Croix*, 19 October 1891.

208. Rollet, *L'Action sociale des catholiques en France*, 262.

209. *La Croix*, 3 October 1889.

210. *Le Temps*, 24 September 1891.

211. *La Croix*, 6 October 1891.

212. *La Croix*, 14 October 1891.

213. *La Croix*, 17 October 1891.

214. See, for example, *La Croix*, 31 August and 21 September 1891.

215. *La Croix*, 17 October 1891.

216. *L'Univers*, as reported in *La Croix*, 30 November 1891.

217. *La Patrie*, 18 October 1891.

218. *L'Estafette*, 15 October 1891.

219. *L'Estafette*, as reported in *Le Monde*, 7 October 1891.

220. *Le Figaro*, 23 September 1891.

221. *Le Figaro*, 7 October 1891.

222. *Le Figaro*, 14 October 1891.

223. *Le Figaro,* 14 October 1891.
224. *Le Voltaire,* 18 October 1891.
225. *Le Radical,* 18 October 1891.
226. *Le Temps,* 7 October 1891.
227. *Le Temps,* 4 October 1891.
228. *Le Temps,* 4 October 1891.
229. *La Petite République,* 15 September 1891.
230. *La Petite République,* 4 October 1891.
231. *La Lanterne,* 18 October 1891.
232. *La Lanterne,* 5 October 1891.
233. *La Lanterne,* 5 November 1891.
234. *La Lanterne,* 28 October 1891.
235. See, for example, *La Lanterne,* 7 and 18 October 1891; and *La Petite République,* 18 October 1891.
236. Domenico to Rampolla, 1 November 1891, Protocollo 4082, Fascicolo 3, Rubrica 248, Anno 1892, ASV.
237. All the major newpapers carried the substance of the 26 October meeting in the Chamber of Deputies. Among them were *Le Voltaire,* 27 October 1891, and *Le Figaro,* 27 October 1891. Ribot's private sentiments corresponded to those expressed before the Chamber of Deputies. See Domenico to Rampolla, 15 October 1891, Protocollo 3987, Fascicolo 1, Rubrica 248, Anno 1892, ASV.
238. Vol. 1106, CP: Rome, August–October 1891, AAE.
239. Béhaine to Ribot, telegram, n.d., Affaires Diverses Politiques, Saint-Siège, Vol. 21, 1891, AAE.
240. Béhaine to Ribot, telegram, 3 October, Affaires Diverses Politiques, Saint-Siège, Vol. 21, 1891, AAE.
241. Cardinal Langénieux to Ribot, 30 October 1891, Affaires Diverses Politiques, Saint-Siège, Vol. 21, 1891, AAE.
242. Billot to Ribot, 7 October 1891, CP: Rome, Vol. 1106, August–October 1891, AAE.
243. Béhaine to Ribot, 7 October 1891, CP: Rome, Vol. 1106, August–October 1891, AAE.
244. Béhaine to Ribot, 20 October 1891, CP: Rome, Vol. 1106, August–October 1891, AAE.
245. Domenico, Archbishop of Thessalonica, Papal Nuncio, to Cardinal Rampolla, 4 October 1891, Protocollo 3740, Fascicolo 3, Rubrica 248, Anno 1892, ASV.
246. Ribot to Billot, 3 October 1891, CP: Italie, Vol. 100, October–December 1891, AAE; and Billot to Ribot, 4 October 1891, CP Italie, Vol. 100, October–December 1891, AAE.

247. Billot to Ribot, 10 October 1891, CP Italie, Vol. 100, October–December 1891, AAE.

248. C. Ressman to Monsieur le Ministre, 12 October 1891, CP Italie, Vol. 100, October-December, AAE.

249. Billot to Ribot, 8 October 1891, CP Italie, Vol. 100, October–December 1891, AAE.

250. Billot to Ribot, 15 October 1891, CP Italie, Vol. 100, October–December 1891, AAE.

251. Billot to Ribot, 1 January 1892, CP: Italie, Vol. 101, January–March 1892, AAE.

252. Billot to Ribot, 25 January 1892, CP: Italie, Vol. 101, January–March 1892, AAE.

253. See, for example, Billot to Ribot, 26 February, 2 March, 6 March 1892, CP: Italie, 101, January–March 1892, AAE.

254. Mémoires et Documents, Italie, Vol. 44, 1887, 1888, 1889, AAE.

255. Béhaine to Ribot, 10 November and 18 December 1891, CP: Rome, Vol. 1107, AAE.

256. Francis Joseph, member of the Habsburg dynasty, ruled Austria from 1848 to 1916. Plagued by ethnic problems within the Austro-Hungarian Empire, Austria was dominated militarily and politically by its more powerful neighbor to the north, Germany.

257. Béhaine to Ribot, 30 November and 8 December 1891 and 8 January 1892, CP: Rome, Vols. 1107 and 1108, AAE.

258. Charles, Prince zu Löwenstein, 22 October 1891, to Leo XIII, Protocollo 4222, Fasciolo 4, Rubrica 248, Anno 1891, ASV.

259. Domenico, Archbishop of Thessalonica, Papal Nuncio, to Cardinal Rampolla, 4 October 1891, Protocollo 3786, Fascicolo 3, Rubrica 248, Anno 1892, ASV.

260. Léon Harmel to Cardinal Rampolla, 31 October 1891, Protocollo 4186, Fascicolo 5, Rubrica 248, Anno 1892, ASV.

261. Bishop of Montpellier to Cardinal Rampolla, 5 November 1891, Protocollo 4046, Fascicolo 5, Rubrica 248, Anno 1892, ASV.

262. Protocollo 4173, Fascicolo 5, Rubrica 248, Anno 1892, ASV.

263. Rollet, *L'Action sociale des catholiques en France,* 262.

264. Rollet, *L'Action sociale des catholiques en France,* 255.

265. Wallace, *Leo XIII and the Rise of Socialism,* 328.

266. Halperin, "Leo XIII and the Roman Question," 111.

267. Halperin, "Leo XIII and the Roman Question," 112–113.

268. Wallace, *Leo XIII and the Rise of Socialism,* 310.

CHAPTER FIVE   New Directions

An earlier version of this chapter appeared as "The Aix Affair of 1891: A Turning Point in Church-State Relations before the Separation?" in *French Historical Studies* 21 (1998): 543–559.

1. Monsieur Bishop,

> You are acquainted with the regrettable incidents that recently occurred in Rome during the course of the pilgrimages known as those of the "French workers."
>
> You have too much feeling for national interests not to be aware that the authorities of the country must avoid being compromised by these demonstrations which easily can lose their religious character.
>
> I have, consequently, the honor of inviting you to abstain, for the moment, from all participation in these pilgrimages.
>
> Rest assured of my high regard.
>
> A. Fallières
> Minister of Justice and Religious Affairs

2. BB/18/1855, Dossier 1617, A91, AN. Born in 1820 at Saint-Jean-la-Vère in the Loire, Gouthe-Soulard was named professor of philosophy at the Institution Secondaire des Minimes shortly after his ordination, then in succession *curé* at Saint Vincent de Paul and *curé* at Saint Peter of Vaise, both in Lyons. Saint Peter's was a workers' parish, and Gouthe-Soulard was popular with his parishioners. In 1886 he was named archbishop of Aix, an unusual promotion in that it had been a half century since a simple priest had become an archbishop without first serving as bishop. No doubt in response to his popularity with workers, contemporaries thought of him as a "liberal." *Le Figaro,* 21 October 1891. But historians of the period characterized him as an "unrepentant royalist and without subtlety." Jean-Baptiste Duroselle, *La France et les français, 1900–1914* (Paris: Éditions Richelieu, 1972), 123.

3. "Je ne vois pas pourquoi, disait-il, vous nous invitez à ne pas nous compromettre dans des manifestations qui peuvent, dites-vous, perdre facilement leur charactère religieux.... Nous n'avions pas besoin de votre invitation ni pour le passé ni pour le present, et rien ne vous autorise à nous la faire pour l'avenir. Du reste, nous savons nous conduire. Le Comité organisateur a suspendu les pèlerinages; quand ils se rétabliront, ju ferai ce que je voudrai dans l'intérêt de mon diocese.... Vous aviez mieux à faire que de vous presser à nous écrire cette letter, qui

devient un triste et odieux contresens. De Plus, elle n'est appuyée sur rien de sérieux. La paix est quelquefois sur vos lévres, la haine et la persecution sont toujours dans vos actes, parce que la franc-maçonnerie, cette fille ainée de Satan, gouverne et commande; mille fois aveugle volontaire qui ne le voit pas. Pour moi, ju suis vivement blessé dans ma dignité de Français, de Catholique et d'évêque."

As printed in, Domenico Cardinal Ferrata, *Mémoires* (Paris: Prix, 1922), 115–116.

4. Ferrata, *Mémoires,* 115–116; Gouthe-Soulard to Monsieur le Ministre, 8 October 1891, Protocollo 4012, Fascicolo 3, Rubrica 248, Anno 1892, ASV.

5. Adrien Dansette, *Histoire religieuse de la France comtemporaine,* 2 vols. (Paris: Flammarion, 1951), 2:136.

6. Domenico, Archbishop of Thessalonica, Papal nuncio to Cardinal Rampolla, 17 October, Protocollo 3981, Fascicolo 3, Rubrica 248, Anno 1892, ASV.

7. Guy Chapman, *The Third Republic of France* (London: St. Martin's Press, 1962), 295.

8. Chapman, *The Third Republic of France,* 295.

9. Rampolla to Domenico, 22 October 1891, Protocollo 3981, Fascicolo 3, Rubrica 248, Anno 1892, ASV.

10. Domenico to Rampolla, 22 October 1891, Protocollo 4082, Fascicolo 3, Rubrica 248, Anno 1892, ASV.

11. Domenico to Rampolla, 15 October 1891, Protocollo 3987, Fascicolo 3, Rubrica 248, Anno 1891, ASV.

12. Rampolla to Domenico, 27 October 1891, Protocollo 4082, Fascicolo 3, Rubrica 249, Anno 1892, ASV.

13. Rampolla to Domenico, 24 October 1891, Protocollo 4012, Fascicolo 3, Rubrica 248, Anno 1892, ASV.

14. Rampolla to Domenico, n.d., Protocollo 4364, Fascicolo 4, Rubrica 248, Anno 1892, ASV.

15. Domenico to Rampolla, n.d., Protocollo 4454 and Protocollo 4364, Fascicolo 4, Rubrica 248, Anno 1892, ASV.

16. Rampolla to Domenico, 27 October 1891, Protocollo 4082, Fascicolo 3, Rubrica 248, Anno 1892, ASV.

17. Ribot, Minister of Foreign Affairs, to Monsieur le Comte Lefèbvre de Béhaine, Ambassador of the French Republic to the Vatican, 17 December 1891, Protocollo 5151, Fascicolo 8, Rubrica 248, Anno 1892, ASV.

18. Domenico to Rampolla, 1 November 1891, Protocollo 4082, Fascicolo 3, Rubrica 248, Anno 1892, ASV.

19. Fallières to Ribot, n.d., F/19/1945, AN.

20. Béhaine to Ribot, 11 December 1891, Vol. 1107, CP: Rome, November–December 1891, AAE.

21. Gouthe-Soulard, *Mon procès, mes avocats* (Paris: E. Deptu, 1891).

22. BB/18/1855, Dossier 1617, A91, AN.
23. BB/18/1855, Dossier 1617, A91, AN.
24. Domenico to Rampolla, 25 November 1891, Protocollo 4454, Fascicolo 4, Rubrica 248, Anno 1892, ASV.
25. Béhaine to Ribot, 10 November 1891, Vol. 1107, CP: Rome, November–December, AAE.
26. Béhaine to Ribot, 10 November 1891, Vol. 1107. CP: Rome, November–December, AAE.
27. Domenico to Rampolla, 1 December 1891, Protocollo 4626, Fascicolo 4, Rubrica 248, Anno 1892, ASV.
28. Rampolla to Domenico, 30 November 1891, Protocollo 4517, Fascicolo 4, Rubrica 248, Anno 1892, ASV.
29. Béhaine to Ribot, 29 November 1891, Vol. 1107, CP: Rome, November–December AAE.
30. Rampolla to Domenico, 23 and 25 November 1891, Protocollo 4454 and Protocollo 4426, Fascicolo 4, Rubrica 248, Anno 1892, ASV.
31. Béhaine to Ribot, 12 December 1891, Vol. 1107, CP: Rome, November–December, AAE.
32. Béhaine to Ribot, 19 December 1891, Vol. 1107, CP: Rome, November–December, AAE.
33. Rampolla to Domenico, 8 November 1891, Protocollo 4257, Fascicolo 4, Rubrica 248, Anno 1892, ASV.
34. Rampolla to Domenico, 9 November 1891, Protocollo 4222, Fascicolo 4, Rubrica 248, 248, Anno 1892, ASV.
35. Rampolla to Domenico, 9 November 1891, Protocollo 4222, Fascicolo 4, Rubrica 248, ASV.
36. Ribot to Béhaine, 17 December 1891, Protocollo 5151, Fascicolo 8, Rubrica 248, Anno 1892, ASV.
37. Domenico to Rampolla, 7 December 1891, Protocollo 4656, Fascicolo 4, Rubrica 248, Anno 1892, ASV.
38. Domenico to Rampolla, 13 December 1891, Protocollo 4837, Fascicolo 4, Rubrica 248, Anno 1892, ASV.
39. Rampolla to Domenico, 19 December 1891, Protocollo 4837, Fascicolo 4, Rubrica 248, Anno 1892, ASV.
40. Rampolla to Domenico, 19 December 1891, Protocollo 4837, Fascicolo 4, Rubrica 248, Anno 1892, ASV.
41. Leo XIII, *Au Milieu des Sollicitudes,* Claudia Carlen, I. H. M., *The Papal Encyclicals, vol. 2, 1878–1903* (Raleigh: Pierian Press, 1981), 278. For a more complete discussion of the background and results of the Ralliement letter, see Lillian Parker Wallace, *Leo XIII and the Rise of Socialism* (Durham: Duke University Press, 1966), 282–308.

42. Leo XIII, *Au Milieu des Sollicitudes,* Carlen, *Papal Encyclicals, 1878–1903,* 2:280.

43. For an interesting discussion of this concept in a different context, see François Furet, *Marx and the French Revolution* (Chicago: University of Chicago Press, 1988), 18.

44. Study of Jean-Marie Mayeur and Marie Zimmermann in *Lettres de Carême des Évêques de France (1861–1959)* as cited in Pierre Pierrard, *L'Église et les ouvriers en France (1840–1940)* (Paris: Hachette, 1984), 395–396.

45. Emile Poulat, Introduction, in *Christianisme et monde ouvrier,* ed. François Bédarida and Jean Maitron (Paris: Les Éditions Ouvrières, 1975), 62.

46. Georges Guitton, S.J., *Léon Harmel, 1829–1915,* 2 vols. (Paris: Action Populaire, 1927), 2:77.

47. Gordon Wright, *France in Modern Times* (New York: W.W. Norton, 1995), 239.

48. Maurice Larkin, *Church and State after the Dreyfus Affair* (New York: Harper & Row, 1973), 48–51.

49. John McManners, *Church and State in France, 1870–1914* (New York: Harper & Row, 1972), 134–145.

50. Wright, *France in Modern Times,* 227–230.

51. Billot to Ribot, 22 October 1891, Vol. 100, CP: Italie, October–December 1891, AAE.

52. Billot to Ribot, 9 December 1891, Vol 100, CP: Italie, October–December 1891, AAE.

53. Guitton, *Léon Harmel, 1829–1915,* 1:203.

54. Protocollo 7349, Fascicolo 1, Rubrica 12, Anno 1892, ASV.

55. L'Abbé Emmanuel Barbier, *Le Progrès du libéralisme catholique en France sous le pape Léon XIII,* 2 vols. (Paris: P. Lethielleux, 1907), 2:114.

56. *La Croix,* 28 July, 4 August, 6 August 1897.

57. Parker Thomas Moon, *The Labor Problem and the Social Catholic Movement in France* (New York: Macmillan, 1921), 366.

58. *La Croix,* 7 August, 10 August, 12 August, and 13 August 1897.

59. *La Laterne,* 9 August 1897; *La Petite République.*

60. *Le Voltaire,* 10 August 1897.

61. Barbier, *Le Progrès du libéralisme catholique,* 2:226.

62. See, for example, Protocollo 49139, Fascicolo 4, Rubrica 12, Anno 1898, ASV; Protocollo 49624, Fascicolo 1, Rubrica 17, Anno 1899, ASV; and Léon Harmel, *Lettres de Léon Harmel à ses enfants, voyage à Rome, février 1899,* 80K, 4650, p. 37, BN.

63. Jean Chelini and Henry Branthomme, *Les Chemins de dieu* (Paris: Hachette, 1982), 339.

64. Barbier, *Le Progrès du libéralisme catholique*, 2:92.

65. McManners, *Church and State in France*, 94; Henri Rollet, *L'Action sociale des catholiques en France, 1871–1914* (Paris: Desclée de Brouwer, 1958), 339; Paul Misner, *Social Catholicism in Europe*, (New York: Crossroad, 1991), 222; Jean-Marie Mayeur, *Catholisme social et démocratie chrétienne: Principes, romains, experiences françaises* (Paris: Éditions du Cerf, 1986), 7.

66. Robert Talmy, *Le Syndicalisme chrétien en France (1871–1930)* (Paris: Éditions Bloud & Gay, 1965), 38.

67. Misner, *Social Catholicism in Europe*, 218.

68. Rollet, *L'Action sociale des catholiques en France*, 341, 381–384.

69. Misner, *Social Catholicism in Europe*, 227; Barbier, *Le Progrès du libéralisme catholique*, 2:199.

70. Rollet, *L'Action sociale des catholiques en France*, 350–351.

71. Rollet, *L'Action sociale des catholiques en France*, 249, 350.

72. Rollet, *L'Action sociale des catholiques en France*, 386–388.

73. Rollet, *L'Action sociale des catholiques en France*, 341.

74. McManners, *Church and State in France*, 94; Moon, *The Labor Problem*, 366.

75. Rollet, *L'Action sociale des catholiques en France*, 338–339, 342–345, 357; McManners, *Church and State in France*, 94; Barbier, *Le Progrès du libéralisme catholique*, 2:115.

76. Le père Charcosset, in *Un Livre du famille*, Chapter 2, as cited in Guitton, *Léon Harmel, 1829–1915*, footnote 1, 2:77.

77. Guitton, *Léon Harmel, 1829–1915*, 2:77.

78. Misner, *Social Catholicism in Europe*, 228.

79. Léon Harmel in a speech entitled "Les Hommes nouveaux," 1892, as reported in *La Croix*, Ch. 982, AM.

80. Léon Harmel to R. P. Bailly, 19 March 1892, Ch. 982, AM.

81. Barbier, *Le Progrès du libéralisme catholique*, 2:93.

82. For further detail on the Christian democratic congresses, their principal leaders, and the movement in general, see Rollet, *L'Action sociale des catholiques en France*, esp. chap. 11 (338–389); Alec R. Vidler, *A Century of Social Catholicism 1820–1920* (London: SPCK, 1964); Theodore Zeldin, *France, 1848–1945*, vol. 1 (Oxford: Oxford University Press, 1973); Larkin, *Church and State after the Dreyfus Affair*; McManners, *Church and State in France*, esp. chap. 11 (94–117); Misner, *Social Catholicism in Europe*, esp. chap. 12 (227–239) and chap. 15 (288–318); Barbier, *Le Progrès du libéralisme catholique*, 1:162–165 and all of vol. 2.

83. Léon Harmel in a speech at the regional congress held at Blois, 3 April 1899, Ch. 982, AM.

84. Vidler, *A Century of Social Catholicism*, 129.
85. Vidler, *A Century of Social Catholicism*, 129–131.
86. Misner, *Social Catholicism in Europe*, 232.
87. Misner, *Social Catholicism in Europe*, 232.
88. Police report, F7 12482, AN.
89. Joseph N. Moody, *Church and Society: Catholic Social and Political Thought and Movements, 1789–1950* (New York: Arts 1953), 156.
90. McManners, *Church and State in France*, 99.
91. Vidler, *A Century of Social Catholicism*, 128.
92. Police reports, F7 12482, AN.
93. Police reports, F7 12482, AN; Guitton, *Léon Harmel, 1829–1915*, 2:26–27; McManners, *Church and State in France*, 98.
94. McManners, *Church and State in France*, 98.
95. Rollet, *L'Action sociale des catholiques en France*, 361.
96. Léon Harmel to the director of *L'Univers*, 24 September 1900, as printed in *Mouvement sociale revue catholique internationale*, November 1900.
97. Rollet, *L'Action sociale des catholiques en France*, 363.
98. Y.-M. Hilaire, "Les Ouvriers de la region du Nord devant l'église catholique (XIXe–XXe siècle)," in *Christianisme et monde ouvrier*, ed. François Bédarida and Jean Maitron (Paris: Les Éditions ouvrières, 1975), 234.
99. François Sellier, "France," in *Labor in the Twentieth Century*, ed. John T. Dunlap and Walter Galenson (New York: Academic Press, 1978), 220, 222. During the Popular Front government (1937–1938) of Léon Blum, the socialist prime minister initialed the Matignon Accord, which set into motion the structure for collective bargaining and therefore dialogue between management and labor. However, because of the short duration of the Popular Front government—a mere thirteen months—lasting communication between employers and employees did not occur until 1968.
100. Rollet, *L'Action sociale des catholiques en France*, 366–370; Robert Talmy, *L'Association catholique des patrons du Nord, 1884–1895* (Lille: Facultés Catholique, 1962), 181–184.
101. Rollet, *L'Action sociale des catholiques en France*, 380.
102. Stephen Wilson, *Ideology and Experience* (East Brunswick, N.J.: Associated University Presses, 1982), 170.
103. Wilson, *Ideology and Experience*, 173, 248.
104. David McCullough, *The Path between the Seas* (New York: Simon and Schuster, 1977), 205. For a shorter version of the French phase of the building of the Panama Canal, see Sanford J. Mock, "The Panama Canal—Part I—The French Attempt," *Manuscripts* 53, no. 3 (Summer 2001): 193–211.
105. McCullough, *The Path between the Seas*, 206.

106. Incidents that resulted in bloodshed and death of Italian immigrants occurred in Vat (1884), Meuse and Aube (1885), Isère (1886), Aisne (1888), Haute-Marne (1889), Lorraine (1895), and Isère (1901). Eugen Weber, *France Fin de Siècle* (Cambridge, Mass.: Harvard University Press, 1986), 134–135. See also Gérard Noiriel, "French and Foreigners," in *Realms of Memory,* ed. Pierre Nora (New York: Columbia University Press, 1996), 1:154; and Jeremy D. Popkin, *A Modern History of France* (Englewood Cliffs, N.J.: Prentice Hall, 1994), 202.

107. Weber, *France Fin de Siècle,* 135.

108. For perhaps the most detailed account of the Panama Canal Scandal, and certainly the whole project of building the Central American canal, see McCullough's *Path between the Seas.* A more general rendering can be found in Wright, *France in Modern Times,* 240–242.

109. McCullough, *The Path between the Seas,* 209.

110. McCullough, *The Path between the Seas,* 204.

111. Jean-Marie Mayeur and Madeleine Rebérioux, *The Third Republic from Its Origins to the Great War, 1871–1914* (New York: Cambridge University Press, 1987), 200.

112. Weber, *France Fin de Siècle,* 131.

113. Wilson, *Ideology and Experience,* 290.

114. Jean-Denis Bredin, *The Affair* (New York: George Brazillier, 1986), 26.

115. Pierre Birnbaum, "Grégoire, Dreyfus, Drancy, and the Rue Copernic: Jews at the Heart of French History," in Nora's *Realms of Memory,* 1:393, 395–397.

116. For a thorough discussion of this whole subject, see Birnbaum, "Grégoire, Dreyfus, Drancy, and the Rue Copernic," 1:379–423.

117. Perhaps the most detailed account of the scandal can be found in Bredin, *The Affair.* Also useful is Mayeur and Rebérioux, *The Third Republic from Its Origins to the Great War, 1871–1914,* 179–208; Popkin, *A Modern History of France,* 203–206; Weber, *France Fin de Siècle,* 130–133; and Wright, *France in Modern Times,* 242–245.

118. McManners, *Church and State in France,* 119.

119. Birnbaum, "Grégoire, Dreyfus, Drancy, and the Rue Copernic," 1:383; Wilson, *Ideology and Experience,* 334–336.

120. Mayeur, *Catholicisme social et démocratie chrétienne,* 161.

121. Police reports, F7 12482, AN.

122. General Georges Boulanger became war minister of France in 1886. He became a popular hero by extending student deferments, permitting soldiers to have beards, suggesting the abolishment of St. Cyr, trying to construct military installations in Lorraine, and conducting unauthorized military maneuvers on France's eastern border. The government dismissed him from his cabinet post, partially in response to protestations by Bismarck, but this action only increased

his popularity. He ran for political office in 1889 and achieved a great electoral victory. But before he could claim its rewards, he fled to Brussels with his mistress. When she died of tuberculosis in July, he committed suicide on her grave on September 30, 1889. Significantly, he stirred up *revanche,* the desire for revenge against Germany, and represented patriotism and popularism.

123. McManners, *Church and State in France,* 122.

124. Freemasonry arose during the Enlightenment as a secular alternative to the Roman Catholic Church, and it was characterized by its belief in the "Great Architect of the Universe" and by its lodges and rituals. In 1738, the Catholic Church condemned Freemasonry.

125. Léon Harmel to R. P. Bailly, 19 March 1892, Ch. 982, AM.

126. Léon Harmel in a speech given at Congrès Ouvrier de Tours, 5 June 1897, Ch. 982, AM.

127. Léon Harmel in a speech before the Assemblée Générale des Catholiques du Nord et du Pas-de-Calais, 1892, Ch. 982, AM.

128. Léon Harmel to R. P. Bailly, 19 March 1892, Ch. 982, AM.

129. Léon Harmel in a speech delivered in Reims at the Conférences Populaires, 8 January 1890, Ch. 982, AM.

130. Larkin, *Church and State after the Dreyfus Affair,* 95.

131. Larkin, *Church and State after the Dreyfus Affair,* 94–95.

132. In addition to his encyclical *Humanum Genus* (20 April 1884), Leo XIII denounced Masonry in the following encyclicals: *Dall'Alto Dell'Apostolico Seggio* (15 October 1890), *Custodi Di Quella Fede* (8 December 1892), and *Inimica Vis* (8 December 1892).

133. Police reports, F7 12482, AN.

134. Mayeur, *Catholicisme social et démocratie chrétienne,* 163.

135. Jean-Marie Mayeur claims 1889. Mayeur, *Catholicisme social et démocratie chrétienne,* 210.

136. Wilson, *Ideology and Experience,* 285.

137. Mayeur, *Catholicisme social et démocratie chrétienne,* 211.

138. Mayeur, *Catholicisme social et démocratie chrétienne,* 210.

139. Rollet, *L'Action sociale des catholiques en France,* 241.

140. Wilson, *Ideology and Experience,* 289.

141. Wilson, *Ideology and Experience,* 288.

142. Léon Harmel in speech delivered at Sacré-Coeur in Montmartre, 27 June 1897, Ch. 982, AM.

143. Léon Harmel to "Eminentissime Seigneur," 1 July 1897, Protoccolo 38693, Fascicolo 1, Rubrica 17, Anno 1897, ASV.

144. Léon Harmel to "Eminentissime Seigneur," 1 July 1897, Protoccolo 38693, Fascicolo 1, Rubrica 17, Anno 1897, ASV.

145. Léon Harmel to "Eminentissime Seigneur," February 1899, Protocollo 49139, Fascicolo 4, Rubrica 12, Anno 1898, ASV.

146. Leo XIII, *Humanum Genus,* Carlen, *Papal Encyclicals, 1878–1903,* 2:99.

147. Mayeur, *Catholicisme social et démocratie chrétienne,* 194.

148. Léon Harmel to "Très Saint-Père," 3 March 1896, Portocollo 29637, Fascicolo 1, Rubrica 9, Anno 1896, ASV.

149. Pierre Trimouille, *Léon Harmel et l'usine chrétienne du Val des Bois* (Lyon: Centre d'Histoire du Catholicisme de Lyon, 1974), 185–186.

150. Jean-Marie Mayeur, "Tiers-ordre franciscain et catholicisme social en France à la fin du XIXe siècle," *Revue d'Histoire de l'Église de France* 70, no. 1 (1984): 187.

151. Police reports, F7 12482, AN.

152. Police reports, F7 12482, AN.

153. Trimouille, *Léon Harmel et l'usine chrétienne,* 35.

154. Trimouille, *Léon Harmel et l'usine chrétienne,* 187–196.

155. McManners and Misner claim that the first meeting of the Semaines Sociales was held at Lyon in 1904. McManners, *Church and State in France, 1870–1914,* 111; Misner, *Social Catholicism in Europe,* 288.

156. A canon is a clergyman serving in a cathedral or collegiate church.

157. Rollet, *L'Action sociale des catholiques en France,* 494–500; Trimouille, *Léon Harmel et l'usine chrétienne,* 187–196.

158. The Seminary of Saint-Sulpice, founded in 1642, served the Sulpician religious community. The order is not strictly speaking a religious order but rather a society of diocesan priests; that is, its religious men had as their primary mission the operation of Church parishes and attendant institutions in dioceses. The Seminary of Saint-Sulpice was regarded as a model seminary. Not only did it prepare the priests of Paris and its suburbs, but young men came from all over France, Ireland, Switzerland, and the United States to study at one of two campuses. The original campus is located in the heart of Paris at 6 rue du Regard in the sixth *arrondisement;* the second campus is located outside of Paris proper in Issy-Les-Moulineaux.

159. For a more complete account of the effects of the Military Law of 1889 on the clergy of France, see Joan L. Coffey, "For God and France: The Military Law of 1889 and the Soldiers of Saint-Sulpice," *Catholic Historical Review* 88, (October 2002): 677–701.

160. Trimouille, *Léon Harmel et l'usine chrétienne,* 192.

161. Rollet, *L'Action sociale des catholiques en France,* 500, says that the year was 1901; while Trimouille, *Léon Harmel et l'usine chrétienne,* 192, claims 1902.

162. Léon Harmel to "Eminentissime Seigneur," n.d., Protocollo 28466, Rubrica 223, Anno 1896, ASV.

163. Léon Harmel to "Eminentissime Seigneur," 8 April 1899, Protocollo 49571, Fascicolo 4, Rubrica 12, Anno 1898, ASV.

164. Concern with clerical education was not confined to the French. In addition to *Depuis Le Jour*, Leo XIII issued two subsequent encyclicals on the subject: *Paternae* (18 September 1899) to the archbishops and bishops of Brazil and *Fin Dal Principio* (8 December 1902) to the bishops of Italy.

165. Leo XIII, *Depuis Le Jour*, Carlen, *Papal Encyclicals, 1878–1903*, 2:457.

166. Leo XIII, *Depuis Le Jour*, Carlen, *Papal Encyclicals, 1878–1903*, 2:460.

167. Leo XIII, *Depuis Le Jour*, Carlen, *Papal Encyclicals, 1878–1903*, 2:460.

168. Leo XIII, *Depuis Le Jour*, Carlen, *Papal Encyclicals, 1878–1903*, 2:458.

169. Leo XIII, *Depuis Le Jour*, Carlen, *Papal Encyclicals, 1878–1903*, 2:460.

170. Leo XIII, *Depuis Le Jour*, Carlen, *Papal Encyclicals, 1878–1903*, 2:460–461.

171. Trimouille, *Léon Harmel et l'usine chrétienne*, 192.

172. Lester K. Kurtz, *The Politics of Heresy* (Berkeley: University of California Press, 1986), 9–15.

173. Kurtz, *The Politics of Heresy*, 161.

174. Paul M. Cohen, *Piety and Politics* (New York: Garland, 1987), 32.

175. Kurtz, *The Politics of Heresy*, 9–15.

176. Kurtz, *The Politics of Heresy*, 9–15.

177. Kurtz, *The Politics of Heresy*, 9–15.

178. Leo XIII, *Longinqua*, Carlen, *Papal Encyclicals, 1878–1903*, 2:364.

179. Leo XIII, *Longinqua*, Carlen, *Papal Encyclicals, 1878–1903*, 2:367.

180. Leo XIII, *Longinqua*, Carlen, *Papal Encyclicals, 1878–1903*, 2:367.

181. Leo XIII, *Longinqua*, Carlen, *Papal Encyclicals, 1878–1903*, 2:364–365.

182. Beginning with the papacy of Pope Clement V (r. 1305–1314), who left Rome for Avignon, and continuing for the next seventy years, the Church entered one of the most troubled periods in its history. The Great Schism (1378–1415) divided western Christendom into two warring camps with two and sometimes three popes. France and its supporters recognized the pope in Avignon, while England and most of the German states recognized the pope in Rome. The result was the weakening of the papacy and strengthening of the conciliar movement within the Church. The notion of the Roman Church ruled by a council of bishops lost ground with the resurgence of the papacy after 1450.

183. *The Great Encyclicals of Pope Leo XIII*, 452.

184. Kurtz, *The Politics of Heresy*, 35.

185. Leo XIII, *Graves de Communi Re*, Carlen, *Papal Encyclicals, 1878–1903*, 2:483.

186. Leo XIII, *Graves de Communi Re*, Carlen, *Papal Encyclicals, 1878–1903*, 2:481.

187. Leo XIII, *Graves De Communi Re,* Carlen, *Papal Encyclicals, 1878–1903,* 2:484.

188. See McManners, *Church and State in France,* 104–117.

189. Misner, *Social Catholicism in Europe,* 238, 288, 290.

190. Léon Harmel, 19 February 1899, *Lettres de Léon Harmel à ses enfants, voyage à Rome,* 8.

191. Harmel, 22 February 1899, *Lettres de Léon Harmel à ses enfants, voyage à Rome,* 8.

192. See, for example, Protocollo 52209, Fascicolo 15, Rubrica 248, Anno 1900, ASV; and Harmel, February 14, 1899, *Lettres de Léon Harmel à ses enfants, voyage à Rome,* 3.

193. Léon Harmel to "Très Saint-Père," 14 September 1901, Protocollo 65520, Fascicolo 7, Rubrica 17, Anno 1901, ASV.

194. Léon Harmel writing in *La France du travail à Rome,* October–December, 1905.

195. The Sillon ("furrow") was a Paris-based organization that united intellectuals and workers in a nonconfessional communal brotherhood for the purpose of alleviating class tension. It opposed anti-Semitism, monarchism, anticlericalism, and integral nationalism. Under the direction of Marc Sangnier, it published a newspaper and a review, and wanted to organize a republican party based on Christian principles. See the following for a more detailed discussion of Sangnier and his organization: Vidler, *A Century of Social Catholicism,* 133–139; McManners, *Church and State in France,* 99–103, 170–172; Misner, *Social Catholicism in Europe,* 298–305.

196. McManners, *Church and State in France,* 170.

197. Guitton, *Léon Harmel, 1829–1915,* 2:358.

Conclusion

1. Léon Bourgeois (1851–1925) promoted Solidarism nationally and internationally. A member of the Radical Party, he at various times served the government of the Third Republic as minister of the interior, education and justice minister, foreign minister, minister of labor, and prime minister. In 1920 he was awarded the Nobel Peace Prize for his efforts to establish world peace under the banner of Solidarism. J.E.S. Hayward, "The Official Philosophy of the French Third Republic: Léon Bourgeois and Solidarism," *International Review of Social History* 6 (1961): 21, 26.

2. Georges Guitton, S.J., *Léon Harmel, 1829–1915,* 2 vols. (Paris: Action Populaire, 1927), 2:379–383.

3. Judith F. Stone, *The Search for Social Peace* (Albany: State University of New York Press, 1985), 14.

4. Stone, *The Search for Social Peace*, 62.

5. François Sellier, "France," in *Labor in the Twentieth Century*, ed. John T. Dunlap and Walter Galenson (New York: Academic Press, 1978), 238.

6. It was discontinued as a general benefit in 1971, after which it was only paid to those with low incomes. Sellier, "France," 238.

7. Sellier, "France," 218.

8. Stone, *The Search for Social Peace*, 15.

9. Léon Harmel to Monsieur le Vicaire Générale, 23 June 1914, AM.

10. Carl Strikwerda, "Catholic Working Class Movements in Europe," *International Labor and Working Class History* 34 (Fall 1988): 3.

11. Léon Harmel to Monsieur le Vicaire Générale, 23 June 1914, AM.

12. Sellier, "France," 219.

13. Sellier, "France," 222.

14. Sellier, "France," 220–222.

15. Léon Harmel to Monsieur le Vicaire Générale, 23 June 1914, AM.

16. David McLellan, *Marxism and Religion* (New York: Harper & Row, 1987), 51, 159.

17. McLellan, *Marxism and Religion*, 2.

18. Parker Thomas Moon, *The Labor Problem and the Social Catholic Movement in France* (New York: Macmillan, 1921), 179–181.

19. Cited in Moon, *The Labor Problem and the Social Catholic Movement in France*, 182.

20. Police reports, F7 12482, AN.

21. Protocollo 28205, Fasciolo 8, Rubrica 248, Anno 1900, ASV.

22. Jules Guesde, *Double réponse* (Paris: Publications de la Société Nouvelle de Librarie Éditions, 1906).

23. Léon Harmel to M. Krafft, 1 October 1879, 59 J 13, AM.

24. Léon Harmel to Abbé Leroy Quimper, 21 November 1881, and 13 December 1881, 59 J 17, AM.

25. Léon Harmel speaking before the Congrès des Directeurs des Associations Ouvrières Catholique, 1879, Ch. 982, AM.

26. Harmel speaking before the Congrès des Directeurs des Associations Ouvrières Catholique, 1879, Ch. 982, AM.

27. Léon Harmel's report to the Congrès d'Autun, August 1882, as reported in *L'Association Catholique*, 15 August–15 September 1882, Ch. 982, AM.

28. Harmel's report to the Congrès d'Autun, August 1882, as reported in *L'Association Catholique*, 15 August–15 September 1882, Ch. 982, AM.

29. Harmel's report to the Congrès d'Autun, August 1882, as reported in *L'Association Catholique*, 15 August–15 September 1882, Ch. 982, AM.

30. Léon Harmel in a speech before the Congrès des Directeurs des Associations Ouvrières Catholiques, 1881, Ch. 982, AM.

31. Léon Harmel in a speech before the Patrons du Nord at Mouveaux, 15 July 1894, 80R Piece 9630, BN.

32. Léon Harmel in a speech to the Cercle Vaugirard de Paris, 9 January 1898, Ch. 982, AM.

33. John XXIII, *Pacem in Terris*, as cited and discussed in McLellan, *Marxism and Religion*, 136.

34. John Paul II, *Laborem Exercens* (14 September 1981) in Claudia Carlen, I. H. M., *The Papal Encyclicals, vol. 5, 1958–1981* (Raleigh: Pierian Press, 1981), 312.

35. Police reports, F7 12482, AN; *French Socialist Congresses, 1876–1914* (New York: Clearwater Publishing Co., n.d.).

36. For a fuller discussion of Solidarism, see Hayward, "The Official Philosophy of the French Third Republic," 22–25; Theodore Zeldin, *France, 1848–1973*, vol. 1 (Oxford: Oxford University Press, 1973), 655–671; Stone, *The Search for Social Peace*, xii–xv, 100–139, 163, 173; John H. Weiss, "Origins of the French Welfare State: Poor Relief in the Third Republic, 1871–1914," *French Historical Studies* 13 (Spring 1983): 47–78.

37. Hayward, "The Official Philosophy of the French Third Republic," 22–25.

38. Marianne Debouzy, "Permanence du paternalisme?" *Le Mouvement Social* 144 (July–September 1988): 3.

39. Michelle Perrot as cited by Debouzy, "Permanence du paternalisme?" 7.

40. Perrot as cited by Debouzy, "Permanence du paternalisme?" 7.

41. Pierre Trimouille, *Léon Harmel et l'usine chrétienne du Val des Bois* (Lyon: Centre d'Histoire du Catholicisme de Lyon, 1974), 137.

42. Strikwerda, "Catholic Working Class Movements in Europe," 2.

43. Strikwerda, "Catholic Working Class Movements in Europe," 20.

44. Strikwerda, "Catholic Working Class Movements in Europe," 3.

45. Léon Harmel to Monsieur le Vicaire Générale, 23 June 1914, AM.

46. Strikwerda, "Catholic Working Class Movements in Europe," 28.

47. John F. Cronin and Harry W. Flannery, *The Church and the Workingman* (New York: Hawthorn Books, 1965), 26, 56. But see also, of course, Pius XI, *Quadragesimo Anno*, in Carlen, *Papal Encyclicals, 1903–1939*, 3:415–443.

48. Richard L. Camp, *The Papal Ideology of Social Reform* (Leiden: E. J. Brill, 1969), 25–37.

49. Pius XI in *Quadragesimo Anno*, as cited in Peter Riga, *John XXIII and the City of Man* (Westminster, Md.: Newman Press, 1966), 8.

50. Jean-Yves Calvez, S. J., *The Social Thought of John XXIII* (Chicago: Henry Regnery, 1964), 15–53. But also refer to John XXIII, *Mater et Magistra*, Carlen, *Papal Encyclicals, 1958–1981*, 5:59–90.

51. Calvez, *The Social Thought of John XXIII*, 4–12.

52. Paul VI, *Populorum Progressio,* Carlen, *Papal Encyclicals, 1958–1981,* 5:183–201.

53. John Paul II, *Laborem Exercens* (14 September 1981), Carlen, *Papal Encyclicals, 1958–1981,* 5:300. The pope delayed issuing his encyclical on labor until September because of hospitalization. He had prepared the document in time for the May 15 anniversary, but did not have time to review it until later. John Paul II, *Laborem Exercens,* Carlen, *Papal Encyclicals, 1958–1981,* 5:325.

54. John Paul II, *Laborem Exercens,* Carlen, *Papal Encyclicals, 1958–1981,* 5:310.

55. John Paul II, *Laborem Exercens,* Carlen, *Papal Encyclicals, 1958–1981,* 5:320.

56. John Paul II, *Laborem Exercens,* Carlen, *Papal Encyclicals, 1958–1981,* 5:301.

57. Guitton, *Léon Harmel, 1829–1915,* 2:394–398.

BIBLIOGRAPHY

Archival Sources

Segretaria de Stato, Archivio Vaticano (Vatican Archives)

Anno 1890
Rubrica 1   Worker pilgrimages to Rome
Anno 1891
Rubrica 248
     Fascicolo 1   Pantheon incident
     Fascicolo 3   Pantheon incident
     Fascicolo 4   European support of Holy See
Anno 1892
Rubrica 12
     Fascicolo 1   Worker pilgrimages
Rubrica 248
     Fascicolo 1   Pilgrimage of 1891 and future plans after Fallières Circulaire
     Fascicolo 2   Pantheon incident and Ralliement letter
     Fascicolo 3   Pilgrimage of 1891, Pantheon incident
     Fascicolo 4   Pilgrimage of 1891, Pantheon incident, Fallières Circulaire
     Fascicolo 5   Pilgrimage of 1891 and trial of Monseigneur Gouthe-Soulard

Fascicolo 6	Letters of support in aftermath of Pantheon incident
Fascicolo 7	Additional correspondence in aftermath of Pantheon incident
Fascicolo 8	Vatican response to diocesan catechisms in France; correspondence between Rome and French minister of foreign affairs

Anno 1894
Rubrica 12

Fascicolo 1	Correspondence between Harmel and the Vatican; socialism

Anno 1895
Rubrica 12

Fascicolo 2	Correspondence between Harmel and Vatican; Christian democracy

Anno 1896
Rubrica 9

Fascicolo 1	Correspondence between Harmel and Vatican; Third Order of St. Francis

Rubrica 223

Fascicolo 2	Correspondence between Harmel and Vatican; Christian democracy

Anno 1897
Rubrica 17

Fascicolo 1	Correspondence between Harmel and Vatican; fruits of *Rerum Novarum*
Fascicolo 4	Correspondence between Harmel and Vatican

Rubrica 220

Fascicolo 4	Correspondence between Harmel and Vatican; pilgrimages

Anno 1898
Rubrica 12

Fascicolo 4	Correspondence between Harmel and Vatican; Christian democracy

Anno 1899
Rubrica 17

Fascicolo 1	Correspondence between Harmel and Vatican; L'Union Fraternelle, Christian worker congresses, worker pilgrimages

Anno 1900
Rubrica 248

Fascicolo 8	Correspondence between Harmel and Vatican; Albert de Mun, Christian democracy; French elections
Fascicolo 15	Correspondence between Harmel and Vatican; social action of the French clergy

Anno 1901
Rubrica 17
    Fascicolo 7   Correspondence between Harmel and Vatican; worker pilgrimages, L'Union Fraternelle

Archives Nationales (Paris)

Série BB_{18}, Dossiers of the Criminal Division from 1890 to 1955
  1855   Trial of Monseigneur Gouthe-Soulard
Série BB_{30}, Discharges of the Department of Justice
  1484   Diverse material relating to Pantheon incident and Gouthe-Soulard Affair
Série F_7, General Police Records
  12477   Surveillance of political parties and movements
  12478   Surveillance of political parties and movements
  12482   Surveillance of political parties and movements
  12483   Surveillance of political parties and movements
Série F_{19}, Cultes
  1332   Monseigneur Gouthe-Soulard
  1943   Reports between France and Rome under the Third Republic
  1945   Relations between Third Republic and the Holy See
  2552   Archbishops and Bishops
  2566   Archbishops and Bishops
  5562   Worker pilgrimage of 1889; press clippings
  5563   Worker pilgrimage of 1891 and Pantheon incident; press clippings
  5564   Diverse material, including pilgrimages and Episcopal responses to Fallières Circulaire and Aix Affair; press clippings
  5565   Press clippings from the Aix Affair
  5614   Chamber of Deputies' discussions of ecclesiastical material

Archives du Ministère des Affaires Etrangères (Paris)

Vol. 21 CP Rome Correspondence between Ministry of Foreign Affairs and French representative to the Holy See
Vol. 44 Italie   Memoirs and documents

Vol. 100 Italie　　　　　　Correspondence between Ministry of Foreign Affairs and French representative to Italy
Vol. 101 Italie　　　　　　Correspondence between Ministry of Foreign Affairs and French representative to Italy
Vol. 1106 CP Rome　　　　Correspondence between Ministry of Foreign Affairs and French representative to the Holy See
Vol. 1107 CP Rome　　　　Correspondence between Ministry of Foreign Affairs and French representative to the Holy See
Vol. 1108 CP Rome　　　　Correspondence between Ministry of Foreign Affairs and French representative to the Holy See

Archives de la Marne (Châlons-sur-Marne)

59 J 13　　　　Correspondence of Léon Harmel
59 J 15　　　　Correspondence of Léon Harmel
59 J 16　　　　Correspondence of Léon Harmel
59 J 17　　　　Correspondence of Léon Harmel
59 J 18　　　　Correspondence of Léon Harmel
59 J 19　　　　Speeches and correspondence of Léon Harmel
59 J 20　　　　Correspondence of Léon Harmel
59 J 21　　　　Correspondence of Léon Harmel
59 J 72　　　　Speeches and correspondence of Léon Harmel
Ch. 982　　　　Speeches and correspondence of Léon Harmel, booklets on Val-des-Bois
Ch. 982 *bis*　　Speeches of Léon Harmel, booklets on Val-des-Bois
A 241　　　　　*La France du travail à Rome* (newspaper of the worker pilgrimages)

Archives of the Archdiocese of Paris

IDX.22　　　　General commentary on the state of the Church

Archives de la Compagnie de Saint-Sulpice (Paris)

Circulaires des supérieurs généraux de Saint-Sulpice 1875–1905
Le Faisceau, news bulletin of the Seminary of Saint-Sulpice, 1907–1909
Bulletin Trimestriel 1914–1918, letters from the Front

Published Sources

Journals and Newspapers

Journel official, October–December 1891
La France du travail à Rome, 1905
La Semaine religieuse de Paris, 1891
L'Autorité, 1891
L'Association Catholique, 1876–1915
La Cocarde, 1891
Le Cri du people, 1885, 1887, 1889, 1891
La Croix, 1885, 1887, 1889, 1891
L'Estafette, 1889, 1891
Le Figaro, 1885, 1887, 1889, 1891, 1897
Le Gaulois, 1891
L'Intransigeant, 1889
Le Jour, 1891
La Justice, 1891
La Laterne, 1885, 1887, 1889, 1891, 1897
Le Matin, 1891
Le Monde 1891
La Petite République, 1891
Le Radical, 1891
Le Rappel, 1891
La République
Le Siècle, 1891
Le Soleil, 1891
Le Temps, 1885, 1887, 1889, 1891, 1897
L'Univers, 1889, 1891
Le Voltaire, 1885, 1887, 1889, 1891, 1897

Anonymous and Unsigned Works

Congrès de l'union fraternelle. Paris: Rondelet et Cie.
Congrès of Nouveaux. Roubaix: Auguste Roussel, 1894.
Exposition universelle de 1900—Harmel Frères. Reims: Imprimerie cooperative, n.d.
French Socialist Congresses, 1876–1914. New York: Clearwater Publishing Company, n.d.

General Assembly (1912) of the Oeuvre des Cercles Catholiques. Bibliothèque Nationale. 8oR 7711.
La France du travail à Rome, 1888–1905.
"Les Congrès nationaux de la démocratie chrétienne à Lyon," *Revue d'histoire modern et contemporaine* (July–September 1962).
Seven Great Encyclicals. Glen Rock: Paulist Press, 1939.
"Socialisme et charité." Bibliothèque Nationale. 8oR 7713.
"Socialisme et l'église." *La Revue Socialiste* 38 (1903): 35–52.
Seven Great Encyclicals. Glen Rock: Paulist Press, 1939.
The Great Encyclical Letters of Pope Leo XIII. Chicago: Benziger Brothers, 1903.

Books, Pamphlets, and Secondary Sources

Accampo, Elinor A. *Industrialization, Family Life, and Class Relations.* Berkeley: University of California Press, 1989.
Accampo, Elinor A., Rachel G. Fuchs, and Mary Lynn Stewart. *Gender and the Politics of Social Reform in France, 1870–1914.* Baltimore: Johns Hopkins University Press, 1995.
Agulhon, Maurice. *The French Republic, 1879–1992.* Cambridge, Mass.: Blackwell Publishers, 1993.
Amdur, Kathryn E. "The Making of the French Working Class." In *The Transformation of Modern France,* edited by William B. Cohen, 66–96. New York: Houghton Mifflin, 1997.
Anderson, R. D. *France, 1870–1914.* Boston: Routledge & Kegan Paul, 1977.
Aquinas, Thomas. *Summa Theologica.* Chicago: Encyclopedia Britannica, 1952.
Barbier, L'Abbé Emmanuel. *Le Progrès du libéralisme catholique en France sous le pape Léon XIII.* 2 vols. Paris: P. Lethielleux, 1907.
Barrows, Susanna. *Distorting Mirrors.* New Haven: Yale University Press, 1981.
Beaune, Henri. *La Participation aux benefices dans l'industrie et le commerce.* Lyon: Auguste Cote, 1893.
Bellanger, Claude, Jacques Godechot, Pierre Guiral, and Fernand Terrou. *Histoire Générale de la presse française.* Tome III, *De 1871 à 1940.* Paris: Presses Universitaires de France, 1972.
Bédarida, François, and Jean Maitron. *Christianisme et monde ouvrier.* Paris: Les Éditions Ouvrières, 1975.
Beevers, John. *The Sun Her Mantle.* Westminster, Md.: Newman Press, 1953.
Berenson, Edward. *Populist Religion and Left-Wing Politics in France, 1830–1852.* Princeton: Princeton University Press, 1984.
Bergeron, Louis. *L'Industrialisation de la France au XIXe siècle.* Paris: Hatier, 1979.
Berlanstein, Lenard R. *The Working People of Paris, 1871–1914.* Baltimore: Johns Hopkins University Press, 1984.

Berth, Edouard. "Religion et socialisme." *Revue socialiste* (July 1900): 20–43. Musée Social, Paris, France.

Billot, Albert. *La France et l'Italie*. Paris: Librairie Plon, 1905.

Birnbaum, Pierre. "Grégoire, Dreyfus, Drancy, and the Rue Copernic: Jews at the Heart of French History." In *Realms of Memory*, vol. 1, edited by Pierre Nora, 379–423. New York: Columbia University Press, 1996.

Black, Anthony. *Guilds and Civil Society in European Political Thought from the Twelfth Century to the Present*. Ithaca: Cornell University Press, 1984.

Bossenga, Gail. "Protecting Merchants: Guilds and Commercial Capitalism in Eighteenth-Century France." *French Historical Studies* 15 (Fall 1988): 693–703.

Boulard, Fernand. *Essor ou déclin du clergé français?* Paris: Éditions du Cerf, 1950.

———. *Premiers itineraries en sociologie religieuse*. Paris: Éditions Ouvrières Economie et Humanisme, 1954.

Boxer, Marilyn J., and Jean H. Quataert. "Women in Industrializing and Liberalizing Europe." In *Connecting Spheres*, edited by Marilyn J. Boxer and Jean H. Quataert. New York: Oxford University Press, 1987.

Boxer, Marilyn J., and Jean H. Quataert, eds. *Connecting Spheres*. New York: Oxford University Press, 1987.

Bredin, Jean-Denis. *The Affair*. New York: George Brazillier, 1986.

Bruhat, Jean. "Anticlericalisme et mouvement ouvrier en France avant 1914." *Le Monde Social*, no. 57 (October–December 1966): 61–100.

———. "Anticlericalisme et mouvement ouvrier en France avant 1914." In *Christianisme et monde ouvrier*, edited by François Bédarida and Jean Maitron, 79–115. Paris: Éditions Ouvrières, 1975.

Byrnes, Robert F. *Antisemitism in Modern France: The Prelude to the Dreyfus Affair*. 2 vols. New Brunswick: Rutgers University Press, 1950.

Calvez, Jean-Yves. "Association et corporation chez les premiers commintateurs de *Rerum Novarum*." *Chronique Sociale de France* 65 (3 December 1957): 647–673.

———. *The Social Thought of John XXIII*. Chicago: Henry Regnery, 1964.

Calvez, Jean-Yves, and J. Perrin. *Église et société économique*. Paris: Aubier, 1959.

Cameron, Rondo. *France and the Economic Development of Europe, 1800–1914*. Princeton: Princeton University Press, 1961.

Camp, Richard L. *The Papal Ideology of Social Reform*. Leiden: E. J. Brill, 1969.

Canetti, Elias. *Crowds and Power*. New York: Viking Press, 1963.

Capéran, Louis. *L'Anticléricalisme et l'affaire Dreyfus*. Toulouse: Imprimerie Régionale, 1948.

Carlen, Claudia, I. H. M. *The Papal Encyclicals*. 5 vols. Raleigh: Pierian Press, 1981.

Caron, François. *An Economic History of Modern France*. New York: Columbia University Press, 1979.

Chabod, Federico. *Italian Foreign Policy*. Princeton: Princeton University Press, 1996.
Chapman, Guy. *The Third Republic of France*. London: St. Martin's Press, 1962.
Chelini, Jean, and Henry Branthomme. *Les Chemins de dieu*. Paris: Hachette, 1982.
Cholvy, Gérard. *Être chrétien en France au XIXe siècle, 1790–1914*. Paris: Éditions du Seuil, 1997.
Cholvy, Gérard, and Yves-Marie Hilaire. *Histoire religieuse de la France contemporaine, 1880–1930*. Toulouse: Bibliothèque Historique Privat, 1986.
Clark, Linda L. *Schooling the Daughters of Marianne*. Albany: State University of New York Press, 1984.
Clark, Martin. *Modern Italy, 1871–1982*. New York: Longman, 1984.
Coffey, Joan L. "Of Catechisms and Sermons: Church-State Relations in France, 1890–1905." *Church History* 66 (1997): 54–66.
———. "For God and France: The Military Law of 1889 and the Soldiers of Saint-Sulpice." *Catholic Historical Review* 88 (October 2002): 677–701.
Cohen, Paul M. *Piety and Politics*. New York: Garland, 1987.
———. "Heroes and Dilettantes: The Action Française, Le Sillon, and the Generation of 1905–14." *French Historical Studies* 15 (Fall 1988): 673–687.
Cohen, William B. "The Development of an Urban Society." In *The Transformation of Modern France*, edited by William B. Cohen, 47–65. New York: Houghton Mifflin, 1997.
Connerton, Paul. *How Societies Remember*. New York: Cambridge University Press, 1989.
Cronin, John F. *Social Principles and Economic Life*. Milwaukee: Bruce Publishing Company, 1959.
Cronin, John F., and Harry W. Flannery. *The Church and the Workingman*. New York: Hawthorn Books, 1965.
Dansette, Adrien. *Histoire religieuse de la France contemporaine*. 2 vols. Paris: Flammarion, 1951.
Dassonville, J. "La Famille ouvrière du Val-des-Bois." *Revue de l'Action Populaire* (10 January 1914): 14–22; (10 February 1914): 121–130; (20 March 1914): 210–217; (10 April 1914): 263–270.
Debouzy, Marianne. "Permanence du paternalisme?" *Le Mouvement Social* 144 (July–September 1988): 3–16.
Desan, Suzanne. "Redefining Revolutionary Liberty: The Rhetoric of Religious Revival during the French Revolution." *Journal of Modern History* 60 (March 1988): 1–27.
Dorr, Donal. *Option for the Poor*. Maryknoll, N.Y.: Orbis Books, 1983.

Dreyfus, François. *Les Evêques contre le pape.* Paris: Bernard Grasset, 1985.
Dubois, M. le Dr. (President of the General Council of the Seine). "De l'Assistance des vieillards simples par le placement familial." Rouen: Imprimerie Cagniard, 1898.
Dupront, Alphonse. *Du Sacré.* Paris: Éditions Gallimard, 1987.
Duroselle, Jean-Baptiste. *Les Débuts du catholicisme en France, 1822–1870.* Paris: Presses Universitaires de France, 1951.
———. *La France et les français, 1900–1914.* Paris: Éditions Richelieu, 1972.
Engels, Friedrich. "On the History of Early Christianity." *Basic Writings on Politics and Philosophy: Karl Marx and Friedrich Engels.* Garden City, N.Y.: Anchor Books, 1959.
Faquet, Emile. *L'Anticléricalisme.* Paris: Société Française d'Imprimerie et de Librairie, 1906.
Ferrata, Cardinal Dominique. *Mémoires.* Paris: Prix, 1922.
Fiero, Gloria. "The *Dits:* The Historical Context." In *Three Medieval Views of Women,* edited by Gloria Fiero, Wendy Pfeffer, and Mathé Allain, 28–83. New Haven: Yale University Press, 1989.
Fiero, Gloria, Wendy Pfeffer, and Mathé Allain, eds. *Three Medieval Views of Women.* New Haven: Yale University Press, 1989.
Fogarty, Michael P. *Christian Democracy in Western Europe, 1820–1953.* Notre Dame: University of Notre Dame Press, 1957.
Ford, Caroline. "Religion and the Politics of Cultural Change in Provincial France: The Resistance of 1902 in Lower Brittany." *Journal of Modern History* 62, no. 1 (March 1990): 1–33.
———. "Religion and Popular Culture in Modern Europe." *Journal of Modern History* 65 (March 1993): 152–175.
———. "Violence and the Sacred in Nineteenth-Century France." *French Historical Studies* 21 (Winter 1998): 101–112.
Frader, Laura L. "Doing Capitalism's Work: Women in Western European Industrial Economy." In *Becoming Visible,* edited by Renate Bridenthal, Susan Mosher Stuard, and Merry E. Wiesner, 295–325. New York: Houghton Mifflin, 1998.
Fuchs, Rachel G. *Poor and Pregnant in Paris.* New Brunswick: Rutgers University Press, 1992.
Furet, François. *Marx and the French Revolution.* Chicago: University of Chicago Press, 1988.
Gargan, Edward T., ed. *Leo XIII and the Modern World.* New York: Sheed and Ward, 1961.
Gibson, Ralph. *A Social History of French Catholicism, 1789–1914.* New York: Routledge, 1989.

Gildea, Robert. *Education in Provincial France, 1800–1914.* New York: Oxford University Press, 1983.

Gilson, Etienne. *The Church Speaks to the Modern World.* Garden City, N.Y.: Image Books, 1954.

Gordon, David M. "Industrialization and Republican Politics: The Bourgeois of Reims and Saint-Étienne under the Second Empire." In *French Cities in the Nineteenth Century,* edited by John M. Merriman, 117–138. New York: Holmes & Meier, 1981.

———. *Liberalism and Social Reform.* Westport, Conn.: Greenwood Press, 1996.

Gouthe-Soulard, Monseigneur. *Mon procès, mes avocats.* Paris: E. Deptu, 1891.

Green, Hannah. *Little Saint.* New York: Modern Library, 2001.

Gregoire, Léon [Goyau, Georges]. *Le Pape, les catholiques et la question sociale.* Paris: Perrin et Cie, 1893.

Guesde, Jules. "Essai de catéchisme socialiste" (1876).

———. "Lettre à Monsieur Leo XIII" (1878).

———. "Christianisme et socialisme, conference contradictoire avec Marc Sangnier" (1905).

———. "Le Catéchisme des travailleurs" (1906).

———. *Double réponse.* Paris: Publications de la Société Nouvelle de Librarie Editions, 1906.

———. *Jules Guesde: Textes Choisis, 1867–1882.* Paris: Éditions Sociales, 1970.

Guilbert, Madeleine. "L'Evolution des effectives du travail feminine en France Depuis 1866." *Revue Française du Travail* 2 (September 1947): 747–777.

———. *Les Functions des femmes dans l'industrie.* Paris: Mouton, 1966.

Guitton, Georges, S.J. *Léon Harmel, 1829–1915.* 2 vols. Paris: Action Populaire, 1927.

Halperin, S. William. "Leo XIII and the Roman Question." In *Leo XIII and the Modern World,* edited by Edward T. Gargan, 101–124. New York: Sheed and Ward, 1961.

Hanna, Martha. *The Mobilization of the Intellect.* Cambridge, Mass.: Harvard University Press, 1996.

Hareven, Tamara K. *Family Time and Industrial Time.* New York: Cambridge University Press, 1982.

Harmel, Léon. *Le Val des Bois (exposition de l'organisation).* Bibliothèque Carnegie, Reims, France. Ch. B. M1837.

———. *Organisation chrétienne de l'usine, par un industriel.* Paris, 1874. D. 89780. Bibliothèque Nationale.

———. *Manuel d'une corporation chrétienne.* Tours, 1876.

———. *Conférence du cercle catholique de Seéz,* October 1881. Bibliothèque Nationale. 6,8R Piece 2284.

---. *Exposé sommaire de l'oeuvre pronouncé à Lyon le 27 novembre 1887*. Paris, 1888. Bibliothèque Nationale. 8oR 4120.
---. *Catéchisme du patron*. Paris, 1889.
---. *Congrès des Patrons du Nord*. Nouveaux, 1894. Bibliothèque Nationale. 8oR 9630.
---. "Le Commerce et l'église." Speech delivered at the annual meeting of the Union Fraternelle. Paris: Rondelet et Cie, 1898. Bibliothèque Nationale. 8oH 717.
---. Speech given by Harmel to the Cercle Vaugirard of Paris. Reims: Imprimerie de l'archevêché, 1898. Bibliothèque Nationale. 80 7735.
---. *Lettres de Léon Harmel à ses enfants, voyage à Rome, février 1899*. Bibliothèque Nationale. 8oK 4650.
---. *Souvenir de Felix Harmel*. Blois, 1900.
---. *La Démocratie dans l'usine—le Conseil d'Usine du Val des Bois, 1907*. Reims: Imprimerie Cooperatives, 1907.
---. *Le Cardinal Langénieux et le Val des Bois* (1910). Bibliothèque Nationale. 8oR 25690.
Hause, Steven C., with Anne R. Kenney. *Women's Suffrage and Social Politics in the French Third Republic*. Princeton: Princeton University Press, 1984.
Hayward, J.E.S. "The Official Philosophy of the French Third Republic: Léon Bourgeois and Solidarism." *International Review of Social History* 6 (1961): 19–48.
Henry, Pierre. *Le Mouvement patronal catholique en France*. Paris, 1936.
Herlihy, David. *Women in Medieval Society*. Houston: University of St. Thomas, 1971.
Hilden, Patricia. *Working Women and Socialist Politics in France: 1880–1914*. Oxford: Clarendon Press, 1986.
Hilaire, Y.-M. "Les Missions intérieures face à la dechristianisation pendant la seconde moitie du XIX siècle dans la region du Nord." *Revue du Nord* 46 (1964): 51–68.
---. "Les Ouvriers de la region du Nord devant l'église catholique (XIXe–XX siècle)." *Le Mouvement Social* 57 (October–December 1966): 181–201.
---. "Les Ouvriers de la region du Nord devant l'église catholique (XIXe–XX siècles)." In *Christianisme et monde ouvrier*, edited by François Bédarida and Jean Maitron, 223–243. Paris: Les Éditions Ouvrières, 1975.
Hoog, Georges. *Histoire du catholicisme social en France, 1871–*. Paris: Nouvelle Édition, 1946.
Horne, Alistair. *The Fall of Paris*. New York: Penguin Books, 1966.
Horvath-Peterson, Sandra. *Victor Duruy and French Education*. Baton Rouge: Louisiana State University Press, 1984.

Houdoy, J. *La Filature de coton dans le Nord de la France.* Paris: Librairie Nouvelle de Droit et de Jurisprudence, 1903.
Hufton, Olwen. *The Prospect before Her.* New York: Vintage Books, 1995.
Hyams, Edward. *Pierre-Joseph Proudhon.* New York: Taplinger, 1979.
Hyman, Paula. "The Dreyfus Affair: The Visual and the Historical." *Journal of Modern History* 61, no. 1 (March 1989): 88–109.
Ionescu, Ghita, ed. *The Political Thought of Saint-Simon.* Oxford: Oxford University Press, 1976.
Irving, R. E. M. *Christian Democracy in France.* London: George Allen & Unwin, 1973.
Isambert, François-André. *Christianisme et classe ouvrière.* Tournoi: Casterman, 1961.
Jardin, André, and André-Jean Tudesq. *Restoration and Reaction, 1815–1848.* New York: Cambridge University Press, 1988.
Jarlot, Georges. *Le Régime corporatif et les catholiques sociaux.* Paris: Flammarion, 1938.
———. "Les Avant projets du *Rerum Novarum* et les 'Anciennes corporations.'" *Nouvelle Revue Theologique* (January 1959): 60–77.
Jaubert. *L'Organisation actuelle du Val des Bois.* Blois: Imprimeries Reunies du Centre, 1904.
Johnson, Humphrey. *The Papacy and the Kingdom of Italy.* London: Sheed and Ward, 1926.
John Paul II. *Laborem Exercens* (1981). In *The Papal Encyclicals,* edited by Claudia Carlen, I. H. M., 5:299–326. Raleigh: Pierian Press, 1981.
John XXIII. *Mater et Magistra* (1961). In *The Papal Encyclicals,* edited by Claudia Carlen, I. H. M., 5:59–90. Raleigh: Pierian Press, 1981.
Jonas, Raymond. *France and the Cult of the Sacred Heart.* Berkeley: University of California Press, 2000.
Judt, Tony. *Marxism and the French Left.* Oxford: Clarendon Press, 1986.
Kale, Steven D. "Architects of Tradition: Legitimism and the Reconstruction of French Society, 1852–1883." Ph. D. diss., University of Wisconsin–Madison, 1987. Published as *Legitimism and the Reconstruction of French Society, 1852–1883.* Baton Rouge: Louisiana State University Press, 1992.
Kaplan, Steven L. "Social Classification and Representation in the Corporate World of Eighteenth-Century France: Turgot's 'Carnival.'" In *Work in France: Representations, Meaning, Organization and Practices,* edited by Steven L. Kaplan, and Cynthia J. Koepp, 176–228. Ithaca: Cornell University Press, 1986.
Kselman, Thomas A. *Miracles and Prophecies in Nineteenth-Century France.* New Brunswick: Rutgers University Press, 1983.

———. *Death and the Afterlife in Modern France*. Princeton: Princeton University Press, 1993.
Kuisel, Richard F. "The French Search for Modernity." In *The Transformation of Modern France*, edited by William B. Cohen, 28–46. New York: Houghton Mifflin, 1997.
Kurtz, Lester K. *The Politics of Heresy*. Berkeley: University of California Press, 1986.
Lafargue, Paul. "Droit à paresse" (1883). In *Pamphlets socialistes*. Paris: V. Giard & E. Briere, 1900.
———. "Pie IX au paradis" (1890).
———. "La Religion du capital." In *Pamphlets socialistes*. Paris: V. Giard & E. Briere, 1900.
———. "La Religion et capital" (1907).
Landes, David S. "French Entrepreneurship and Industrial Growth in the Nineteenth Century." *Journal of Economic History* 9 (1949): 45–61.
———. *The Unbound Prometheus*. New York: Cambridge University Press, 1969.
Langer, William L. *The Franco-Russian Alliance, 1890–1894*. New York: Octagon Books, 1967.
Langlois, Claude. "Catholics and Seculars." In *Realms of Memory*, edited by Pierre Nora, 1:108–143. New York: Columbia University Press, 1996.
Larkin, Maurice. *Church and State after the Dreyfus Affair*. New York: Harper & Row, 1973.
———. "The Vatican, France and the Roman Question, 1898–1903." *Historical Journal* 27 (1984): 177–197.
———. *Religion, Politics and Preferment in France since 1890*. Cambridge University Press, 1995.
Latreille, A., and R. Rémond. *Histoire du catholicisme en France*. Vol. 3. Paris: Spes, 1962.
Laumonier, M. L'Abbé. *Guide du pèlerin à Rome*. Val des Bois, 1898.
Lefevre, Emile. *Le Val des Bois: Étude économique*. Paris: Charles Amat, 1911.
Lefranc, Georges. *Le Mouvement socialiste sous la III Republique*. Paris, 1963.
Leo XIII. *Quod Apostolici Muneris* (December 1878). In *The Papal Encyclicals*, edited by Claudia Carlen, I. H. M., 2:11–15. Raleigh: Pierian Press, 1981.
———. *Etsi Nos* (February 1882). In *The Papal Encyclicals*, edited by Claudia Carlen, I. H. M., 2:63–68. Raleigh: Pierian Press, 1981.
———. *Auspicato Concessum* (September 1882). In *The Papal Encyclicals*, edited by Claudia Carlen, I. H. M., 2:69–74. Raleigh: Pierian Press, 1981.
———. *Nobilissima Gallorum Gens* (February 1884). In *The Papal Encyclicals*, edited by Claudia Carlen, I. H. M., 2:85–89. Raleigh: Pierian Press, 1981.

———. *Humanum Genus* (April 1884). In *The Papal Encyclicals,* edited by Claudia Carlen, I.H.M., 2:91–101. Raleigh: Pierian Press, 1981.

———. *Immortale Dei* (November 1885). In *The Papal Encyclicals,* edited by Claudia Carlen, I.H.M., 2:107–119. Raleigh: Pierian Press, 1981.

———. *Sapientiae Christianae* (January 1890). In *The Papal Encyclicals,* edited by Claudia Carlen, I.H.M., 2:211–223. Raleigh: Pierian Press, 1981.

———. *Dall'Alto Dell'Apostolico Seggio* (October 1890). In *The Papal Encyclicals,* edited by Claudia Carlen, I.H.M., 2:225–232. Raleigh: Pierian Press, 1981.

———. *Rerum Novarum* (May 1891). In *The Papal Encyclicals,* edited by Claudia Carlen, I.H.M., 2:241–261. Raleigh: Pierian Press, 1981.

———. *Au Milieu des Sollicitudes* (February 1892). In *The Papal Encyclicals,* edited by Claudia Carlen, I.H.M., 2:277–283. Raleigh: Pierian Press, 1981.

———. *Inimica Vis* (December 1892). In *The Papal Encyclicals,* edited by Claudia Carlen, I.H.M., 2:297–299. Raleigh: Pierian Press, 1981.

———. *Custodi di Quella Fede* (December 1892). In *The Papal Encyclicals,* edited by Claudia Carlen, I.H.M., 2:301–305. Raleigh: Pierian Press, 1981.

———. *Longinqua* (January 1895). In *The Papal Encyclicals,* edited by Claudia Carlen, I.H.M., 2:363–370. Raleigh: Pierian Press, 1981.

———. *Spesse Volte* (August 1898). In *The Papal Encyclicals,* edited by Claudia Carlen, I.H.M., 2:439–443. Raleigh: Pierian Press, 1981.

———. *Depuis Le Jour* (September 1899). In *The Papal Encyclicals,* edited by Claudia Carlen, I.H.M., 2:455–464. Raleigh: Pierian Press, 1981.

———. *Paternae* (September 1899). In *The Papal Encyclicals,* edited by Claudia Carlen, I.H.M., 2:465–467. Raleigh: Pierian Press, 1981.

———. *Graves de Communi* (January 1901). In *The Papal Encyclicals,* edited by Claudia Carlen, I.H.M., 2:479–485. Raleigh: Pierian Press, 1981.

———. *In Amplissimo* (April 1902). In *The Papal Encyclicals,* edited by Claudia Carlen, I.H.M., 2:495–496. Raleigh: Pierian Press, 1981.

———. *Fin dal Principio* (December 1902). In *The Papal Encyclicals,* edited by Claudia Carlen, I.H.M., 2:511–515. Raleigh: Pierian Press, 1981.

Le Play, Frédéric. *La Réforme sociale en France.* 2 vols. Paris: H. Plon, 1864.

———. *L'Organisation du travail.* Paris: Alfred Mame et Fils, 1870.

———. *L'École de la paix sociale.* Tours: Alfred Mame et Fils, 1881.

———. *On Family, Work, and Social Change.* Edited, translated, and introduced by Catherine Bodard Silver. Chicago: University of Chicago Press, 1982.

Lerner, Gerda. *The Creation of Patriarchy.* New York: Oxford University Press, 1986.

———. *The Creation of Feminist Consciousness.* New York: Oxford University Press, 1993.

Levillain, Philippe. *Albert de Mun*. Paris: École Française de Rome, 1983.
Lipsey, Roger. *Have You Been to Delphi?* Albany: State University of New York Press, 2001.
Lowe, C. J., and F. Marzari. *Italian Foreign Policy, 1870–1940*. Boston: Routledge & Kegan Paul, 1975.
Magraw, Roger. *A History of the French Working Class*. Vol. 1, *The Age of Artisan Revolution, 1815–1871*. Cambridge, Mass.: Blackwell Publishers, 1992.
———. *A History of the French Working Class*. Vol. 2, *Workers and the Bourgeois Republic*. Cambridge, Mass.: Blackwell Publishers, 1992.
Malon, Benoit. "Socialisme et charité." *La Revue Socialiste* (January 1884).
———. "Le Catholicisme social." *La Revue Socialiste* (July 1885).
———. "Religion et socialisme." *La Revue Socialiste* (July 1900).
Marquigny, Eugene, S.J. *La Constitution des oeuvres de la famille ouvrières*. Lyon: P. Trat Ainé, 1875.
———. *La Réforme des ateliers*. Lyons: P. Trat Ainé, 1876.
Martin, Benjamin F. *Count Albert de Mun*. Chapel Hill: University of North Carolina Press, 1978.
Masse, Benjamin L., S.J., ed. *The Church and Social Progress*. Milwaukee: Bruce Publishing Company, 1966.
Mayeur, Jean-Marie. *La Séparation de l'église et l'état*. Paris: René Juillard, 1966.
———. "Le Catholicisme social en France à la fin du XIXe siècle." *Le Mouvement Social* 57 (October–December 1966): 211–216.
———. "Catholicisme intransigeant, catholicisme social, démocratie chrétienne." *Annales* (March–April 1972): 483–499.
———. "Tiers-ordre franciscain et catholicisme social en France à la fin du XIXe siècle." *Revue d'Histoire de l'église de France* 70, no. 1 (1984): 181–194.
———. *La Vie politique sous la troisième république, 1870–1940*. Paris: Éditions du Seuil, 1984.
———. *Catholicisme social et démocratie chrétienne: Principes, romans, experiences françaises*. Paris: Éditions du Cerf, 1986.
Mayeur, Jean-Marie, and Madeleine Rebérioux. *The Third Republic from Its Origins to the Great War, 1871–1914*. New York: Cambridge University Press, 1987.
McCullough, David. *The Path between the Seas*. New York: Simon and Schuster, 1977.
McDougall, Mary Lynn. "Protecting Infants: The French Campaign for Maternity Leaves, 1890s–1913." *French Historical Studies* 13 (Spring 1983): 79–105.
McLellan, David. *Marxism and Religion*. New York: Harper & Row, 1987.
McManners, John. *Church and State in France, 1870–1914*. New York: Harper & Row, 1972.

McMillan, James F. *Housewife or Harlot: The Place of Women in French Society, 1870–1940.* New York: St. Martin's Press, 1981.
Mellor, Alec. *Histoire de l'anticléricalisme français.* Tours: Mame, 1966.
Misner, Paul. *Social Catholicism in Europe.* New York: Crossroad, 1991.
Mitchell, Allen. *Victors and Vanquished: The German Influence on Army and Church in France after 1870.* Chapel Hill: University of North Carolina Press, 1984.
———. *The Divided Path.* Chapel Hill: University of North Carolina Press, 1991.
Moch, Leslie Page. *Paths to the City.* Beverly Hills, Calif.: Sage Publications, 1983.
Mock, Sanford J. "The Panama Canal—Part I—The French Attempt." *Manuscripts* 53, no. 3 (Summer 2001): 193–211.
Moody, Joseph. *Church and Society: Catholic Social and Political Thought and Movements, 1789–1950.* New York: Arts, 1953.
———. "The Dechristianization of the French Working Class." *Review of Politics* 20 (January 1958): 46–69.
Moon, Parker Thomas. *The Labor Problem and the Social Catholic Movement in France.* New York: Macmillan, 1921.
Moon, S. Joan. "Feminism and Socialism: The Utopian Synthesis of Flora Tristan." In *Socialist Women,* edited by Marilyn Boxer and Jean H. Quataert, 19–50. New York: Elsevier, 1978.
Moses, Claire Goldberg. *French Feminism in the 19th Century.* Albany: State University of New York Press, 1984.
Moss, Bernard H. *The Origins of the French Labor Movement.* Berkeley: University of California Press, 1976.
Mosse, George L. "The French Right and the Working Classes: Les Jaunes." *Journal of Contemporary History* 7 (July–October 1972): 185–207.
Mun, Albert de. *Ma vocation sociale.* Paris: P. Lethielleux, 1908.
Murtagh, James G. "Theory of the Family Wage." In *The Church and Social Progress,* edited by Benjamin L. Masse, S. J., 87–90. Milwaukee: Bruce Publishing Company, 1966.
Noiriel, Gérard. *Les Ouvriers dans la société française XIX–XX siècle.* Paris: Éditions du Seuil, 1986.
———. "'Du Patronage au paternalisme': La restructuration des formes de domination de la main d'oeuvre ouvrière dans l'industrie metallurgique Française." *Le Mouvement Social,* no. 144 (July–September 1988): 17–35.
———. "French and Foreigners." In *Realms of Memory,* edited by Pierre Nora, 1:146–178. New York: Columbia University Press, 1996.
Nolan, Mary Lee, and Sidney Nolan. *Christian Pilgrimage in Modern Western Europe.* Chapel Hill: University of North Carolina Press, 1989.
Nora, Pierre. "Conflicts and Divisions." In *Realms of Memory,* edited by Pierre Nora, 1:21–23. New York: Columbia University Press, 1996.

———. "General Introduction: Between Memory and History." In *Realms of Memory*, edited by Pierre Nora, 1:1–20. New York: Columbia University Press, 1996.

Nord, Philip. "Republicanism and Utopian Vision: French Freemasonry in the 1860s and 1870s." *Journal of Modern History* 63, no. 2 (June 1991): 213–229.

———. "The Welfare State in France, 1870–1914." *French Historical Studies* 18 (Spring 1994): 821–838.

Offen, Karen. "Feminism, Antifeminism, and National Family Politics in Early Third Republic France." In *Connecting Spheres*, edited by Marilyn J. Boxer and Jean H. Quataert, 177–186. New York: Oxford University Press, 1987.

Paul VI. *Populorum Progressio* (March 1967). In *The Papal Encyclicals*, edited by Claudia Carlen, I.H.M., 5:183–201. Raleigh: Pierian Press, 1981.

Périn, Charles. *Les Économistes, les socialistes et le christianisme*. Paris, 1849.

———. *La Richesse dans les sociétés chrétiennes*. Paris: Jacques Le Coffre, 1861.

———. *Le Socialisme chrétien*. Paris, 1879.

———. *La Patron, sa fonction, ses devoirs, ses résponsabilités*. Lille: Desclée de Brouwer, 1886.

———. *Premiers principes d'économie politique*. Paris: Librairie Victor Le Coffre, 1896.

Pernoud, Régine, and Marie-Véronique Clin. *Joan of Arc*. New York: St. Martin's Press, 1999.

Perrot, Michelle. *Les Ouvriers en grève*. Tome I. Paris: Mouton and École Pratique des Hautes Études, 1974.

Pierrard, Pierre. *L'Église et les ouvriers en France (1840–1940)*. Paris: Hachette, 1984.

Piou, Jacques. *Questions religieuses et socials*. Paris: Librairie Plon, 1910.

Pius X. *Vehementer Nos* (February 1906). In *The Papal Encyclicals*, edited by Claudia Carlen, 3:45–51. Raleigh: Pierian Press, 1981.

———. *Pieni L'Animo* (July 1906). In *The Papal Encyclicals*, edited by Claudia Carlen, 3:57–61. Raleigh: Pierian Press, 1981.

———. *Gravissimo Officii Munere* (August 1906). In *The Papal Encyclicals*, edited by Claudia Carlen, 3:63–65. Raleigh: Pierian Press, 1981.

———. *Une Fois Encore* (January 1907). In *The Papal Encyclicals*, edited by Claudia Carlen, 3:67–70. Raleigh: Pierian Press, 1981.

———. *Pascendi Dominici Gregis* (September 1907). In *The Papal Encyclicals*, edited by Claudia Carlen, 3:71–98. Raleigh: Pierian Press, 1981.

———. *Singulari Quadam* (September 1912). In *The Papal Encyclicals*, edited by Claudia Carlen, 3:135–138. Raleigh: Pieran Press, 1981.

Pius XI. *Quadragesimo Anno* (May 1931). In *The Papal Encyclicals*, edited by Claudia Carlen, 3:415–443. Raleigh: Pierian Press, 1981.

———. *Ad Catholici Sacerdotti* (December 1935). In *The Papal Encyclicals,* edited by Claudia Carlen, 3:497–516. Raleigh: Pierian Press, 1981.

———. *Divini Redemptoris* (March 1937). In *The Papal Encyclicals,* edited by Claudia Carlen, 3:537–554. Raleigh: Pierian Press, 1981.

Plessis, Alain. *The Rise and Fall of the Second Empire, 1852–1871.* New York: Cambridge University Press, 1987.

Popkin, Jeremy D. *A History of Modern France.* Englewood Cliffs, N.J.: Prentice Hall, 1994.

Poulat, Emile. "La Société religieuse en France et le changement." *Revue Française de Sociologie* 3 (1966): 291–305.

———. Introduction. In *Christianisme et monde ouvrier,* edited by François Bédarida and Jean Maitron, 13–64. Paris: Les Éditions Ouvrières, 1975.

Prestwich, Patricia E. "Food and Drink in France." In *The Transformation of Modern France,* edited by William B. Cohen, 160–181. New York: Houghton Mifflin, 1997.

Rearick, Charles. *Pleasures of the Belle Époque.* New Haven: Yale University Press, 1985.

Rebérioux, Madeleine. "Socialisme et religion: Un inédit de Jaurès." *Annales* 16 (November–December 1961): 1096–1120.

———. *La republique radicale? 1898–1914.* Paris: Éditions du Seuil, 1975.

Reddy, William M. *The Rise of Market Culture.* New York: Cambridge University Press, 1984.

Remond, René. *Les Deux congrès ecclesiastiques de Reims et Bourges, 1896–1900.* Paris: Sirey, 1974.

———. *L'Anticléricalisme en France de 1815 à nos jours.* Paris: Librairie Fayard, 1976.

Renouvin, Pierre. *Histoire des relations internationals.* 6 vols. Paris: Librairie Hachette, 1954.

Riga, Peter. *John XXIII and the City of Man.* Westminster, Md.: Newman Press, 1966.

Rollet, Henri. *L'Action sociale des catholiques en France, 1871–1914.* Paris: Desclée de Brouwer, 1958.

Sàcquin, Michèle. *Entre Bossuet et Maurras: L'Antiprotestantisme en France de 1814 à 1870.* Paris: École des Chartres, 1998.

Schmidt, Martin E. *Alexandre Ribot: Odyssey of a Liberal in the Third Republic.* The Hague: Martinus Nijhoff, 1974.

Sedgwick, Alexander. *The Ralliement in French Politics, 1890–1898.* Cambridge, Mass.: Harvard University Press, 1965.

Seeley, Paul. "O Sainte Mère: Liberalism and the Socialization of Catholic Men in Nineteenth-Century France." *Journal of Modern History* 70 (December 1998): 862–891.

Sellier, François. "France." In *Labor in the Twentieth Century*, edited by John T. Dunlap and Walter Galenson, 197–240. New York: Academic Press, 1978.
Sewell, William H., Jr. *Work and Revolution in France: The Language of Labor from the Old Regime to 1848*. London: Cambridge University Press, 1980.
Simon, Jules. *L'Ouvrière*. Paris: Hachette, 1861.
Smith, Bonnie G. *Ladies of the Leisure Class*. Princeton: Princeton University Press, 1981.
Soubiran-Paillet, Francine. *L'Invention du syndicat (1791–1884)*. Paris: Le Réseau Européen Droit et Société à La Maison des Sciences de L'Homme, 1999.
Spencer, Philip. *Politics of Belief in Nineteenth-Century France*. London: Faber and Faber, 1953.
Standaert, Eugene. *Chez le bon père*. Bruges: Verbeke-Loys & Fils, 1902.
Stearns, Peter. *Revolutionary Syndicalism and French Labor*. New Brunswick: Rutgers University Press, 1971.
———. "Early Strike Activity in France." In *The Working Class in Modern Europe*, edited by Mary Lynn McDougall, 22–35. Lexington, Mass.: D.C. Heath, 1975.
———. *Paths to Authority*. Chicago: University of Illinois Press, 1978.
Stewart, Mary Lynn. *Women, Work and the French State*. Montreal: McGill-Queen's University Press, 1989.
Stone, Judith F. *The Search for Social Peace*. Albany: State University of New York Press, 1985.
Strikwerda, Carl. "The Divided Class: Catholics vs. Socialists in Belgium, 1880–1914." *Comparative Studies in Society and History* 30 (April 1988): 333–359.
———. "Catholic Working Class Movements in Europe." *International Labor and Working Class History* 34 ((Fall 1988): 1–10.
———. "France and the Belgian Immigration of the Nineteenth Century." In *The Politics of Immigrant Workers: Essays on Labor Activism and the World Economy since 1830*, edited by Camille Guerin-Gonzales and Carl Strikwerda, 101–131. New York: Holmes and Meier, 1991.
———. *A House Divided: Catholics, Socialists, and Flemish Nationalists in Nineteenth-Century Belgium*. Lanham, Md.: Rowman & Littlefield, 1997.
Strumingher, Laura S. *Women and the Making of the Working Class: Lyon, 1830–1870*. St. Alban's, Vt.: Eden Press Women's Publications, 1979.
Sweets, John F. "Hold That Pendulum! Redefining Fascism, Collaborationism, and Resistance in France." *French Historical Studies* 15 (Fall 1988): 731–758.
Talmy, Robert. *L'Association catholique des patrons du Nord, 1884–1895*. Lille: Facultés Catholique, 1962.

———. *Aux Sources de catholicisme social.* Tournai: Desclée & Co., 1963.
———. *Le Syndicalisme chrétien en France (1871–1930).* Paris: Éditions Bloud & Gay, 1965.
Tannenbaum, Edward R., and Emiliana P. Noether. *Modern Italy.* New York: New York University Press, 1974.
Tilly, Louise A., and Joan W. Scott. *Women, Work, and Family.* New York: Holt, Rinehart and Winston, 1978.
Tournier, Jules. *Le Cardinal Lavigerie (1863–1892).* Paris: Perrin et Cie, Libraires-editeurs, 1913.
Trimouille, Pierre. *Léon Harmel et l'usine chrétienne du Val des Bois.* Lyon: Centre d'Histoire du Catholicisme de Lyon, 1974.
———. "Léon Harmel et les patrons du Nord: La crise de 1893–1894." *Revue du Nord* 73 (April–September 1991): 271–282.
Troeltsch, Ernst. *The Social Teaching of the Christian Churches.* Vol. 1. New York: Harper & Row, 1960.
Turmann, Max. *Le Développement du catholicisme social depuis l'encyclique "Rerum Novarum."* Paris: Libraires Félix Alcan et Guillamin Réunis, 1909.
Turner, Victor, and Edith Turner. *Image and Pilgrimage in Christian Culture.* New York: Columbia University Press, 1978.
Vaussard, Maurice. *Histoire de la démocratie chrétienne.* Paris: Éditions du Seuil, 1956.
Vidler, Alec R. *A Century of Social Catholicism, 1820–1920.* London: SPCK, 1964.
Vincent, K. Steven. *Pierre-Joseph Proudhon and the Rise of French Republican Socialism.* New York: Oxford University Press, 1984.
Wallace, Lillian Parker. *Leo XIII and the Rise of Socialism.* Durham: Duke University Press, 1966.
Ward, James E. "Leo XIII and Bismarck: The Kaiser's Vatican Visit of 1888." *Review of Politics* 24 (July 1962): 392–414.
Weber, Eugen. *Peasants into Frenchmen.* Stanford: Stanford University Press, 1976.
———. *France Fin de Siècle.* Cambridge, Mass.: Harvard University Press, 1986.
Weiss, John H. "Origins of the French Welfare State: Poor Relief in the Third Republic, 1871–1914." *French Historical Studies* 13 (Spring 1983): 47–78.
Willard, Claude. "Les Attaques contre Notre-Dame dans l'usine." In *Christianisme et monde ouvrier,* edited by François Bédarida and Jean Maitron, 245–250. Paris: Éditions Ouvrières, 1975.
Williams, Stuart, ed. *Socialism in France.* New York: St. Martin's Press, 1983.
Wilson, Stephen. "Catholic Populism in France at the Time of the Dreyfus Affair, the Union Nationale." *Journal of Contemporary History* 10 (October 1975): 667–705.

———. *Ideology and Experience.* East Brunswick, N.J.: Associated University Presses, 1982.
Wright, Gordon. *France in Modern Times.* New York: W.W. Norton, 1995.
Zeldin, Theodore. *France, 1848–1945.* Vol. 1. Oxford: Oxford University Press, 1973.
Zola, Émile. *The Debacle.* New York: Penguin Group, 1972.

INDEX

Page references in italics refer to illustrations which appear on unnumbered pages following page 100 of the text.

accident insurance, 82, 123, 211, 235
Action Française, 122
Aeterni Patris (Leo XIII), 135
agricultural industry, 53–54
Aix Affair, 195–204, 231, 239, 244
Albani, Stanislao Medolago, 137
alcohol abuse, 65–67, 87
Alexander III, tsar of Russia, 175
Americanism, 195, 207, 224–29
André, Hyppolite, 131
Annum Sacrum (Leo XIII), 19
anticlericalism, 3, 65, 68, 87, 130, 146, 174–75, 198, 202
anti-Protestantism, 70
anti-Semitism, 3, 29, 116, 195, 202, 213–20, 231, 238–39
apprenticeships, 41, 88–89, 94–95, 235

arbitration, 236
Archiconfrérie de Notre Dame de l'Usine, l', 43
Aristotle, 140
artisanal associations. *See* guilds
Association catholique, L', 117, 121, 125–26
Association Catholique de la Jeunesse Française (ACJF), 126, 181, 183
Association Catholique des Patrons du Nord, L'. *See* Patrons du Nord
associations, religious, 74–77, 93, 156, 208
Au Milieu des Sollicitudes (Leo XIII). *See* Ralliement directive

Aumôniers d'Usines, 5, 220, 222, 228, 231. *See also* factory chaplains
Auspicato Concessum (Leo XIII), 219
Austria, 169, 189–90
automobile industry, 51, 53

Belgium, 14–15, 51, 133, 180, 220
Benedict XV, pope, 230
benefits, worker: accident insurance and, 82, 123, 211, 235; *boni corporatif* and, 81, 83–84, 247; health insurance and, 82, 235; housing and, 41, 90–91, 112; mutual aid societies and, 14, 41, 81–82, 90–91, 109, 142, 235, 242; profit-sharing programs and, 81, 83–84, 90–91, 121, 247; retirement/pension plans and, 81–82, 84–85, 90–91, 109, 123, 211–12, 235; savings banks and, 14, 73, 81, 90–91, 242; unemployment compensation/insurance and, 109, 211
Bergson, Henri, 215
Billot (French ambassador to Italy), 184, 187–88
bishops, appointment of, 203
Bismarck, Otto von, 170, 174–75, 287n. 143
Black, Anthony, 37
Blanc, Louis, 102, 106–7, 109
Bois de la Coudrette, Le, 234
boni corporatif, 81, 83–84, 247
Boniface VIII, pope, 135, 154
Bosco, Dom, 161, 177
Boulanger, Georges, 216
Boulanger Affair, 3, 148, 192
Boulard, Fernand, 67
Bourgeois, Léon, 233, 241

Brandts, Franz, 131
Buchez, Philippe, 16, 102, 106–7, 109, 118, 128, 137–38

cabarets, 65–67, 87, 208
Carnegie, Andrew, 27, 229
Catéchisme du patron (Harmel), 5, 114
Catholic Church: anticlericalism and, 3, 65, 68, 87, 130, 146, 174–75, 198, 202; bishops, appointment of, in, 203; church-state separation and, 4, 68, 194, 196–98, 200, 203, 225–26, 230, 244; clergy/seminarians of, 4–5, 30–31, 48, 67–69, 76–77, 194, 220–24, 228, 231; de-/re-Christianization and, 4, 14, 18, 28, 32–36, 42–43, 48, 65–71, 73–77, 118–20; Dreyfus Affair and, 216; feminization of religion and, 67, 152, 222; religious orders and, 4, 33, 70; role of, 29–30. *See also* encyclicals; *individual popes (e.g., Boniface VIII)*
Catholic science, 31, 38
Cercles Chrétiens d'Études Sociales, Les, 5, 43, 207–9, 231
Chambord, Henri Dieudonné d'Artois, Comte de, 18, 124
Chapelier Law (1791), 25, 93
charity, 36, 46, 77, 113, 140–41, 159, 166
Charles VII, king of France, 18
Charles X, king of France, 18
child labor, 41, 61–63, 85, 123, 130
Cholvy, Gérard, 6
Choncray, Eugène, 181
Christian democratic movement, 3–4, 9, 118, 144, 191, 202,

205–10, 244–45; anti-Protestantism and, 70; anti-Semitism and, 195, 213, 245; congresses of, 5, 195, 209–13, 216, 220, 228, 231; encyclical on, 227–29; Freemasonry and, 195; Modernism/Americanism and, 195, 226; as pressure group, 194, 208
Christianization, de-/re-. *See* de-/re-Christianization
Christine de Pizan, 32
church-state separation, 4, 68, 194, 196–98, 200, 203, 225–26, 230, 244. *See also* Ralliement directive
civic education, 108
class stratifications: *boni corporatif* and, 84; clergy and, 69, 116; corporatism and, 109–10; industrial revolution and, 15, 62; as natural hierarchies, 38, 92–93; private property and, 140–41; reconciliation of, 105–6, 115–16, 166–67; *Rerum Novarum* and, 138–39; revolutionary disruptions and, 127, 150; workshop/factory size and, 54
clergy and seminarians: class stratifications and, 69, 116; education of, 5, 30–31, 48, 194, 220–24, 228, 231; as factory chaplains, 76–77, 120, 194, 220–24, 243; military service of, 4, 68, 194, 222; religious vocations and, 67–68
Clovis, king of the Franks, 17
Cobden-Chevalier Treaty, 57, 169
Cocarde, La, 214
collective bargaining, 93, 212, 236
Collinet, Léon, 137
Comte, Auguste, 110

Concordat, French (1801), 4, 42, 69–70, 173, 197–98, 203
Confédération Français du Travail Chrétien, 245
Confédération Générale du Travail, 245
Conseil d'Atelier, 94
Conseil des Études, 117–21, 125–29, 136
Conseil des Prud'hommes, 61, 124, 236–37
Conseil d'Usine, 43, 80, 93–95, 101, 112, 136, 142, 212, 222, 236–37, 243
consumer cooperatives, 73, 81, 83–84, 95, 106–7, 110, 217
cooperatives, 90–91, 212; *boni corporatif* and, 81, 83–84, 247; consumer, 73, 81, 83–84, 95, 106–7, 110, 217; producer, 106–9, 217
corporatism, 37, 102–14, 229, 246–47
Council of Trent, 149
Creusot Firm, 269n.190
Cri du peuple, 161
criminal activities, 67, 89
Crispi, Francesco, 168–70
Croix, La, 163, 164, 168, 179, 183–84, 210

Dabry, Pierre, 210
Dansette, Adrian, 195
Déchelette, Eugène, 131
Declaration des droits de l'homme (Bourgeois), 233, 241
Decurtins, Kaspar, 137
de Gaulle, Charles, 245
Dehon, Léon, 210, 220–21
de Mun, Albert: Aix Affair and, 199; Oeuvre des Cercles and, 102,

de Mun, Albert (*cont.*)
114–17, 122–26, 207–8; as organizer of worker pilgrimages, 152, 157, 161–63, 182, 205; Pantheon incident and, 187; Patrons du Nord and, 128, 131; personal pilgrimages of, 117, 150; press coverage of, 186; Ralliement directive and, 202; socialism and, 237–38; state intervention in social welfare and, 138; youth organizations and, 183

Denis, Saint, 18, 145

Depuis Le Jour (Leo XIII), 223

de-/re-Christianization, 4, 14, 18, 28, 32–36, 42–43, 48, 65–71, 73–77, 118–20

de Rouvroy, Claude-Henri, 102

Desan, Suzanne, 69

Dreuze, Michel, 181

Dreyfus Affair, 3, 148, 192, 202–3, 215–16, 239, 244

Drumont, Edouard, 213–14, 216, 220

Durkheim, Émile, 24, 93, 215

d'Ursel, Jean, 137

Duruy, Victor, 88–89

Dutilleul, Alfred, 131

Easter duty, observance of, 4, 65, 69–70, 75

education, 4; civic, 108; of clergy/seminarians, 5, 30–31, 48, 220–24, 228, 231; elementary, 20, 41, 81, 85, 235; at Val-des-Bois, 85–88. *See also* vocational training

egoism, 27, 39

encyclicals: *Aeterni Patris* (Leo XIII), 135; *In Amplissimo* (Leo XIII), 227; *Annum Sacrum* (Leo XIII), 19; *Auspicato Concessum* (Leo XIII), 219; *Depuis Le Jour* (Leo XIII), 223; *Etsi Nos* (Leo XIII), 172–73; *Exeunte Iam Anno* (Leo XIII), 134; *Graves de Communi Re* (Leo XIII), 227–29; *Humanum Genus* (Leo XIII), 141, 217, 219; *Immortale Dei* (Leo XIII), 134–35; *Laborem Exercens* (John Paul II), 248–49; *Libertas Praestantissimum* (Leo XIII), 134; *Longinqua* (Leo XIII), 225; *Mater et Magistra* (John XXIII), 246–47; *Pacem in Terris* (John XXIII), 240; *Populorum Progressio* (Paul VI), 247–48; *Providentissimus Deus* (Leo XIII), 133; *Quadragesimo Anno* (Pius XI), 246; *Quod Apostolici Muneris* (Leo XIII), 134; *Rerum Novarum* (Leo XIII), 5, 9, 103, 116, 118, 120, 126, 130, 134–44, 137–38, 140–44, 147, 176, 178, 182, 191–92, 194, 202, 206–8, 211, 213, 218, 223–24, 244–46, 261n.196; *Sapientiae Christianae* (Leo XIII), 135; *Testem Benevolentiae* (Leo XIII), 226, 229; *Unam Sanctum* (Leo XIII), 135

Enlightenment, 104, 115

entertainments, 14, 65–67, 87, 90, 208, 234

Estafette, L', 167, 184–85

Etsi Nos (Leo XIII), 172–73

Exeunte Iam Anno (Leo XIII), 134

factory chaplains, 75–77, 120, 194, 220–24, 243

factory councils, 5, 43, 81

factory inspections, 130
Fallières, Armand, 182, 195–96, 198–99
Fallières Circulaire, 188, 190, 192, 195–204, 231, 244
families, sanctification of, 22–37, 90, 106, 111–12, 118, 138
family allowances, 235
family wage, 5, 78–79, 81, 91, 112, 121, 141, 208, 212, 235, 246
fascism, 37, 120, 122, 246
Féron-Vrau, Camille, 131, 213
Ferrata, Cardinal Domenico, 195–96
Ferry, Jules, 62, 85
Figaro, Le, 168, 185
Fourier, Charles, 16, 102, 105–6, 137–38
Fournier, Félix, 131
France: and bishops, appointment of, 203; church-state separation in, 4, 68, 194, 196–98, 200, 203, 226, 230, 244; education laws in, 85, 87; German influences on, 3–4; immigration laws in, 97; industrial revolution and, 50–53, 62, 64, 71, 132; labor laws in, 63, 80, 83, 85–86, 93, 123–24, 129–31, 142, 212, 217; relations with Italy, 168–76, 180–81, 187–89, 203–4; social Catholicism in, 15–16, 133; treaties of, 57. *See also* Ralliement directive
France du travail à Rome, La, 152
France libre, La, 210
Francis Joseph, emperor of Austria, 189
Franco-Prussian War, 1–3, 5, 18, 85, 146, 150, 170, 214
Freemasons, 46, 195–96, 216–20, 231

French Concordat. *See* Concordat, French (1801)
French Revolution. *See* Revolution of 1789
Fribourg Union, 136–38, 143

Gambetta, Léon, 214
Garnier, Théodore, 210
Gaulois, La, 214
Germany, 3–4, 15, 27, 51, 82, 169, 174–75, 189–90. *See also* Franco-Prussian War
Germinal (Zola), 50, 90, 148
Gibbons, Cardinal James, 226–27
Gibson, Ralph, 67–68
Gordon, David, 91
Gouthe-Soulard, Xavier, archbishop of Aix, 195, 197, 199
Graves de Communi Re (Leo XIII), 227–29
Great Britain, 26–27, 50–51, 53, 56–57
Grégoire, Maurice, 181
Guarantees, Law of (1871), 171
Guesde, Jules, 216, 239
guilds, 24, 30, 37, 92–93, 104, 110–11, 118, 142
Guitton, Georges, 6

Halperin, S. William, 287n.131
Harmel, Albert (cousin), 98–99
Harmel, Alexandrine Tranchart de Rethel (mother), 13–14, 19, 21–22, 34, 156
Harmel, Ernest (brother), 22, 98–99
Harmel, Felix (son), 97, 177
Harmel, Gabrielle (wife), 5, 19, 23
Harmel, Gabriel (son), 168
Harmel, Jacques (grandfather), 12–13

Harmel, Jacques-Joseph (father), 2, 13–15, 17, 19, 81, 156, 242
Harmel, Jules (brother), 19, 98–99
Harmel, Léon: anti-Semitism of, 38, 46, 216–19; canonization of, 21, 234; death of, 5–6, 19, 249–50; education of, 19–20, 86; evaluations of, 6; family roots of, 12–22, 33; health of, 177; inheritance of Val-des-Bois and, 2, 12, 19; Leo XIII, relationship with, 5, 12, 162, 166, 176–79, 205, 207; marriage of, 23; personal pilgrimages of, 17, 117, 150, 156; photographs of, *Figs. 1–3*; political orientation/activities of, 17, 25, 124, 194, 209–10; publications of, 5, 114, 136, 139, 152, 221; religious faith of, 21–22, 45–47; ultramontanism of, 16–17, 207, 229
health insurance, 82, 235
Helleputte, Georges, 137
Hilaire, Yves-Marie, 69, 70
Hilden, Patricia, 61
hours of work, 30, 40, 42, 63–65, 80–81, 123–24, 211, 217, 235
housing, 41, 90–91, 112
Humanum Genus (Leo XIII), 141, 217, 219
Humbert, king of Italy, 180–82, 189

immigrants, 74–75; Belgian, 59, 68, 97–98; Italian, 97, 214; Jewish, 215
Immortale Dei (Leo XIII), 134–35
In Amplissimo (Leo XIII), 227
individualism, 27, 37, 103–4, 229
indulgences, 154, 176
industrial revolution, 2, 15, 50–53, 62, 64, 71, 132, 150

infallibility, doctrine of, 171, 225
insurance, workers', 82, 109, 123, 211, 235
Integrists, 225, 230
Intransigeant, L', 167
Italy: industrial revolution and, 51; reaction to pilgrimages in, 164–65, 168, 177, 180, 182; relations with France, 168–76, 180–81, 187–89, 203–4; Roman Question and, 170–74, 182–83, 189, 191–92, 204, 243; social Catholicism and, 15

Jaurès, Jean, 143
Jesuits, 75, 128, 176, 224–25
Jews. *See* anti-Semitism
Joan of Arc, 17–18
John XXIII, pope, 240, 246–47
John Paul II, pope, 240, 247–49
Jonas, Raymond, 18
Jubilee Years, 154
Justice sociale, La, 210

Karl zu Löwenstein, Prince, 137, 190
Ketteler, Wilhelm Emmanuel von, 4, 115
Kuefstein, Franz, 137
Kuisel, Richard F., 51
Kulturkampf, 174

Laborem Exercens (John Paul II), 248–49
labor shortages, 74–75
Lafargue, Paul, 143, 237
Lamennais, Félicité de, 15–16, 31
Lamy, Etienne, 238
Landes, David, 61, 98
Langénieux, Cardinal Benoit-Marie: Aix Affair and, 199; as organizer

of worker pilgrimages, 152, 157, 161–63, 165, 177, 205; Pantheon incident and, 182, 188; press coverage of, 186
Langlois, Claude, 28
Lanterne, La, 167, 186
Lateran Accord (1929), 171
La Tour du Pin, René de: Conseil des Études and, 118–19; decentralization of government and, 246; Fribourg Union and, 136–37; Oeuvre des Cercles and, 102, 114–17, 120–22, 125–26, 207–8; personal pilgrimages of, 117, 150; Ralliement directive and, 202; wages and, 141
Law of Guarantees (1871), 171
Lazarists, 75
Le Bon, Gustave, 148
Lefèbvre de Béhaine, Comte, 161, 163, 177, 181, 188–89
Legitimism, 16–19
Lemire, Jules, 210
Leopold, king of Belgium, 133
Leo XIII, pope, 132–36, 226–28; Aix Affair and, 197, 199–200, 203; anti-Semitism and, 220; audiences with worker pilgrims, 161–62, 166, 177–78, 182, 205; Cercles Chrétiens and, 209; Christian democratic movement and, 191, 194, 205, 209, 226, 227–28; church-state separation and, 226; encyclicals of, 19, 133–35, 137, 141, 172–73, 217, 219, 223, 225–28; Freemasons and, 217–18, 220; on government, 134–35; Harmel, relationship with, 5, 12, 162, 166, 176–79, 205, 207; health of, 165; Jubilee Years and, 154; on liberalism, 137; Ralliement directive and, 116, 135, 201–2, 206, 228, 231; republican government and, 17, 116, 124, 201–2, 204; Roman Question and, 172–76, 182–83, 191–92; on socialism, 206; Third Order of St. Francis and, 219; Union Fraternelle and, 219; on Val-des-Bois, 136. *See also Rerum Novarum* (Leo XIII)
Le Play, Frédéric, 102, 110–12, 114, 118
Lerner, Gerda, 32–33
Levillain, Philippe, 112
liberalism, 26–28, 36, 46, 103–4, 113, 115, 130, 132, 134, 207
Libertas Praestantissimum (Leo XIII), 134
life expectancies, 63–64, 85
Longinqua (Leo XIII), 225
Louis VIII, king of France, 17
Louis XVI, king of France, 18
Lourdes, France, 156–57
Luca (Signor), 181, 184
Luger, Karl, 216
Luther, Martin, 33

Magraw, Roger, 61
Maignen, Maurice, 115, 117–20, 141, 207
Mame, Alfred, 131
Manuel d'une corporation chrétienne (Harmel), 5, 136, 139, 221
Marcellot, M., 131
Marian devotion, 4, 32, 43, 149–50, 152–53, 191
Marquigny, Eugene, 128
Marx, Karl, 53, 118, 237

Mater et Magistra (John XXIII), 246–47
maternity leaves, 83, 235
Maurras, Charles, 122
May Day activities, 159–60, 209
Mayeur, Jean-Marie, 143
McKinley tariff, 57, 97
McManners, John, 92
Méline Tariff, 57
Mermillod, Msgr. Gaspar, 137
Merry del Val, Monsignor, 203
Military Law (1889), 68, 222
military service, 4, 68, 194, 222
missionaries, 42, 70, 75–76, 120
Moch, Leslie, 71
Modernism, 195, 207, 224–29
monarchists, 16, 116, 124, 130, 202
Monde, Le, 168
Moody, Joseph, 69, 70
motherhood, 32–35, 41
Mouvement Républicain Populaire, 245
mutual aid societies, 14, 41, 81–82, 90–91, 109, 142, 235, 242

Napoléon I, 69–70, 150, 170–71
Napoléon III, 1, 16, 146
nationalism, 3, 203
Naudet, Paul, 210
New Imperialism, 38, 55–56
Neyrand, Charles, 131
nihilism, 134
Noiriel, Gérard, 2
Notre Dame de l'Usine, 43, 109, 208

Oeuvre des Cercles Catholiques d'Ouvriers, L', 5, 43, 102–3, 109, 114–27, 207–8
Offenbach, Jacques, 215
Organic Articles (1801), 42, 197–98, 203

Osservatore romano, L', 188
Ozanam, Antoine-Frédéric, 16

Pacem in Terris (John XXIII), 240
Panama Canal Affair, 3, 148, 192, 213–214
Paris Commune, 3, 109, 146
Parti du Rassemblement du Peuple Français, 245
Pasteur, Louis, 31, 44
paternalism, 37–41, 43–44, 91–92, 101, 114, 129, 131, 139, 208, 242–43
Patrie, La, 184
Patrons du Nord, 5, 50, 102, 109, 122, 127–32, 212–13
Paul VI, pope, 247–48
pauperism, 15, 26–27, 46, 57
Pecci, Gioacchino Vincenzo Raffaele Luigi. *See* Leo XIII, pope
Pelloux, General, 184
pension plans. *See* retirement and pension plans
Périn, Charles, 102, 113–14, 118, 125
Perrot, Michelle, 92, 97, 148, 242
Petite république, La, 186
Peuple français, Le, 210
Pierrard, Pierre, 68–69
pilgrimages, 4, 5, 67, 145–92, 243–44; of 1885, 152, 157, 160–61, 166, 182, 191; of 1887, 138, 161–64, 174, 182, 189, 191, 243; of 1889, 140–41, 160, 164–68, 174, 182, 189, 191, 228–29, 243; of 1891, 144, 174, 176–91, 205, 243; of 1897, 205–6, 219; of 1905, 152; of 1912, 207; costs of, 157, 165; Fallières Circulaire and, 188, 190, 194, 195–204; goals of, 159–60, 177, 191; housing

arrangements for, 159, 164–65, 177; Italian reaction to, 164–65, 168, 177, 180, 182; as journeys to sacred places, 17, 148–50, 153–54; Pantheon incident and, 9, 179–83, 191, 231, 239, 244; participants on, 152–53, 156–57, 160–61, 177–78, 205; press coverage of, 160–61, 163–64, 167–68, 179, 183–90, 206, 243; *Rerum Novarum* and, 137, 144, 147, 176, 178, 182, 191–92, 244; resumption of, 204–7
Pius VII, pope, 69–70, 197
Pius IX, pope: appointments of, 133; audiences of, 17; Italian monarchy and, 289n.189; Marian devotion and, 149; *Quanta Cura* and, 104, 132; Roman Question and, 171–72; *Syllabus of Errors* and, 104, 116, 132, 171
Pius X, pope, 203, 207, 228, 229–30
Pius XI, pope, 245–46
political parties: Catholic, 198, 200, 208; socialist, 91
Popkin, Jeremy, 51
Popolo romano, 188
Populorum Progressio (Paul VI), 247–48
press coverage, 9; of Aix Affair, 196, 198, 200; anticlericalism of, 130; anti-Protestantism of, 70; of Christian democratic movement, 210; of Panama Canal Affair, 214; of pilgrimages, 160–61, 163–64, 167–68, 179, 183–90, 206, 243
Prestwich, Patricia, 66
private property, 111, 115–16, 121, 140–41

producer cooperatives, 106–9, 217
profit-sharing programs, 81, 83–84, 90–91, 121, 247
proselytism, 42–43, 69–70, 75–76, 120
Protestants, 42, 69–70, 149
Proudhon, Pierre-Joseph, 102, 106–9, 137–38, 146
Proust, Marcel, 215
Providentissimus Deus (Leo XIII), 133

Quadragesimo Anno (Pius XI), 246
Quanta Cura, 104, 132
Quirinal Palace, 172, 174–75
Quod Apostolici Muneris (Leo XIII), 134, 137, 141

racial inequalities, 38
Radical, Le, 185
radicalism, 192
railroad travel, 157–59, 165
Ralliement directive, 116, 135, 201–2, 206, 228, 231
Rampolla del Tindaro, Cardinal Mariano, 175, 176, 199, 230
re-Christianization. *See* de-/re-Christianization
recreational facilities, 81, 90
Reinsurance Treaty, 175
relief funds. *See* mutual aid societies
religious orders, 4, 33, 70
religious practices/observance, 4, 14, 43, 65, 68–70, 75
religious vocations, 67–68
Rerum Novarum (Leo XIII), 9, 118, 136–44, 202, 223–24, 245–46, 261n.196; anti-Semitism and, 218; Christian democratic movement and, 194, 206; clergy and, 194; Oeuvre des Cerles and,

Rerum Novarum (cont.)
116; private property and, 140–41; socialism/communism/nihilism condemned by, 134, 137–38; study of, 5, 194, 207–8; Thomism and, 135; trade unions and, 120, 130, 142–43; Val-des-Bois and, 103; wages and, 141, 211, 213; worker pilgrimages and, 137, 144, 147, 176, 178, 182, 191–92, 244; young people and, 126
retirement and pension plans, 81–82, 84–85, 90–91, 109, 123, 211–12, 235
Revolution of 1789, 3, 24–25, 30, 69, 104, 115, 146, 150
Revolution of 1830, 127, 146, 150
Revolution of 1848, 13, 16, 25, 109, 127, 146, 150
Revolution of 1871, 109, 127, 145–46, 150
Ribot, Alexandre, 175–76, 187–88, 197–98, 200, 203
Richard de la Vergne, Cardinal François-Marie-Benjamin, 177
Riforma, La, 168
Roman Question, 170–74, 182–83, 189, 191–92, 204, 243
Rome, as pilgrimage site, 17, 153–54
Roosevelt, Theodore, 27
Rothschild family, 213, 215
Rudinì, Antonio di, 170, 176, 188–89, 204
Russia, 51, 53, 175–76, 180

Sacred Heart, devotion to, 4, 18–19
Saint-Simon, Comte de, 102, 105–6, 110, 137–38
Saint-Sulpice Seminary, 221–22
Sangnier, Marc, 222, 230

Sapientiae Christianae (Leo XIII), 135
Saturdays, as work holidays, 235
savings banks, 14, 73, 81, 90–91, 242
Schindler, Franz, 137
Secolo, Il, 179
Sée, Camille, 85
Sée Law (1880), 87
Seeley, Paul, 153
Semaines religieuses, Les, 164
Semaines Sociales, 5, 31, 220–24, 228, 231
seminarians. *See* clergy and seminarians
sexual harassment, 35, 94
Sillon, Le, 118, 228, 230
Simon, Jules, 26
Six, Paul, 210
social Catholicism, 3–4, 15–16, 102, 115, 122, 133, 167, 227
Social Darwinism, 38
socialism, 93, 108, 127, 206–7; anti-Semitism and, 216; encyclicals against, 132, 134, 137–38; pre-Marxist, 15; religious, 103–5, 108–9; revolutionary, 167, 177, 237–40; Revolution of 1848 and, 16
Société de Secours Mutuels, 81–82
Society of St. Joseph, 15, 76
Society of St. Vincent de Paul, 16
solidarism, 103, 240–41
Soubiran-Paillet, Francine, 93
Spuller, Eugene, 238
Stearns, Peter, 90
Stone, Judith, 80
strikes, labor, 42, 60, 80, 97, 128, 139, 146, 148, 159
Strikwerda, Carl, 236
Summa Theologica, 47, 136, 140, 223
Sundays, as rest days, 30, 40, 65, 80, 123, 211, 235

Syllabus of Errors, 104, 116, 132, 171
syndicalism and syndicalists, 108–9, 121, 141–42
syndicats: mixte, 45, 92, 107, 113, 119–20, 123, 126–29, 137, 142–43, 190, 211–12; *professionnel,* 92–93, 99, 124, 211; *séparés,* 45, 120, 122, 125–26, 129–30, 137, 142–43, 190, 211–12, 231

Talmy, Robert, 118, 120
Temps, Le, 167, 185, 187, 206
Testem Benevolentiae (Leo XIII), 226, 229
textile industry, 50–65, 80, 83, 88
Thiers, Adolph, 146
Thiollière, Camille, 131
Third Order of St. Francis, 46, 218–20, 228, 231
Thomas Aquinas, Saint, 47, 115, 135–36, 139–40, 223
tourism, 156
trade unions, 92–95; Catholic, 245; collective bargaining and, 93, 212, 236; legalization of, 93, 123, 129, 142, 148, 212; membership growth in, 236; religious affiliation disassociation and, 217; as *syndicats mixte,* 45, 92, 107, 113, 119–20, 123, 126–29, 137, 142–43, 190, 211–12; as *syndicats professionnel,* 92–93, 99, 211; as *syndicats séparés,* 45, 120, 122, 125–26, 129–30, 137, 142–43, 190, 211–12, 231
Treaty of Frankfurt, 146
Trimouille, Pierre, 6–7, 27, 75, 95–96, 243
Triple Alliance, 169–70, 175, 186
Turner, Edith, 148
Turner, Victor, 148

ultramontanism, 16–17, 19
Unam Sanctum (Leo XIII), 135
unemployment compensation/insurance, 109, 211
Union Fraternelle, L', 5, 218–20, 231
Union Générale Bank, 213
unions. *See* trade unions
United States, 27, 51, 56–57, 225
Univers, L', 164, 167–68, 184, 210
Urban II, pope, 154
usury, 29

Val-des-Bois, 1–2, 5, 13, 58, 72, 95–100, 243; apprenticeships at, 88, 235; chapel at, 69, 74; communal improvement in, 77–92, 95, 142, 242; cultural life of, 90; education at, 85–88; factory chaplains and, 75–76, 120, 194, 220–24, 243; fires in, 43, 55, 95–96; hiring practices of, 59, 74–75, 96–98; housing at, 90, 112; missionaries and, 71; modernization of, 55–56, 58, 96, 105, 228; photographs of, *Figs. 4–5;* religious objects/practices in, 43, 73–77, 112; shared responsibility at, 91–95; standard setting by, 91, 118, 122, 130–32, 136, 166, 211; *syndicat mixte* in, 45, 92, 107, 129, 143, 212, 222, 236; wages and payment methods in, 67, 77–79; workday hours in, 63, 80–81; working conditions and, 61, 82–83, 94–95, 235. *See also* Conseil d'Atelier; Conseil d'Usine
Vatican Councils, 46, 171
Vichy, France, 156
Victor Emmanuel, king of Italy, 171, 179–80

Villermé, Louis-Réne, 26, 60–61, 66, 110
Vincent de Paul, Saint, 70
Viviani, René, 101
vocational training, 81, 87–89
Voix de la France, La, 210
Voltaire, Le, 167, 179, 185

wages, 61–63, 77–79, 94; for children, 61–62; commensurability of, 41–42, 211–13; family allowances and, 235; family wage and, 5, 78–79, 81, 91, 112, 121, 141, 208, 212, 235, 246; payment methods for, 14, 67, 79; for women, 60–61, 79
Wallace, Lillian Parker, 137, 192
Weber, Eugen, 66, 68, 156
welfare states, 247
William II, emperor of Germany, 2, 174–75, 189
women: as business partners, 14; Christian democratic congresses and, 211; education of, 86–87; life expectancies of, 63–64; Marian devotion and, 191; maternity leaves for, 83, 235; as moralizing influence, 32–36, 48, 87, 110–11; motherhood and, 32–35, 41; pilgrimages and, 152–53, 162–63; religious associations and, 76–77; strikes and, 60; wages for, 60–61, 79; workday hours and, 63, 211; in the workforce, 26, 35–36, 59–60, 78
work, philosophy of, 36–45
workday. *See* hours of work
worker councils, 44, 236
worker pilgrimages. *See* pilgrimages
worker priests, 31, 220
working conditions, 60–61, 82–83, 94–95, 235
World War I, 2, 5–6, 233–34
Wright, Gordon, 61

Zimmermann, Marie, 143
Zola, Émile, 50, 90, 148

JOAN L. COFFEY

is associate professor of history at Sam Houston State University.

www.ingramcontent.com/pod-product-compliance
Lightning Source LLC
Chambersburg PA
CBHW071359300426
44114CB00016B/2113